62 0040952 4 TELEPEN

£ 28·20

WITHDRAWN
FROM THE LIBRARY

D0302810

DOCTORS AND

MEDICINE IN MEDIEVAL ENGLAND

1340–1530

ROBERT S. GOTTFRIED

# DOCTORS AND MEDICINE IN
# MEDIEVAL ENGLAND

## 1340 – 1530

PRINCETON UNIVERSITY PRESS

PRINCETON, NEW JERSEY

COPYRIGHT © 1986 BY PRINCETON UNIVERSITY PRESS

PUBLISHED BY PRINCETON UNIVERSITY PRESS, 41 WILLIAM STREET

PRINCETON, NEW JERSEY 08540

IN THE UNITED KINGDOM

PRINCETON UNIVERSITY PRESS, GUILDFORD, SURREY

ALL RIGHTS RESERVED

LIBRARY OF CONGRESS CATALOGING IN PUBLICATION

DATA WILL BE FOUND ON THE LAST PRINTED PAGE OF THIS BOOK

ISBN 0–691–05481–9

PUBLICATION OF THIS BOOK HAS BEEN AIDED BY A GRANT FROM THE

ANDREW W. MELLON FOUNDATION

THIS BOOK HAS BEEN COMPOSED IN LINOTRON JANSON

CLOTHBOUND EDITIONS OF PRINCETON UNIVERSITY

PRESS BOOKS ARE PRINTED ON ACID-FREE

PAPER, AND BINDING MATERIALS

ARE CHOSEN FOR STRENGTH

AND DURABILITY

★

MEDICAL LIBRARY
QUEEN'S MEDICAL CENTRE

Class  WZ 54 GOT

Fund  270-005

Book No.  6200409524

Jc

PRINTED IN THE UNITED STATES OF AMERICA

BY PRINCETON UNIVERSITY PRESS, PRINCETON, NEW JERSEY

*To*
*Willie and Phil*

# CONTENTS

# LIST OF ILLUSTRATIONS

# LIST OF TABLES

# ACKNOWLEDGMENTS

I have had much help and support in writing this book. In Britain I used the facilities of: the British Library, the British Museum, London; the University Library, Cambridge University; the Bodleian Library, Oxford University; the Wellcome Library for the History of Medicine, London; the Public Record Office, London; the Guildhall Library, London; the Corporation of London Library, London; the Institute of Historical Research, The University of London; and have used or corresponded with the archives and archivists in Kent, Essex, Sussex, Suffolk, Norfolk, Hampshire, Hertfordshire, Leicestershire, Gloucestershire, and Yorkshire record offices. In the United States I have used the Alexander Library, Rutgers University; the Firestone Library, Princeton University; the library of the Institute for Advanced Study, Princeton; and the Regenstein Library, the University of Chicago. Librarians and archivists were, without exception, gracious and helpful to me. Thanks are also due to the editors and staff of Princeton University Press, especially Miriam Brokaw, Joanna Hitchcock, and Gretchen Oberfranc.

I have also received generous financial support. The Charles and Johanna Busch Memorial Fund of Rutgers University provided me with funds from 1980 through 1984. The American Council of Learned Societies gave me a fellowship for 1982–1983. And the Institute for Advanced Study in Princeton allowed me that ultimate luxury, a fellowship there in 1983. It was in the idyllic setting of the Institute that I wrote the crucial first draft of this book.

As in the past, scholars have given generously of their time to read and criticize my work in its various states of preparation. John Elliot, Felix Gilbert, Marshall Clagett, and Allan Silver were among many people at the Institute for Advanced Study who listened to my papers, read my drafts, and gave me advice. Lawrence Stone of Princeton University did the same, as did audiences at Princeton University, Indiana University, the University of British Columbia, Rutgers University, and the University of Toronto. Parts of my research have appeared in articles in *The Bulletin of the History of Medicine*. I thank the readers of that journal for their comments. And, as he has always done, my colleague Maurice Lee has waded through page after page in draft after draft of the book manuscript, pointing out my shortcomings in prose and conception.

Finally—and rather oddly—I should like to thank Charles H. Talbot, the preeminent historian of medieval English medicine. I have met Talbot just once, and then only briefly. Throughout the course of this book I shall take issue with many of the concepts, and even facts in his published works. But his work is fundamental, a starting point for anyone interested in the history of medicine. It would have taken me far longer to do my research and write without the foundation of his book and articles, and the medical register he compiled with E. A. Hammond. In all, this book could not have been written without the help of the librarians and archivists. It would not have been written without the financial support, and it would have been far weaker without the help of my readers and those authors whose studies I have drawn on.

# LIST OF ABBREVIATIONS

| | |
|---|---|
| *BHM* | *Bulletin of the History of Medicine.* |
| B.M. | The British Library, the British Museum. |
| *BRUC* | A. B. Emden, *Biographical Register of the University of Cambridge to A.D. 1500* (Cambridge: Cambridge University Press, 1963). |
| *BRUO* | A. B. Emden, *Biographical Register of the University of Oxford to A.D. 1500*, 3 vols. (Oxford: Oxford University Press, 1957–1959). |
| CCR | Calendar of Close Rolls Preserved in the Public Record Office, Edward I–Henry VII. 46 vols. |
| CChR | Calendar of Charter Rolls Preserved in the Public Record Office, 1226–1516. 6 vols. |
| CFR | Calendar of Fine Rolls Preserved in the Public Record Office. 20 vols. |
| CPR | Calendar of Patent Rolls Preserved in the Public Record Office. 56 vols. |
| C.U.L. | Cambridge University Library. |
| *DNB* | *Dictionary of National Biography to 1900*, 22 vols., eds. Sir Leslie Stephen and Sir Sidney Lee (London, 1885–1900). |
| EETS | Early English Text Society. |
| Guildhall | London Guildhall Library. |
| Hustings Wills | *Calendar of Wills Proved and Enrolled in the Court of Husting, London*, 2 vols., ed. R. R. Sharpe (London: 1889–1890). |
| *JHM* | *Journal of the History of Medicine.* |
| L–B | London Letter Books. |
| London Com. Court | Wills of the Commissary Court of London, Guildhall Library. |
| *LPFD* | *Letter and Papers, Foreign and Domestic . . . of the Reign of Henry VIII Preserved in the Public Record Office.* |
| *MH* | *Medical History* |
| O.U. Bod. | Bodleian Library, Oxford University. |
| PCC | Prerogative Court of Canterbury Wills, The Public Record Office, London. |
| PRO | Public Record Office, London. |

Riley, *Memorials of London* — Henry Thomas Riley, *Memorials of London and London Life* (London: Longmans, 1861).

Rot. Parl. — *Rotuli parliamentorum et petitiones.*

Rymer, *Foedera* — Thomas Duffus Hardy, *Syllabus of Rymer's Foedera* (London: Longmans, 1869).

*T&H* — C. H. Talbot and E. A. Hammond, *The Medical Practitioners in Medieval England* (London: Wellcome Historical Medical Library, 1965).

Wellcome — Wellcome Historical Medical Library.

DOCTORS AND

MEDICINE IN MEDIEVAL ENGLAND

1340–1530

These physicians
That help men die

—ANONYMOUS, *Fourteenth Century*


War is the only real school for surgeons.

—HIPPOCRATES

This is a study of English doctors and medicine from the Black Death to the foundation of the Royal College of Physicians. The dates of these two events, 1348 and 1518, are not followed exactly. Many of the methods and institutions of practitioners, especially physicians, were carryovers from the classical and high medieval past. And some of the changes characteristic of the late middle ages began in the thirteenth century, while others did not run their course until the 1540s and beyond. But 1348 and 1518 are turning points in the history of English medicine.

The first date marks the onset of the second plague pandemic in the British Isles. Plague dealt England's medical community a series of blows from which it never recovered.[1] The Black Death killed influential physicians, medical teachers, and authors. With them went many of the old ideas and concepts. And this was just the beginning of the change. The doctors who survived were unable to cure plague or even assuage the pains of those who were afflicted. Many practitioners, especially physicians, were hard-pressed to develop new systems of epidemiology, and continued to rely on traditional concepts which were based on Greek and Arabic theories devised five hundred to a thousand years before the fourteenth century and its new viruses and bacteria. Consequently, much of what was left of the pre-plague medical community was discredited. After 1348 new kinds of practitioners, often surgeons rather than physicians, came to the forefront. Surgeons and even barber-surgeons dealt with disease the same way they treated more mundane ailments, through practice rather than the theoretical manipulations of physic. It would be from the surgeon's scalpel and not the physician's manuscript that clinical medicine would evolve.

The Black Death was not the only cause for the rise of surgery. Almost as important was the frequency of war. Medieval English kings were usually warlike, but never quite so sanguinary as when they tried to conquer France. Beginning with Edward III and the Crecy campaign—though it might be argued that the trend was in fact begun by

[1] I have dealt with these issues in *The Black Death* (New York: The Free Press, 1983). Pages 104–128 treat medicine.

Edward I during his campaigns in the 1290s—and ending with Henry VIII's expedition of 1513–1514, English kings recruited teams of doctors, most of whom were surgeons, to accompany their armies and treat the wounded. Such experience in combat afforded surgeons opportunities they could never have acquired in civilian practice. For on the battlefield they were able to experiment with techniques and develop, if only by trial and error, an effective and systematic method. They were able to dissect bodies without interference from civil or ecclesiastical authorities. And they were able to share these methods and other ideas with colleagues in an atmosphere the intensity of which could never be duplicated at home.

There was also a political benefit to military service. If successful—and generally, they seem to have been—surgeons home from the wars could expect to partake in the fruits of royal patronage. They might, for example, be brought to court to serve as royal doctors. And the kings who did most of the campaigning—Edward III, Henry V, Edward IV—were among the more astute monarchs, and hence the best patrons. It was, for example, veteran surgeons of the Agincourt campaign who, with Henry V's blessings, established in 1423 the College of Medicine, and then filled out the ranks of the London-based Fellowship of Surgeons, the two most enlightened medical institutions in later medieval England.

The success of the surgeons did not last. The opportunities for combat service diminished after 1450. And late in the fifteenth century new ideas about anatomy and physiology that linked physic and surgery were introduced into England from Italy. These ideas helped revive physic just as surgery was beginning to lose some of its luster—and much of its royal support. Hence, when Henry VIII wished to reform medical practice in 1518 he turned to the physicians. Surgeons were excluded from the Royal College of Physicians. In effect, the nature of the faculty and the curriculum of the college, coupled with the demise of military surgery, ensured that physic would again dominate medical practice. But physic remained text-bound and ineffective. Many historians regard the foundation of the Royal College as a new beginning in English medicine and the first step toward modern practice.[2] I will argue precisely the opposite—that the college marked the end of the period of

[2] The best example is Sir George N. Clark, *A History of the Royal College of Physicians*, i (Oxford: Clarendon Press, 1964).

innovation, discouraged clinical practice, and was less innovative than its fifteenth-century antecedent, the College of Medicine.

Most historians of medieval medicine have followed one of four models: biographies of great men, histories of ideas, examinations of institutions, or studies in the course and treatment of particular diseases.[3] I have tried to include elements of all these approaches, and to add a discussion of the social and cultural lives of practitioners, ordinary ones as well as the distinguished, and an investigation of their larger role in society.

I will also argue that some of the practitioners, mostly physicians and surgeons but also a few apothecaries and barber-surgeons, were part of a bourgeois middle class, or at least, in the words of Sylvia L. Thrupp, a "middle strata of the kingdom."[4] By the fifteenth century this middle stratum had begun to assume what Vern L. Bullough has described as "the professional image."[5] With lawyers, and perhaps scrivenors and stationers, these doctors formed the core of a growing professional class of increasing importance. Medieval professionalism was not quite like its modern counterpart, wherein the word suggests expertise in a particular task, though many medieval practitioners had become expert by 1400. Rather, it was primarily a socio-cultural phenomenon that allowed practitioners to protect their status, wealth, and position. It made them a kind of appendage, albeit a junior one, to the traditional governing classes, whose privilege rested on title and ownership of land, and to the great merchants of London, whose influence was based on wealth.

I will also try to reestablish the medical reputations of late medieval English doctors. Most historians have looked askance at the quality of practice in the fourteenth and fifteenth centuries, not only by comparison with the quality of English medicine in other epochs, but also when measured against the achievements of doctors on the continent. Charles Talbot, for example, wrote: "The century or more that elapsed between

---

[3] Examples are, respectively: H. P. Cholmeley, *John Gaddesden and the Rosa Medicinae* (Oxford: Oxford University Press, 1912); Allen G. Debus, *The English Paracelsians* (London: Oldbourne, 1965); Rotha Mary Clay, *The Medieval Hospitals of England*, 2nd ed. (London: Frank Cass, 1966); and Charles Creighton, *A History of Epidemics in Britain*, i, 2nd ed. (London; Frank Cass, 1965).

[4] Sylvia L. Thrupp, *The Merchant Class of Medieval London, 1300–1500* (Chicago: University of Chicago Press, 1948), p. 288.

[5] Vern L. Bullough, *The Development of Medicine as a Profession* (New York: Hafner, 1966), p. 111.

the introduction of English as a vehicle for medical writings and the foundation of the College of Physicians showed no significant advance in medical knowledge.[6]

Historians of early modern England tend to limit discussion to the role of medicine in the Scientific Revolution of the seventeenth and eighteenth centuries. Those who concentrate on the origins of the revolution begin early in the sixteenth century with Thomas Linacre and the foundation of the Royal College. Sir George N. Clark, for example, in his three-volume study of the college, chose not to discuss its late medieval background in any detail. Rather, he wrote on "why England was medically backwards."[7] Even Margaret Pelling and Charles Webster, two of the most knowledgeable and perceptive historians of medicine, tend to dismiss the period between the outbreak of the Black Death and the foundation of the Royal College: ". . . at the beginning of the [sixteenth] century, England lagged far behind Italy in the organization of its medical profession, in medical education, and in general medical culture."[8]

Such attitudes help explain why so little has been attempted on the history of late medieval English doctors and medicine. Edward Kealey has written on the late Anglo-Saxon and Norman periods, and Charles Talbot, Stanley Rubin, and others on the twelfth and thirteenth centuries.[9] There have been a number of studies on specialized aspects of late medieval medicine, including several by Bullough on education, training, and the process of professionalization.[10] But there has been no attempt to present a systematic, synthetic view, either of the practice of medicine or the nature of medical practitioners. And many of the spe-

---

[6] Charles H. Talbot, *Medieval Medicine in England* (London: Oldbourne, 1967), p. 198.

[7] Clark, *History of the Royal College*, i, p. 34.

[8] Margaret Pelling and Charles Webster, "Medical Practitioners," in Charles Webster, ed., *Health, Medicine and Mortality in Sixteenth Century England* (Cambridge: Cambridge University Press, 1979), p. 165.

[9] Edward J. Kealey, *Medieval Medicus: A Social History of Anglo-Norman Medicine* (Baltimore: Johns Hopkins University Press, 1981); Talbot, *Medicine in Medieval England*; Stanley Rubin, *Medieval English Medicine* (New York: Barnes and Noble, 1974).

[10] A complete list is provided in the bibliography. For Bullough, see *Development of Medicine*. Examples of excellent particular studies include: Darrel W. Amundsen, "Medieval Deontology and Pestilential Disease in the Later Middle Ages," *JHM*, 23, 1977, pp. 172–203; Ida B. Jones, "Popular Medical Knowledge in Fourteenth Century English Literature," *BHM*, 5, 1937, pp. 405–451; and James K. Mustain, "A Rural Medical Practitioner in Fifteenth Century England," *BHM*, 46, 1972, 469–476.

cialized studies have been based more on theories than on the analysis of evidence.

The neglect of late medieval medicine is unwarranted. It can be argued that the 170 years between the inception of the Black Death and the foundation of the Royal College were the most important in English medicine until the 1620s, when the works of William Harvey began to appear. The later middle ages was a period of change. There were developments in addition to the omnipresence of plague and the rise of surgery. Doctors began, albeit slowly and in small numbers, to affiliate with hospitals. Hospitals, in turn, began to evolve from almshouses, pensions, and isolation wards into clinics where doctors attempted to heal rather than just to isolate patients. New methods of sanitation were tried, at times successfully, and in some towns public health laws were passed. Medical texts were written in English as well as Latin, enabling more people to read them. If it did nothing else, the spread of vernacular texts helped remove the mysteries of the more nonsensical treatises.

A final theme runs throughout this book. Late medieval doctors inherited two distinct traditions and corpuses of medical theory, training and practice. One was classical, and primarily Greek. It was based on the works of Hippocrates and his school at Cos, and on Galen. Much of this Greek corpus was lost to Western Europe during the early middle ages, but was passed on to and prospered in the Islamic world. Hence, when it came back to the West in the twelfth century, it came with glosses and commentaries from Arabic-language authors, some of whom, notably Avicenna, Albucasis, and Rhases, became authorities in their own right. This Greek-based, Arabic-amended corpus was predicated on logic. But while much of it was empirical, most of it was theoretical. Very little—at least as it came to be used by English practitioners—was taken from clinical experience. They based their treatments on Greek humoral theory, and emphasized cure through changes in diet or the use of drugs. Given the imprecision of medieval pharmacy and the sorry state of iatrochemistry, such treatments were rarely effective.

The second tradition was more practical—the common experience of folk medicine. In Northern Europe, especially in England, this practical, partly clinical tradition was especially strong. In part this was owing to England's remoteness, and the relative absence of the classical tradition in medieval English culture. But it was also the result of an active approach taken by Anglo-Saxon leeches that advocated that the leech deal directly with his patient. Leeches used drugs, but they also per-

formed surgery. All in all, they developed a clinical tradition that served
as an alternate to the theoretical one of the Greeks. This practical, clinical tradition was not as comprehensive as its rival. Much of it was swal-
lowed up after the Norman Conquest and the development of the English universities, which adopted the Greek model. But it did persist
among surgeons, barbers, and village leeches. It was even carried on in
some of the English monasteries, particularly those of the Benedictines.
Thus, while by 1200 the Greek theoretical approach had become the
dominant one in English medicine, the alternative clinical tradition remained.

In my attempt to treat these themes I have used the traditional sources
in the time-proven ways. But I have also used them to collect information on 2,282 men and women who practiced medicine between 1340
and 1540 and to create a doctors' "data bank."[11] Each individual could
have as many as fifty-three bits of information about his or her personal,
professional, and public life; and while most have far fewer, the file still
enables me to answer with some certainty many basic questions about
the nature and character of late medieval doctors and medical practice.
I believe the file is one of the largest and most comprehensive data banks
yet assembled for any group of late medieval Englishmen.

Finally, I will try to answer two larger questions. If many of the medical practitioners were prosperous and bourgeois, can they provide a
clue to that omnipresent historical problem of the "rise of the middle
class"? Could a middle class, or at least middle strata, having arisen in
fifteenth-century England, become established and not have to rise anymore? And if, as I shall argue, the later middle ages was so important
an epoch in the history of English medicine, why was there no medical
and indeed scientific revolution in the fifteenth and sixteenth centuries?
Raising these questions is, I think, fundamental to an understanding of
later medieval England. For they place the history of medicine where it
ought to be, in the mainstream of social and cultural history.

[11] There is a fine biographical register of doctors compiled by Charles H. Talbot and
E.A. Hammond, *The Medical Practitioners in Medieval England* (London: Wellcome Historical Medical Library, 1965). Faye Marie Getz of the Wellcome is updating it. My file includes all those listed by Talbot and Hammond who practiced in my time period, plus
barber-tonsors and apothecaries, whom they decided not to include, plus over five
hundred physicians, surgeons, and barber-surgeons they did not include for whatever reason. The doctors' data bank is discussed throughout the text, but especially below, pp.
249–251. See too Robert S. Gottfried, "English Medical Practitioners, 1340–1530," *BHM*,
58, 1984, pp. 164–182.

# I

## THE CORPORATE FRAMEWORK
## OF MEDICINE

Fundamental to the change of post-plague medicine of late medieval doctors was the building—or at least improving—of medical institutions.[1] This process was in turn affected by the corporate nature of medieval English society, a characteristic that successive epidemics and social, economic, and cultural changes would help break down but never destroy, and that was still evident in early modern England. The English constitution and government were relatively sophisticated and successful. But the royal bureaucracy was small, and its powers diminished as one traveled farther from Westminster or wherever the king was holding court. Like everyone else, doctors had to look after their own interests. Hence, a corporate structure was necessary for both building and protecting their positions and privileges.

Late medieval medical institutions had common features. Most were local, especially municipal. They were organized according to the status and function of the practitioners, and were multifarious and overlapping. Many doctors belonged to several, and did not regard the various oaths of fealty and loyalty which they took as creating any conflict of interest. The purpose of the corporation was, after all, protective. Yet it

[1] There is no definitive or even singular study of late medieval medical institutions. There is not even a detailed study of a particular institution, such as Sir George N. Clark's, *A History of the Royal College of Physicians*, i (Oxford: Clarendon Press, 1964). The most synthetic interpretation has been presented in a series of articles by Vern L. Bullough; they are listed, below, p. 332; and are, in turn, summarized in his *The Development of Medicine as a Profession* (New York: Hafner, 1966). Among other studies are: R. Theodore Beck, *The Cutting Edge; Early History of the Surgeons of London* (London: Lund Humphries, 1974); John Flint South and D'Arcy Power, *Memorials of the Craft of Surgery in England* (London: Cassell and Co., 1886); Charles H. Talbot, *Medicine in Medieval England* (London: Oldbourne, 1967); Jessie Dobson and R. Milnes Walker, *Barbers and Barber-Surgeons of London* (London: Blackwell, 1979); Young, *Annals of the Barber-Surgeons*; and Caroline Rawcliffe, "Medicine and Medical Practice in Later Medieval London," *Guildhall Studies in London History*, 5, 1981, pp. 13–25. Beck, South and Power, and Young reprint many of the important institutional records. I will not discuss another medical, or at least quasi-medical institution, hospitals. A good reference, albeit somewhat dated, is Rotha Mary Clay, *The Hospitals of Medieval England*, 2nd ed. (London: Frank Cass, 1965). See too the various Victoria County Histories.

provided for other things as well, most notably the training and supervising of doctors, the establishing of parameters of practice, and, when
necessary, discipline and penalties.

Medical institutions were affected by the church.[2] Despite the damage dealt it by plague and the other difficulties of late medieval life, the
church continued to exert a great deal of influence over the practice of
medicine. Ecclesiastical authorities played a large role in the universities, the training ground of physicians, even after 1453, when doctors
were allowed to marry.[3] They retained some supervisory role over the
corporations of other types of practitioners, particularly the confrater-
nities, the socio-religious societies formed within most guilds.[4] Further,Christian dogma affected the philosophy of medicine. Theologians
argued that the soul was more important than the body.[5] This affected
what could be taught, and prevented the development in the universities
of medical specialities like anatomy and physiology.

Medical institutions were also affected by the competition among the
different kinds of practitioners. Occasionally different organizations
worked together, as in 1423, when the physicians and surgeons founded
the College of Medicine. But more often the differences led to rivalries
and quarrels. Each group had special skills and interests, and their corporations tended above all to protect these interests. Ironically, the bit-
terest battles that medical practitioners and their corporations fought
were among themselves. The tensions inherent in such competition
made these intrinsically conservative institutions even more protective
and insular than they might otherwise have been.

[2] See, for example: Huling E. Ussery, *Chaucer's Physician: Medicine and Literature in Fourteenth-Century England* (New Orleans: Tulane Studies in English, 1971), pp. 5–20; Benjamin Lee Gordon, *Medieval and Renaissance Medicine* (New York: Philosophical Library,
1959), particularly the chapters on anatomy, surgery and English medicine; David Riesman, *The Story of Medicine in the Middle Ages* (New York: Hoebner, 1935), especially pp.
17–47; Stanley Rubin, *Medieval English Medicine* (London: David and Charles, 1974), especially pp. 15–16.

[3] Erwin H. Ackerknecht, *A Short History of Medicine*, 2nd ed. (Baltimore, Md.: Johns
Hopkins University Press, 1982), p. 85. For instances, see: *Calendar of Papal Registers, ix,
1431–1447*, ed. J. A. Tremlow (London: HMSO, 1912), pp. 227–228; *Cal. Pap. Reg.—Petitions, i, 1342–1419*, ed. W. H. Bliss (London: HMSO, 1896), p. 7. See too Beck, *Cutting
Edge*, pp. 120–144.

[4] Bullough, *Development of Medicine*, pp. 74–101.

[5] Darrel W. Amundsen, "Medieval Canon Law on Medical and Surgical Practice by the
Clergy," *BHM*, 52, 1978, pp. 22–44.

Until 1518 physicians did not have a peculiar medical corporation. If they held any institution in common it was the universities. Yet both Oxford and Cambridge were ineffective. To use their curricula as examples, they changed hardly at all from the thirteenth century to the 1520s.[6] This was one of the reasons that medicine remained a minor discipline. It was moribund, and must have seemed to the best students less prestigious than theology or law, and more boring than the natural sciences and other arts programs.

There were other problems. For at least a century after their foundations neither university had separate medical faculties; the first reliable reference at Oxford comes in 1303, while that at Cambridge dates fifty years later.[7] Even after their foundations the faculties remained small and undistinguished. A glimpse at the lists of faculties at selected colleges, presented in Table 1.1, confirms this. To take Balliol as an example, between 1300 and 1540 it had just four fellows who can clearly be identified as physicians. Only Merton had what might be called a medical community, and it would be a mistake to make too much of this,

[6] For English universities, see: Vern L. Bullough, "Medical Study at Mediaeval Oxford," *Speculum*, 36, 1961, pp. 600–612; Bullough, "The Medieval Medical School at Cambridge," *Mediaeval Studies*, 24, 1962, pp. 161–168; Ussery, *Chaucer's Physician*, pp. 5–11; A.H.T. Robb-Smith, "Medical Education at Oxford and Cambridge Prior to 1850," in F.N.L. Poynter, ed., *The Evolution of Medical Education in Britain* (London: Pitman Medical Publishing Co., 1966), pp. 19–52; Humphrey D. Rolleston, *The Cambridge Medical School* (Cambridge: Cambridge University Press, 1932); Margaret Pelling and Charles Webster, "Medical Practitioners," in Webster, ed., *Health, Medicine and Mortality in the Sixteenth Century* (Cambridge: Cambridge University Press, 1979), pp. 189–207. For European universities see: Pearl Kibre and Nancy G. Siraisi, "The Institutional Setting," in David C. Lindberg, ed., *Science in the Middle Ages* (Chicago: University of Chicago Press, 1978), pp. 120–144; Nancy G. Siraisi, *Taddeo Alderotti and His Pupils* (Princeton: Princeton University Press, 1981); Siraisi, *Arts and Science at Padua* (Toronto: University of Toronto Press, 1973); G. W. Corner, "The Rise of Medicine at Salerno in the Twelfth Century," *Annals of Medical History*, 3, 1931, pp. 1–16; Sonoma Cooper, "The Medical School at Montpellier in the Fourteenth Century," *Annals of Medical History*, 2, 1930, pp. 164–195; Michael McVaugh, "Quantified Medical Theory and Practice at Fourteenth Century Montpellier," *BHM*, 43, 1969, pp. 397–413; Vern L. Bullough, "Mediaeval Bologna and Medical Education," *BHM*, 32, 1958, pp. 201–215; Bullough, "The Mediaeval Medical University at Paris," *BHM*, 31, 1957, pp. 197–211; Bullough, "The Development of the Medical University at Montpellier to the End of the Fourteenth Century," *BHM*, 30, 1956, pp. 508–523; Hastings Rashdall, *The Universities of Europe in the Middle Ages*, 3 vols., ed. F. M. Powicke and A. V. Emden (Oxford: Oxford University Press, 1936) is still useful.

[7] This is nicely summarized in Talbot, *Medicine in Medieval England*, pp. 67–69.

since a 1284 injunction discouraged its practice in the college.[8] Indeed, in 1414 there was just one man on the entire faculty of Oxford with an M.D.—and he was a foreigner.[9] There is evidence that early in the fourteenth century the royal physician Nicholas Tingewick read lectures on physic at something called "the Physic School" on Cat Street, on the site of the cloisters of All Souls College.[10] But there is no other record of it, and it was probably only a lecture hall. Nor is there much solace in the case of John Major. Major was an Oxford M.D.[11] In 1426 a testimonial letter praised him for his distinguished teaching, and for reviving the university's medical program.[12] But this came in the very year he incepted. Later in the year he entered the service of John Duke of Bedford, with whom he remained until 1435. Major continued in private practice until his death in 1447, apparently never teaching again.[13]

The problems of the English universities are illustrated by the case of Thomas Brown.[14] In 1396 Brown presented himself for admission to the faculty of medicine at the University of Paris. He produced a notarized certificate claiming that he had studied medicine at Oxford for six and a half years, and asked that it be recognized toward his course at Paris.[15] This was a standard procedure; while the Parisians rarely gave full credit for studies at another university they usually gave at least half.

[8] "Ordinances of Archbishop Peckham, 1284: Injunction to Visitors," in George C. Broderick, *Memorials of Merton College* (Oxford: Oxford Historical Society, 1855), pp. 25, 37, 154.

[9] Talbot, *Medicine in Medieval England*, p. 68. The Talbot text does not have footnotes, making it difficult to use. I have looked in *T&H* and in the data bank, and cannot find him.

[10] Talbot, *Medicine in Medieval England*, p. 108; *T&H*, pp. 229–230. Talbot seems to have taken his information from Robert T. Gunther, *Early Science in Oxford* (Oxford: Oxford University Press, 1925), iii, p. 9.

[11] *T&H*, pp. 165–166.

[12] *Epistolae Academicae*, ed. H. Astey (Oxford: Oxford University Press, 1898), i, p. 20.

[13] *T&H*, p. 165. Even after 1520, when new ideas about anatomy, physiology, and surgery were brought to the universities by Englishmen who had studied in Italy, the medical programs at Oxford and Cambridge generated very little excitement. At Cambridge a total of just seven M.B.s and seven M.D.s were granted by the colleges between 1500 and 1530. Pelling and Webster, "Medical Practitioners," p. 198, from whom this is taken, believe that this lack of interest and subsequent mediocrity of practice persisted well into the sixteenth century, and ended only in the 1540s, with the endowment of the Regius professorships in medicine. In this way, the Regius professorships serve as a terminus of medieval medicine. See too Talbot, *Medicine in Medieval England*, p. 69.

[14] *T&H*, p. 336; Talbot, *Medicine in Medieval England*, p. 68.

[15] *Chartularium Universitatis Parisiensis*, iv, ed. Heinrich Denifle, pp. 12–13.

But this was not to be with Thomas Brown. After deliberation the Parisians decided that Brown was not skilled enough even to gain first-year admission.[16]

Because the universities were geared toward teaching and not practice, they were ineffective as corporations for practitioners. Until the middle of the fifteenth century they did not even require clinical training as part of their programs.[17] Another look at the Merton College dons (Table 1.1) confirms this. Merton was a major center for the study of natural and physical science.[18] Thomas Bradwardine, William Heytesbury, Richard Swineshead, John Dumbleton, and their associates provided the college with a reputation unmatched by any other at Oxford or Cambridge. It produced distinguished physicians, including John Chamber, John Gaddesden, Simon Bredon, and Thomas Linacre. Surviving manuscripts even suggest creative teaching.[19] But from 1300 to 1520 I have records of just twenty physicians, a paltry total for two centuries at the best medical program in England. By contrast, evidence has been found for over twenty mathematicians in the 1330s alone.[20] Most of the Merton physicians were required to take higher clerical orders.[21] And, since priests were forbidden to lecture in medicine, some of the twenty were unable even to share their medical knowledge.[22]

There were similar problems at other Oxford colleges. The New College statutes of 1379 listed seventy fellows.[23] Of these, twenty-two were

[16] *Ibid.*

[17] Talbot, *Medicine in Medieval England*, p. 68.

[18] Gunther, *History of Science*, ii, pp. 43–69; Annaliese Maier, "The Concept of Function in Fourteenth-Century Physics," in Steven D. Sargent, ed., *On the Threshold of Exact Science: Selected Writings of Annaliese Maier on Late Medieval Natural Philosophy* (Philadelphia: University of Pennsylvania Press, 1982), pp. 61–75.

[19] For example, see O.U. Bodley Ms. Digby 176.

[20] Gunther, *History of Science*, ii, pp. 96–99. And there was the injunction against medical practice. See above, note 8.

[21] Of the 20 Merton physicians listed in Table 1.1, 19 took higher orders, and there is no evidence for the twentieth, Walter Stanton. Following John Baldwin, *The Scholastic Culture of the Middle Ages, 1000–1300* (Lexington, Mass.: D. C. Heath and Company, 1971), p. 47, I am taking as major orders priests, deacons, and subdeacons; and as minor orders psalmists, readers, and acolytes.

[22] Ackerknecht, *Short History of Medicine*, pp. 82, 88–93; Talbot, *Medicine in Medieval England*, pp. 69–71. See too note 8.

[23] Talbot, *Medicine in Medieval England*, p. 69. The statutes are in the *Munimenta Academia, or Documents Illustrative of Academic Life and Studies at Oxford*, 2 vols., ed. H. Anstey (London: Rolls Series, 1868).

TABLE 1.1: Physicians at Oxford and Cambridge

| College | Dates | College | Dates |
|---|---|---|---|
| 1. OXFORD | | Nicholas Lynn | 1380–1400 |
| | | John Malden | 1387–1402 |
| *All Souls* | | John Martok | 1440–1503 |
| Richard Bartlett | 1470–1557 | John Maudith | 1309–1343 |
| William Goldwin | 1455–1482 | Robert Sherborn | 1454–1536 |
| Nicholas Halswell | 1468–1528 | Walter Stanton | 1386–1402 |
| Thomas Linacre | 1460–1524 | Henry Sutton | 1440–1500 |
| John Racour | 1467–1487 | John Wik | 1357–1387 |
| *Bailliol* | | *New* | |
| John Free | 1430–1465 | Thomas Bentley | 1475–1521 |
| Simon Holbech | 1307–1340 | Thomas Boket | 1427–1467 |
| William Leverton | 1321–1348 | Thomas Edmunds | 1417–1481 |
| John Malverne | 1393–1422 | John Morer | 1429–1472 |
| *Canterbury* | | John Raundes | 1400–1435 |
| John Cokkes | 1435–1475 | Robert Sherborn | |
| John Talbot | 1498–1550 | (also Merton) | 1454–1536 |
| *Corpus Christi* | | John Swanich | 1390–1448 |
| Gilbert Kymer | 1411–1463 | Robert Thurbarn | 1370–1450 |
| | | John Wittenham | 1380–1413 |
| *Exeter* | | *Oriel* | |
| John Arundell | 1420–1477 | John Landreyn | |
| Henry Beaumond | 1372–1415 | (also Exeter) | 1349–1409 |
| John Landreyn | 1349–1409 | William Lynch | 1472–1517 |
| William Parkhouse | 1506–1541 | John Malden | |
| Henry Whitfield | 1335–1388 | (also Merton) | 1387–1402 |
| | | Thomas Wilton | 1381–1448 |
| *Magdalen* | | | |
| Thomas Gamme | 1485–1507 | *Queens* | |
| William Hasard | 1486–1509 | Thomas Southwell | 1406–1441 |
| | | Henry Whitfield | |
| *Merton* | | (also Exeter) | 1335–1388 |
| John Bilsden | 1435–1484 | | |
| Simon Breden | 1310–1372 | *University* | |
| Thomas Bloxham | 1446–1473 | John Middleton | 1360–1429 |
| John Chamber | 1470–1549 | John Sparwell | 1445–1489 |
| Nicholas Colnet | 1391–1421 | William Wymondham | 1350–1377 |
| Thomas Duncan | 1400–1461 | *Other Oxford physicians without an accurate* | |
| John Ellis | 1390–1457 | *college fellowship* | |
| Edward Finch | 1504–1539 | Peter Alcomlowe | 1461–1468 |
| Geoffrey Fromand | 1335–1351 | Thomas Aston | 1325–1401 |
| John Gaddesden | 1280–1349 | William Bokenham | 1479–1480 |
| Walter Knightly | 1440–1501 | William Bari | 1490 |
| Thomas Linacre | | William of Exeter | 1300–1359 |
| (also All Souls) | 1460–1524 | | |

| College | Dates | College | Dates |
|---|---|---|---|
| *Other Oxford physicians, cont.* | | William Ordew | 1445–1470 |
| Peter Fernandez | 1488–1533 | Richard Pettifer | 1453–1489 |
| Henry Hawte | 1491–1508 | William Skelton | 1440–1471 |
| John Hert | 1457 | John Somerset | 1390–1455 |
| William Hobbes | 1459–1488 | Thomas Whetley | 1450–1478 |
| John Major | 1426–1447 | *Michaelhouse* | |
| Geoffrey Melton | 1377–1411 | John Tesdale | 1389 |
| Simon Moene | 1312–1325 | | |
| Henry Neuton | 1301–1342 | *Pembroke* | |
| William Newton | 1359–1366 | John Kim | 1428–1432 |
| William Phillips | 1452–1507 | *Peterhouse* | |
| Robert Sidesterne | 1287–1316 | John Frye | 1400–1433 |
| John Somerset | 1390–1455 | William Hatclif | |
| Thomas Sutton | 1464–1500 | (also Kings) | 1430–1480 |
| Nicholas Tyngewick | 1291–1339 | Simon Holbeche | 1307–1335 |
| | | Walter Lacy | 1450–1512 |
| II. CAMBRIDGE | | Roger Marshall | 1417–1477 |
| *Gloucester* | | John Martin | 1339–1350 |
| William Leinster | 1444–1487 | Roger Oudbey | 1350–1393 |
| | | Thomas Reed | 1430–1504 |
| *Gonville Hall* | | John Stockton | 1314–1361 |
| Edmund Albon | 1461–1485 | *University* | |
| William Rougham | 1360–1393 | Henry Bagot | 1478–1525 |
| *Kings* | | Master Brinkley | 1464–1475 |
| John Argentine | 1442–1508 | Master Burton | 1486 |
| Edmund Arnold | 1445–1465 | Lewis Caerlyon | 1465–1493 |
| John Clerke | 1440–1477 | James Frise | 1460–1488 |
| Thomas Cliffe | 1445–1483 | Thomas Hall | 1489–1527 |
| Thomas Dalton | 1431–1488 | John Paul | 1477–1486 |
| William Hatclif | 1430–1480 | Master Pownce | 1482–1483 |
| Lewis Kery | 1472–1510 | John Preston | 1504–1505 |
| Walter Leinster | | John Stale | 1461–1474 |
| (also Gloucester) | 1444–1487 | John Willis | 1456–1480 |
| Roger Marshall | 1417–1477 | Robert Yaxley | 1460–1540 |
| Philip Morgan | 1454–1521 | | |

in what might be called the professions. Ten specialized in canon law, ten in civil law, and two in medicine. Throughout the fourteenth, fifteenth, and early sixteenth centuries I have identified just nine New College men who were or would become physicians, and this was the second highest total, after Merton. At Magdalen late in the fourteenth century two of forty fellows were studying medicine—and this after receiving permission from the provost of the college.[24] Of the others, only All Souls produced as many as five physicians for whom evidence survives. As Charles Talbot wrote: "It is not surprising that the number of masters of medicine from Oxford was small."[25]

The situation was a bit better at Cambridge. This was ironic, for though some of the Oxford colleges, like Merton, had achieved a European-wide reputation, Cambridge was a backwater.[26] Yet it may have been precisely because Cambridge was a minor university that medicine, a second-rate discipline, was given more attention than it was at Oxford. There was, as noted, a distinct medical faculty by 1350, and perhaps as early as 1300.[27] By the mid-fourteenth century Pembroke College had designated one of its thirty fellows to specialize in medicine.[28] Peterhouse seems to have had at least fourteen physicians among its fellows, and King's ten. And Gonville Hall, later Gonville and Caius, was developing into a center for medical studies.[29] In 1351 two of its fellows were designated to study medicine, probably in response to the Black Death.[30] Edmund Albon was a don at Gonville from 1466 to 1475 and later a royal physician.[31] In 1486 he endowed "the master and fellows of the college of Our Lady, called Gonville Hall, Cambridge" with lands and shops whose value he estimated at the considerable sum of one hundred marks.[32]

But here too it would be dangerous to assume too much. Albon did

---

[24] Kenneth Bruce MacFarlane, *The Origins of Religious Dissent in England*, 2nd ed. (New York: Collier Books, 1966), pp. 17–41.

[25] Talbot, *Medicine in Medieval England*, p. 69.

[26] It is harder to get complete figures for Cambridge than it is for Oxford because most of the university's records were destroyed in the 1381 riots. Furthermore, much more editing has been done on the Oxford records, particularly by the Oxford Historical Society.

[27] Talbot, *Medicine in Medieval England*, pp. 68–69.

[28] *Ibid.*

[29] *Ibid.*

[30] *Ibid.*

[31] *T&H*, pp. 38–39.

[32] *CCR*, 1485–1500, p. 29.

not specify that his bequest be used for medicine, and Gonville did not blossom fully until 1550.[33] Like the program at Oxford, that at Cambridge was generally moribund. Like Oxford, Cambridge attracted few of the best or even the worst students to its medical programs. From 1488 until 1511, when the Parliamentary Licensing Act gave authority to the bishops to sanction medical practice, both universities had 3,827 degree candidates. Of these, twenty-eight, less than one percent, were in medicine.[34] As late as 1450 the statutes of Cambridge had to make special provision for the university preceptors to present their candidates for medical degrees. So few doctors of medicine were available that it was sometimes necessary to go outside the university to find qualified examiners.[35]

Finally, Oxford and Cambridge were ineffective as physicians' corporations because they were located in provincial towns rather than in London. London offered opportunities for fame, fortune, and patronage that Oxford and Cambridge could never match.[36] The best physicians, whether they were educated at English universities or abroad, whether they were denizen or alien, gravitated to London. This was one reason Oxford and Cambridge found it so difficult to maintain proper medical faculties. It has been claimed that both universities were forced to accept part-time students, that is, those who did not plan to complete the medical course, and to allow them to study other subjects.[37] Otherwise, interested students might leave to learn from the masters in London.

Yet, despite the weakness of the universities, the physicians remained the social and to some degree the professional elite among doctors. University degrees retained their prestige, and university chancellors kept the power to license medical practice. This is not surprising. At the time of the Black Death physicians were the leading medical practitioners, and their positions seemed unassailable. As long as the university authorities kept the authority to license practice, physicians did not need other institutions. It was only when medical corporations representing

[33] Pelling and Webster, "Medical Practitioners," pp. 189–206; Talbot, *Medicine in Medieval England*, p. 69.

[34] Pelling and Webster, "Medical Practitioners," p. 198.

[35] Bullough, "Mediaeval Medical School at Cambridge," pp. 61–68.

[36] Bullough, *Development of Medicine*, pp. 80–81; F.N.L. Poynter, "The Influence of Government Legislation on Medical Practice in Britain," in Poynter, ed., *The Evolution of Medical Practice* (London: Pitman Medical Publishing Company, 1961), pp. 5–15.

[37] Bullough, *Development of Medicine*, p. 81.

rival practitioners began to challenge the physicians' seminal role that physicians developed additional institutions, in particular, the Royal College of 1518.

Surgeons enjoyed no inherent advantages.[38] To the contrary, they labored under the stigma of being craftsmen, a designation carried since antiquity and which implied that they were less proficient than physicians.[39] Institutionalization was essential to their success. Excluded or at least discouraged from matriculating at the universities, the surgeons turned to building their own corporation in London, home to the wealthiest patients, and close by the seat of royal authority and patronage in Westminster.

Surgeons first organized after the Black Death, though there is dispute as to when. Unwin, an authority on guilds, said it was 1353.[40] But his evidence is unclear, and others have settled on 1368–1369, when the Fellowship of Surgeons was formed.[41] The first years of the Fellowship are obscure. The earliest references are indirect, and if a charter or list of regulations was drawn up it has not survived. Most of what is known comes from the fifteenth century, and we can only surmise that the Fellowship was formed at least in part as the surgeons' response to the failure of physicians to deal with the plague. The Fellowship was not a guild and was never incorporated. Rather, it was an association of surgeons with common interests, but without the strictures and rules that characterized guilds. In 1369 John Dunheved, John Hyndstoke, and Nicholas Kyldesby were "admitted as Master Surgeons of the City and allowed to practice."[42] This was done so that they would:

[38] There are several studies of surgeons. See: Hedley Atkins, *The Surgeon's Craft* (Manchester: Manchester University Press, 1965); Beck, *Cutting Edge*; William J. Bishop, *The Early History of Surgery* (London: Robert Hale, 1960); George Gask, *Essays in the History of Medicine* (London: Butterworth, 1950); Geoffrey Parker, *The Early History of Surgery in Great Britain* (London: A. C. Black, 1920); and South and Power, *Memorials of the Craft of Surgery*.

[39] See below, pp. 62–72. Some of the prejudices are discussed in Elizabeth L. Eisenstein, *The Printing Press as an Agent of Change* (Cambridge: Cambridge University Press, 1979), pp. 537–541, 566–574.

[40] George Unwin, *The Gilds and Companies of London*, 4th ed. (London: Frank Cass Reprints, 1966), p. 88.

[41] South and Power, *Memorials of the Craft of Surgery*, p. xi, in which they argue for 1368, probably in confusion over the starting date of the new year; Beck, *Cutting Edge*, pp. 30–54; Young, *Annals of the Barber Surgeons*, pp. 36–38; Dobson and Walker, *Barbers and Barber-surgeons*, p. 9–30. The reference they cite, presumably, is L-B G, p. 21, when four surgeons, addressed as masters, adjudicated a malpractice case.

[42] L-B G, p. 236. It is reprinted in Riley, *Memorials*, p. 337.

. . . well and faithfully serve the people, in undertaking cures, would take reasonably from them, etc., would faithfully follow their calling, and would present to the said Mayor and Alderman the defaults of others undertaking cures, so often as should be necessary; and that they would be ready, at all times when they should be warned, to attend the maimed or wounded and other persons, etc.; and would give truthful information to the officers of the city aforesaid, as to such maimed, wounded and others, whether they be in peril of death or not, etc. And also faithfully to all other things touching their calling.[43]

The act gave the Fellows authority over the practice of surgery in London, and an institutional bearing which, if not quite the same as incorporation, fitted them into the hierarchical structure of the city's corporations.

The Fellows' power was demonstrated a few years later when Dunheved and two other surgeons, John Garlikhuth and Nicholas Surgeon, gave expert testimony in a malpractice case involving Richard Cheyndut.[44] Cheyndut was imprisoned for undertaking to cure Walter de Hull "of a malady of his left leg, whereby owing to his lack of care and knowledge, the patient was in danger of losing his leg."[45] Dunheved and his associates examined the leg and told the mayor and alderman that "it would require great experience, care and expense if the leg were to be cured without permanent injury."[46] The jury found for the plaintiff to the amount of fifty shillings, and Cheyndut apparently did not practice again.

Another example came in 1417.[47] John Severelle, also known as John Love and described as a leech from Salisbury, wanted to practice surgery in London.[48] He was not a member of the Fellowship, and could not provide evidence of surgical training. To complicate matters, this was a time when many surgeons were making a name for themselves in military service. Love wanted certification so that he could travel abroad in the retinue of the king's brother, Thomas Duke of Clarence. He recog-

[43] *Ibid.*

[44] *Calendar of Pleas and Memorial Rolls . . . of the City of London at the Guildhall, 1364–1381*, ed. A. H. Thomas (Cambridge: Cambridge University Press, 1929), p. 236.

[45] *Ibid.*

[46] *Ibid.*

[47] There are, literally, dozens of cases. See, for example. CPR, 1348–1350, p. 175, for a case involving Thomas Goldington, a prominent fourteenth-century physician. Barbara A. Hanawalt of Indiana University has shown me two virtually identical cases from the coroners' rolls: PRO, Just. 2/105, m6d; and Just. 2/67, m30.

[48] Riley, *Memorials*, p. 657.

nized an old debt of £20, then gave cash security of £10 so that he "should take any man under his care, as to whom risk of maiming or of his life might ensure, and within four days should not warn the Wardens of the Craft of Surgery thereof, then such recognizance should hold good."[49] Ironically, the security went for naught. Two days later the sheriff of London reported that Clarence and his retinue had departed from the city without Love, whose license to practice was suspended.

As the cases of Cheyndut and Love indicate, the Fellows had two clear goals. They wanted to ensure the quality of surgery. And they wanted to establish control over the practice of uplanders and aliens, that is, surgeons from outside London and those who were not members of the Fellowship. If outsiders wished to practice in or around the city they had to meet the Fellows' standards and line their pockets. The Fellows had the power to back up their rules, even though they remained unincorporated. For they were supported by the mayor and the aldermen, who policed surgery because, among other reasons, they kept half the fines paid by violators.[50]

The surgeons had rivals. Principal among them were the barber-surgeons, elite members of a mystery within the larger company of barbers, most of whose members were barber-tonsors. The barbers organized around 1300 and were chartered in 1376, whence began a century of bickering. The Fellows relied primarily on their superior medical skills, and for much of the fifteenth century managed to keep the barber-surgeons at bay. The surgeons also benefited from continuing malpractice.[51] And they sought the help of the physicians. Their timing was perfect. For in 1421 several London physicians, also distressed at the increase in malpractice, petitioned in Parliament that Henry V crack down on "false surgeons."[52] The physicians claimed that quackery and its proliferation throughout England endangered the community of the realm, not to mention their own social and medical position. They argued for a distinction between "Fisik, a science, and surgeons, *les meistres de cell' arte*."[53] Yet the physicians were not attacking the Fellows—and

---

[49] *Ibid.*

[50] *Ibid.*, p. 337.

[51] As mentioned in note 47, there are dozens of cases. See, for example, the case involving the surgeon Nicholas Bradmore, the physician Lawrence Marks, and the barbers John Morris and John de Calais in CCR, 1399–1413, pp. 99 and 101.

[52] *Rot. Parl.* iv, ff. 130b, 158a.

[53] *Ibid.*

such an attack would probably have done them little good. Henry V was the surgeons' keenest and most powerful patron. He had called them to service in his French ventures, and they had responded and performed well. Thomas Morstede, the leader of the Fellowship, was the king's personal surgeon, favorite doctor, and friend. Nor were the physicians threatened by the surgeons. They simply wanted some control over other practitioners so as not to jeopardize their own positions. If gaining such control meant associating with an elite group of surgeons favored by the Crown, then so much the better. The surgeons must have been delighted. They could now rub shoulders with university-trained practitioners and, by implication, turn the barbers into second-class medical citizens.

The result was the foundation in 1423 of the College of Medicine, consisting of the surgeons of the Fellowship and the university-trained physicians practicing in London.[54] A petition was drawn up and put before the mayor and aldermen, which set up an alternate medical program to those at the universities. It allowed for organization as well as curriculum:

> Master Gilbert Kymer, Doctor of Medicine and Rector of Medicine in the City of London, Master John Suntbreshete, Commissioner in Medicine, and Master Thomas Southwell, bachelor in medicine, bring the two surveyors of the Faculty of Physic in the same city, together with Thomas Morstede and John Harrow, the two masters of the craft of surgery, and all other surgeons, to the mayor and alderman, for authority to found a joint college for better education and control of physicians and surgeons in London and its liberties.[55]

The college was headed by a rector of medicine, the first of whom was Gilbert Kymer, one of the most distinguished physicians of the early fifteenth century.[56] It was chartered not only to police quacks but also to supervise the practice of other doctors, including barber-surgeons, barber-tonsors, apothecaries, and midwives.[57] Provision was made for common exams, benevolence, and medical care for the indigent sick. There

[54] L–B K, p. 11.

[55] *Ibid*. South and Power, *Memorials of the Craft of Surgery*, pp. 47–55; and Beck, *Cutting Edge*, pp. 124–125, discuss the foundation. The charter is reprinted in Appendix B, pp. 298–306, of South and Power. It is ironic that approval came from municipal rather than royal or parliamentary sources.

[56] *T&H*, pp. 61–63; also, see below, pp. 116–117.

[57] L–B K, p. 11; South and Power, *Memorials of the Craft of Surgery*, Appendix B.

was a small endowment, including three tenements in London. One was designated as a common reading and study hall, and the other two for the assembly and consultation of, respectively and separately, the physicians and surgeons.

The College of Medicine could have changed the format not only of medicine but also of English higher education. But it failed. For all the high-minded rhetoric of its charter, the old prejudices between physician and surgeon persisted, the separate houses being one example. Further, many members regarded the college as a convenience, or just another institution designed to ensure their medical monopolies. In fact, physicians and surgeons had little in common. And in some ways, the college itself was a one-issue institution, conceived as the result of a series of malpractice cases. It was the creation of men with strong personalities—Henry V, Gilbert Kymer, Thomas Morstede—and needed them to keep it together. But Henry was dead when the foundation was established, Kymer was plunged into a lawsuit that threatened to ruin his career, and Morstede was left with a college that most of the physicians cared little about.[58]

The college was also challenged by the London Barbers' Company. There were more barbers and even barber-surgeons in London in the 1420s than there were physicians and surgeons combined.[59] The barbers were quick to grasp the realities of urban politics. Few of them, even the most successful barber-surgeons, were as wealthy or prominent as the surgeons of the Fellowship. Acting alone or in small groups they could not threaten the doctors of the college. But taken together, barber-surgeons and barber-tonsors could be formidable. They chafed at control by the collegians, sanctioned as it was by king and Parliament, and turned, with cash in hand, to the municipal authorities of London. In 1427 the barbers got succor from the mayor:

> Masters of the faculty of Surgery in the Mystery of the Barbers of the City [that is, the mystery of barber-surgeons] shall exercise the said faculty [that is, the practice of their kind of surgery] as fully as they did in the days of Thomas Fauconer, late Mayor of London [that is, before 1423], and other mayors, notwithstanding the claim which the Rector and Surveyors of Physicians and the Masters of Surgery now newly impose upon the said

---

[58] *Cal. Plea Mem. Rolls*, 1413–1437, p. 174. Kymer himself was not initially involved, but he and many other members of the college, including Thomas Morstede, were soon dragged in.

[59] See below, Tables 7.1–7.3.

barber by virtue of a certain ordinance made during the mayoralty of William Walderne. . . .[60]

This did not concern the physicians. Their practice was not threatened by surgeons of any stripe, and their principal concern about surgery was malpractitioners. They did not challenge the pretensions of the barbers, and by 1427 most of them seem to have lost interest in the College of Medicine. It was this combination of factors that doomed the college. There are no subsequent records of it, and it had collapsed by 1430. Physicians and surgeons went their separate ways and continued their different kinds of practice. As continental, or at least Italian, physic and surgery grew closer, they drifted apart in England.

In 1435, perhaps convinced that any revival of the College of Medicine was unlikely, the surgeons drew within and had the Fellowship's regulations confirmed.[61] It is likely that they were a reiteration of those drawn up when the Fellowship was founded. They were important because they set the structure and nature of surgery for the next hundred years. Seventeen surgeons signed them (Table 1.2), the largest number of members the Fellowship ever enrolled. By contrast, there were just eight members in 1492, seven in 1493, twelve in 1514, and eleven in 1517 (Table 1.3).[62] Such low figures were characteristic of the Fellow-

TABLE 1.2: 1435 Petitioners of the Fellowship of Surgeons

| | |
|---|---|
| William Bradwardine | John Polley |
| John Hatfield | Thomas Ward |
| John Corby | Henry Stratford |
| John Ford | Geoffrey Constantine |
| Robert Wilton | Robert Branch |
| William Wells | Robert Saxton |
| John Cosyn | Henry Ashburn |
| John Bacton | Thomas Morstede |
| Thomas Hertford | |

[60] L–B K, p. 36.

[61] Guildhall Ms. 5244, f. 234. The text is reprinted in South and Power, *Memorial of the Craft of Surgery*, pp. 307–308; and Beck, *Cutting Edge*, pp. 130–135.

[62] The sources are as follows: 1435, Guildhall Ms. 5244, f. 234, reprinted in Beck, *Cutting Edge*, pp. 130–135, and South and Power, *Memorials of the Craft of Surgery*, p. 307; for 1492, L–B L, p. 29, excerpted in Beck, *Cutting Edge*, p. 127; for 1493, *Journal of the Common Council*, Corporation Library, reprinted in Beck, *Cutting Edge*, pp. 147–148; for 1514, L–B M, f. 216, reprinted in Beck, *Cutting Edge*, p. 120; for 1517, L–B N, 144b, reprinted in

TABLE 1.3: Numbers of Members of the Fellowship
of Surgeons

| Date | Number |
|------|--------|
| 1435 | 17 |
| 1492 | 8 |
| 1493 | 7 |
| 1514 | 12 |
| 1517 | 11 |

ship, and had both a good and a bad effect. On one hand, the membership remained elite. Fellows were well trained and highly skilled, respected and in demand. They got ample fees for their services. But few
surgeons could meet these exacting standards. By the sixteenth century
the officers represented a third of the membership. The Fellows apparently continued to feel that, given their small numbers, incorporation
was unnecessary. This prevented them from having any real influence
in the corporate world of London politics.

The regulations were commonplace, and dealt more with institutional
and administrative than medical issues. There was an annual meeting at
which four members were selected masters, or wardens, of the Fellowship. The masters were confirmed in their authority to supervise surgical practice in and around London; to set new rules of practice, both
in technique and format; and to discipline delinquents. A schedule of
fines was established, though, excepting when they were collected by
municipal authorities, it is hard to imagine how a dozen or so surgeons
could police the activities of between eighty and two hundred barbers
and at least that many non-professional practitioners.[63] Hence the mas-

---

Beck, *Cutting Edge*, and Thomas Vicary, *Anatomie of the Bodie of Man*, ed. F. J. Furnivall
and P. Furnivall (London: EETS, 53, 1888), pp. 210–212. By 1525 Vicary claims, pp. 212–
213 that there were just eight left. See below, p. 301.

[63] I have not found complete annual lists of memberships in the London Barbers' Company. The best records are probably those culled for masters and wardens by Young, *Annals of the Barber-Surgeons*, pp. 1–19. See too Dobson and Walker, *Barbers and Barber-Surgeons*, pp. 129-131, who have used the freemen's rolls, which survive from the 1520s. They
can be found in Guildhall Ms. 5265, "Register of Admissions to the Freedom of the Worshipful Company of Barber-Surgeons of London, 1522–1664." For the sixteenth-century
figures of apprenticeships, see Sir D'Arcy Power, "The Education of a Surgeon Under
Thomas Vicary," in his *Selected Writings* (Oxford: Clarendon Press, 1931), pp. 67–94. See
also below, pp. 302–303.

terships were a burden. They cut down on the number of patients who might be treated, and could be frustrating and even dangerous. No surgeon was expected to serve more than two consecutive terms.

Provisions were made for charity. Each member was to give at least eight pence a year to the poor, a rather minute sum for wealthy men.[64] Each surgeon was required to provide free service for those who could not pay. But even assuming the fullest cooperation by the surgeons—a rather far-fetched assumption—there were too few Fellows to treat the many Londoners who fell sick yet could not afford their fees. By contrast, there were enough barbers to treat a large number of charity cases. When they adopted such a policy in the sixteenth century it brought a great deal of good will.[65]

The Fellowship regulations also dealt with deontology, or medical ethics. Surgeons were advised on setting and collecting fees, and warned against interfering with the morals of the patients, especially female ones.[66] Foreign surgeons were forbidden to practice unless they paid an entry fee and passed a competency test. There were to be no secrets among the Fellows, a key provision. The prestige of the Fellowship was based on the members' skills and innovation; they had risen to prominence because of their effective treatment. Keeping a new technique under wraps hurt the practice of the other Fellows, and it was expected that any new methods would be shared.

In some ways the 1435 regulations were like those of the craft guilds. There were common funds and feasts, and obligations of social security. Apprentices, who trained for between seven and ten years—though there are instances of terms of up to twelve years—could not be held back, nor could journeymen be monopolized by individual surgeons.[67] There were common oaths to bind the Fellows together. The authority of the masters was absolute, but since the office rotated no individual could accumulate too much power, at least not easily and without the

[64] Guildhall Ms. 5244. The regulations are reprinted in South and Power, *Memorials of the Craft of Surgery*, pp. 307–309; and Beck, *Cutting Edge*, pp. 130–135. See Tables 7.12–13.

[65] Thomas Forbes, "Barber-Surgeons Help the Sick Poor," *JHM*, 31, 1976, pp. 461–462. This 1528 record comes from *The Repertory Book of the City of London*.

[66] Guildhall Ms. 5244, f. 234. Some of the deontology may have been taken from John Arderne, *Treatise of Fistula in Ano*, ed. D'Arcy Power (London: EETS, 1910), pp. 4–8.

[67] Guildhall Ms. 5244, f. 234. Interestingly, in L–B D, p. 151, Thomas de Mangrave was said to have been apprenticed to Richard le Barber for twelve years.

conveyance of a circle of friends. The masters regulated the quality of surgery, and were empowered to fine those who did not meet the accepted standards at rates of up to one hundred shillings. There was nothing unusual about any of this; indeed, the regulations were much like those of the barbers, whom the surgeons despised. It is worth reiterating that while the surgeons distinguished themselves medically their fellowship was quite ordinary. This contributed to their decline.

Barbers organized in London and the larger provincial towns throughout the later middle ages.[68] By 1450 they played an important if not crucial role in municipal government. Barbers and most barber-surgeons were undistinguished as medical practitioners. They performed menial tasks and received modest fees, and the most skilled of them did not perform at the high levels of the surgeons. Many barber-tonsors were illiterate, and even barber-surgeons had to offer grooming services to supplement their incomes. But, as noted, there were many of them— in London at least ten barbers for every surgeon; and in the provincial towns a more lopsided ratio. Institutionalization and strength through numbers brought privilege. The London Barbers' Company was well run. The masters did not pretend to the power of the physicians, and in most instances did not challenge the authority of the surgeons. Barbers simply wanted to practice with a minimum of supervision or interference.

The first evidence of the London company comes in 1307. Mayor John Le Blund objected to the way in which barbers were advertising their surgery: they were hanging bloody rags on poles outside their shops, and putting buckets of blood *en leur fenestres*.[69] Le Blund asserted that the barbers were overstepping their authority and expertise; their traditional medical privileges were limited to letting blood only when a physician was present. Loosely organized, the barbers drew back, offering no resistance whatsoever. A year later they were in trouble again. Some of them were accused of turning the therapeutic municipal baths, called *bagnios*, or stews, into brothels.[70] Mayor Sir Nicholas Farndon told Richard le Barber, whom he addressed as the master of the company:

---

[68] For general references to the barbers, see the works cited in note 41, especially Young and Dobson and Walker.

[69] Young, *Annals of the Barber-Surgeons*, p. 23. Young claims the source is L–B D, p. 157. I cannot find it.

[70] L–B C, p. 165; it is reprinted in Young, *Annals of the Barber-Surgeons*, pp. 23–24.

to have supervision over the trade of the barbers. . . . And he was admitted and made oath that every month he would make security throughout the whole of his trade, and if he should find any among them keeping brothels, or acting unseemingly in any other way, and to the scandal of the trade, he was to distrain upon them.[71]

This is the first reliable record of a barbers' organization in England. The mastership seems to have been by appointment of the mayor and held for an extended period. In these first years the barbers had no real corporate power, and there was little distinction between the barber-surgeons and the barber-tonsors. Perhaps this was the reason the barbers acceded to any challenges; they were a minor company, and most members made their living by cutting hair and shaving beards.

This changed, slowly at first, and then more quickly after the Black Death. Cooperation with municipal officials was to pay dividends. In 1309 barbers were admitted as freemen of the city.[72] Since only freemen could exercise political power, this was a crucial step. And it represented an early victory over the rival surgeons, who opposed the barbers' admission and did not gain it themselves until 1312.[73] It is a good example, too, of how the barbers managed to gain influence and the right to broaden and govern their own medical practice. They could not do it through professional expertise. But they recognized the structure of political power in London, and set about to make the best use of it. The masters of the company did not lose sight of the limits of their power; after all, the company never ranked higher than seventeenth of seventy-six guilds. But they wanted to practice medicine, which was more lucrative than cutting hair.

The barbers showed their political acumen a year later when the company became, ex officio, the keepers of Newgate.[74] Members kept general watch, an onerous and time-consuming task, and one from which the surgeons of the Fellowship constantly sought exemption. Yet the barbers' willingness to serve won them good will and eventually led to a medical success. In 1375 they were allowed supervision over London's

[71] L–B C, p. 165; it is reprinted in Young, *Annals of the Barber-Surgeons*, p. 24. It is also in Riley, *Memorials*, p. 67.

[72] Young, *Annals of the Barber-Surgeons*, pp. 256–257. Young is incorrect in claiming that the lists of freemen begin in 1551. London Guildhall Ms. 5265 has records from 1522.

[73] Young, *Annals of the Barber-Surgeons*, p. 25.

[74] L–B D, pp. 212–213; it is reprinted in Young, *Annals of the Barber-Surgeons*, pp. 25–26.

lepers, most of whose houses were adjacent to or near the city gates they watched. They were given it as "the result of their surgical skills."[75]

For the rest of the fourteenth century there are frequent references to individual barbers and their activities, but few to their corporations.[76] Those that do exist show steady gains, not all in medicine. Barbers continued to cut hair, and the company masters did not neglect these activities in their pursuit of medical privileges. In 1375 they managed to gain control over all tonsorial services in London and its suburbs.[77] Unlicensed practitioners, be they denizens, aliens, or uplanders, were prohibited from barbering without the approval of the Londoners. Local amateurs and folk from the countryside had been cutting hair and shaving beards at street stalls without paying a service fee. To enforce their control, the Londoners appointed two of their members as overseers. They even managed to make some medical hay, arguing that these unlicensed barbers were "surgeons . . . little skilled in their craft."[78] This was important in the company's continuing success. It ensured that while the barbers were improving their corporate and medical positions they would not be challenged from below. And what took place in London was doubly important since the London guild served as the model for those in the provincial towns.[79]

In the course of the century, the barbers developed a profitable sideline: they became landlords. In 1381 they acquired a hall on Silver Street, in St. Olav's Ward, and began renting it out.[80] Sometime in the fifteenth century they acquired a second hall, on Monkswell Street in Cripplegate Ward.[81] Both were available to anyone who could pay the hiring fees. Many London companies did this, but the barbers seem to

[75] Young, *Annals of the Barber-Surgeons*, p. 25.

[76] Many individual barbers stand out. Among the more successful were: Roger del Ewerie, whose activities as royal barber are noted in CPR, 1361–1364, p. 395; and Adam de Thorpe, also a royal barber, CPR, 1343–1345, p. 238.

[77] L–B H, p. 20. The full description is in L–B H Ms., f. 26. See Young, *Annals of the Barber-Surgeons*, pp. 35–36; and Riley, *Memorials of London*, pp. 393–394.

[78] South and Power, *Memorials of the Craft of Surgery*, pp. 97–98.

[79] This was especially so in York and Coventry.

[80] B.M. Harl. Ms. 541.

[81] There is controversy over just when this hall was built, with some scholars arguing the 1440s, and others the 1470s. The final word seems to be that of Beck, *Cutting Edge*, pp. xv–xvi. See too R. Theodore Beck, "The Halls of the Barbers, Barber-Surgeons and Surgeons," *Annals of the Royal College of Surgeons*, 47, 1970, pp. 14–29; and Dobson and Walker, *Barbers and Barber-Surgeons*, pp. 77–78.

have done it more than most. In 1422–1423, for example, the hall on Silver Street was rented at least nine times, and became an important source of income for the company.[82]

The barbers also began to accumulate an endowment, mostly of tenements and messuages in and around London. This came from the charitable bequests of members, the most notable of whom was Robert Ferbras.[83] Ferbras, who styled himself a citizen-surgeon, was in fact a barber-surgeon and member of the London company. His will, proved in May, 1473, showed how rich a successful barber-surgeon could become.[84] He had married but had no children, often a circumstance leading to philanthropy, and left much of his estate to his company. This included land, barber shops and equipment, books and cash. His example was followed; while Ferbras was the single greatest benefactor of the London company, many of his colleagues also contributed. John Wilkinson, "citizen and barber," died in 1470.[85] He left the company cash for "the recreation with the fellows of my arts." Richard Estie, a citizen and barber-surgeon, left seven books of surgery, while Thomas Collard left an unspecified "all my books."[86] These became the seed of the company library.

It is instructive to compare the legacies made by the rival surgeons. Because they were richer, their bequests were usually greater. John Dagville I, an executor of Robert Ferbras's will, died in 1477.[87] Also styling himself a citizen-surgeon, Dagville bequeathed books and equipment to the Fellowship, which in the course of the fifteenth century began to build up its library.[88] Thomas Roppisley, another citizen-sur-

---

[82] Dobson and Walker, *Barbers and Barber-Surgeons*, pp. 77–78. See too *Cal. Plea Mem. Rolls, 1458–1482*, pp. xi, 90.

[83] For Ferbras's will see Guildhall Ms. 9826. It is excerpted in Beck, *Cutting Edge*, pp. 137–138. Beck, *Cutting Edge*, pp. 48–54, 73–78, 92–104, 136–144, 158–172, excerpts wills of important surgeons, barber-surgeons and barber-tonsors. See below, pp. 154–156.

[84] Guildhall Ms. 9826.

[85] Commissary Court of London, vi, Wilde Register, f. 55. It is summarized in Beck, *Cutting Edge*, pp. 163–164. See also Marc Fitch, ed., *An Introduction to Testamentary Records in the Commissary Court of London*, i, 1374–1488 (London: British Record Society, 1969).

[86] For Esty, see Com. Court Lon., vi, Wilde Register, f. 192. It is reprinted in Beck, *Cutting Edge*, p. 165. Colard's will is in London Com. Court, vi, Wilde, f. 326; it is excerpted in Beck, *Cutting Edge*, pp. 166–167.

[87] Dagville I's will is Com. Court Lon., Wattys, f. 246. It is excerpted in Beck, *Cutting Edge*, pp. 138–141. This is one of the fullest of late medieval doctors' wills.

[88] Beck, *Cutting Edge*, pp. 140–141.

geon, left cash and books to "my fellowship or craft of the surgeons of London."[89] John Hobbes, seemingly a member of both companies, a royal surgeon and father to the even more prominent William Hobbes, also a member of both companies and a university graduate to boot, left a different kind of legacy: "food, drink, cash to the master, wardens and brothers of my art of surgery."[90] The surgeons were generous. Yet the paradigm of corporate versus particular power held true. Individual surgeons left more than individual barbers. But there were so many more barbers that the total of their legacies was greater than that of the surgeons.[91] And there are no records that the surgeons, sensitive perhaps about their dignity, ever let out their hall. By 1450 the Barbers' Company must have been wealthier than the Fellowship of Surgeons.

Late in the fourteenth century, first in 1376 and then in 1388, the London barbers drew up and had approved their by-laws.[92] These by-laws served as the model for other companies throughout the kingdom, and were a milestone in the development of barbers as doctors. Their inception was prompted when the company masters complained again that unlicensed, unskilled barbers were operating throughout the city, despite earlier proscriptions. In particular, the masters railed against the uplanders, that is, barbers from outside London and its suburbs, who were attracted to the city by the prospect of fat fees. The Londoners claimed:

> [The uplanders] take houses and intermeddle with barbery, surgery and the cure of other maladies, while they know not how to do such things, nor were they instructed in such crafts; to the great danger and in deceit of the people and to the great scandal of all good barbers.[93]

The masters proposed measures that would prevent such abuses:

> . . . there shall always be two good men of the said craft [that is, from the Company of Barbers] chosen by common assent to be wardens of the craft; and that two such persons shall be presented unto the Mayor, Recorder, and Alderman . . . and sworn before them . . . to rule their said craft; and that said masters may inspect the instruments of the said art, to see that

[89] PRO, Prerogative Court of Canterbury Wills, Holgrave, f. 37.

[90] Com. Court Lon., vi, Wilde, f. 85v.

[91] The surgeons' total charity averaged about twenty shillings. The barber-surgeons' total charity averaged 6/8; while that of the barber-tonsors averaged 20 pence.

[92] L–B H, pp. 20, 26; Young *Annals of the Barber Surgeons*, p. 35–37.

[93] The ordinances are printed in Riley, *Memorials of London*, pp. 393–394.

they are good and proper for the service of the people, by reason of the great peril that might ensure thereupon; and that, on complaint of such two masters, all rebellious persons . . . shall . . . pay forty pence. And that from henceforth no man of their craft shall be attested to the franchise [of London] if he be not attested as good and able upon examination before you made. And that no foreigner shall keep house or shop in their craft within the said city and its suburbs thereof.[94]

This was heady stuff, a direct challenge to the authority of the Fellowship, which, it will be recalled, had in 1369 been given control and supervision over the practice of surgery in London. Young claims that this "placed the Barbers on an equal footing with [the Fellowship] in the examination of Surgeons, the inspection of their instruments, etc."[95] He overstated his case. In social status and by law and custom, even when they were performing the same medical tasks—which in fact they seldom did—barbers were assigned an inferior position. But as with many other institutional developments in the fourteenth century the approval of the barbers' by-laws laid the groundwork for their future efforts to achieve parity.

This was also the case in 1388. Richard II ordered all guilds and fraternities in England to report their activities and holdings, and pay a tax.[96] Most of the individual guild reports have been lost, but there is a seventeenth-century copy of that of the London barbers, and the return shows the company's strengths and weaknesses.[97] Though richer than ever, the barbers were still poor when compared with the most influential guilds in the city. Their endowment remained comparatively small. They assembled just once a year, compared with two or even four times for some of the greater companies, and keeping the watch was their sole civic duty.[98] But they had a livery. They provided charity for the poor and social security for widows and orphans. Training was by a seven-year apprenticeship, followed by a period of journey work, which was closely supervised and regulated; a mistake with a patient, after all, was potentially more dangerous than one at a spinning wheel or a forge. Annual dues of forty pence were collected, plus an additional fourteen for

[94] *Ibid.*, p. 394.

[95] Young, *Annals of the Barber-Surgeons*, pp. 36–37.

[96] Beck, *Cutting Edge*, pp. 44–46; and Young, *Annals of the Barber-Surgeons*, pp. 32–34, a reprint from the 1634 record.

[97] Young, *Annals of the Barber-Surgeons*, pp. 32–35.

[98] *Ibid.*, p. 34.

selected fees, and there was a schedule of fines covering every possible violation of the company by-laws. These rules do not disguise the modest power of the London company, especially in medical practice. But again they provided the framework for future expansion.

This was demonstrated in 1410, when the barbers succeeded in getting their rules reconfirmed.[99] The reconfirmation was another direct challenge to the authority of the surgeons, because Mayor Richard Merlawe allowed that the barbers ought to enjoy additional medical prerogatives:

> without the scrutiny of any person or persons of any other craft or trade, under any name whatsoever other than the craft or trade of the said barbers, either as to shaving, making incisions, bloodletting or any other matters pertaining to the art of barbery or surgery, in the craft of the said barbers now practiced or to be practiced thereafter.[100]

The surgeons responded as they always had. They accused the barbers of incompetence and lumped them with malpractitioners.[101] Ironically, the accusation best fitted those barbers against whom the London company had actively campaigned, aliens and uplanders. But the surgeons had managed to denigrate all barbers. In 1415, for example, they argued:

> some barbers of [London], who are inexperienced in the art of surgery, do often times take under their care many sick and maimed persons, fraudulently obtaining possession of very many goods thereby; by reason whereof, they are often times made worse off at their departure that they were at their coming: and that, by reason of inexperience of the same barbers, such persons are often maimed; to the scandal of such skillful and discreet men as practice the art of surgery and the manifest destruction of the people of Our Lord King.[102]

Damnation proved good strategy. London authorities' initial response had been to allow more power to the masters of the Barber's Company. Simon Rolf and Richard Wells, two of the most distinguished barbers in London, were appointed to "maintain close scrutiny and report on mal-

---

[99] L–B I, p. 85; reprinted in Young, *Annals of the Barber-Surgeons*, p. 39.

[100] L–B I, p. 85.

[101] CPR, 1348–1350, p. 561.

[102] L–B I, p. 135; it is reprinted in Young, *Annals of the Barber-Surgeons*, p. 40 and Riley, *Memorials of London*, p. 606.

practice."[103] They were to test, supervise, and check the skills, practices, and cures of all barber-surgeons in the city. A tangible result was
the composition of an impressive code of ethics.[104] But well-meaning
though Rolf and Wells might have been, their reforms and policing faculties were inadequate. By 1415 there were at least 200 and perhaps as
many as 500 practicing barbers in London.[105] There were continuing
complaints against them of abuse and malpractice. Ultimately, it was
these allegations that prompted the physicians to join with the surgeons
and found the College of Medicine.

As noted, the barbers protested. Rebuffed by king, parliament, and
their more learned peers, they went to municipal authorities, and within
the year they were successful. Mayor John Mitchell confirmed their
rights, at least within the city.[106] Such inconsistent behavior by government officials was common, and proved a major obstacle in the development of a system of public health.[107] A few kings, like Henry V, did
have a sort of plan, and tried to improve health care. But most kings,
Parliamentarians, and municipal officials did not. This was a reflection
of and indeed a cause of corporate society. Medical standards were left

[103] L–B I, p. 135.

[104] Young, *Annals of the Barber-Surgeons*, p. 41. The code reads: "Well and faithfully
[were barbers] to watch over and oversee all manners of barbers practicing the art of surgery, and within the liberty of the said city dwelling; to maintain and observe the rules
and ordinances of the craft or practice aforesaid; no one to spare for love, favor, gain or
hate, diligently, without concealment . . . faithfully to examine wounds, bruises, hurts
and other infirmities . . . and all other things to do and perform which right are befitting
or requisite for the master or overseers of such practice."

[105] See Table 7.1. There may have been more. By 1550 the number of apprentices presented annually was 150. Since the term of apprenticeship was about seven years, there
may have been 1,000 apprentices at any given time.

[106] L–B K, p. 36; it is reprinted in Young, *Annals of the Barber-Surgeons*, p. 43. The reference reads: "The Masters and faculty of surgery within the craft of barbers do exercise the
same faculty even as fully and entirely as in the times of Thomas Fauconer, the late mayor
and other mayors, [as] it was granted unto them, notwithstanding the false accusation
which the rector and supervisors of Physic and the Masters of Surgery pretend concerning
a certain ordinance made in the time of William Walderne, late mayor [in 1423, when the
College was chartered] and entered in L–B K, f. 6, the which they now endeavor to enjoin
upon the barbers."

[107] This can be compared with the situation in Italian cities, where municipal government constituted the principal authority, and a coherent system of public health was in
place by the fourteenth century. See Carlo M. Cipolla, *Public Health and the Medical Profession in the Renaissance* (Cambridge: Cambridge University Press, 1976), pp. 1–66.

to the corporations themselves, and their principal interests were privilege and monopoly. If the barbers were willing to pay to have their medical rights reinforced, one mayor wàs prepared to countermand the actions of another. No one seemed to think this was odd, and the barbers came to expect that they would pay every few years to have their privileges confirmed.

The surgeons' response to the barbers' reassertion of medical privilege was to continue to remain aloof. They believed that their association with the physicians strengthened their position, and they continued to have faith in their superior surgical skills. For a time, this was true. In 1424 the physicians and surgeons of the College of Medicine, in their only recorded official act, adjudicated a case of malpractice.[108] Three prominent doctors were involved. One, John Dalton, was a barber. The second was Simon Rolf, the barber-surgeon who ten years earlier had himself been assigned to investigate malpractice. The third was John Harrow, a surgeon and one of the supervisors of the Fellowship. Hence, the litigants represented all levels of surgical practitioners. The three were accused by one William Forest of ignorance and malpractice in treating a wound of his hand, which he claimed they had crippled. A board of inquiry was established, including some of the most prominent doctors in England—Gilbert Kymer, John Suntsbrethete, Thomas Southall, John Corby, Thomas Morstede, William Bradwardine, Henry Ashburn, and John Ford. Not surprisingly, the panel found their colleagues innocent of malpractice of any kind, and the case was dismissed.

But, as noted, this was the only action of the College. The physicians drifted away, and the advisers of the new king, Henry VI, proved as disinterested in medicine as Henry V had been interested. The surgeons continued to remain small and elite, and draw praise for their work. But they ignored the corporate realities of late medieval politics, especially in London. As a result, the barbers caught up. In 1450 the master and wardens of the London company were allowed additional powers of medical enforcement.[109] Attendance at meetings was made mandatory, an important stricture for a guild that relied on numbers rather than on quality, and the fines levied for just about everything were increased.

---

[108] *Cal. Plea Mem. Rolls*, p. 174.

[109] L–B K, p. 250. They are reprinted in South and Power, *Memorials of the Craft of Surgery*, pp. 321–325; and Young, *Annals of the Barber-Surgeons*, pp. 42–47.

And it became virtually impossible for foreign barbers to practice, a response to the influx of Netherlanders in the 1430s and 1440s.[110]

In effect, the powers of the masters were strengthened and centralized. In a small organization like the Fellowship of the Surgeons, this might not have mattered. Seventeen or fewer practitioners, all highly skilled and probably egocentric, plus an office rotated every two years, made it very difficult for anyone to dominate. But in a large company like the barbers, with an elite mystery of barber-surgeons, it was possible for a few men to rise to the top, even with a short term of office. A core of about twenty to thirty barber-surgeons took control of the company, set on the idea that their mystery, if not the entire company, could reach parity with the Fellowship. In 1451 the barber-surgeons made another gain: they were granted a coat-of-arms.[111] This underscored their special privileges within the company, and threw up one more challenge to the surgeons of the Fellowship, who did not receive a similar privilege for over fifty years.[112]

The coat-of-arms was a prelude to greater success. In 1462, in the reign of a new, strong, and avaricious king, Edward IV, the entire Barbers company was incorporated.[113] The granting charter was explicit in permitting a medical role. Indeed, its preamble declared that incorporation was necessary so that medical standards could be kept high:

> [The Company] of Barbers of Our City of London, exercising the Mystery of the Art of Surgery, as well as respecting wounds, bruises, hurts and other infirmities of our liegemen, and healing and curing the same, as in letting blood, and drawing the teeth of our liegemen, have for a long time undergone and supported, and daily do undergo and support, great and manifold applications and labors; and also how through ignorance, negligence and stupidity of some men of the said barbers, as well as freemen of the said city, and who daily resort to the said city, and in the mystery of Surgery are not sufficiently skilled, whereby very many and almost infinite evils have before this time happened to many of our liegemen, in their wounds, hurts, bruises, and other infirmities, by such Barbers and Surgeons, on account of their defect in healing and curing; from which cause, some of our said liegemen have gone the way of all flesh, and others,

[110] CPR, 1429–1436, pp. 548–581.

[111] Young, *Annals of the Barber-Surgeons*, p. 432. He reproduces the design.

[112] *Ibid.*, pp. 69, 433.

[113] CPR, 1461–1467, p. 109. They are reprinted in Young, *Annals of the Barber-Surgeons*, pp. 52–62. See also South and Power, *Memorials of the Craft of Surgery*, pp. 326–330.

through the same cause, have been all given over as incurable and past relief, and it is to be dreaded, that similar or greater evils may be in the future
arise on this head, unless proper remedy is by us, speedily provided for the
same. We therefore, heartily weighing and considering that such evils do
happen to our liegemen for want of the examinations, corrections, and
punishments by a due supervision of such Barbers and surgeons as are sufficiently skilled and instructed in the said mysteries or arts aforesaid; have
at the humble request of our aforesaid, beloved, honest and freemen of the
said Mystery of Barbers in our said city, granted to them that the said Mystery and all men of the said mystery aforesaid, may be in deed and name
on body and one perpetual community, and that two principals of the said
community may, with the consent of twelve persons, or at least eight of the
said community who are best skilled in the mystery of surgery, every year
elect and make out of the Community two Masters or Governors of the ut-
most skill, to superintend, rule and govern the Mystery and Community
aforesaid and all men of the mystery, and of the business of the same for-
ever.[114]

The charter continued in rambling fashion, but making several important points. First, it confirmed the existence of the elite mystery of
barber-surgeons within the larger company. This allowed the barber-
surgeons to have their cake and eat it too—to have the advantages of a
small, well-trained elect, on one hand, and the corporate power of larger
numbers, on the other. And, second, a consequence of the new role of
the mystery, the charter was concerned more with medicine than with
barbering. Ethics and standards were stressed, qualities that the surgeons had always argued were unique to them. Yet the barber-surgeons
did not forget what it was that enabled them to challenge the surgeons
in the first place; they strengthened and extended the company's constitution. Tight controls were confirmed to the masters, who had the
power to fine and regulate all practices and professional activities.[115] The
positions were still rotated so that no individual could accrue too much
power. But power was oligarchic, vested in the hands of twenty or so
members of the mystery of barber-surgeons.

The Barbers' Charter of 1462 made two other important points. The
property rights and privileges of the company, with all their rents, incomes, and guarantees, were assured for the future. While the manage-

---

[114] Young, *Annals of the Barber-Surgeons*, p. 56.
[115] They may have had more power than the masters and wardens of most other companies. See Unwin, *Gilds and Companies of London*, pp. 64–175.

ment of the endowment was vested with the masters and wardens, they could use funds only for the benefit of the company. And the "benefit" was to be decided by all the members.[116] This became especially important when in 1470 a regulation from the Crown allowed that property, particularly tenements, could be held for corporate purposes.[117] Finally, the barbers were allowed to teach surgery, giving them another opportunity to achieve parity with surgeons of the Fellowship.[118] Constitutionally, if not yet medically, the barbers, in Young's words, were "with the possession of their charter . . . in an unassailable position, and we hear no more of their molestation by the Guild of Surgeons."[119]

While the barbers were making their gains, there is virtually no record of activity from the surgeons. It is more likely that the Fellowship, whose membership was shrinking (Table 1.3), was inactive. Its privileges were essentially unchallenged by the rise of the barbers. The surgeons still hoped to associate with the physicians, and probably felt secure in their relations with the barbers. But the barbers continued to be active and persistent in their demands, and to participate in medical activities. In 1482, the Privy Council approved more regulations for what was now called "the science of barbery."[120] The barber-surgeons also asked that additional powers fall to them. Despite the allusion to science, the new regulations were constitutional rather than medical. They tightened the master's control over journeymen and apprentices, yet did so without improving their training. Indeed, so complete was the rise of the barber-surgeons that many Fellows began to hedge their bets and seek a double livery, that is, membership in the Barbers' Company as well as their own guild, a possibility since the Fellowship remained unincorporated.[121] This became fashionable as well as politic when Edward IV and Richard III became members of the barber surgeons' mystery in the 1480s.[122]

The rise of the London Barbers' Company was not without setback.

---

[116] Young *Annals of the Barber-Surgeons*, pp. 53–54.

[117] Beck, *Cutting Edge*, pp. 131–150, makes much of this.

[118] Bullough, *Development of Medicine*, pp. 68–76; Young, *Annals of the Barber-Surgeons*, pp. 361–362; Pelling and Webster, "Medical Practitioners," pp. 173–177.

[119] Young *Annals of the Barber-Surgeons*, p. 61.

[120] L–B L, p. 191; Young, *Annals of the Barber-Surgeons*, pp. 61–65.

[121] Among the many were John and William Hobbes, as noted, and Richard Esty. See Beck, *Cutting Edge*, p. 145.

[122] *Ibid.*, p. 146.

The incorporation charters of 1462 and 1483 heightened the differences between the barber-surgeons and the barber-tonsors, and occasionally those differences boiled over. In 1487 the barber-surgeon masters of the company presented more ordinances to the mayor.[123] The ordinances were not really new, but they reflected the tensions within the company and generally showed off the advantages of the barber-surgeons. Barber-tonsors were subjected to a battery of examinations in order to "ensure high medical standards."[124] Practitioners in London and its suburbs were to be under the complete control of the company officers, all of whom were barber-surgeons. Foreign and upland practitioners, most of whom were barber-tonsors, were reminded of their subservience to the barber-surgeons. The masters were confirmed in their control over all journeymen and apprentices, including those of the barber-tonsors. Some barber-tonsors chafed at these prospects, but they did not rebel. For the mystery of barber-surgeons still recruited members from among the barber-tonsors, and it had become profitable to be a barber-surgeon. By the 1480s the barber-surgeons had attained a kind of parity with the surgeons. What as recently as 1460 had seemed preposterous—a union between the surgeons and the barber-surgeons—was now possible. In part, of course, this was due to the corporate successes of the barbers and the small numbers of the surgeons. But it was also due to a decline in skills among the Fellows. It will be argued in Chapters Four and Six that the surgeons' medical successes were predicated on the skills they picked up on the battlefields of the Hundred Years War. Suffice it to say here that by the 1480s the great campaigns had ended, very few surgeons who had served in the last battles were still alive, and the expertise of the Fellows was not as great as it once had been.[125]

The surgeons of the Fellowship must have realized this because in the 1490s they began to concentrate on securing their corporate position. In 1492, they were granted a coat-of-arms, albeit forty years after the barber-surgeons got theirs.[126] In the same year, they won several privileges and exemptions.[127] Yet the text explicating these privileges suggests the surgeons' problem:

[123] L–B L, p. 244; Young, *Annals of the Barber-Surgeons*, pp. 62–64.
[124] *Ibid.*
[125] See below, pp. 130–167.
[126] Young, *Annals of the Barber-Surgeons*, pp. 69, 433.
[127] L–B L, pp. 286-287.

The wardens and other good folk of the Fellowship of Surgeons enfranchised in the City of London, not passing in number eight persons, before
the mayor and Alderman, and presented a petition praying that in consideration of their small numbers, they might continue to be discharged from
serving as constables and from any office bearing arms, as well as from ju-
ries, as they had been accustomed time out of mind, and further, to continue to have search of all foreigners using the fraternity of surgery in the
city.[128]

Here was the dilemma: to be exclusive demanded being small, a dangerous characteristic in a corporate society. There were just eight Fellows
in 1492, and they had to be exempted from the very service that had
made them important to begin with.[129]

This led in 1493 to "The Agreement Between the Fellowship of Surgeons and the Company of Barbers."[130] Medical historians have been arguing about the effects of the agreement for a hundred years. South and
Power, historians of the surgeons, dismissed it as inconsequential.[131]
Young, a historian of the barbers, regarded it as epoch-making, and said
it brought equality.[132] He claimed that the surgeons and barbers continued on a cooperative path until their union by act of Parliament in 1540.
Beck, a historian of surgery, generally followed Young, playing up what
he calls the new "professionalism" of the barber-surgeons.[133] Bullough,
a social as well as medical historian, regarded it as a triumph of physicians, those who worked with their minds, over all surgical practitioners, who worked with their hands.[134] The answer probably lies some-
where between all these interpretations, but closest to that of Bullough.
In the end, the physicians would triumph, though that was not obvious
until the 1530s. In 1493 the Fellowship of Surgeons still remained elite,
aloof, and apart. The Fellowship and the Company were not yet joined.
Each continued to elect its own masters and wardens, set its own policies

[128] The text is reprinted in Beck, *Cutting Edge*, pp. 127–128.

[129] Their ranks were still small when Henry VIII granted them a similar exemption
twenty years later. See *LPFD*, i, 1509–1514, #4848; Vicary, *The Anatomie of the Bodie*, pp.
210–212.

[130] Guildhall Ms. 5244, f. 23v. It is reprinted in South and Power, *Memorials of the Craft
of Surgery*, pp. 333–334; Young, *Annals of the Barber-Surgeons*, pp. 66–68; and Beck, *Cutting
Edge*, pp. 147–148.

[131] South and Power, *Memorials of the Craft of Surgery*, p. 82.

[132] Young, *Annals of the Barber-Surgeons*, p. 66.

[133] Beck, *Cutting Edge*, p. 147.

[134] Bullough, *Development of Medicine*, pp. 86–92.

and medical standards, and attract different kinds of patients.[135] In some instances they acted jointly. But the essence of the agreement was that the surgeons would not try to regulate the practices of the barbers—something that, in fact, they had not been able to do for a half century. And both groups agreed that no one could practice surgery of any kind in or around London without their joint approval.

The surgeons and barbers generally continued to go their own ways. In 1495, Henry VII approved a petition from the Mystery of the Barber-Surgeons.[136] Several barber-surgeons, seemingly enamored of the surgeons, had ceased to attend the ceremonies of the Barbers' Company. Any such breach in the corporate structure of the company was potentially disastrous, and the other barber-surgeons asked the king to help them preserve their unity. He did, and the errant barber-surgeons were fined and forced back into the fold. The barber-surgeons acted, too, to mollify the barber-tonsors. In 1497 a diploma was awarded by the master and wardens of the Barbers' Company to one of their members, Robert Anson, presumably a barber-tonsor, allowing him to practice surgery.[137] But the barber-surgeons were careful not to jeopardize their new professional standing. Anson was required to pass a series of examinations before "a great audience of many right well expert men in surgery and others. . . ."[138] One of the "others" was a noted physician,

TABLE 1.4: Signatories of the 1493 Agreement between the Surgeons and the Barbers

| Name | Guild | Name | Guild |
|------|-------|------|-------|
| Robert Taylor | surgeon | Robert Scarlot | barber |
| Robert Haliday | barber | Robert Beverley | surgeon |
| William Wetwang | surgeon | John Johnson, Sr. | barber |
| John Johnson, Yr. | barber | Richard Knight | surgeon |
| Thomas Roppisley | surgeon | James Scott | barber |
| Richard Hayward | barber | John Wells | barber |
| Thomas Thornton | surgeon | James Ingoldesby | barber |
| Harry Tile | barber | John Taylor | barber |
| John Hart | surgeon | Richard Snoddenham | barber |
| Richard Newell | barber | Nicholas Levering | barber |
| John Pyncham | barber | Andrew Oliver | barber |
| John Markham | surgeon | John Wilson | barber |

[135] See below, pp. 286–295.

[136] L–B L, p. 156.

[137] Guildhall Ms. 5244; Beck, *Cutting Edge*, pp. 149–150; Young, *Annals of the Barber-Surgeons*, pp. 69–70.

[138] Guildhall Ms. 5244; Beck, *Cutting Edge*, p. 150.

John Smith.[139] And, in 1499, the masters obtained from Henry VII, ever eager to fill his coffers, a confirmation of the charter of incorporation of 1462.[140] They even managed a few changes. The number of masters was raised from two to four, and the mystery of barber-surgeons was again recognized. All this cost just twenty shillings, the same price as the original charter twenty-seven years earlier.

There are several interesting aspects to these developments. First, the barber-surgeons recognized the continuing importance of corporate unity, and were quick to discipline members of their own mystery who violated the rules of the larger company. Further, the barber-surgeons used this as an opportunity to reiterate their rules and reassert their own dominance in the company; office and control continued to be vested in their mystery. They were concerned with the quality of the medical care they offered. But when they sought help they turned, not to the surgeons, but to the physicians. And it is easy to see why the barber-tonsors accepted the continuing domination of the company by the barber-surgeons. It was always possible to rise through the ranks as Robert Anson had. Most important, by 1500 the barber-surgeons of London, if not yet the barber-tonsors, had become indistinguishable from the surgeons of the Fellowship.

Outside London and the university towns there was less competition and strife between medical corporations because there were fewer kinds of practitioners.[141] Most provincial doctors were barbers.[142] There were physicians and surgeons in the larger towns like Bristol, Norwich, and York. But they were few in number and charged high fees; the real competition barbers faced came from below, from lay and folk practitioners. Further, most provincial barbers offered medical and tonsorial services, eliminating the kind of internal rivalry that plagued their London counterparts. In all, barber-tonsors dominated licensed medical practice out-

---

[139] *T&H*, p. 183.

[140] Young, *Annals of the Barber-Surgeons*, pp. 70–71. The manuscript is in the Corporation of London Library, L–B M, f. 216. According to Beck, *Cutting Edge*, p. 150, the charter changed the company name to Barber-Surgeons.

[141] I will not discuss the unique situation of medical institutions in the university towns. See Bullough, *Development of Medicine*, pp. 74–92; and Pelling and Webster, "Medical Practitioners," pp. 188–206. The discussion will generally cover barbers. A good article on apothecaries is T. D. Whittet, "The Apothecary in Provincial Guilds," *MH*, 8, 1964, pp. 245–273.

[142] The precise figure from the file is 75.1% See Table 7.2.

side London. And they consciously modelled their organizations on the example of the London Barbers' Company.

The best evidence of provincial medical institutions comes from York.[143] As befitted the capital of the north, with its own court and social life, York was one of the county towns from which there are records of different kinds of doctors. There was a physicians' organization as early as 1299 and a barbers' guild by 1350.[144] The first continuous sources are the Freemen's Rolls.[145] The 1381 rolls are particularly good; they show one physician, apparently with a university degree, and eighteen barbers.[146] These nineteen practitioners—and they surely underenumerate the actual total of doctors in York—provided the substantial doctor/patient ratio in a town of about 7,500 of one to 400.[147] Further, the number of barbers held steady throughout the fifteenth century, as York's overall population began to decline. By 1450 the company may have had between twenty and thirty masters, making it the largest service guild in the town.[148]

[143] For York, the best sources are B.M. Egerton Ms. 2572; *Register of the Freemen of York, 1272–1558*, Surtees Society, 96, 1897; and *Register of the Guild of Corpus Christi*, Surtees Society, 57, 1872. See too *The Victoria History of the Counties of England, Yorkshire; The City of York*, ed. P. M. Tillott (London: Institute of Historical Research, 1961), pp. 25–116; Margaret C. Barnet, "The Barber-Surgeons of York," *MH*, 12, 1968, pp. 19–30; G. A. Auden, "The Gild of the Barber-Surgeons of the City of York," *Proceedings of the Royal Society of Medicine*, 21, 1927, pp. 70–76; and Vern L. Bullough, "Training of Nonuniversity Educated Medical Practitioners in the Later Middle Ages," *JHM*, 14, 1959, pp. 446–458.

[144] Auden, "Gild of Barber-Surgeons," pp. 70–76.

[145] *Register of Freemen*, pp. 35–253.

[146] A question arises as to the interpretation of the York and other freemen's rolls. Do they represent entrants for a year, or do they represent a periodic renewal of freemen status in which all or some guild members periodically reaffirm their status? Barnet, "Barber-Surgeons of York," pp. 19–20, seems to think the latter, for she implies that the 18 barbers of 1381 represented the entire guild. I am not so sure. See R. B. Dobson, "Admissions to the Freedom of the City of York," *Ec.H.R.*, 2nd series, 25, 1973, pp. 1–21.

[147] According to *The World Health Statistics Annual, 1978*, iii (Geneva: W.H.O., 1979), England and Wales had a population of 49,195,000. It had 64,000 physicians, 14,200 dentists, and 13,626 pharmacists.

[148] *VCH: City of York*, pp. 84–85. For comparable figures for other towns, see: Robert S. Gottfried, *Bury St. Edmunds and the Urban Crisis, 1290–1539* (Princeton: Princeton University Press, 1982), pp. 117–122; W. G. Hoskins, "English Provincial Towns in the Early Sixteenth Century," in his *Provincial England* (London: Macmillan, 1963), pp. 68–85; and Charles Phythian-Adams, *Desolation of a City: Coventry and the Urban Crisis of the Late Middle Ages* (Cambridge: Cambridge University Press, 1979), pp. 74–124.

The York barbers set themselves up like those of London.[149] They were governed by two masters, who were given absolute power, but were elected for a term of just one year. The members met annually for a general business meeting. Accounts were rendered, fines paid, and new rules and applicants for admission were discussed. Aliens and uplanders—ironically, practitioners like the York barbers were the uplanders against whom the Londoners railed—were proscribed from practice unless they paid a fine of six shillings, eight pence. This set the tone for the regulations. There were rules about the conduct of medical practice, but few about its substance. There seem not to have been, for example, exams to test the competence of barbers, guild members or otherwise. This was typical of practice outside London. There were many practitioners, but the quality of their skills was variable.

The guild officers in York were called supervisors, an appropriate designation. They watched over all guild members, from apprentices to masters. They ran spot checks on barber shops in order to police the hours of practice, and fined violators. Before the Black Death, the York medical establishment, like those elsewhere in England, was confident of its practice. Membership was restricted, and hours of operation were circumscribed. Few journeymen made master, and Sunday work was prohibited.

After the commencement of the plagues this changed.[150] Unlicensed practitioners operated more boldly than before, and offered services at all hours. The York barbers responded by allowing night and even Sabbath hours in order to keep the competition at bay. Easy entry and general fluidity also became characteristic. Aliens and uplanders had only to pay a small fee to practice.[151] This reflected a new attitude: quacks and charlatans would practice anyway. Why not sanction them and make some profit to boot? Nor were guild masters subjected to rigorous standards. They paid six shillings and eight pence for the continuing right to practice. If a master violated a regulation, he was placed on probation for three months, after which he was restored to full guild membership unless, quite literally, he killed someone. Journeymen had to pay the customary six and eight and serve a three-month probation. Afterward,

[149] York's medical history is discussed by Auden and Barnett. The guild book is B.M. Egerton 2572.
[150] Barnet, "Barber-Surgeons of York," pp. 19–30.
[151] Ibid.

they were required to pay another fee of forty shillings, and then became guild masters. It was even possible to remain outside the guild and still practice; such barbers simply had to pay a monthly fee, also forty shillings. Throughout the regulations there is hardly a word about the quality of medical practice. The closest reference was to the livery, developed by 1400: a red and white striped pole, with a bleeding dish on the top.[152]

By the late fifteenth century conditions had changed again. Perhaps standards had so deteriorated that, as had been the case in London, municipal authorities demanded real medical reforms. Or perhaps the surfeit of practitioners had made medicine less profitable, and fewer aliens, uplanders, and local journeymen sought to become practitioners. In any case their corporate structure and power intact, the barbers turned to the quality of the medical care.[153] The 1487 guild regulations showed increasing concern with techniques of surgery, widespread literacy among the barbers, and a new deontology.[154] Even their art work showed new perspective: the frontispiece of the guild book was a drawing of Ss. Cosmas and Damian, hardly firm evidence of clinical practice, but at least a clear reference to the patron saints of surgery, something for which earlier barbers seemed to care little. By the end of the fifteenth century the York barbers' guild looked remarkably like that of London. The difference was that in York the barbers were unchallenged. There were few physicians, surgeons, or apothecaries to constrain them, and no tension between the barber-surgeons and barber-tonsors, primarily because there was little distinction between the two. The results were mixed. The barbers were successful, stable, and had some power in town government. But they lacked proper medical training and did not have competitors to spur them on. As a result, the quality of medical care, even after the reforms of the 1480s, was poor.

Of the other county towns Bristol, Norwich, and Coventry have the best records. The Bristol Barbers' Guild was comprehensive and broadbased.[155] Among its members were practitioners who in London would

[152] *Ibid.*

[153] B.M. Egerton Ms. 2572, ff. 17–19.

[154] *Ibid.*, ff. 17–50.

[155] Sources for Bristol are: *The Little Red Book of Bristol*, ed. F. Bickley, 2 vols. (Bristol: W. Crofton Hemmons, 1900); and *Calendar of the Bristol Apprentice Book, 1532–1565*, ed. D. Hollis, Bristol Record Society, 14, 1948. See too: *The Victoria History of the Counties of England: Gloucestershire*, vols. 1, 3, 4; George Parker, "Early Bristol Medical Institutions:

TABLE 1.5: Barbers' Guilds and the Dates of Their Inceptions

| Town | Date | Town | Date |
|------|------|------|------|
| York | 1345 | Dublin | 1446 |
| Norwich | 1349 | Salisbury | 1458 |
| Lincoln | 1369 | Durham | 1468 |
| London | 1376 | Ipswich | 1474 |
| Bristol | 1395 | | |
| Coventry | 1421 | Exeter | 1487 |
| Beverley | 1430 | Hereford | 1503 |
| Newcastle | 1442 | Chester | 1540 |

have been members of the Fellowship of Surgeons. Indeed, by an act of Parliament in 1363 every doctor in Bristol save university-educated physicians had to belong to the guild.[156] The company regulations, laid out in *The Little Red Book* in 1395 and confirmed and incorporated by 1418, were similar to those of the London and York guilds.[157] By 1439 the Bristol guild was licensed, along with those from London, York, Newcastle, Salisbury, Exeter, and Durham, in a general Parliamentary ordinance.[158] Such reiterations of corporate identity and the sense of tradition they nurtured were important. They established the legitimacy of the Bristol barbers, especially against unlicensed and non-professional practitioners, and helped prevent surgeons and perhaps even physicians from forming autonomous organizations. In Bristol, as in York, the members of the barbers' guild were unchallenged in their practices.

There were a few distinct characteristics of the Bristol guild. The first, as noted, was the barbers' control over all other practitioners save physicians.[159] Bristol barbers were more powerful than their counterparts in any other major town in England. This circumstance developed in the generation after the Black Death, when the practitioners were preoccupied with their failures and worried about maintaining their position. Unlike the York barbers those in Bristol decided to restrict guild

The Mediaeval Hospitals and Barber-Surgeons," *Transactions of the Bristol and Gloucestershire Archaeological Society*, 44, 1922, pp. 155–177; and R. Milnes Walker, "The Barber-Surgeons of Bristol," *Bristol Medico-Chirurgical Journal*, 90. 1975, pp. 51–53.

[156] Walker, "The Barber-Surgeons," p. 51. Also, see Charles E. Boucher, "The Black Death in Bristol," *Transactions of the Bristol and Gloucestershire Archaeological Society*, 60, 1938, pp. 31–46.

[157] *Little Red Book*, ii, pp. 69–71 for 1395; and pp. 135–141 for 1418.

[158] *Ibid.*, pp. 152–158.

[159] Parker, "Early Bristol Medical Institutions," pp. 155–166.

membership, and complained constantly about practice by "ignorant
. . . and unlearned people."[160] Their traditional rivals were not uplanders or aliens, but Bristol tailors, fullers, weavers, and waxmakers, all of
whom wished to practice surgery. In 1430, the waxmakers, whose claim
to being practitioners rested on the fact that they, like barbers, used wax
for embalming, made a legal challenge to try to break the barbers' monopoly.[161] This was not without precedent, for waxmakers in other
towns, including Chester, Newcastle, and Norwich, had won some
medical privileges. But the Bristol barbers demanded that town officials
test the waxmakers' surgical skills, arguing that they were undisciplined
and poorly trained. Apparently they were, for the mayor ruled for the
barbers, and the monopoly was not challenged again.

A second peculiarity was the prominent role the barbers' company
played in civic ritual. All medieval guildsmen were expected to participate in town affairs and, to varying degrees, all did. To have forsworn
such rituals would have jeopardized a guild's civic position. In most
towns the barbers were limited to relatively unimportant tasks, such as
the night watches of the Londoners. But in Bristol the opposite was true;
they participated at the highest levels. An example was their prominent
role in the *Corpus Christi* pageant, one of the most important events on
the town calendar, and a chance to display individual success and flaunt
corporate power.[162] This in turn was a reflection of their power in the
town and domination over medical practice.[163]

The Norwich guild resembled that of Bristol, for the barbers were
powerful.[164] Membership included some physicians and surgeons as

[160] *Little Red Book*, p. 136.

[161] *Ibid*. This was the case with waxchandlers in other places. See Clark, *History of the
Royal College*, i, p. 9. See too Geoffrey Parker, *The Early History of Surgery in Great Britain*
(London: A.C. Black, 1920), pp. 58–70.

[162] Charles Phythian-Adams, "Ceremony and Citizen: The Communal Year in Coventry, 1450–1550," in Paul Slack and Peter Clark, eds., *English Towns in Transition, 1500-
1700* (London: R.K.P., 1972), pp. 57–85, has shown the importance of these events.

[163] Walker, "The Barber-Surgeons," pp. 52–53.

[164] The best sources for Norwich's medical history are freemen's rolls and a 1388 royal
writ that described the organization of the barbers' guild. See: *Calendar of Freemen of Norwich, 1317–1603*, ed. Walter Pye (London: Elliott Stock, 1880); *An Appendix of Indentures
of Norwich Apprentices*, eds. Winifred M. Rising and Percy Millican, *Norfolk Record Society*,
29, 1959; *Records of the City of Norwich*, 2 vols., ed. William Hudson and John Cottingham
Tingay (Norwich: Jarrold, 1910); and *An Introduction to the Obedientiary and Mannor Rolls of
Norwich Cathedral Priory*, ed. (Norwich: Jarrold, 1930). See too Charles William, *Masters
Wardens and Assistants of the Gild of the Barber-Surgeons of Norwich* (Norwich: Jarrold, 1900).

well as barber-surgeons and barber-tonsors.[165] Further, guild regulations were more concerned with medical practice than were those of the
other barbers' companies, and included discussion of a range of specialities and treatments, including dentistry, the making and selling of
drugs, bonesetting, and the more typical cupping and leeching that provincial barbers usually performed.[166] In Norwich, as in York and Bristol, the barbers so outnumbered the other practitioners that there was
relative harmony in the medical community. This harmony was enhanced by the 1511 Parliamentary Licensing Act. Power of regulation
passed, as prescribed, to the bishop of Norwich; he turned to the barbers for advice on enforcement, enabling them to add the authority of
the church to their already formidable powers.[167]

The Norwich guild, like those of London, York, and Bristol, had a
substructure of fraternities and charities, with their attendant obligations.[168] Around 1300, membership ranged from twelve to twenty masters, making it smaller than those in the other towns. But, given Norwich's population of around 10,000, plus the presence of a few
physicians and surgeons who did not join the guild and the inevitable
substrata of unlicensed practitioners, the doctor to patient ratio of at
least 1 to 650 was still quite good.[169] And there is evidence suggesting an
even higher ratio after the Black Death, when population fell to perhaps
6,000, and never rose to above 8,000.[170] Seventeen barbers were admitted to the freedom between 1349 and 1396, thirty-eight between 1400
and 1449, and thirty-one between 1450 and 1498.[171]

In some ways the Norwich barbers were distinct. There was more
family continuity than in other towns, with about a tenth of the total
number of practitioners having sons, daughters, or nephews who followed them into practice.[172] And there was a separation, unique in

[165] Williams, *Masters, Wardens and Assistants*, pp. 1–17.

[166] *Ibid.*, pp. 5–9.

[167] Young, *Annals of the Barber-Surgeons*, pp. 575–577.

[168] Williams, *Masters, Wardens and Assistants*, pp. 5–9.

[169] See below, p. 253.

[170] For Norwich's population, see James Campbell, *Norwich* (London: Scolar Press,
1975), pp. 10–17; and Barbara Green and Rachel M. R. Young, *Norwich: The Growth of a
City* (Norwich: City of Norwich Museum, 1972), pp. 15–18.

[171] *Calendar of Freemen's Rolls*, pp. 1–155. They are arranged alphabetically, and not by
date.

[172] *Ibid.*, pp. 3, 4, 5, 8, 12, 17, 22, 29, 32, 36, 39, 42, 44, 45, 48, 50, 52, 53, 54, 57, 62,
68, 72, 76, 78, 84, 85, 86, 87, 100, 104, 110, 112, 116, 126, 132, 137, 140, 141, 143, 146,

county towns, between barber-surgeons and barber-tonsors. As in London the barber-surgeons dominated the barbers' guild; unlike London,
this meant that they also dominated medical practice throughout the
town and its environs.

A final example of provincial medical organization comes from Coventry. There are good records of the barbers, mostly from the town leet
court books.[173] In 1449 Coventry's mayor ordered a general muster,
with all guilds required to participate. Twenty-three guilds returned a
total of 603 men, fifteen of them barbers.[174] This suggests that Coventry
had perhaps twenty to thirty active barbers in the middle of the fifteenth
century; with a town population of perhaps 6,500, this would make for
a doctor/patient ratio of about 1/200, even better than those in the other
major county towns, and providing excellent medical coverage.[175] But
quantity did not necessarily mean quality. The muster also ranked the
guilds, using a combination of factors, including size, wealth, and traditional prestige. The barbers placed fifteenth of twenty-three, a lower-
middling position which gives interesting perspective on the place of
practitioners in the county towns. In Bristol and Norwich, doctors
rubbed shoulders with the town elite. There were enough of them to
provide adequate medical coverage, but not so many as to breed too
much competition. York and Coventry had very large numbers of barbers. In both towns, medical practice brought limited wealth and prestige. Even the wealthiest practitioners in Coventry were less successful
and influential than textile merchants and most victuallers.[176]

Coventry's barbers were incorporated in 1445.[177] Their rules and regulations were like those of the other barbers' guilds, and need not be discussed. One aspect of practice in Coventry does stand out, however: the

---

151, 152, 153. A fourteenth-century family of smiths is the Dephams, p. 42; a fifteenth-
century family of grocers is the Southertons, p. 127.

[173] *The Coventry Leet-Book, or Mayor's Register*, ed. Mary D. Harris, 2 vols. (London:
EETS, 1907–1913; *Register of the Guild of the Holy Trinity, St. Mary, St. John the Baptist and St.
Katherine of Coventry*, i, ed. Mary D. Harris, *Dugdale Society*, 13, 1935; *Statute of the Mer-
chant Roll of Coventry, 1392–1416*, ed. Alice Beardwood, *Dugdale Society*, 17, 1939. See too
Phythian-Adams, *Desolation of a City*.

[174] *Coventry Leet-Book*, pp. 224–226.

[175] The information comes from the doctors' file.

[176] The wealth measure is discussed below, pp. 442–445. For comparison, see Hoskins,
"English Provincial Towns," pp. 68–85; and Phythian-Adams, *Desolation of a City*, pp.
204–220.

[177] *Coventry Leet-Book*, pp. 224–226.

struggle over whether to keep Sunday hours.[178] In itself, this was not unique. Barbers in Canterbury London and, as noted, York, also faced this problem.[179] But in Coventry working on the Sabbath became a preoccupation. The barbers said it was their duty to offer services every day; if this is to be taken literally it is a remarkable assertion of nascent professionalism. But the barbers had other motives. They alleged that when they did not practice, unlicensed practitioners from surrounding villages came into town and did, to the detriment of the public weal. Further, the barbers pointed out that people got sick every day, and that they had to offer their cures when needed. This point was conceded by Coventry's mayor and bishop.[180] In 1421, barbers were allowed to open Sunday "if he [the patient] be a sick man or a wayfaring man that come to this city."[181]

The barbers did not restrict their practice; it was soon reported that they were treating anyone, and shaving and cutting hair to boot. In 1436, the mayor asked that the Sunday rule be changed and, ironically, was supported by the barbers.[182] The barbers now claimed that work on the Sabbath was sacrilegious and, besides, they were tired and wanted a day of rest just like other guildsmen. Further, they pushed for municipal authorities to police uplanders and unlicensed practitioners who operated in violation of guild bylaws. This they did not get, and the dispute simmered and occasionally erupted over for the next decade, the barbers trying to assert their monopoly, and the town fathers trying to offer general medical services. This was particularly important in Coventry, since it stood at the crossroads of the Midlands, and was visited regularly by travelers. Finally, in 1445 the mayor and aldermen, who came from guilds more powerful than that of the barbers, prevailed.[183] Barbers and members of another service guild, the blacksmiths, were forced to open every day.

[178] *Ibid.*, p. 225.

[179] For York, see Barnet, "The Barber-Surgeons of York," pp. 19–30. In 1413 the archbishop of Canterbury protested against the Sunday practice of the London barbers. See L–B I, pp. 115–116; and Young, *Annals of the Barber-Surgeons*, pp. 47–49. For Canterbury, see Leslie G. Matthews, "Spicers and Apothecaries in the City of Canterbury," *MH*, 9, 1965, pp. 289–291.

[180] *Coventry Leet-Book*, p. 226.

[181] *Ibid.*, pp. 185, 224–226.

[182] *Ibid.*

[183] *Ibid.*, p. 225.

This setback was temporary. For reasons that are not clear, the Coventry barbers grew confident. In 1495 they held a pageant at Holy Trinity Church, together with the skinners.[184] Such public festivities, like the *Corpus Christi* processions in Bristol, were an important part of urban life, and a continuing demonstration of corporate presence and power. Soon after the Holy Trinity procession the barbers posted a new series of regulations for medical practice.[185] These required that all surgeons and leeches—leeches probably being practitioners of physic who did not have a university degree—acknowledge the authority and sovereignty of what was now styled as the "Fellowship and Craft of Barbers."[186] Further, the guildsmen requested that the town supplement the "Craft of Barbers" so that they could hold more festivals.

Here, then, is another example of medical practice in the county towns. An overwhelming majority of the doctors were barbers. They organized into guilds and controlled local medical practice. Yet the largest of these towns—York, Bristol, Norwich, Coventry—seem to have had another, much smaller but more elite band of doctors, physicians with at least some university training, and surgeons trained in the fashion of the London Fellows. This elite was not organized and did not resist the pretensions of the barbers. They did not have to. The barbers were never powerful enough, even in Bristol or Norwich, to impose their will on the town elites, most of whom came from textiles and victualling rather than service guilds. These town elites, mayors and aldermen, were the final word in questions of municipal policy. And it is likely that the mayors and aldermen were treated not by barbers but by physicians and surgeons.

At least ten other towns have evidence of medical institutions between the Black Death and the 1511 Licensing Act (Table 1.5).[187] Most of the records are freemen's lists or guild fragments, and are similar to those from York, Bristol, Norwich, and Coventry. There is, however, a peculiarity from the Lincoln Barbers' Guild by-laws.[188] The Lincoln

[184] *Ibid.*, p. 564.

[185] *Ibid.*, p. 569.

[186] *Ibid.*

[187] Useful studies are: R.M.S. McConaghey, "History of Rural Medical Practice," in Poynter, ed., *Evolution of Medical Practice*, pp. 91–111; R. S. Roberts, "Personnel and Practice of Medicine in Tudor and Stuart Medicine in Tudor and Stuart England," ii, *MH*, 7, 1964, pp. 217–234; Whittet, "The Apothecary in Provincial Gilds."

[188] It is reprinted in Young, *Annals of the Barber-Surgeons*, pp. 576–579.

guild allowed women as full practitioners.[189] Furthermore, there is evidence from individual cases if not guild rules that other barbers' companies also allowed them. This distinguished them from physicians and surgeons, and would seem to be a point in their favor: it suggests an open and fluid membership and, since many women were versed in folk practice, an additional medical perspective. The reality, however, was not so enlightening. In Lincoln and everywhere else, women practitioners were invariably the spouses of dead barbers who took over their husbands' practices.[190] Most barbers were as close-minded and monopolistic as physicians: they were just less able to impose their will.

The restriction of women practitioners set the tone for medical institutions. The institutions were, generally, inflexible and bent on preserving the *status quo* and the monopoly of the masters, be they physicians, surgeons, or barbers. They were more concerned with administration than with training and regulation. They were, with the occasional exception of the London Fellowship of Surgeons, uninterested in innovation and change—and, it sometimes seems, in the practice of medicine itself. Yet placed in context this is hardly surprising. English society was corporate, and the road to success was traveled most easily in large and powerful organizations. Guilds with large memberships like the London barbers had an advantage over loosely organized fellowships like that of the London surgeons. Medical institutions did not have to neglect the actual practice and skills of medicine. But the energies of guild leaders were usually channeled into making rules and securing benefits. Furthermore, medical institutions were traditionally organized by kinds of practitioners, something not even the members of the College of Medicine could overcome. Medical institutions hardened, then preserved, the differences among practitioners and practices. They insured competition, but competition aimed at achieving privilege rather than at producing better doctors. The result was an institutional framework that proved to be the major obstacle to a better system of medical care.

[189] *Ibid.*, p. 578.

[190] L–B L, pp. xxx–xxxii. Of the sixteen female barbers in the file, at least ten followed their husbands in practice. See London Com. Court Litchfield, ff. 11v–12; and 139. See too Dobson and Walker, *Barbers and Barber-Surgeons*, p. 24; and two London Com. Court Wills, Litchfield, ff. 11v–12; and 139.

# 2

## MIRRORS OF MEDICAL
## PRACTICE

Late medieval society was hierarchical as well as corporate. As doctors were organized into guilds, colleges, and fellowships, so too did they fall into social groups. Indeed, as suggested in Chapter One, the institutional history of English medicine is sometimes best understood in the context of social conflict. Physicians lodged atop the social structure, and looked down on the other practitioners, even the surgeons, who stood second. They in turn ignored the barber-surgeons, who sneered at the barber-tonsors, who railed at unlicensed practitioners. But medical social structure was more complicated than this. A case in point is the situation of the apothecaries. In the practitioners' world they rated with the barber-surgeons, skilled craftsmen who compounded the drugs used by physicians. Yet many apothecaries, especially those in London, were members of powerful and prosperous grocers' companies, and marketed the goods of an increasingly lucrative overseas trade. Hence, they were often very rich, and merchants before doctors.

There was also a problem of context. Most practitioners were bourgeois. Though they fitted into a medical hierarchy, they were also part of an urban social structure. They had to find their place in a setting in which "money makes the man."[1] And late medieval English society was fluid—"an age of ambition," as it has been styled.[2] Success as a doctor was not always enough. Practitioners often found themselves competing in a larger urban as well as medical environment. But, unlike many London merchants, most were happy as doctors and showed little interest in

[1] B.M. Reg. Ms. 17B, xlvii. The quote is discussed in Sylvia L. Thrup, *The Merchant Class of Medieval London, 1300–1500* (Ann Arbor, Mich.: University of Michigan Press, 1962), p. 317.

[2] F.R.H. DuBoulay, *An Age of Ambition* (New York: Viking Press, 1970). In my opinion, this is the best social history of late medieval England. Less satisfactory but interesting in its discussion of the professions is Paul Murray Kendall, *The Yorkist Age: Daily Life During the Wars of the Roses* (New York: Norton, 1970), pp. 281–327. Social structure is discussed in Huling E. Ussery, *Chaucer's Physician* (New Orleans: Tulane Studies in English, 1971), p. 31.

becoming gentlemen.[3] Rather, they wanted their children to follow
them in medical careers. In Chapter Seven practitioners will be presented as prosperous, bourgeois, and middle class; herein their roles, re-
sponsibilities, and public and private images will be discussed.

Physicians were the social elite of late medieval doctors. This was the
case in 1340, and remained so even in 1500, when their medical inadequacies had been exposed, examined, and raked over for a century and
a half, and the surgeons had proved their mettle. Part of the physicians'
continuing prestige was owing to their university educations and, in
some cases, clerical status. But part also came from the nature of their
practice, which was predicated on theory and not action. They used
their minds, not their hands. This theory had a classical base; physicians
read, wrote, and sometimes talked in Latin, the language of Christendom's first order. Historians used to stress that physicians were forbidden to shed blood, and that this determined the nature of their practice.[4]
Recent scholarly studies suggest that this has been overplayed, that not
all physicians were clerics and some were clinicians.[5] It may be an over-
simplification to picture the physician, hand cupped over mouth, eyes
cast aside, barking directions to a blood-splattered barber, who was bus-
ily cutting away at a patient, or directing an apothecary in the compounding of a balm or salve.[6] Chaucer's physician, after all, was noted
for his physic *and* surgery.[7]

Yet there was more truth than not in the traditional image. With their
university educations, physicians were familiar with the Roman arguments that separated the head and the hand, the things produced of the

[3] Thrupp, *Merchant Class*, pp. 234–287. Lawrence Stone and Jeanne C. Fawtier Stone,
*An Open Elite: England, 1540–1880* (Oxford: Clarendon Press, 1984), call into question
many of Thrupp's conclusions.

[4] The most recent article, which discusses and debunks much of the historiography, is
Darrel W. Amundsen, "Medieval Canon Law on Medical and Surgical Practice by the
Clergy," *BHM*, 52, 1977, pp. 22–44.

[5] This is borne out by the data from the doctors' file. Slightly more than five percent of
the doctors in the file were clerics; of these about sixty percent took higher orders. See
below, pp. 258–259. Yet the case of the Mertonians, discussed above, p. 13*n*21, is
worth noting.

[6] See for example, the splendid illustrations in Loren MacKinney, *Medical Illustrations
in Medieval Manuscripts* (London: Wellcome Historical Medical Library, 1965), especially
those on pp. 209–210.

[7] Geoffrey Chaucer, *The Canterbury Tales*, ed. Nevill Coghall (New York: Penguin
Books, 1977), p. 30.

free man from those of the slave.[8] Parker claims that there was little distinction between physic and surgery among the Arabs and in the early
medieval West.[9] While he overstates his case, he is basically correct. But
from the twelfth century onward, as a growing list of new and corrected
classical texts were made available to Western doctors, the separation of
practitioners became more distinct.[10] It became more pronounced still
with the appearance of newer and better translations in the fourteenth
and fifteenth centuries. Humanists like Petrarch and Salutati, while de-
faming physic when it was elevated to the rank of a liberal art, lauded it
in comparison with surgery.[11]

The classical distinctions were reinforced by two social theories: trifunctionalism and the blood taboo. Trifunctionalism, which became
popular about the same time as the new texts appeared, posited an au-
thoritarian, highly structured, and stable society.[12] Its first class, which
was constituted by thinkers, included the university-educated physicians. The third class, the workers, included all other practitioners,
even surgeons. At the same time, surgeons suffered from the stigma of
the blood taboo.[13] Occupations were divided into those which were licit,
and those which were not. One of the things which made an occupation

---

[8] This is best seen in the two most popular works of surgery of Hippocrates, *Fractures*
and *Joints*. A Roman physician who argued for the integration of physic and surgery was
Cornelius Celsus, *De medicina*. The appropriate works of Hippocrates and Celsus are listed
below, pp. 322–323. See E. D. Phillips, *Greek Medicine* (London: Thames and Hudson,
1973); and Erwin H. Ackerknecht, *A Short History of Medicine*, rev. ed. (Baltimore: Johns
Hopkins University Press, 1983), pp. 47–78.

[9] George Parker, *The Early History of Surgery in Great Britain* (London: A. C. Black,
1920), p. 15.

[10] Charles H. Talbot, "Medicine," in David Lindberg, ed., *Science in the Middle Ages*
(Chicago: University of Chicago Press, 1978), pp. 391–428.

[11] This is nicely summed up, with excerpted quotations, in Elizabeth L. Eisenstein, *The
Printing Press as an Agent of Change* (Cambridge: Cambridge University Press, 1979), pp.
251–254. Nancy G. Siraisi, *Arts and Sciences at Padua: The Studium of Padua Before 1350* (Toronto: Pontifical Institute of Mediaeval Studies, 1971), p. 162, points out that Petrarch was
an intermittent resident of Padua, and felt that physicians there put too much value on
teaching the *practica*, as opposed to theory that the *studium* offered.

[12] The works of George Dumezil are fundamental. See: *Mythe et epopees*, 3 vols. (Paris:
Bibliothèque de sciences humaines, 1968–1973); and *Les dieux souverains des Indo-Européens*
(Paris: Gallimard, 1977). See too George Duby, *The Three Orders: Feudal Society Imagined*,
trans. Arthur Goldhammer (Chicago: University of Chicago Press, 1980).

[13] Jacques Le Goff, "Licit and Illicit Trades in the Medieval West," in his *Time, Work
and Culture*, trans. Arthur Goldhammer (Chicago: University of Chicago Press, 1980), pp.
58–70.

illicit was the blood taboo—that is, an occupation that in some way caused bleeding. Thus butchers, executioners, barbers, and even surgeons were burdened not just with being craftsmen, but of being tainted craftsmen to boot.

 As some elements reinforced the primary role of physicians, others chipped away at it. Most important was the Black Death. Physicians had established the standards of practice before 1348, and got credit when the system worked; concomitantly, they took most of the blame when it failed. Physicians treated the Black Death with new twists on old theories, or with traditional advice on diet and calls for modera- *surgeons* tion.[14] They rarely came in contact with the afflicted, which was per- *gained more* haps not such a bad idea, but their images suffered. Surgeons, cutting *respect.* and sawing, using opiates and ointments, and above all always taking a direct and active approach, were not much more successful than the physicians. But they seemed at least to be trying. It is not surprising that the most critical anti-medical sentiments expressed in the late middle ages were aimed at the physicians (see Illus. 1).

Printing, too, hurt the physicians' image. Elizabeth Eisenstein has discussed the relationship between printing and medicine, and I need only summarize her conclusions.[15] Beginning around 1475 and becoming pronounced around 1500, printers began making medical books, especially those on surgery and anatomy in the vernacular. This was the continuation of an earlier trend, which in England had begun before the introduction of the press.[16] These vernacular texts were aimed not only at medical professionals but also at intelligent laymen, and were often presented as self-help manuals.[17] Many of them drew on materials written and compiled by surgeons rather than physicians. Before the Black Death, traditional works of physic based on Galen, Hippocrates, and John Gaddesden were most popular. After it, especially by 1500, they

[14] This is discussed in Robert S. Gottfried, *The Black Death* (New York: The Free Press, 1983), pp. 104–128. See too Anna Montgomery Campbell, *The Black Death and Men of Learning* (New York: Columbia University Press, 1931).

[15] Eisenstein, *The Printing Press*, pp. 246–270, 533–574.

[16] Charles H. Talbot, *Medicine in Medieval England* (London: Oldbourne, 1967), pp. 186–197.

[17] Paul Slack, "Mirrors of Health and Treasures of Poor Men: The Uses of the Vernacular Medical Literature of Tudor England," in Charles Webster, ed., *Health, Medicine and Mortality in the Sixteenth Century* (Cambridge: Cambridge University Press, 1979), pp. 237–273. See too the essays in A.S.G. Edwards, ed., *Middle English Prose: A Critical Guide to Major Authors and Genres* (New Brunswick, N.J.: Rutgers University Press, 1984), especially Laurel Braswell, "Utilitarian and Scientific Prose," pp. 337–388.

*From 1500* were replaced by works taken from the surgeons John Arderne, Guy de Chauliac, and Lanfranc of Milan, or from collections of short, practical tracts and recipes.[18] Further, when the texts were in Latin they could be interpreted only by highly trained physicians, who could make sense of the hundreds of references, allusions, and syllogisms. This gave them a mystique. When translated many texts were exposed for the gobbledygook that they were. By contrast, the practical manuals, sometimes misleading and misinformed, were generally direct, explicit, and to the point.

Hence, as the Roman tradition, trifunctionalism, and the blood taboo worked to preserve the position of physicians, the Black Death, physic's practical inadequacies, printing, and the spread of vernacular texts were deleterious and threatening. Physicians were hard-pressed to retain their positions and privileges—but they did. At the royal court, always a barometer of social status, physicians remained the best paid and, with a few exceptions, most influential practitioners.[19] In 1452 they were freed from a considerable bond when Pope Nicholas V allowed physicians in lower orders to marry—something many of them had been doing for a hundred years without papal sanction.[20] This reversed an earlier trend, dating back to the twelfth century, whereby papal pronouncements such as those of the Council of Clermont in 1131 had forbidden monks to practice medicine and restricted the opportunities of physicians.[21]

Further, in an age of increasing material consumption and sumptuary laws, physicians were permitted to wear more elaborate and ostentatious costumes than the other practitioners. In 1428, for example, the royal physician John Somerset was allowed, among other rewards for long and faithful service to the king and the citizens of London, "to have a livery with fur and lining, as other royal physicians have."[22] Physi-

[18] This judgment is drawn from my reading of medical manuscripts. See below, pp. 196–203, 214–234, and 260–262. Fernand Braudel, *Civilization and Capitalism*, 1 (New York: Harper and Row, 1979), p. 80, points out that Guy went through sixty-nine printed editions between 1478 and 1895.

[19] A. R. Myer, *The Household of Edward IV* (Manchester: University of Manchester Press, 1959), pp. 225–296. See below, pp. 91–129. For a comparison, see Guido Ruggiero, "Status of Physicians and Surgeons in Renaissance Venice," *JHM*, 36, 1981, pp. 168–184.

[20] Ackerknecht, *Short History of Medicine*, p. 85.

[21] *Ibid.*, p. 82.

[22] CPR, 1422–1429, p. 460.

cians had previously been permitted special dress. In 1406 Parliament passed one of several postplague sumptuary laws.[23] Nobles were placed at the top of the social ladder, followed by gentlemen and the clergy, a departure from the traditional trifunctional ordering. Then came royal officials, masters of divinity, doctors of law, regents of the universities, and masters of physic. Physicians were allowed to wear a combination of squirrel and rabbit, with trims of mustelids.

Most physicians could afford such dress. They were among the wealthiest bourgeoisie in England.[24] Witness Chaucer's marvelous description:

> Hippocrates, and Haly and Galen
> Serapion, Rhazes and Avicen
> Averroes, Gilbert and Constantine
> Bernard and Gaddesden and John Damescene
> In diet he was measured as could be
> Including naught of superfluity
> But nourishing and easy. It's no libel
> To say that he read but little in the Bible
> In blue and scarlet he went clad, withal,
> Lined with a taffeta and with sendal [a thin, fine silk
> material, worn as a garment]
> And yet he was right chary with expense
> He kept the gold he gained from pestilence
> For gold in physic is fine cordial
> And therefore he loved gold exceeding all.[25]

Some physicians were involved in business. This brought them more money, which brought more status. The most obvious commercial sideline, as Chaucer noted, was trading in the spices they used for medicines. But some physicians were involved in other kinds of deals as well, especially real estate. In the decade before the Black Death, John of York and Ludovico de Arecia, the latter presumably an Italian, bought and sold land in and around London.[26] A century later John Spencer was a large landholder and active businessman in London.[27] So too was Ed-

---

[23] *Rot. Parl.*, 111, p. 593a. For more detail, see Elspeth M. Veale, *The English Fur Trade in the Later Middle Ages* (Oxford: Oxford University Press, 1966), especially pp. 1–21.

[24] See below, pp. 265–268, for practitioners' wealth.

[25] Chaucer, *Canterbury Tales*, pp. 30–31.

[26] See for instance, L–B F, p. 131.

[27] *T&H*, p. 186; for example, CCR, 1447–1454, p. 33.

mund Albon, doctor to Edward IV and benefactor of Gonville Hall, Cambridge.[28] Albon was the holder of enough property to seek approval at the beginning of the reign of Henry VII, lest his possession of certain tenements be questioned.[29] And his contemporaries John Smith,[30] William Lacy,[31] Thomas Hall,[32] and Thomas Linacre,[33] all prominent physicians, also dabbled in real estate.

These business interests may explain why other observers were not as gentle as Chaucer in treating the physicians' "love of gold." Such criticisms did not begin in the late middle ages. John of Salisbury, writing in the twelfth century, claimed that physicians had two maxims they never violated: "Never mind the poor; never refuse money from the rich."[34] In the thirteenth century Roger Bacon continued this theme and added another, claiming that most physicians were ignorant, especially of the drugs they favored for treatment.[35] Consequently, they left compounding to apothecaries. Apothecaries were even worse; they were cheats and scoundrels to boot, who regularly deceived physicians.[36]

These criticisms paled besides those that came after the Black Death. One of the most scathing was written by Petrarch and then taken up by other humanists, including many in England a century later:

> Carry out your trade, mechanic [the physician], if you can. Heal bodies, if you can. If you can't, murder; and take the salary . . . for your crimes. . . . But how can you dare relegate rhetoric to a place inferior to medicine? How can you make the mistress inferior to the servant, a liberal art to a mechanical one? It is your business to look after bodies. Leave the care and education of the mind to genuine philosophers and orators.[37]

English critics were less eloquent than Petrarch but no less vitriolic. William Langland, like Chaucer, resented their love of gold and fancy dress. But he was more critical:

[28] *T&H*, pp. 38–39.

[29] CCR, 1485–1500, p. 29.

[30] *Ibid.*, p. 366.

[31] *Ibid.*, p. 150.

[32] *Ibid.*, p. 303.

[33] *Ibid.*, p. 347.

[34] As quoted in Talbot, *Medicine in Medieval England*, p. 136.

[35] Sir John Charles, "Roger Bacon on the Errors of Physicians," *MH*, 4, 1960, pp. 269–282.

[36] *Ibid.*, p. 270.

[37] Eisenstein, *The Printing Press*, pp. 251–252.

If you follow these instructions, I'll bet you the doctors will soon be selling their ermine hoods and their fine cloaks of Calabrian fur with gold tassels, to get themselves a square meal; and you'll see them gladly giving up their medicine for farm work to avoid starvation.[38]

In *The Testament of Cressida*, Chaucer himself was more critical:

> Doctor in physic, clad in scarlet gown
> And furred well, as sic and ought to be
> Honest and good, and not would any world would care he.[39]

Others were more critical still:

> . . . while men go after a leech,
> the body is buried.[40]

And Langland again:

> For these doctors are mostly murderers, God help them.
> Their medicines kill thousands before their time.[41]

Piers the Ploughman stressed their dishonesty. He had physicians—and apothecaries—offer shelter to the Liar:

> Then the doctors were annoyed, and sent him an urgent letter asking him to join them, and help them analyze urine. And the grocers also sought his help for hunting out their wares, for he knew something of their trade, and had all the drugs and spices at his command.[42]

The author of *The Play of the Sacrament* concurred:

> What disease or sickness it ever you have
> He [the physician] will never leave you till you be in your grave.[43]

This theme of incompetence was also picked up by the author of *The Romance of the Rose*:

[38] William Langland, *Piers the Ploughman*, ed. J. F. Goodridge (New York: Penguin Books, 1966), p. 88. Many of these statements are collected and edited in Ida B. Jones, "Popular Medical Knowledge in Fourteenth Century English Literature," i, *BHM*, 1937, pp. 405–451. I have used more recent and modernized translations or transcriptions whenever possible.

[39] Chaucer, *The Testament of Cressida*, as quoted in Jones, "Popular Medical Knowledge," p. 413.

[40] Jones, "Popular Medical Knowledge," p. 420.

[41] Langland, *Piers the Ploughman*, p. 88.

[42] *Ibid.*, p. 44.

[43] As quoted in J. J. Jusserand, *English Wayfaring Life in the Middle Ages*, 2nd ed. (London: Methuen), p. 97.

Physician and advocate
Gone right by the same gate
They sell the science for winning
And haunt her craft for great getting
They will not worsen in no wise
But for lucre and covetness.[44]

And most critical of all, from the anonymous fourteenth-century "A Poem on the Times of Edward II":

. . . these physicians
That help men die.[45]

The image of avarice, if not incompetence, is also in the writing of the physicians themselves. Some scholars have cited the development of a deontology as an important step in the growing professionalization of late medieval medicine.[46] Rightly so: but as one reads the codes of ethics, the doctors' desire to collect proper fees seems as strong as their will to cure the sick. A good example comes from Henri de Mondeville's *La chirurgie* which, its subject notwithstanding, was used by English physicians:

Thus [the doctor should] give his advice only to five classes of people: to those who are really poor, for love of God . . . ; to his friends, from whom he does not wish to receive a fixed revenue or a definitive sum of money . . . ; to those whom he knows to be grateful after a complete recovery . . . ; to those who repay poorly, such as our seigneurs and their relatives, chamberlains, justices, bailiffs, advocates, and all those whom he does not dare refuse counsel; and to those who pay completely in advance.[47]

John Arderne generally followed Mondeville, adding just a few touches. He was particularly concerned with collecting fees, about which he wrote:

After [the patient] inquires about the state of his health, the physician should ask boldly for more or less [in fees], but he ever be wary of scarce

[44] As quoted in Jones, "Popular Medical Literature," p. 415.

[45] Thomas Wright, ed., *Political Songs of England* (London: Camden Soc., 6 1839), stanza 39.

[46] Vern L. Bullough, *The Development of Medicine as a Profession* (New York: Hafner, 1966), pp. 93–111.

[47] Henri de Mondeville, *La Chirurgie*, ed. E. Nicaise (Paris: Felix Alcan, 1893), p. 110. It and other parts of *La Chirurgie* are translated in Bullough, *Development of Medicine*, pp. 93–106.

asking, for over scarce asking sets at naught both the market and the thing [that is, the service offered by the doctor].[48]

And, as a counterpoise to these ethics, the author of *The Seven Deadly Sins* claimed that the poor were not given the same medical care as physicians offered the rich:

> It must be a criect, a crowned weight
> That knows that names from beans and peas
> Or else their medicine they have no might
> To give a man license to live in ease.[49]

The attack is nicely summed up in the graphically named poem *Death to the Physician*:

> Master of Physic which on your urine
> So look and gauge and stare against the sun
> For all your craft and study of medicine
> All the practice and science that ye can
> Your life's course so far is run
> Again we might your craft may not endure
> For all the goals that you thereby have won.

To which the physician replies:

> Full long agony. That I unto physic
> But sit my wit with diligence
> In speculative and in practice
> To get a name through excellence
> To find out against pestilence
> Preservations to staunch it and to fine
> But I dare say shortly in sentence
> Against death is worth no medicine.[50]

Such bitterness occasionally boiled over into practice, especially when a physician was judged to have committed an atrocious act of malpractice. The chronicler Thomas Walsingham describes the case of one London practitioner in 1382. An allegation was presented against a "false physician," who claimed to cure the sick with a parchment charm.[51] The mayor found him guilty, and decided that:

[48] John Arderne, *Treatise of Fistula in Ano*, ed. D'Arcy Power (London: EETS, 1910), p. 5.

[49] *The Seven Deadly Sins*, as quoted in Jones, "Popular Medical Knowledge," p. 417.

[50] Jones, "Popular Medical Knowledge," pp. 415–416.

[51] Thomas Walsingham, *Chronica Monasterii S. Albani*, ed. H. T. Riley (London: Longmans, 1867–1869), pp. 464–466.

he should be led through the middle of the city with trumpets and pages, he riding on a horse without saddle, the said parchment and a whetstone . . . being hung around his neck, a urinal also being hung before him, and another urinal on his back."[52]

In response, physicians remained silent and aloof. There are few defenses of physic, literary or medical, because physicians remained secure in their practice. Indeed, when they responded at all it was to attack the other practitioners, especially their principal challengers, the surgeons. Physicians lambasted the very nature of surgical practice. The author of one popular manuscript started by saying:

Here begins a treatise of all manner of infirmities of man's body
Both within, as touching physic, and without, as touching surgery.[53]

Another wrote:

For to staunch blood. A surgeon is a worker with hand outward in man's body, that may be seen with man even as the wounds, postumes, fleons, fistulas and chancres and such others, and first to staunch the blood, for that must be done first. But then have the name of that man or woman, then go to church and say his charm.[54]

And the author of a fifteenth-century *Ars medica* wrote an entire section called "On the Nobility of Medicine" in which he praised physic at the expense of other kinds of medicine, especially surgery.[55] He blamed all public dissatisfaction on other practitioners.[56]

A few physicians were supportive of surgery, and noted its dynamism.[57] Another fifteenth-century *Ars medica* urged that physicians and surgeons cooperate and share their secrets and skills so that they "can heal and help all diseases and sores within . . . medicine."[58] But calls for cooperation were rare, isolated incidents like the foundation of the Col-

[52] *Ibid.* See too D. W. Robertson, *Chaucer's London* (New York: John Wiley, 1968), who discusses the incident on pp. 205–208.

[53] o.u. Bod. Add. Ms. B 60, f. 1.

[54] o.u. Bod. Ms. Ashmole 1443, f. 401.

[55] o.u. Bod. Ms. Rawlinson c 328, f. 156.

[56] *Ibid.*

[57] o.u. Bod. Ms. Rawlinson c 299, f. 53.

[58] *Ibid.* The manuscript, a collection of recipes and brief tracts, once belonged to John Roberts, a coroner of Middlesex County who died in 1476, and seems to have been written by Thomas Ward, a prominent London doctor. Roberts is not in *T&H*; Thomas Ward is, pp. 358–359.

lege of Medicine in 1423 and the few malpractice cases its members adjudicated.[59] Indeed, physicians even presented their case for superiority before Parliament. The famous 1421 "Ordinances Between Practitioners of Physic and Surgery" led to the College, but they were also a forum for physicians to proclaim publicly their superiority.[60] As noted, a careful distinction was made for regulation and examination by "*Fisk en les Universities et les Surgeons entre les meistres de cell'arte.*"[61] Later in the year the physicians pressed home their separation in the "Petition of the Physicians."[62] They stressed the roles of the three sciences, divinity, medicine, and law, which they argued, dealt respectively with the soul, the body, and worldly goods. The physicians claimed that their science, as they called it, could be properly used only by men of great skills, who had had long arduous training. Otherwise, physic was harmful. They asked that only those trained in the universities be allowed to practice it, and asked for a ban on all women practitioners, whom they regarded as particularly dangerous and incompetent.[63]

This sequence of Parliamentary petitions and decisions is of great interest. The physicians may have been worried primarily about malpractitioners and quacks, but they also took pains to distance themselves from their erstwhile allies, the surgeons. Yet the very fact that physicians bothered to petition suggests the new conditions of the post-plague period. Before the Black Death physicians would never have deigned to respond to their challengers—indeed, they had no challengers. Afterward it was necessary for the most distinguished of them—and such stalwarts as Gilbert Kymer were among the petitioners—to seek legislative approval and assurances.[64]

Surgeons came next in the medical hierarchy, both before and after the Black Death. But after the plague, despite the gratuitous attacks and patronizing attitudes of physicians, their prestige as doctors and their public image rose considerably. Some of the reasons for their success have been suggested; surgical treatment was direct and, barring post-operative infections, effective. Surgeons were practical; they were per-

[59] See above, p. 34.

[60] *Rot. Parl.* iv, f. 130b.

[61] *Ibid.*, f. 130b.

[62] *Ibid.* ff. 158a–158b.

[63] *Ibid.*

[64] *Cal. Plea Mem Rolls, 1413–37*, pp. 174–175. Details on institutions and practice are in Chapters One and Five.

ceived as men of action who got results, a striking contrast with the pro-
crastinating physicians. Additionally, surgeons benefited from military
service, acquiring valuable skills treating the wounded on the battlefield,
and gaining royal support when their treatments were successful. Some
members of the Fellowship of Surgeons had attended university. All
seem to have been literate, and many wrote medical treatises. Some, like
John Arderne and Thomas Morstede, were among the most famous doctors of their time. The joint foundation in 1423 with the physicians of
the College of Medicine was in its own right a tribute to their newly acquired social and professional standing.

Lay critics acknowledged the skills of the surgeons. Distinctions were
made between their success and physicians' failure. Chaucer stressed
this in "The Tale of Melibus":

> Then a surgeon, by leave of and voice of all present who were wise, rose
> up and spoke to Melibus, as you shall hear. "Sir," said he, "as for us sur-
> geons, it belongs to us that we can do for everyone the best that we can,
> when we have been retained, and that we do no harm to our patients.
> Wherefore it happens, many times and oft, that when two men have
> wounded one another, the same surgeon heals them both. Therefore it
> does not become us to foment warfare nor to support factions. And cer-
> tainly, as to healing your daughter, although she is dangerously wounded,
> we will be so attentive, by day and night, that, with God's grace, she shall
> be made sound and whole again, and that as soon as may be possible."[65]

So did the author of *The Book of the Knight of Le Tour Landry*:

> And also she had her medicine and surgeons for to heal and medicine all
> such as were needed.[66]

William Caxton made the same distinction in his *Dialogues in French and
English*:

> And the masters of medicines
> And the surgeons also.[67]

The differences having been established, most authors and commentators then expressed a clear preference for the surgeons. So Chaucer's

---

[65] This is not in the Coghill edition of *The Canterbury Tales*. This transcription is from
the edition by J. U. Nicholson (Garden City, L.I.: Collectors Library), p. 192.

[66] *The Knight de la Tour Landry*, ed. Thomas Wright (London: EETS, 33, 1868), Chap.
103.

[67] *Caxton's Dialogues, English and French*, ed. Henry Bradley (London: EETS, 1900), p. 25.

surgeon "by leave and voice of all present who were wise rose up and spoke. . . ."[68] Indeed, except for those coming from the physicians it is difficult to find critical remarks about the surgeons' prowess, a marked contrast with the multitude of such comments about physicians.[69]

A look at the achievements of individual surgeons confirms this. About forty percent of the surgeons in the data bank were in royal service.[70] They benefited accordingly. An outstanding example was John Leche, who used his royal contacts to secure several plums and must have been one of the larger non-aristocratic landholders in England.[71] By the time of his death early in the fifteenth century Leche had stopped calling himself a surgeon—an exception to the general pattern—and had affected a coat-of-arms.[72] A century later Antony Ciabo, surgeon to Henry VIII, was given among other gifts the franchise to import 600 tuns of Gascon wine, which he did at a considerable profit.[73] Like Leche, he became armigerous.[74] Indeed, surgeons became nearly as wealthy as the physicians.[75] Yet they never seem to have brought upon themselves the scorn and criticism that physicians did. For rich and arrogant though they may have been, the surgeons performed their allotted functions.

Another reason for the surgeons' popularity was their charity and public service. Virtually all the surgeons in the data file who left wills made bequests to pious charity; fifteen percent of the physicians did not.[76] Surgeons gave about a fifth of their traceable movable wealth, physicians apparently less than a tenth.[77] Some of the donations were

---

[68] "The Tale of Melibus" is not included in the Coghill edition of *The Canterbury Tales*. I have again used the Nicholson edition, cited above, p. 192.

[69] This does not seem to have been the case in Europe. In Italy, it might be explained by the integration of physic and surgery. See, for example, Nancy G. Siraisi, *Taddeo Alderotti and His Pupils* (Princeton: Princeton University Press, 1981). But in France, where the two disciplines were distinct, as in England, surgeons do not seem to have enjoyed a better reputation. See Bullough, *Development of Medicine*, pp. 81–88.

[70] See below, Chapter Four, for details.

[71] *T&H*, pp. 161–162; CPR, 1374–1377, p. 402; CPR, 1385–1389, p. 228; CPR, 1388–1392, p. 456; CPR, 1381–1385, p. 527; CPR, 1399–1401, p. 203.

[72] CPR, 1405–1408, pp. 169–170.

[73] *Foedora*, p. 777 (Henry VI, pp. 111, 37); See too Beck, *Cutting Edge*, p. 169.

[74] Beck, *Cutting Edge*, p. 169.

[75] See the data on wealth, below, pp. 263–268.

[76] *Ibid*. Eighty-five percent is, of course, a fair rate in its own right.

[77] *Ibid*., pp. 269–271.

ostentatious enough to be highly visible. Thomas Thornton himself the
founder through charitable bequest of Elsing's Hospital for the blind in
London, was willed £5.[78] The bequest to Thornton was made so that he
could provide medical care for the city's poor "to pay for their leechcraft."[79] Thomas Morstede, esquire, court surgeon, war hero, famous
author, and driving force behind the foundation of the College of Medicine, is another case in point.[80] He became rich and famous because of
his surgical skills. According to H. L. Gray, who has printed his
1447 tax assessment, Morstede had £154 worth of land, making him one
of the richest men in the city.[81] He had his own coat-of-arms, was a
member of the Fishmongers' Company, one of the four predominant
guilds of London, and at one time was owed debts of up to £200.[82]
Morstede was also civic-minded. He served at least twice as chief-of-sur-
geons in the royal armies in France. He adjudicated a number of malpractice cases. In 1413, he was appointed Searcher of the Port of London, a post he held for twenty-five years.[83] The Searcher was akin to a
harbor-master and was potentially a very lucrative position; it paid an
annual salary of £10 and offered the possibility of almost unlimited corruption. Yet there is no evidence or even suggestion that Morstede
abused this or any other posts he held. He was imbued with a sense of
*noblesse oblige*, and despite—or perhaps because of—his position at court
was never subjected to professional, ethical, or personal criticism.

John Harrow is another case in point.[84] He too became one of the
wealthiest men in fifteenth-century London—a member of the Fishmongers' Company, a financier owed many debts, and the holder of
much property inside and out of London.[85] Harrow was in royal service,
and acted as chief surgeon during two French campaigns; he was a
founder of the College of Medicine, a judge in malpractice cases, and a
Searcher for the Port of London.

It is not surprising that Harrow and Morstede were widely admired.

[78] *Dugdale*, vi, 2, p. 706.

[79] *Ibid*.

[80] *T&H*, pp. 350–352; Beck, *Cutting Edge*, pp. 76–79; below, pp. 144–149.

[81] H. L. Gray, "Incomes from Land in England," *English Historical Review*, 49, 1934,
p. 637.

[82] Thrupp, *Merchant Class*, pp. 260–261.

[83] CFR, 1413–1422, p. 35.

[84] *T&H*, pp. 154–155; below, pp. 150–151.

[85] For example, see CPR, 1422–1429, p. 610.

Consider, however, the careers of the brothers John and Nicholas Brad-more.[86] Notable during the reign of Henry IV, they too were rich and successful—military and royal surgeons, landholders with flourishing London practices, civil servants. But they were also criminals. The Bradmores were arrested for breach of contract, trespassing, and counterfeiting—a rather common allegation against surgeons, many of whom were also members of the Goldsmiths' Company—and were unreliable in their royal service.[87] Yet neither man was ever convicted of wrongdoing, neither was ever subjected to public criticism, and both were praised for the high quality of their surgical skills.[88] They benefited from the good will and praise that virtually all surgeons, especially members of the London Fellowship, enjoyed.

The surgeons did have problems of social acceptance. At the height of their careers a few of them, including John Bilsden, William Hobbes, and William Holm went to the expense and trouble of getting university degrees, and styled themselves as physicians.[89] They must have thought they were better off. And the foundation of 1423 notwithstanding, the surgeons' effort to gain acceptance by the physicians was never completely successful. The barber-surgeons challenged the surgeons from the end of the thirteenth century onward, arguing that there was little difference between the two practices. Outside of London, as noted, this was often true, and the barbers' challenges were usually successful. Some provincial surgeons were even lumped together with other craftsmen. In Newcastle and York, they were linked with waxchandlers, on the theory that embalming, which many provincial surgeons practiced to supplement their incomes, gave the two "trades" the common denominator of wax.[90] In Oxford, surgeons were associated with waferers, in Kingston-upon-Hull with weavers, and in Salisbury with silk-weavers.[91] Such was also the case on the continent. In Amsterdam, surgeons

[86] *T&H*, pp. 123–124, 218–219.

[87] CCR, 1396–1399, p. 488; *ibid.*, p. 208; CCR, 1399–1402, p. 199; CCR, 1392–1396, p. 488; CCR, 1402–1405, p. 182.

[88] CCR, 1402–1405, p. 336; CPR, 1405–1406, p. 454; CFR, 1405–1413, p. 104. Indeed, they are even credited with developing a new instrument for extracting arrows. See Beck, *Cutting Edge*, pp. 55–56.

[89] See *T&H*, pp. 128–129, 401–402; Myers, *Household of Edward IV*, pp. 58, 182.

[90] *Register of Freemen of Newcastle-upon-Tyne* (Newcastle: Newcastle-upon-Tyne Records Committee, iii, 1923), pp. 1–5; *Register of the Freemen of York, 1272–1558*, Surtees Society, 96, 1897, pp. 34–261.

[91] *The Ancient Trade Guilds and Companies of Salisbury*, ed. Charles Haskins (Salisbury:

were linked with wooden shoemakers, and in parts of Italy with stone-cutters.[92] And because the London Fellowship was unincorporated, surgeons could take liveries in other companies. These combinations, even with successful companies like the Fishmongers' and Goldsmiths', were often ill-advised, for they compromised the surgeons' claims to be full-time and professional medical practitioners.

The physicians fought the surgeons by criticizing surgery; the surgeons tried to defend their status by emphasizing their skills. One way to do this was to prosecute malpractice cases, especially when barbers were involved.[93] In 1348, before the London Fellowship was even founded, a few surgeons complained to Edward III that a hospital warden was exercising the "office of surgery" without proper training.[94] The warden, they said, "neglected the dues of wardenship and has dissipated and consumed goods and alienated lands to the great neglect of the hospital."[95] In 1354 master surgeons Adam de la Poultrie and David of Westmoreland testified in the London Hustings Court against John le Spicer, probably an apothecary, who was accused of negligence while attending a wound.[96] Spicer had apparently set a broken jaw, a task normally reserved for surgeons. When the jaw did not heal properly the patient complained; Spicer countered by claiming the jaw had been inoperable from the start. The patient then went to de la Poultrie and Westmoreland, who resented the infringement of surgical privilege and worried about their own reputations and status. The mayor ruled for the surgeons and warned others who attempted surgery without a license.[97] Nor was the surgeons' preoccupation with the quality of surgery limited

---

Bennett Brothers, 1912), pp. 363–369; Sir George N. Clark, *A History of the Royal College of Physicians*, i (Oxford: Clarendon Press, 1964), p. 10.

[92] Clark, *History of the Royal College*, i, p. 11; Eisenstein, *The Printing Press*, pp. 252–253.

[93] As the only recorded act the officers of the College of Medicine performed was the judgment of such a case it might be argued that this was as much a reason as medical parity for the surgeons' desire for association with the physicians. I have been able to find evidence of about fifty of these malpractice cases.

[94] CPR, 1348–1350, pp. 175–176.

[95] *Ibid.*

[96] Riley, *Memorials of London Life*, pp. 273–274.

[97] *Ibid.* The cases of malpractice involving Richard Cheyndut and John Severelle Love will be remembered from Chapter 1, above, pp. 19–20. See *Cal. Plea Mem. Rolls*, 1364–1381, p. 236; and Riley, *Memorials of London Life*, p. 651.

to London or to barbers. In 1539 surgeons in Norwich sued an apothecary for practicing surgery "without license or skill."[98]

Surgeons' skills were sometimes recognized by other doctors. A few late medieval medical authors, in stressing the differences between physic and surgery, argued that surgeons were better.[99] Others stressed the similarities, urged cooperation, and suggested the two disciplines be taught as one. John Mirfield wrote:

> that the distinction [between physic and surgery] was rather artificial. To be a good physician one has to be a good surgeon. A physician must know how to bleed and even shave, and much of the distinction between the practices was due to the arrogance of the physician.[100]

Mirfield wrote early in the fourteenth century. By the end of the fifteenth century his perspective had been adopted by others. One of the reasons for this, as noted, was the spread of printing; as the proliferation of texts hurt physicians, so it helped surgeons.[101] Perhaps a third of the books printed in England in the 1480s and 1490s were books of medicine translated into the vernacular.[102] The books were largely unchanged from the twelfth and thirteenth centuries and seemed nonsensical in light of the new epidemiological conditions of the later middle ages.[103] This was important, because it helped "demystify" physicians' texts to a reading public that consisted to a large degree of practical, hardheaded merchants.[104] And the surgical books that were printed were more direct and straightforward—indeed, generally explicable, the kind of text a mercer or draper could appreciate and understand.

The printing of surgical books also worked in a more subtle way. The most common editions were derivations of John Arderne and Guy de Chauliac.[105] Appropriately enough, they were the best written, organized, most comprehensive, and original of all late medieval medical

---

[98] *Records of the City of Norwich*, ii, eds. William Hudson and John Cottingham Tingay (Norwich: Jarrold, 1916), p. 168.

[99] John Mirfield, *Surgery*, ed. James B. Coltan (New York: Hafner, 1969), pp. 5–6.

[100] *Ibid*.

[101] Talbot, *Medicine in Medieval England*, pp. 186–192.

[102] Slack, "Mirrors of Health," in Webster, *Health, Medicine and Mortality*, pp. 237–274.

[103] Campbell, *Black Death and Men of Learning*, pp. 49–125.

[104] For books and readers see H. S. Bennett, *English Books and Readers, 1475–1557*, 2nd ed. (Cambridge: Cambridge University Press, 1969), pp. 97–109, 165.

[105] This is taken from my reading of the texts. See below, Chapter Six.

texts. Both stressed deontology and the importance of dignity and reserve. Both stressed the importance in medicine of using the hand, the
tool of the surgeon, *with* the brain, the tool of the physician, and the
folly of separating the two. And printing served far better another principal feature of surgical manuals, illustrations. Manuscript illustrations
were often inaccurate and even unintelligible. But if a printer got good
illustrations he could reprint them as long as his plates were serviceable.
This applied to anatomy texts as well, which like those of surgery pro-
liferated after 1476.[106]

An example of the new perspective is a much-copied Oxford manuscript from about 1480, later printed, which included a segment entitled
"An Ancient Treatise of Leechcraft on Medicine and Surgery."[107] The
author played down the distinction between physic and surgery, emphasizing like John Mirfield the importance of integrated practice. He
then offered an admonition:

> The man that well of leechcraft lere [learn]
> Read one this book and you will hear
> Many a medicine both good and true
> To heal sores, both old and new
> Here are medicines without flew [fault]
> To heal all sores that been durable
> Of sword and knife and arrow
> Be the wound wide or be it narrow
> Of spear or quarrel or dagger or dart
> To make him heal in likely part
> So that the sick will do nicely
> And keep himself from surfeity
> Be the wound not so deep
> I have of there him take no keep
> So he drink same or Antioch
> Him there not dread of Antrage
> Be that 20 days be crimson and yone
> He shall heal both flesh and bone
> Do read and go in likely plane
> Through the might of good grain
> Thus saith Ypocras the good suran
> And Socrates, the good and gallidan [Galen]
> That were philosophers good all three

---

[106] Eisenstein, *The Printing Press*, pp. 537–554. See too the works cited above, note 17.
[107] O.U. Bod., Ashmole Ms. 1477, ff. 1–47.

That time the best in any otre [other]
In all this world were now three pere
As for any may back here
Christ's practice now medicine through God's
To find men's lives in distant plain.[108]

In this otherwise traditional call for excellence in medicine, physicians and surgeons were not distinguished, and war wounds and the other ailments usually identified with surgery were lumped together for treatment by all practitioners.

Another late-fifteenth-century manuscript, purportedly assembled by a team of five physicians and four surgeons, shows this attempt at an integrated practice.[109] It was a general *Ars medica* that could have served as a reference for any practitioner. But it differed from earlier *Ars* in its presentation of physic and surgery in integrated fashion. More compelling still is a third manuscript from the late fifteenth century.[110] The author addressed the traditional distinction between physic and surgery, and supported it in theory. But he claimed that practice was another issue, and argued that a skilled practitioner must be the master of all theories and techniques. A good doctor thought about causes and treatments; he contemplated the humors and natural conditions, since the latter demonstrated the essence of the former.[111] Diagnosis came from theory, and treatment could begin with drugs and the manipulation of diet. But these traditional approaches of the physician were seldom enough. If they failed, good practitioners of any ilk turned to surgery.[112]

Surgeons, then, enjoyed a good public image. Increasingly, they won a measure of respect from their peers and their patients. They ranked second to the physicians in the medical hierarchy, and in a few instances won parity. They were rich and like the physicians something of a self-perpetuating elite—indeed, even more so since none of them were clerics, as nearly half the physicians were, and more of them had children. Of the members of the London Fellowship, about a third left records of families; of these twenty percent had sons who also became surgeons.[113] There are records of ten families in which there were surgeons for three

[108] *Ibid.*, ff. 112–114.
[109] *Ibid.*, Ashmole Ms. 1481, f. 33.
[110] *Ibid.*, Ashmole Ms. 1498, f. 57–62.
[111] *Ibid.*, f. 59.
[112] *Ibid.*
[113] For more details see below, pp. 268–270.

generations or more.[114] Yet there was also social mobility. Some surgeons became physicians. High mortality rates, a demographic maxim of the fourteenth and fifteenth centuries, meant that there was always need for new members, however restrictive the Fellowship's entry rules might be.[115] And surgery was lucrative and prestigious enough to attract men from other occupations. Some surgeons, like the Bradmores, were members of the Goldsmiths' Company, and several goldsmiths became surgeons.[116] Both the surgeons and goldsmiths were dexterous and worked with precious metals, and it has been argued that the goldsmith-surgeons were among the leading bankers in London.[117]

Yet, for all their success, surgeons remained the social inferiors of physicians. Some sons of the gentry became physicians; none, despite Power's claim for John Arderne, seem to have become surgeons.[118] Some surgeons came from the ranks of the barber-surgeons, especially in the county towns. The York freemen's rolls show that Richard Shipton, whose father called himself a barber, was listed as a surgeon.[119] Others repeated this pattern at least four times late in the fourteenth century.[120] And social mobility worked in the other direction. Two sons of the surgeon Richard Moberley, also of York, became buckle-makers.[121] So did the son of William Appleton, who combined buckle-making with the more traditional goldsmithing.[122] Richard Shipton's father was also a barker.[123] Nicholas Brereton, son of a merchant, became a barber-surgeon.[124] And so it went; in all, some of York's surgeons and

[114] *Ibid.*

[115] Thrupp, *Merchant Class*, pp. 191–231; Robert S. Gottfried, *Epidemic Disease in Fifteenth Century England* (New Brunswick, N.J.: Rutgers University Press, 1978), pp. 187–224.

[116] CCR, 1454–1461, p. 145; CCR, 1461–1468, p. 208.

[117] Talbot, *Medicine in Medieval England*, pp. 195–196. See too T. F. Reddaway and Lorna E. M. Walker, *The Early History of the Goldsmiths' Company* (London: Edward Arnold, 1975).

[118] See the introduction of D'Arcy Power, ed., John Arderne, *Treatise on Fistula in Ano* (London: EETS, 1911), p. x. See too D'Arcy Power, "English Medicine and Surgery in the Fourteenth Century," in his *Selected Writings*, 2nd ed. (New York: Augustus M. Kelley, 1970), pp. 29–47.

[119] *Registers of the Freemen of York*, p. 170.

[120] *Ibid.*, p. 40.

[121] *Ibid.*, p. 134.

[122] *Ibid.*, p. 132.

[123] *Ibid.*, p. 170.

[124] *Ibid.*, p. 181.

barber-surgeons came from families in which the father was a fletcher, a water-lader, cook, merchant, fishmonger, carver, tailer, butcher, mason, and painter.[125] Clearly, more surgeons came from the ranks of craftsmen than from those of merchants or gentlemen. English surgeons, then, enjoyed a better social position and were more prosperous by the fifteenth century than ever. But they never had as exalted a position as did their Italian counterparts, and they were never quite equal with the physicians.[126]

Barbers came next in the medical hierarchy. Though there were distinct differences between barber-surgeons and barber-tonsors in training and practice, social commentators usually considered them as one. And they usually treated them with little regard. To some degree, this was justified. Barbers were the most poorly trained of the licensed practitioners. They provided the most mundane treatments and charged the lowest rates, and most of them offered tonsorial as well as medical services. They were far and away the most common kinds of practitioners, comprising well over half the London doctors, over three-quarters in the county towns, and close to sixty percent in the countryside.[127] And in London, their authority and even autonomy was as often as not countermanded by the physicians and surgeons.

But to some degree this tarnished reputation was undeserved. Most barber-surgeons in London were competent; some were good, and a few were among the better practitioners of their day. This was the case, for example, with Simon Rolf and Thomas Vicary.[128] In most of the county towns barbers dominated practice altogether, and in a few held high social position.[129] But they could never escape identification as craftsmen,

---

[125] *Ibid.*, pp. 185, 203, 204, 212, 241; 215, 234, 245; 236, 244.

[126] Siraisi, *Taddeo Alderotti*, pp. 268–302. An interesting comparison is Christopher R. Friedrichs, *Urban Society in an Age of War: Nordlingen, 1580–1720* (Princeton: Princeton University Press, 1979), p. 88.

[127] For more data, see below, pp. 254–256. For a sixteenth-century perspective see Margaret Pelling and Charles Webster, "Medical Practitioners," in Webster, ed., *Health, Medicine and Mortality*, pp. 165–235.

[128] For Rolf, see *T&H*, pp. 325–326; for Vicary, *DNB*, 20, pp. 300–301.

[129] A few barber families suggest social mobility. The son of the London barber-tonsor Walter Field, for example, was a canon at Merton College. See London Com. Court, Sharpe, f. 88. For the countryside, see Margaret Pelling, "Occupational Diversity: Barber Surgeons and the Trades of Norwich, 1550–1640," *BHM*, 56, 1982, pp. 484–511; and Pelling, "A Survey of East Anglian Medical Practitioners, 1500–1640," *Local Population Studies*, 25, 1980, pp. 54–65.

and unlike the surgeons there could be no real attempts to change this. Hence, the challenge for the barbers was to win acceptance as skilled craftsmen, the social equals of the gold- and silversmiths, and, indeed, the surgeons when they were labelled as men who worked with their hands. This was to prove difficult, and despite the corporate gains in the fifteenth century was achieved only by a handful of London barber-surgeons.

Perhaps the best evidence of the barbers' social dilemma comes from their record of royal service. All kings had royal barbers. But until the middle of the sixteenth century the royal barbers served almost exclusively as hairdressers.[130] They were allowed to draw blood only when a physician or surgeon was present.[131] The barbers did not even benefit much from their affiliation, beginning in the 1490s, with the physicians.[132] Bullough claims that in France physicians, determined to keep the surgeons of the Guild of St. Côme at bay, provided anatomy lectures and financial support to the barbers.[133] Barbers were allowed to wear the short robes traditionally reserved for the surgeons. This did not happen in England, even in the 1530s, when barber-surgeons like Vicary and Andrew Boorde were close to the king and performed and dressed like the surgeons of the Fellowship.[134] Even when the London barber-surgeons established a lecture series in medicine the lectures were given by physicians.[135]

This inability to gain social acceptance in the medical world or among the general public explains the barbers' relentless corporatism. Rules and regulations, in effect the legislation of social status, was their surest path to recognition. And in lieu of social or medical success, corporatism was the best way for the barbers to prevent the spread of unlicensed practitioners, their principal rivals for lower-middling and poorer patients. It explains why the barbers continually sought exemptions from certain municipal duties, even though participation in civic ritual was a time-honored way for craft guildsmen to gain municipal power. The physicians and surgeons, after all, did not have burdensome civic obli-

---

[130] Myers, *Household of Edward IV*, pp. 16, 125.

[131] *Ibid.*, p. 125.

[132] See above, pp. 40–42.

[133] Bullough, *Development of Medicine*, pp. 82–91.

[134] Vicary, *Anatomie of the Bodie*, pp. 89–122.

[135] Young, *Annals of the Barber-Surgeons*, pp. 69–72.

gations; if the barbers were to prove their equals they too needed some exemptions.

The lack of social recognition also accounts for the barbers' stiff resistance to practice by foreigners, whom the barbers claimed were "little skilled in their craft."[136] It explains why the barbers of London were so concerned with the upkeep and use of their halls and the constant reiteration of their guild charters. And it helps explain why the barber-surgeons wanted a coat-of-arms. Few barbers, even barber-surgeons, made much of an individual success. None until Vicary in the middle of the sixteenth century had the ear of the king or his advisers. It is even difficult to find references to or about them—in some ways, the most telling critique of their lack of status and identity. The few descriptions that do survive are bland and matter-of-fact: witness Chaucer's barber, who does not evoke either the respect or curiosity that his physician, surgeon, or even apothecary does:

> A merry child he was, so God save me
> Well could he let blood, clip and shave.[137]

And:

> There were all of Martes division
> The barber and the butcher and the smith.[138]

Langland, in a reference to barbers as dentists who often carried a belt with teeth to advertise successful extractions, affected a similar tone:

> Dawn, the dicker with a dozen harlots
> of potours and of pikers and plied tooth-drawers.[139]

And John Arderne was suspicious of their practice in general. He urged that the surgeons not tell the barbers how to cure piles:

for if barbers knew their doing would usurp this cure, appropriate it themselves unto unworship and not little harm of the masters [of the Fellowship of Surgeons].[140]

Barbers who made their mark usually did it outside the barbery. In

[136] Riley, *Memorials of London*, p. 393.
[137] *Canterbury Tales*, lines A 3326–3328.
[138] *Ibid.*, lines A 2024–2025.
[139] c text is not in the Goodridge edition. See W. W. Skeat, *Piers the Ploughman* (London: EETS, 1886), c, vii, l, 369–370.
[140] Arderne, *Treatise in Fistula*, p. 71.

1485 a London mercer, William Burwell, took his brother Thomas, a barber, into the mercery.[141] The mercers were one of the three great companies of London, and membership in it was a boon, especially for someone coming from a minor company like the barbers. Thomas paid £5, was made a freeman, and began trading in cloth. But he continued to practice barbery, and his association with the mercers probably benefited his colleagues in the Barbers' Company. Perhaps it was this kind of dual membership, even in incorporated companies, that led the barber-surgeons of the London mystery to form another, even more select group, the yeomanry.[142] In the fifteenth century royal barbers had won the designation "yeoman."[143] The title was prestigious, but there were only a handful of royal barbers per reign. Yet many members of the mystery wanted to be yeoman because it provided the social standing they seemed unable to win on their own. Hence, early in the sixteenth century, the barber-surgeons announced their own designation, paid municipal authorities for its sanction, and proclaimed themselves yeoman of the company and the city of London.[144]

Another success came in 1445, when three barbers from Beverley were selected to help deliver the gaol in York Castle.[145] Gaol delivery could be onerous, but it was prestigious and usually reserved for leading citizens or members of the gentry. Until the sixteenth century it was an honor for craftsmen to be asked. In Salisbury and Somerset in the mid-fifteenth century, two barbers, John Peverell and Thomas Hardy, were moneylenders.[146] Money lending per se did not bring social honor. But it brought wealth, which did. It is not surprising to see barber-entrepreneurs in the countryside, where there was room to wheel and deal. But a few London barbers became rich and famous. One was John King, who early in the fifteenth century exported wool and cloth.[147] There was John Silk, a barber who was also called a woolman, a name generally

[141] Jean M. Imray, "Les Bones Gentes de la Mercerye de Londres: A Study of the Membership of the Medieval Mercers' Company," in A.E.J. Hollaender and William Kellaway, eds., *Studies in London History* (London: Hodder and Stoughton, 1969), p. 163.

[142] Young, *Annals of the Barber-Surgeons*, pp. 276–287; Unwin, *Gilds and Companies*, pp. 226–228.

[143] Myers, *Household of Edward IV*, p. 125.

[144] Dobson and Walker, *Barbers and Barber-Surgeons*, pp. 49–50.

[145] CCR, 1441–1447, p. 441.

[146] CPR, 1452–1461, p. 59.

[147] CCR, 1399–1413, pp. 103, 487, 554.

applied to entrepreneurs who procured fleece from the sheepfolds.[148] Roger Webb and John Vinocur were land brokers in and around London in the fifteenth century, and occasionally traded in textiles.[149] Yet, prominent though these individuals were, their wealth and the positions that came from it were the products of trade, real estate, or money-lending schemes, and never just barbery.[150]

There was a seamier side to the barbers. Their proclivity for turning bathhouses into brothels was mentioned in Chapter One. They were also involved in a number of crimes. All types of practitioners, including physicians and surgeons, occasionally ran afoul of the law. The shady activities of the Bradmore brothers, already mentioned, serve as an example. But crooked physicians and surgeons were exceptional; the number of barbers who committed or were accused of crimes was far larger, even when their greater overall numbers are accounted for.[151] There are cases of trespass, poaching, larceny, assorted felonies, assault, and even murder.[152] One barber, Richard Wanling of London, was wanted for, literally, dozens of criminal violations over a period of twenty years.[153] The reasons for late medieval crime are complex and go beyond the scope of this study.[154] But, clearly, barbers were of a lower socio-economic standing than the other doctors. They were more likely than physicians, surgeons, or apothecaries to be accused, caught, tried, or convicted of any crime. Barbers seemed more prone to committing violent

[148] *Ibid.*, pp. 113, 175, 209, 312, 405, 465, 479, 481.

[149] CCR, 1441–1447, p. 76; CCR, 1447–1454, pp. 33, 56, 504; CCR, 1461–1468, p. 455. Webb left a will, proved in the London Com. Court, 1473, 6, 135ᵛ; and is in *T&H*, pp. 315–316.

[150] One other example illustrates this. In 1461 Richard Dod, barber and citizen of London, was involved in a land dispute which lingered for four years and included property throughout much of eastern England. Dod was a respected barber-surgeon, an owner and perhaps author of a medical text and, for a barber, the scion of an important family. Some of the land in dispute had been in the Dod family for three generations. When his holdership was challenged, Dod fought back tenaciously. Yet he did so as a landholder and London citizen, and not a barber; indeed, in some of his pleas he did not mention his occupation. See CCR, 1461–1468, pp. 80, 303.

[151] In the CPR and CCR from 1350 to 1450 I found less than ten records of pardons for crimes committed by surgeons and physicians; there are over one hundred for barbers.

[152] CPR, 1436–1441, p. 463; *ibid.*, p. 110; CPR, 1452–1461, p. 320; CPR, 1436–1441, p. 554.

[153] CCR, 1396–1399, pp. 69, 425, 429; CCR, 1399–1413, p. 497.

[154] The literature is enormous. A summary treatment is John Bellamy, *Crime and Public Order in England in the Later Middle Ages* (London: R.K.P. 1973).

acts, perhaps because they had less of a stake in the established social order than physicians, surgeons, and apothecaries.

This is borne out by evidence for civil as well as criminal cases. In 1445 barbers, leeches, and surgeons from London, York, and Bristol were involved in a dispute over jurisdiction, trespass, and malpractice.[155] The medical background of one of the leeches was questioned, while one of the barbers was calumniated at as a "laborer." The barbers were arrested and later broke gaol. There is no record of resolution, and it is not certain who was at fault, who precipitated the crisis, how common such relations between barbers in distant cities was maintained, or even who the malefactors were. But the underlying bitterness is clear, as was the tendency of the physicians and surgeons to turn up their noses and assume the barbers guilty of incompetence and wrongdoing simply because they were barbers.

There were similarly bitter cases of suits between surgeons and barbers in London in 1400, 1402, and 1410.[156] The 1410 case involved the physician Lawrence Marks, who had stood bail for the surgeon Henry Ashburn, who was being sued by the barber-surgeon Nicholas Silvester. Ashburn's crime is not specified, and apparently did not concern medicine. But Ashburn had helped Marks earlier in the year when the latter was accused of trespass.[157] And Marks was asked to give assurance that he would keep the peace with the barber John de Calais, with whom he had quarreled.[158] Again, the topic of the disagreement is not certain, and may not have been medical. But the social implications were clear. Both Marks and Ashburn chafed at having to deal with barbers, even the respected Silvester. Both implied that, given their social positions, there could be little doubt that they, the physician and surgeon, were above repute, and that the barber was guilty of wrongdoing. Apparently, the court shared this opinion, for Marks and Ashburn were set free and bail was returned.

A final example suggests the barbers' social problems. In 1405 Richard Asser, a barber, broke his contract and left the services of Nicholas Bradmore.[159] Bradmore, it will be recalled, was a litigious character who operated on both sides of the law. Asser was a Southwark barber whom

[155] CPR, 1441–1446, pp. 304, 334.
[156] CCR, 1399–1413, p. 101.
[157] CCR, 1399–1413, p. 15.
[158] *Ibid.*, pp. 100, 101, and 203.
[159] *Ibid.*, p. 70.

Bradmore employed to do simple surgery; occasionally, surgeons, like physicians, hired barber-surgeons and used them as paramedics. But Assert asserted that Bradmore worked him too hard and did not pay him enough; after leaving service, he filed suit against Bradmore and his brother John for non-payment. The Bradmores counter-sued, and the case lingered for several years.[160] There is no evidence telling who was right or wrong—though their past history suggests some sort of violation by the Bradmores. But sentiment among London's influential folk was clearly with the surgeons. A group of citizens raised bail for Nicholas Bradmore, who then managed to coerce Asser back for the duration of the contract.[161]

Apothecaries were unlike other practitioners. They occupied an important but ambiguous place in the medical hierarchy. For they were more than doctors, and in some cases devoted just a minor part of their professional lives to medical practice. Many of the drugs, especially those prescribed by the university-trained physicians for whom the apothecaries did most of their compounding, derived from spices. Most spices came from South Asia, and were a valuable commodity of the English overseas trade. Consequently, many apothecaries were also spice traders, or at least retailers.[162] In the thirteenth century they had associated with the spicers and pepperers; in the fourteenth century the spicers, pepperers, and apothecaries formed grocers' companies, beginning with that in London in 1345.[163] With the Mercers and Drapers, the Grocers' Company was the most powerful in the city. In addition to reaping fortunes in long-distance trade, grocers held many important municipal offices. In the fifteenth century, of eighty-eight mayors, eighteen, or over twenty percent, were grocers. Only the mercers, with twenty-five (twenty-eight percent) served more frequently. And of 173 aldermen, thirty-one, or almost eighteen percent, were grocers. Again, only the mercers, with forty-one, or close to twenty-four percent, served more frequently.[164]

[160] *Ibid.*, pp. 70, 134; CPR, 1401–1405, p. 244.

[161] *Ibid.*, p. 101.

[162] Leslie G. Matthews, *The Royal Apothecaries* (London: Wellcome Medical Historical Medical Library, 1967). See too Geoffrey E. Trease, *Pharmacy in History* (London: Bailliere, Tindall, and Cox, 1964), pp. 59–79; T. D. Whittet, "The Apothecary in Provincial Guilds," *MH*, 8, 1964, pp. 245–273.

[163] William Herbert, *The History of the Twelve Great Livery Companies of London*, 2nd ed., i (New York: Augustus M. Kelley, 1968), pp. 297–388.

[164] This is taken from C. J. Kingsford, *Prejudice and Promise in Fifteenth Century England*

Here was the ambiguity: by definition, the apothecaries were hand-
maidens to the physicians. They made and sold the drugs that physicians prescribed, and when they treated patients directly they did so as
second-class physicians, using simplified *Ars medica*.[165] As doctors they
ranked below physicians and surgeons and, by some accounting, even
the barbers.[166] But their economic and political clout as grocers and the
social status that accompanied it made for a contradiction. Some apothecaries were more successful, influential, and wealthier than the most
exalted physicians and surgeons, even those in royal service. And this
was true not just in London but in virtually all the larger provincial
towns, where grocers also were dominant members of the urban
elites.[167]

Why, then, did not apothecaries play a larger role among late medieval doctors? Why did they act as physicians wanted them to? One reason, as suggested, was that doctoring was a minor concern to them.[168]
Another is that their failure to specialize cut both ways. Apothecaries
were usually second-class grocers, dominated in the company by the
pepperers and spicers who traded full-time.[169] In Norwich, for example,
the best way to distinguish the apothecaries from the rest of the grocers
was by the far greater wealth of the latter.[170] Further, as noted, in the
fifteenth century apothecaries were joined in their commercial ventures

---

(London: Frank Cass Reprints, 1962), p. 107. Six goldsmiths were mayors and sixteen
goldsmiths were aldermen. Data from 1377 to 1394 show that more aldermen were grocers—108 of 403, or close to twenty-seven percent—than were members of any other company. These are of aldermen who can be identified. The next highest company was the
mercers, with 85 of 403, or twenty-one percent. The goldsmiths, many of whom were
surgeons, were fourth, with 44 of 403, or close to eleven percent. This data comes from
Alfred B. Beaven, *The Aldermen of the City of London* (London: Eden Fisher, 1908–1913), i,
p. 360.

[165] See for example, B.M. Harl. Ms. 5294. This is a clear, well-written herbal, but it is
second-rate physic.

[166] Though this generally agreed perspective is disputed by historians of pharmacy, the
most influential of whom has been Leslie Matthews. In addition to *Royal Apothecaries*, pp.
16–70, see his other works cited in the bibliography, below, p. 337.

[167] Unwin, *Gilds and Companies*, pp. 72–109. Sylvia L. Thrupp, "The Grocers of London: A Study of Distributive Trade," in Eileen Power and Michael M. Postan, eds., *Studies in English Trade in the Fifteenth Century* (London: Methuen, 1933), pp. 247–292.

[168] See Thrupp, "The Grocers," pp. 259–272.

[169] *Ibid.*

[170] Charles Williams, *Masters, Wardens and Assistants of the Gild of the Barber-Surgeons of
Norwich* (Norwich: Jarrold, 1900), pp. 3–7.

by other doctors, especially physicians and even surgeons. Thrupp, the authority on the London grocers, claims that in the fourteenth century many surgeons traded in pharmaceuticals and other spices.[171] And to take a provincial example again, it is often difficult to distinguish Norwich surgeons and apothecaries.[172] Several men used the terms—along with the term grocer—interchangeably at various points in their careers, and masters from one group often had apprentices in the other.[173] To a lesser extent, the same was true in York and Bristol.[174]

This ambiguity extended to royal service. In the household ordinances apothecaries ranked third, after the physicians and surgeons.[175] This did provide a substantial social position, allowing them first to affect the title "yeoman," and later that of "gentleman."[176] Yet they performed few medical tasks, being restricted to compounding physicians' prescriptions and remaining unable to administer drugs unless a physician or surgeon were present.[177] In some royal households, the surgeons did most of the drug-making.[178] Royal apothecaries were primarily vintners and confectioners. But again this ambiguous role complicated the medical hierarchy. For as their medical role diminished the apothecaries' general position at court grew. By 1450 most of them had been taken off salary and put on commission.[179] They became the suppliers to the royal court of drugs, wines, sweets, and other victuals. This proved immensely profitable, and led to their becoming richer and more influential than the royal physicians and surgeons.[180]

There are few contemporary appraisals of apothecaries. Those that

[171] Thrupp, "The Grocers," p. 283.

[172] Williams, *Masters, Wardens and Assistants*, pp. 5–9; *Register of the Freemen of Norwich*, for example, pp. 2, 3, 12, 24.

[173] *Register of the Freemen on Norwich*, pp. 16–18.

[174] For Bristol, see: R. Milnes Walker, "The Barber Surgeons of Bristol," *Bristol Medico-Chirurgical Journal*, 90, 1975, pp. 51–53; George Parker, "Early Bristol Medical Institutions," *Transactions of the Bristol and Gloucestershire Archaeological Society*, 44, 1922, pp. 155–177. For York, see Margaret Barnet, "The Barber-Surgeons of York," *MH*, 12, 1968, pp. 19–30; and *Register of Freemen of York*, pp. 76–214.

[175] Matthews, *Royal Apothecaries*, pp. 53–54.

[176] Myers, *Household of Edward IV*, p. 125.

[177] *Ibid.*, pp. 117–125.

[178] Matthews, *Royal Apothecaries*, pp. 47–48.

[179] *Ibid.* See also his "King John and the English Spicers," *MH*, 5, 1961, pp. 65–76.

[180] Margaret Curtis, "The London Lay Subsidy of 1332," in George Unwin, ed., *Finance and Trade Under Edward III*, 2nd ed. (London: Frank Cass, 1962), pp. 35–92, especially pp. 58–59.

survive are generally temperate and respectful, perhaps a reflection of apothecaries' wealth and position. But apothecaries were also envied, and as Thrupp has pointed out occasionally criticized for their alleged obsession with money.[181] Sometimes this carried over to their role as doctors. Chaucer, for example, in chiding his physician for too great an interest in riches, added the apothecary: "And each made money from the other's guile; They had been friendly for a goodish while."[182] He was referring of course to the close and profitable relationship between those who prescribed the drugs and those who made them. Yet he leaves little doubt that the physician was the medical superior:

> He was a perfect practicing physician.
> These causes being known for what they were,
> He gave the man his medicine then and there.
> All his apothecaries in a tribe.[183]

Apothecaries had the problem of an unfortunate association. Because of the international nature of the spice trade, many of them, particularly in London, were Italians.[184] This was an outgrowth of the Italian domination through most of the later middle ages of the English overseas trade. But London merchants, who were gradually replacing the Italians, resented them, and took advantage of a growing sense of xenophobia among much of the city's populace. There were a number of nasty and a few violent incidents in the first part of the century, and riots in the 1450s.[185]

The apothecaries suffered criticism of their medical skills. They were often reproached by physicians and surgeons for operating in circumstances beyond their skills. The surgeon John Arderne, for example, accused them of meddling—unsuccessfully, to boot—in clinical practice.[186] As one of the most widely read authors of the late middle ages, Arderne's condemnation became a commonplace. Apothecaries who "meddled" were usually restrained and disciplined by other apothecaries, physicians, or surgeons. When they did not desist, they were liable

---

[181] Thrupp, *Merchant Class*, pp. 288–311.

[182] *The Canterbury Tales*, p. 30.

[183] *Ibid.*

[184] CPR, 1429–1436, p. 559. Sylvia L. Thrupp, "Aliens in and Around London in the Fifteenth Century," in Hollaender and Kellaway, *Studies in London*, pp. 249–272.

[185] L–B, K, pp. 316–318.

[186] Arderne, *Fistula in Ano*, pp. 28, 76.

to prosecution. In sixteenth-century Norwich, an apothecary was brought before the convocation of alderman, the highest court in town:

> George Hill, apothecary, of late was committed to prison for that he had used the science of surgery, he not being expert therein, nor yet admitted there unto according to the law, and ministered to diverse persons within this city . . . [whom he] hurt . . . to depart out of this city on this Sunday next come and not to further intermeddle with the same city in the said science of surgery until he shall be there lawfully admitted at his peril.[187]

Not all apothecaries suffered the fate of George Hill. A few expanded their medical practices, and became prominent as doctors rather than merchants. William Burton, a Londoner, was a citizen and grocer, prominent in municipal affairs, and a retailer in anything he could get his hands on.[188] But his will, proved in 1438, shows that he also had a thriving medical practice that went beyond the dispensing of drugs.[189] Further, Burton seems to have practiced without getting the approval of either the physicians or the surgeons; clearly, he benefited from his citizenship. Surgeons, barbers, and even physicians needed the sanction of powerful Londoners to extend and maintain their privileges: yet as often as not the apothecaries who were grocers *were* those powerful Londoners. Like Burton, Roger Smith was a citizen, grocer, and an important Londoner.[190] In 1524 he applied to the royal court for license to "practice physic and surgery in all parts of the realm."[191] In doing so he bypassed the surgeons' and barbers' organizations, and flaunted the regulations of the 1511 Licensing Act and the College of Physicians. The petition was approved, and Smith presumably went on to practice medicine wherever he wanted.

If the role and image of the apothecaries was ambiguous, that of the unlicensed practitioners was downright murky. The most common of these unsanctioned empirics were village leeches. There was a direct correlation between the amount of formal education and the size of the community in which a doctor practiced.[192] Even the largest villages were too small to support a physician or a surgeon in a medical practice, in the unlikely event that he wished to live there. Consequently, most villages

---

[187] *Records of the City of Norwich*, i, p. 168.
[188] Matthews, *Royal Apothecaries*, pp. 39–41.
[189] Hustings Wills, ii, pp. 555–556.
[190] *LPFD*, iv, 1524, p. 131.
[191] *Ibid.*
[192] See below, pp. 254–256.

had only part-time barbers, if in fact they had any licensed practitioner.[193] This accounts for the frequency—and importance—of these
leeches. Few records or descriptions of their practices survive, so it is
difficult to make definitive comments about them. But there must have
been as many of them as there were any other kind of practitioner, including barbers.[194] Their main appeal was the low fees they charged,
and few of them could have made much money. Most had to farm, develop craft skills, or practice medicine in several villages to make ends
meet. Why, then, did they practice at all? Altruism and a love of medicine could well be one reason. But independence was another. Their
counterparts in London—and London and the larger county towns had
empirics in addition to their array of more formally trained doctors—
faced regulations, fines, and penalties. But in the countryside leeches
went unchallenged. They played important roles in community life,
and sometimes became pillars of the establishment.[195]

Leeches were trained in the tradition of folk medicine. Some were
self-taught; others learned at the sides of more experienced leeches; and
all continued to learn through practice. The best of them could compound simple drugs and pastes from herbal, animal, and mineral bases,
and occasionally from more expensive spices.[196] They were probably effective in dealing with minor traumas, low-grade fevers, and other relatively minor problems. Because they were usually of the local population they communicated well with their patients. In some cases, they
might have been more effective than the university-trained physicians,
surgeons, and barbers. Locally, they often had good images. But this
was not the case in the wider world. For, like the apothecaries, the
leeches were victims of an unfortunate association. Rightly or wrongly
they were lumped together with charlatans and quacks. Such malpractitioners had no empirical basis for their medicine, and based their cures
on wild combinations of potions and incantations. Quacks turned up
everywhere, but with doctors in towns better organized the chances of

[193] Pelling, "A Survey of East Anglia Medical Practitioners," pp. 54–65, offers a comparison.
[194] This is discussed by Keith Thomas, *Religion and the Decline of Magic* (London: Wei-
denfeld and Nicholson, 1970), pp. 209–300.
[195] *Ibid.* See too Emmanuel LeRoy Ladurie, *Montaillou: The Promised Land of Error*, trans.
Barbara Bray (New York: George Braziller, 1978), pp. 342–356.
[196] The best study is James K. Mustain, "A Rural Medical Practitioner in Fifteenth Century England," *BHM*, 46, 1972, pp. 469–476.

prosecution there were greater. Hence quacks were most common in the countryside. There they competed with village leeches for patients, and became indelibly associated with them.

Quacks and some empirics traveled the countryside in search of patients. Jusserand wrote a lively account of their practice:

[Quacks] were the folks with a universal panacea, very numerous in the Middle Ages; they went about the world selling health. They established themselves in the village green, or the marketplace, on holidays, spreading a carpet or a piece of cloth on the ground; they displayed their drugs and began to harangue the people. . . .

"Good people . . . I am not one of those poor preachers, nor one of those poor herbalists, who stand in front of churches with their miserable ill-sewn cloaks, who carry boxes and sachets and spread out on a carpet. Know that I am not one of these: but I belong to a lady whose name is Madame Trot of Salerno, who makes a kerchief of her ears, and whose eyebrows hang down as silver chains behind her shoulders: know that she is the wisest lady that is in all four parts of the world. My lady sends us into different lands and countries, into Apulia, Calabria, Burgundy, into the Forest of Arderne to kill wild beasts in order to extract good ointments from them, give medicine to those who are ill in body. . . . And because she made me swear by the saints when I parted from her, I will teach you the proper cure for worms, if you will listen. Will you listen?"[197]

People must have listened. For however much authorities berated them, quacks and the less sensational and more empirical leechs were in great demand. Clark believes this was because both were respected by the peasants and held in great esteem.[198] Perhaps, but it is more likely a function of their willingness to travel to outlying areas and the low fees they charged. Hammond has pointed out that the income of the average country doctor was so modest that it was imperative to have another trade, a plot of land to farm, or a practice that encompassed several villages.[199] Yet these rural doctors, leeches, and quacks filled an important function. In the late middle ages trifunctionalism was still an important social concept, and unlicensed, non-professional practitioners prospered in rural areas, as professional doctors took over the towns.

[197] Jusserand, *English Wayfaring Life*, pp. 95–96.
[198] Clark, *History of the Royal College*, i, p. 18.
[199] E. A. Hammond, "Incomes of Medieval English Doctors," *JHM*, 15, 1960, pp. 154–169.

There are detailed records for one empiric, John Crophill of Essex.[200]
Crophill has left what has been alternatively described as an account
book, a commonplace book, and a treatment book.[201] However it is cat-
egorized, the book helps to explain how the best of the country doctors
operated. Crophill was well educated, and held several positions. His
primary job was bailiff on the manor of Wix Priory in Essex, which he
served for thirty years beginning around 1450. He had a second job as
an ale-conner, and seems also to have considered himself a doctor.[202]
Medical practice may even have been forced on him because he was literate and able to understand the kind of general texts that had become
common in the fifteenth century. The villages in and around Wix
needed someone reliable to treat them; who better than a respected local
bailiff?

Crophill's accounts show that he had patients from at least a dozen
different villages in northern Essex and southern Suffolk, and include
recors of twenty "regulars."[203] He treated a spectrum of patients, including several gentlemen and their wives. His fees were modest, ranging
from twelve pence to two shillings—unfortunately, he did not specify
the cost of particular treatments—but so were his expenses.[204] For in his
role as bailiff he had an opportunity to buy at wholesale some of his medicines. Combined with the work as bailiff and ale-conner, this provided
Crophill a comfortable living. His kind of medicine was physic, and he
followed the Salerno Regimen and urged moderation. His first response
to sickness was usually bleeding, followed by drugs, and guided by the
characteristic Salernitan zodiac man. Crophill, then, was highly regarded and well informed, if not formally trained. He had little theoretical background but was long on practice.

Women constituted a third kind of rural leech.[205] As for other country

---

[200] B.M. Harl. Ms. 1735.

[201] The three major studies are: E. W. Talbert, "The Notebook of a Fifteenth Century
Practicing Physician," *Studies in English*, 21, 1942, pp. 5–30; Rossell Hope Robbins, "John
Crophill's Ale-Pots," *Review of English Studies*, 20, 1969, pp. 82–89; and Mustain, "A Rural
Medical Practitioner."

[202] There is disagreement among the authors. Talbert treats him primarily as a doctor,
Robbins as an ale-conner, and Mustain insists that medicine was the least important of his
three occupations. All suggest that he found medicine most interesting, but Mustain suggests that it was the least profitable of the sidelines.

[203] B.M. Harl. Ms. 1735, f. 36b.

[204] *Ibid.* f. 46b.

[205] See: Lucille B. Pinto, "The Folk Practice of Gynaecology and Obstetrics in the Mid-

doctors, the records of their practice are few and far between. Excepting perhaps their role as midwives, women had little opportunity to enter established medical organizations or get formal training. They were barred from being physicians, and discouraged from entering the surgeons', barbers', and apothecaries' guilds.[206] This left rural areas, where supervision was less exacting; and, indeed, the data in the doctors' file suggests that this is where most women doctors practiced.[207] Like other country doctors, these women drew on folk medicine. Many of them knew the properties of various herbs and plants from cooking, and had household experience with cuts, bruises, and broken bones. And many, as might be expected, served as obstetricians. It is true that men wrote, compiled, or copied the gynecological treatises used in late medieval England, including the various editions of the Trotula manuscripts.[208] Men also dominated the alternative texts, those drawing from the Galenic/Soranic tradition. But women supervised childbirths, and were probably consulted on a wide range of gynecological and obstetric questions. One obstetrix, Marjory Cobbe of Devon, served Elizabeth, wife of Edward IV, and was rewarded with a pension of ten pounds for her services.[209]

Yet the very hazards of childbirth also put female leeches in jeopardy. So great was maternal mortality—as high as twenty percent—that even the best obstetrix would lose many patients.[210] And, like respectable male empirics, female practitioners were tainted by association with quacks. Hence, their skills notwithstanding, the few records that discuss rural women practitioners belittle them and place them at the very bottom of the medical hierarchy. This was the image that poets stressed:

---

dle Ages," *BHM*, 47, 1973, pp. 513–523; Eileen Power, "Some Women Practitioners of Medicine in the Middle Ages," *Proceedings of the Royal Society of Medicine*, 15, 1928, pp. 159–172; Edward F. Tuttle, "The Trotula and the Old Dame Trot: A Note on the Lady of Salerno," *BHM*, 50, 1976, pp. 61–72.

[206] Curtis, "London Lay Subsidy," p. 59. See too Dobson and Walker, *Barber and Barber-Surgeons*, p. 24.

[207] See below, p. 263.

[208] A current edition has been published: Beryl Rowland, ed., *Medieval Women's Guide to Health: The First English Gynecological Handbook* (Kent, Ohio: Kent State University Press, 1981). It is an edition of B.M. Sloane 2463.

[209] *T&H*, pp. 209–210.

[210] See E. A. Wrigley, *Population and History* (New York: McGraw-Hill, 1969), pp. 63–106.

Both hi this conne, hit his peril
To these midwives
For often children show up [alive] quick
I bore too short lives and die
But he alright is christened be
From heaven, every he weaveth.[211]

The few urban women doctors fared better. They were usually wives
or daughters who succeeded a husband or father who was a plenipoten-
tiary in a particular guild. As noted, only the physicians specifically proscribed women practitioners, and a few county town guilds actually
seemed to have welcomed them.[212] Women barbers were most common.
There were, for example, Agnes and Joan Collins, mother and daughter, practicing barbery in Canterbury in the early fifteenth century.[213]
And there were Agnes and Jane Goddeson, also mother and daughter,
practicing in sixteenth-century Bristol. Jane was unusual in that she was
apprenticed to a man.[214] And at least two London barbers left their tools
to their apprentices on the condition that they finish the apprenticeships
under the direction of their wives.[215]

It has been suggested that some female practitioners were of the aristocracy.[216] None occurs in the data bank, but it is unlikely that any of
these aristocrats, if they existed, were practitioners in the traditional
sense. They would not have belonged to doctors' guilds, been trained in
the formal fashion, or even practiced for fees. What we do know of them
comes from a literary tradition, especially poetry. Chaucer wrote of his
prioress:

While she was in Armenia
Both physic and surgery
She had learned of masters great.[217]

---

[211] Jones, "Popular Medical Knowledge," p. 421.

[212] A good example is the Lincoln barbers' statues. See Young, *Annals of the Barber-Surgeons*, pp. 576–579.

[213] *Intrantes: A List of Persons Admitted to the Life and Trade (in Canterbury) from 1392–1592*,
ed. J. M. Cowper (Canterbury: By the Author, 1904), for 1423–1424 and 1432–1434.

[214] *Calendar of the Bristol Apprentice Book, 1532-1565*, ed. D. Hollis, *Bristol Record Society*,
i, 14, 1948, p. 61.

[215] London Com. Court, Alex Sly, Litchfield, f. iiv–12; and London Com. Court,
Thomas Parkin, Litchfield, f. 139.

[216] Jones, "Popular Medical Knowledge," pp. 420–425.

[217] *Canterbury Tales*, A, 3671–3673.

Following Chaucer, some authorities argue that a source of these practitioners was nunneries, where a sophisticated kind of physic was taught and practiced.[218] Here too it is difficult to find institutional records, but there are literary references:

> And at the nunnery the knight was laid
> To help the wounds in his head.[219]

But women barbers, apothecaries, and aristocratic and clerical doctors were a minority. For most women who wanted to be doctors, practice in the countryside was the best alternative, and obstetrics and gynecology the easiest kind of practice. And however skilled they might have been, most female practitioners were, at best, associated with male village leeches, or, at worst, with quacks and charlatans. In either case, they operated on the lowest rung of the medical community.

Practitioners, then, brought together by medicine, were rent apart by social divisions. Physicians stood at the top, followed by surgeons, barbers, and apothecaries. They were followed by unlicensed doctors, including village leeches, quacks, and charlatans, and women. The hierarchy often defied reason. Surgeons could be more effective than physicians; and apothecaries, members of powerful merchant companies and part of another, non-medical bourgeois ladder, commanded greater respect in the outside world. Corporately and formally trained doctors practiced in towns, while those who were self-trained held forth in the countryside. And, with the exception of the surgeons, practitioners suffered from a public image that was usually critical. This helps to account for that final mirror of medical practice: home treatment and the proliferation of "how-to" books on medicine. Hence this passage in *The Canterbury Tales*:

> Though in this town there is no apothecary
> I shall myself to herbs teach you
> That shall be to your health, and for your prowess
> And in our yard through herbs shall I find.[220]

And it explains why Caxton, when printing his *Dialogues in French and English*, included the following poem:

---

[218] Power, "Some Women Practitioners of Medicine," p. 159.

[219] *Romance of Sir Isumbras*, 1485–1486, Thornton Romances, as quoted in Jones, "Popular Medical Knowledge," p. 422.

[220] *Canterbury Tales*, B, 4138–4141.

> For that I am not
> Spicer nor apothecary
> I can not name
> All manners of spices
> But I shall name a part
> Ginger galingale
> Cubibes [berries of the piper cubeba], saffron
> Pepper, cumin
> Sugar white and brown
> Flour of cannell
> Anise, grains of paradise
> Of these things he made confections
> And good powders
> Whereof is made
> And electuaries for medicines.[221]

Laymen might be excused for thinking the advice of this poem to be as effective as an expensive visit to the doctor's office.[222]

[221] Caxton, *Dialogues in English and French*, pp. 19–20.
[222] Braswell, "Utilitarian and Scientific Prose," pp. 337–387.

# 3

## DOCTORS OF THE ROYAL
## COURTS

The surest way for a doctor to gain fame, fortune, and high social position was to serve the king. Royal service allowed any practitioner, physician, surgeon, apothecary, or barber to move in the highest circles in England. It brought instant and automatic respectability. It meant financial gain and immunity from anything unpleasant. It allowed for special privileges and favors, often for family and friends as well as for the practitioner. Being in royal service was the best thing that could happen to a doctor, and most practitioners tried to secure such appointments.

Royal doctors divide into two groups: practitioners of physic and practitioners of surgery. Generally, physicians and their subordinates, apothecaries, were most common and influential at court, while surgeons and their imitators, barbers, were most evident when the king was in transit, especially on campaign. Surgeons and the importance to them of war will be discussed in Chapter Four. Herein, discussion will focus mainly on the practices and careers of the doctors of the royal courts, especially physicians and apothecaries.

Most royal doctors were Englishmen. But many were foreigners who came to England on the invitation of the king, or with the explicit idea of serving him. Hence, while foreign doctors were unimportant in the general history of medicine in late medieval England, they did play a large role at court. At times, as in the early sixteenth century, they brought new ideas and techniques. But basically they practiced the same kind of physic as the Englishmen. This is important, for by studying royal physicians and apothecaries, foreign and domestic, it is possible to get some sense of how the best practitioners of the old medicine went about their business, and how they were able to survive and prosper despite their ineffectual methods.

Household accounts provide the best evidence.[1] Fragments from the

---

[1] The records are: A. R. Myers, ed., *The Household of Edward IV* (Manchester: Manchester University Press, 1959); and *Ordinances and Regulations for the Government of the Royal Household* (London: Society of Antiquaries, 1790).

reign of Edward III are useful because they highlight the differences between service at court and that in the field.[2] Ordinances from 1345 list members of a royal army. Knights, clerks, esquires, men-at-arms, and archers numbering 330 had a single surgeon.[3] By contrast, serjeants-of-arms and their retinue, and esquires of the household and their retinue, totaling 296, had no surgeon, or at least none paid for by the king.[4] Officers of the ministers of the household, with their retinues, totaling 184, had two apothecaries. Yet the minstrels, musicians, "artificers," workmen, and their retinues, including soldiers, also had none, again at least as paid for by the king.[5] In all, the army was said to number 32,391, surely an exaggeration.[6] It included three surgeons; six men alternately called "doctors" and "ductors," who may have been physicians; and an unspecified number of "poticaries."[7] All were paid twelve pence a day "while in the field."[8]

This can be contrasted with evidence from 1348, pertaining to service at court. One surgeon, who ranked with the royal clerks, received an annual wage of forty-six shillings and eight pence.[9] Two physicians, rated with the officers, received eight marks, a mark being two-thirds of a pound.[10] And an unspecified number of apothecaries received forty shillings a year.[11] In addition to being safe at court, the surgeons and physicians supplemented their incomes by treating other patients, while the apothecaries dealt in spices on the side. There is, in all, little question that in the fourteenth century it was better to be a doctor at court than in the field, and best to be a royal physician. And, overall, the pre-plague royal medical entourage was small, probably numbering no more than four.

Royal household ordinances do not deal with doctors again for almost a hundred years. When they do, they show substantial growth. In 1455 Henry VI had seven doctors in attendance, two physicians, three sur-

---

[2] *Ordinances and Regulations*, pp. 3–12.

[3] *Ibid.*, p. 3.

[4] *Ibid.*, p. 4.

[5] *Ibid.*

[6] *Ibid.*, p. 8.

[7] *Ibid.*

[8] *Ibid.*, p. 10.

[9] *Ibid.*

[10] *Ibid.*

[11] *Ibid.*

geons, and two apothecaries.[12] Seven is a great many doctors, even for a king, and Henry may have been atypical. He was sick for long parts of his reign, and the two apothecaries devoted more time to the steward-ship of wines than the making and administering of medicines.[13] The doctors may also have tended members of the royal family. There is, for example, evidence from 1474 in which Edward IV stipulated that his son Prince Edward should always have in attendance "a physician and a surgeon, sufficient and cunning."[14] But, whatever the reservations, the role and opportunities for royal doctors grew enormously in the fif-teenth century.

The best record comes from the reign of Edward IV.[15] A keen and vigorous soldier, a good administrator, and a high liver and over-indul-ger, Edward both organized and needed medical practitioners.[16] In the last ten years of his reign he had six different physicians, two of whom, Dominic de Serego and James Frise, were foreign-born.[17] Edward be-gan a trend which, by the middle of the sixteenth century, would lead to a considerable presence of alien doctors. He also brought doctors to court to serve as consultants; of the six physicians who treated him to-ward the end of his life only two were in residence at any given time. His doctors enjoyed considerable social mobility, even for members of the royal court. One, William Hatclif, became the king's secretary.[18] Another, William Hobbes, began as a surgeon, and ended as a royal physician.[19] Physicians remained the principal doctors, and were paid the highest fees. But the king was treated by equal numbers of physi-cians and surgeons. The self-made Edward appreciated skill and was not afraid of ambition—that, after all, was how he had won the Crown.

Edward's ordinances describe the duties of the court doctors.[20] The physician was to have the freedom of the king's chambers. He was ac-corded a social rank equal to that of the knights and chaplains in court,

[12] *Ibid.*, pp. 18–23.
[13] Leslie G. Matthews, *The Royal Apothecaries* (London: Wellcome Historical Medical Li-brary, 1967), pp. 45–49.
[14] *Ordinances and Regulations*, p. 30.
[15] Myers, *Household of Edward IV*.
[16] Charles Ross, *Edward IV* (Berkeley, Cal.: University of California Press, 1974), pp. 257–277.
[17] *T&H*, pp. 36, 96–98.
[18] *Ibid.*, pp. 398–399.
[19] *Ibid.*, pp. 401–402.
[20] Myers, *Household of Edward IV*, pp. 118–125.

and better than that of the other practitioners. The physician decided what and how much the king would eat and drink, a difficult and thankless task with a sybarite like Edward IV. He was able to purchase whatever supplies and medicine he deemed necessary. His wages were equal those of the royal squires. And one of the two physicians was designated to direct the entire medical staff.[21]

Edward's ordinances reflect the privileges and benefits that royal doctors could expect. There are also examples from other courts, such as that of Elias de Sabboto, Jewish physician to Henry IV.[22] Jews were expelled from England in 1290, but the same royal prerogative that chased them could make exceptions. Elias was a prominent teacher at the University of Pavia, and had a large and lucrative practice. Henry, preoccupied with his health, wanted the best medical care, and sent for him. Elias resisted. He was comfortable in sunny, cultured and relatively tolerant Italy, and did not want to go to that cold backwater, England. He demanded and got a large salary. More prickly still, as an observant Jew he argued that he needed other Jews to constitute a minyan so that he could conduct religious services. Elias asked for and got protection for a dozen Jews. Henry placed all of them, their servants, horses and baggage trains under a royal safe conduct. They stayed in England for a year, serving the king and travelling throughout the kingdom, always without incident. Then Elias returned to Italy, where he became physician to the pope.

Another case in point is Valerius de Poianis, a French physician, who in 1514 was given the king's license to practice anywhere in England, irrespective of local laws and restrictions.[23] Poianis was one of several foreigners, all royal physicians, who were made denizens by proclamation.[24] Sometimes foreigners wanted the help of their royal patients in gaining privileges in their homelands. Walter de Gales was provided property in his native France, while William Radicis was given protec-

---

[21] *Ibid.*, p. 70.

[22] References to Sabboto are: *T&H*, p. 43; Talbot, *Medicine in Medieval England*, pp. 204–205; Rymer, *Foedera*, p. 566 (Hiv,i,184); and Cecil Roth, *History of the Jews in England* (Philadelphia: Jewish Publication Society, 1946), pp. 160, 213–224.

[23] Rymer, *Foedera*, p. 750 (Hvi,i,87).

[24] These included the Greek Thomas Frank, the Venetian Augustine de Augustinus, the Luccan David of Nigarellis, and the Frenchmen Michel Belwell. See Rymer, *Foedera*, p. 662 (Hv,iv,157); p. 770 (Hvi,ii,154); p. 570 (Hiv,ii,8); p. 671 (Hv,i,117).

tion and troops to accompany him on a French tour.[25] The Italian Antony Ciabo was given license to import Gascon wines.[26] English-born royal physicians too could reap unusual benefits from their service. Geoffrey Crook was allowed a letter of marque to sail against the Spanish so that he could recompense the loss from a debt.[27]

Surgeons, as noted, fared best on the battlefield. But they did well at court too, ranking after the physicians. Like the physicians, they were allowed access to the king's apartments, and the chief master surgeon was accorded the rank of squire.[28] A few, like Ciabo and William Hobbes, rose to positions, salaries, and benefits commensurate with those of the physicians, while others, especially during the reigns of Henry V and Henry VI, got salaries at higher than the standard rates.[29] Henry VI employed up to four surgeons, as opposed to two or three physicians.[30] In 1430 he had five of them, and allotted £20 to buy equipment.[31]

The role of the other surgical practitioners, barbers, was never clearly defined. There were always one or two, but ordinarily they only performed the king's toilet. When they did serve as doctors, it was in a minor capacity, such as cupping or lancing.[32] But it was still a good job. In 1340 Adam de Thorpe, described as the king's barber, was allowed a host of privileges, including land and annuities.[33] So too were Roger del Ewerie in 1363, Robert Bolley, and Alexander Donour in 1447, and several others in the fifteenth and early sixteenth centuries.[34] Under Edward IV, they become gentlemen, yeomen, or grooms, surprisingly so, since this placed them on equal social footing with surgeons and apothecaries.[35] Yet the trust and professional respect that was accorded the other doctors was not forthcoming. Barbers did not have access to the royal chambers. Someone, preferably a surgeon, had to be present whenever the king was being shaved. A surgeon also had to be around

---

[25] *Ibid.*, p. 356 (Riii,1,403); p. 402 (Riii,1,437).

[26] *Ibid.*, p. 777 (Hiv,iii,9).

[27] CPR, 1391–1396, p. 330. He was also known as Geoffrey Creek.

[28] Myers, *Household of Edward IV*, pp. 91, 117–121.

[29] *T&H*, pp. 401-402.

[30] *Ordinances and Regulations*, pp. 17–23.

[31] Rymer, *Foedera*, p. 648 (Hiv,iv,157).

[32] Myers, *Household of Edward IV*, pp. 16, 125.

[33] Rymer, *Foedera*, p. 314 (Rii,ii,1117).

[34] *Ibid.*, p. 429 (Rii,ii,708); p. 677 (Hv,i,180); *Rot. Parl.*, ii, f. 33b.

[35] Myers, *Household of Edward IV*, pp. 16, 125.

when the barber cupped, leeched, bled, or performed any of his other already limited medical duties. Still, for most barbers these medical limitations were secondary considerations, superseded by the prospects of riches and social standing.[36]

The role of the royal apothecaries was clouded by their dual status as merchants and doctors. Matthews, the leading authority on the apothecaries, makes much of their medical role.[37] He argues that they prepared and administered the royal medicines, and purchased medical supplies. Further, he claims that they were responsible for making the spiced wines and confectionaries that were used like vitamin pills. Clearly, the royal apothecaries took advantage of the prestige and good connections they established at court to open shops in Westminster and London. There they sold drugs and advised patients, a profitable activity that would be copied by physicians and surgeons.[38]

But duality brought problems. What distinguished doctors from other courtiers was their professional expertise, their ability to advise on a distinct set of problems in a way that no one else could. Here the versatility of the apothecaries worked against them. A thirteenth-century example of this lack of specialization was Richard of Montpellier, spicer to Edward I. He was "designated to come to London for various things needed for the king's malady, as is plainly set forth by the king's physicians."[39] Richard regarded himself as a medical man first and a merchant second, but his medical status was uncertain. It existed, but at the prerogative of the physicians and, as the 1345 ordinances make clear, the surgeons.[40] Even so influential an apothecary as William Burton was not exceptional.[41] Those records that pertain to his service at court show that he always acted as a supplier of spices, and never as a doctor—this in contrast to his active medical career in London.

Another example of the apothecaries' limited medical role came in 1454, when Henry VI's doctors, three physicians and two surgeons,

[36] *Ibid.*

[37] Matthews, *Royal Apothecaries*, pp. 47–48. See too: Matthews, "King John of France and the English Spicers," *MH*, 5, 1961, pp. 65-76; Matthews, "Royal Apothecaries of the Tudor Period," *MH*, 8, 1964, pp. 170–180; and Geoffrey E. Trease, *Pharmacy in History* (London: Balliere, Tindall and Cox, 1964), pp. 59–79.

[38] Matthews, *Royal Apothecaries*, p. 39.

[39] *Ibid.*, p. 18.

[40] *Ordinances and Regulations*, pp. 2–10.

[41] A summary account is provided in Matthews, *Royal Apothecaries*, pp. 39–41.

gathered to prescribe treatment for the king, who had suffered a mental breakdown. They agreed on a medication:

> Electuaries, potions, syrups, confections, laxative medicines in whatever form they thought best, clysters, gargles, baths, complete or partial, removal of the skin, fomentations, embrocations, shaving of the head, ointments, plasters, waxes, scarification, with or without rubifacients, and to do whatever was necessary to relieve and bring back the king's health.[42]

Here was the perfect remedy for a pharmacist, the ideal chance to practice medicine. Matthews believed that Richard Hakedy, the royal apothecary in 1454, "would have been kept busy had he prepared anything like the complete range of medicaments which could be employed."[43] True enough, but even Matthews acknowledges that "the list . . . must have been compiled with the advice of the learned body of physicians and surgeons."[44] In fact, it was drawn up by the physicians and the administration supervised by the surgeons; there is no evidence that the apothecaries even compounded it.[45]

The best evidence of royal apothecaries comes from the household accounts of Edward IV.[46] The apothecary was given the status of yeoman, equal to that of the second of Edward's three surgeons. He took his meals in the great hall, and was seated with the yeoman of royal service, the squires and the gentlemen. He was paid the same wages as the other yeoman, but was provided a special allowance for the purchase of medications, spices, spiced wines, and confectionaries. He was allowed a groom, with whom he shared a bed. He was to be cared for if he fell ill—presumably by a physician or surgeon—and to share in the distribution of gifts from the king. He was given an allowance or, if he chose, a livery at the king's expense. Some medical duties were assigned him in addition to his role as pharmacist. If the surgeons and barbers were absent, the apothecary could draw blood. But he had to do it under supervision, presumably that of the physician. And, unlike the physician and surgeon but like the barber, the apothecary could not enter the king's apartments, and could not treat the king unless the physician or surgeon was present.[47]

[42] CPR, 1452–1461, p. 147.

[43] Matthews, *Royal Apothecaries*, p. 48.

[44] *Ibid.*

[45] This seems clear from an entry in the Patent Rolls, CPR, 1452–1461, p. 147.

[46] Myers, *Household of Edward IV*, pp. 16, 188, 125, 245.

[47] *Ibid.*, pp. 118–125.

Edward IV's apothecary had other, quasi-medical duties. He was charged with maintaining standards of sanitation, especially of the royal bedding and wardrobe. According to the accounts: "These two wardrobes have all their fumigations that the king's robes, doublets, sheets and shirts be fumed all the year of the yeoman apothecary."[48] He was responsible in general for "washing, cleaning and mending," and was to freshen the wardrobe with herbs, flowers, and roots, all to give pleasant fragrances. And he was to purchase food and drug supplies. It seems, then, that the lesser doctors, the apothecary and the barber, were responsible for daily care. But for difficult problems and crises the principal doctors, the physician and surgeon, were called in.

Household ordinances from 1526 show that Henry VIII cut back on the medical role of the apothecaries.[49] Indeed, they even ceased to compound the royal medications.[50] Rather, they joined two new, related officers, the Confectioner and Waferer, and the Spicer, in provisioning the court. Medical treatment was left to two physicians and three surgeons, who performed the same duties that they always had.[51] But specialization did not diminish the appeal of royal service for the apothecaries; on the contrary, it became more attractive than ever. In 1526 the chief royal apothecary was Cuthbert Blackden.[52] He was paid a salary, given meals and the use of a house with a garden, the latter presumably to help in the assembly of herbs and medicines. But Blackden's major source of income came from his principal task, the buying and selling of food and drugs. He bought wholesale and then sold at a considerable profit to the royal household. Matthews estimates that Blackden's bills to Henry VIII in the 1530s averaged £60 a year.[53]

Other evidence suggests the apothecaries' prosperity. There were a lot of them, at least a half dozen at court from the late fifteenth century onward.[54] Blackden had a personal staff of three.[55] The queen had her own apothecary, and he too seems to have had a staff.[56] By 1540 their

[48] *Ibid.*, p. 118.

[49] *Ordinances and Regulations*, p. 166.

[50] Matthews, *Royal Apothecaries*, p. 62.

[51] *Ibid.*

[52] A summary account is in Matthews, *Royal Apothecaries*, pp. 62–66.

[53] *Ibid.*, p. 66.

[54] Matthews, "Royal Apothecaries of the Tudor Period," pp. 170–180.

[55] *Ibid.*

[56] *Ibid.* See also F. D. Blackley and G. Hermansen, eds., *The Household Books of Queen*

social position at court had improved. Thomas Alsop, the chief apothecary, was given the rank of gentleman, a title Henry VIII felt better suited to his servant's wealth and situation than that of yeoman.[57] Like Blackden, Alsop had a staff and became very rich. Henry VIII was often sick in the 1540s, and Alsop kept him supplied with expensive medications. Alsop's salary, forty marks a year (about £27), was modest. But it represented a small part of his total income. He received royal grants of property and trading privileges.[58] Hence, by the end of the middle ages, royal apothecaries were richer and had a more prominent role than ever. But their medical role had all but disappeared.

The privy expenses of Elizabeth of York, daughter of Edward IV, wife to Henry VII, and mother of Henry VIII, also provide information on the doctors of the court.[59] In 1502 and 1503 there are notations about her apothecaries, John Grice and John Pykenham.[60] Grice was a prominent grocer and benefited from his royal service by opening what might be described as a dispensing pharmacy in London.[61] Three bills he submitted to the queen's accountants show how royal doctors got rich. One, from 1502, even includes the cost of a boat ride which took him upriver from his home in London to see the queen in Westminster.[62] This was about the time Elizabeth began a pregnancy which, in February, 1503, would lead to her death in childbirth. During her term she consulted several doctors. One was the surgeon John Johnson, who

---

*Isabella of England, 1311–12* (Edmonton: University of Alberta Press, 1971); and N. H. Nicholas, ed., *Privy Expenses of Elizabeth of York and Wardrobe Accounts of Edward IV* (London: William Pickering, 1830).

[57] For Alsop, see Matthews, *Royal Apothecaries*, pp. 61–73.

[58] *Ibid.*

[59] Nicholas, *Priory Expenses of Elizabeth of York*, pp. 48–49. There is another household book, slightly before my period, for Edward II's queen, Isabella of France, for the years 1311–1312. Oddly enough, the only information about doctors concerns apothecaries, a list of whose medicines is included. They were unextraordinary, the same herbs and spices as had and would be used throughout the middle ages. More interesting is the fact that in the two years covered by the accounts the queen alone employed four apothecaries. One, called "Odin, the queen's apothecary," was the chief adviser; the others, two Frenchmen and an Englishman, did most of the purchasing. And while there is no record of the other doctors, the apothecaries medical role seems limited to the purchase and occasional compounding of medicines, and rarely even their administration. See Blackley and Hermansen, *Household Book of Queen Isabella*, p. 109.

[60] *Ibid.*, pp. 8–105.

[61] Matthews, *Royal Apothecaries*, p. 61.

[62] Nicholas, *Privy Expenses of Elizabeth of York*, pp. 8, 14, 48–49.

charged thirteen shillings and four pence per visit.[63] Another was a Doctor Hallesworth, who was summoned from his home in Kent to see the queen as she lay dying in the Tower.[64] According to the accounts:

> Item, to James Nattras, for his costs going into Kent for Doctor Hallysworth, physician, to come to the Queen, by the king's command. First, for his boat, hire from the Tower to Gravesend and again, 3/4. Item to two watermen abiding at Gravesend unto such time the said James come again, for their expenses, 8 pence. Item, for horse hire and two guides for night and day, 2/3, and for his own expense, 8 pence. Total, 6/8.[65]

Among the other doctors mentioned in Elizabeth's accounts were Benedict Fentre and a Master Lewes.[66] Fentre was paid a retainer of £40 a year, while in 1510 Lewes received the astounding sum £100 in gold.[67] And in 1503, Henry VII, a notorious tightwad, paid an unnamed surgeon twenty shillings to cure him of his French Pox, usually a reference to syphilis.[68] This might provide a clue to the death in childbirth of Queen Elizabeth.

These are the household accounts that provide information on the royal doctors. Other information must be pieced together through a pastiche of sources. There are good records for the apothecaries at the court of Edward III, the most prominent of whom was John Adami.[69] Adami was born in Lucca, the son of a wealthy spice merchant. He first came to London on one of his father's ventures, liked it, and spent most of his adult life there. He became a citizen, in part through royal initiative, was a prominent member of the London spicers' and pepperers' guild, and a force in the foundation of the Grocers' Company in 1345.[70] Adami was involved in real estate in the 1340s and 1350s, and was a partner in many trading ventures.[71] But he was unusual among grocers in that his

---

[63] *Ibid.*, p. 14. For information on Johnson, see *T&H*, p. 158.

[64] *Ibid.*, p. 96; *T&H*, pp. 68–69.

[65] *Ibid.*, pp. 96–97.

[66] *Ibid.* Others included: Master Lynch; Master Lewes, noted as the Queens' physician; Ralph Sentiler; Master Domynyns; Vincent Wolf, a physician; Benedict Fentre, another physician; and another, presumably distinct Master Lewes. Some of these doctors achieved prominence, and will be discussed shortly.

[67] *Ibid.* See too *T&H*, pp. 24–25.

[68] Robert S. Gottfried, *Epidemic Disease in Fifteenth Century England* (New Brunswick, N.J.: Rutgers University Press, 1978), p. 45.

[69] Matthews, *Royal Apothecaries*, pp. 27–28.

[70] CPR, 1350–1354, p. 196.

[71] *Hustings Wills*, ii, p. 4.

predominate interest was in medicine.[72] Perhaps this was what first brought him to Edward III's attention. Adami spent twenty profitable years at the royal court. He was exempted from taxes, endowed with property, and apparently given royal tips in advance of several dubious land deals.[73] His brother, a merchant, was knighted, and his two sons followed him as apothecaries in the London Grocers' Company.[74] Adami's will, proved in 1358, contained a £100 bequest to his brother.[75] In many ways he was the quintessential royal doctor—rich, successful, arrogant, and foreign.

Two of Edward's other apothecaries, Bartholomeo Mine and Vivian Rogeroni, were Italian.[76] Rogeroni was a Luccan and associate of John Adami.[77] Mine was a Lombard, a member of the London Grocers' Company, and a prominent merchant.[78] There are, literally, dozens of references to his activities in the royal calendars, and judging by the prices he charged for his spices he must have become quite wealthy.[79] The other two, William de Stanes and Coursus de Gangeland, were native Londoners.[80] Gangeland served in the first years of the reign, and traveled with the king. In 1345 he was granted a lifetime annuity for restoring Edward's health when the king fell ill on his Scottish campaign. Stanes succeeded Gangeland, and probably became Edward's chief apothecary after John Adami died.[81] With Rogeroni and Mine, he was mostly a supplier of drugs, and received in addition to his salary several royal trading licenses as compensation for his service.[82] He was a partner in a number of ventures, and owned several tenements in London.[83]

---

[72] He was, for example, one of the seven governors of the apothecaries' mystery in the company. *Cal. Plea Mem. Rolls*, 1323–1364, p. 237.

[73] Many apothecaries were involved in land deals in the mid-fourteenth century, a reflection of a group with ready cash taking advantage of the flux of the postplague land market. See, for example, L–B F, pp. 24, 113, 139, 157, 179, 182, 190, 191.

[74] *Hustings Wills*, ii, p. 4.

[75] *Ibid.*

[76] Matthews, *Royal Apothecaries*, p. 29.

[77] Facsimile of Ms. Archives of the Company of the Grocers of the City of London, London Guildhall Library, pp. 35, 45.

[78] See, for example, CCR, 1374–1377, p. 413.

[79] *Ibid.*

[80] Matthews, *Royal Apothecaries*, p. 29.

[81] Matthews, *Royal Apothecaries*, pp. 28–29.

[82] Postan and Power, *Studies in English Trade*, p. 249.

[83] *Hustings Wills*, ii, p. 72; CPR, 1370–1374, p. 442.

Among his many royal gifts was a lifetime annuity of 100 shillings, granted in 1376, a year before Edward's death.[84] In all, the reign of Edward III was a fine time to be a court doctor, and especially an apothecary. Edward was busy and cosmopolitan; he had an international reputation, interests on the continent, and a large and sumptuous court. During his reign, the spicers, pepperers, and apothecaries gave shape and then birth to the powerful London Grocers' Company.[85]

Apothecaries did less well at the court of Richard II. They continued to supply drugs and victuals.[86] To this was added a new and profitable task, caretakers of the royal silver, ordinarily a position reserved for surgeons.[87] But their lack of specialization began to hurt. Richard preferred physicians, paid them higher salaries, allowed them more land and gifts, and accorded them more respect and better social position.[88] This continued during the reigns of the Lancastrians. Henry IV liked foreign physicians, and was uninterested in the kind of medical advice that apothecaries offered. He made less use of them than any other late medieval king. Those apothecaries who were brought to court came strictly as part-timers and exclusively as suppliers.

Henry IV's only apothecary of note was the aforementioned William Burton. Citizen and officer of the Grocers' Company, Burton supplied the king with spices and drugs, no small matter in the reign of Henry IV, who was frequently ill and generally a hypochondriac. He was well rewarded; in 1401 Henry provided him an annual salary of £20 for what must have been just a few weeks' work each year, and later allowed him

[84] Matthews, *Royal Apothecaries*, p. 28.

[85] A final example is that of Thomas de Martins, a Dutchman, Fleming or Frenchman, who may have been a sixth royal apothecary to Edward III. There is no firm evidence of his actually being at court. But he was involved with Edward, members of his court, and some of his apothecaries in a series of business deals which brought considerable profits to everyone. See CPR, 1343–1345, p. 113; and Eilert Eckwall, *Two Early London Subsidy Rolls* (Lund: C.W.K. Gleerup, 1951), p. 46.

[86] Matthews, *Royal Apothecaries*, pp. 28–30, 36–41.

[87] CCR, 1337–1381, p. 23.

[88] For example, see CPR., 1396–1399, pp. 41, 482, 525, 527. Richard also had a personal interest in the spice trade; in 1389, he regulated its trade throughout England, and in doing so restricted the role of foreigners. His motives are not clear, though personal profit, antipathy toward the Italians who still dominated trade, and the rising power of the London Grocers must have been factors. Indeed, Richard's regulations were an important step in the grocers' rise to power. This meant new opportunities for the apothecaries, especially out of medicine. See *Statutes of the Realm* (London: Society of Antiquaries, 1816), 16 Ric. II, c.1–3.

a lifetime annuity.[89] He supplied the court with victuals as well as drugs, and opened two shops in Cambridge in addition to the one he had in London.[90] His star continued to rise, and in 1405 he represented London in Parliament.[91] All this sounds more like the career of a successful capitalist than that of a doctor—but that, of course, was what William Burton really was.

Like his father, Henry V employed apothecaries as victualers.[92] He did advocate the use of treacle as an antidote for infections from battlefield wounds, but believed it ought to be applied by surgeons.[93] Henry VI, whose court became a center of medical practice, was different. His apothecaries did act as doctors. This was partly owing to the skills, influence, and prestige of Richard Hakedy, the most prominent of late medieval apothecaries, and the one most interested in medicine.[94] Like Burton and the others, Hakedy was a citizen of London and an important member of the Grocer's Company. His first royal appointment came in 1441, about the time Henry VI ended his minority and began to make his own decisions. Hakedy was provided with the substantial though not spectacular salary of forty marks, but soon improved his position. Within a year he was made a gentleman and one of two garbellers for the ports of London, Sandwich, and Southampton.[95] The royal garbellers controlled customs, and the possibilities for graft were unlimited; a clever man could quadruple his salary without bringing upon himself royal censure.[96]

For all his worldly success it was his medical skills that distinguished Hakedy. He had a special interest in preparing medicines. Hakedy was not an innovator; rather, he worked entirely within the existing pharmaceutical tradition. But he felt that new combinations could be made of the old mixtures, and worked scrupulously and diligently to come up with more effective medicines. It would be incorrect to make too much

[89] CPR, 1401–1405, p. 28.

[90] CFR, 1399–1405, pp. 208–209; CPR, 1401–1405; *Cal. Plea Mem. Rolls*, 1413–1427, p. 229.

[91] L–B I, pp. 121, 251.

[92] See below, pp. 145–146.

[93] These are discussed by Matthews, *Royal Apothecaries*, p. 42.

[94] *Ibid.*, pp. 45–48, has a nice summary on Hakedy.

[95] CPR, 1436–1441, p. 525.

[96] CCR, 1441–1447, p. 86; Leslie G. Matthews, *A History of Pharmacy in Britain* (London: 1962), pp. 358–359.

of Hakedy as a researcher or innovator. As noted, when Henry VI suffered his breakdown, it was the physicians and surgeons who were called on to prescribe treatments. But those same physicians and surgeons respected Hakedy as a doctor. And Hakedy, at the very least, set a medical rather than mercantile model for other apothecaries; success and riches could be had in medicine as well as in grocery.

Hakedy served Henry until his death late in 1456 or early in 1457.[97] Subsequently, there are records showing a clear and regular succession of royal apothecaries for a hundred years.[98] John Clerk was the next notable royal apothecary.[99] He began serving Edward IV in 1452, mostly on a daily basis, at the modest salary of eight pence a day. But he was persistent and made his presence felt; increasingly, he spent long stretches at court, and by the end of his second year was receiving an annual salary of £88, about four times that of Hakedy, a generation earlier.[100] And there is no mistaking the medical nature of his service; it was "for certain physic supplied for the king's own use and administered him under the advice of the king's physicians."[101] Clerk did not have direct access to the king, and he supplied the court with food as well as drugs. But his principal duties were those of a doctor. Eventually he became responsible for ensuring that Edward actually took his medicine, won the king's trust, and remained in service until Edward's death.[102]

Clerk's career outside the royal court is interesting. Matthews believed he was a citizen of London and a master in the Grocers' Company from 1427.[103] This is possible, but unlikely; it would have made him a very old man by the time he entered royal service, and so prominent a character would probably have been called before the king earlier in his working life. The John Clerk who was a grocer and citizen in the 1420s may have been a relative, perhaps even father to the royal apothecary. In any circumstance, the John Clerk who served Edward IV was a sub-

---

[97] His will was proved in PCC, Stokton, 1446, f. 15. The PCC, of course, reserved probate for testators with property in several jurisdictions—that is, the wealthiest folk in the kingdom.

[98] William Godfrey and Thomas Babham succeeded Hakedy. See Matthews, *Royal Apothecaries*, pp. 49, 52.

[99] *Ibid.*, pp. 49–52.

[100] CCR, 1461–1468, pp. 118, 223.

[101] *Ibid.*, p. 223.

[102] He too had his will proved in the Prerogative Court. See PCC, Logge, 1483, f. 8.

[103] Matthews, *Royal Apothecaries*, p. 51.

stantial figure by the 1440s, and a man of considerable means.[104] He held property in London, Essex, and perhaps Kent; had drug shops in London and probably in Coggeshill, Essex; and was a member of several local and royal commissions even before he began serving at court.[105] Clerk was also an official in London, and used his business skills, political connections, and medical knowledge to become a supplier of medicines during the London plague of 1471.[106] Another of his medical tasks came in 1472, when Clerk, sixteen other apothecaries, and two physicians were appointed by the mayor of London to examine a suspect shipment of treacle imported from Italy.[107] When he died in 1483 he was one of the richer men in London.[108]

John Grice and John Pakenham, apothecaries to Henry VII, have been mentioned. As befitted the comparatively modest kingship of the first Tudor, neither was as prominent nor as well paid as Clerk had been.[109] Each was granted a lifetime annuity of £10.[110] Grice also received several gifts of property, including seven houses in London.[111] Like their predecessors, they supplied the court with food and drugs. But Grice's duties were broadened to include the preparation and supply of the newly popular, quasi-medical confectionaries and sweet meats for the royal table.[112] And with a third royal apothecary, Thomas Pierson, Grice resumed the fourteenth-century tradition of becoming general merchants at court.[113] Perhaps this was necessary because their salaries were lower than those of Hakedy and Clerk. Or perhaps most fifteenth-century royal apothecaries were more interested in trade than in business.

Like Henry V, Henry VIII was interested in medicine.[114] But unlike his predecessor, he was interested in physic and pharmacy rather

---

[104] For example, CCR, 1441–1447, p. 458; CCR, 1447–1454, p. 19; CCR, 1468–1476, pp. 14, 416.

[105] Ibid., 1476–1488, pp. 72, 98, 449; CPR, 1467–1477, pp. 70–71.

[106] Matthews, *Royal Apothecaries*, p. 51.

[107] L–B L, p. 93.

[108] For Clerk's will, see Matthews, *Royal Apothecaries*, p. 52.

[109] Ibid., pp. 61–63.

[110] CPR, 1485–1494, p. 251.

[111] Ibid., pp. 360, 469; CPR, 1494–1509, pp. 115, 136, 164, 203.

[112] Matthews, *Royal Apothecaries*, pp. 61–62.

[113] Ibid., pp. 63–64.

[114] J. J. Scarisbrick, *Henry VIII* (Berkeley, Cal.: University of California Press, 1968), pp. 97–134.

than in surgery. One result was a collection of medical recipes, dating about 1510, dedicated to and often attributed to the king.[115] Henry VIII had several apothecaries, including Thomas Pierson. More notable was Richard Babham, a member of the Grocers' Company of London, hired in 1516 at £10 per year.[116] Like John Grice, Babham served as Serjeant of the Confectionary, and made a substantial profit on the victuals he supplied to the court. But Babham was also a pharmacist. A list of his supplies from 1518 includes primarily spices, over·half of which were medicines.[117]

In 1519 Henry added two more apothecaries. One, John de Soto, was a Spaniard, and served Queen Catherine of Aragon.[118] De Soto was one of several foreigners, but the only one who was not Italian. The other new man was Cuthbert Blackden, already mentioned, and, like William Burton, Richard Hakedy, and John Clerk, one of the most important royal apothecaries of the late middle ages.[119] Blackden began as an assistant to Babham, but quickly rose to a position of authority and influence; when Henry VIII reorganized his household in 1526, it was Blackden who provided still another direction for the royal apothecaries.[120] Once again the apothecaries became merchants, now supplying the court with spices and condiments.

The reasons for this change were twofold. First, with the foundation of the Royal College in 1518 physicians assumed a more commanding role among doctors than they had for a century and a half.[121] Henry VIII asked his physicians, not his apothecaries, about medications. And, second, as English merchants came to play a larger role in the spice trade, the gains that could be realized from it were far greater than those that could be made from medical practice. Blackden was, above all, an entre-

---

[115] B.M. Sloane Ms. 1047. It is unlikely that Henry wrote any of it. The manuscript lists as contributors four royal physicians, Doctors Butts, Cromer, Chamber, and Augustine, the later Agostino deglo Agostino, physician not to Henry but to Cardinal Wolsey. Composed in English and Latin and elegantly written, it was probably intended for royal use. The recipes are direct, easy to follow, and simplistic. Most are plasters or balms of one sort or another, and Henry probably could have compounded them himself. The manuscript has no illustrations, and was meant to be used in cookbook fashion. But it suggests Henry's interest in pharmacy.

[116] Matthews, *Royal Apothecaries*, pp. 63–64.

[117] *LPFD*, Henry VIII, iii, ii, p. 1515.

[118] See below, p. 286.

[119] Matthews, *Royal Apothecaries*, pp. 64–67.

[120] *Ordinances and Regulations*, pp. 163, 166, 167, 178–180.

[121] See below, pp. 295–300.

preneur who realized that the royal court was a major center of consumption. It has been estimated that through the 1530s he made annual profits of over £50 just on the sale of drugs to the king.[122] He gathered about him a staff of assistants, all of whom became rich, and by his death in 1540 he like Clerk was one of the wealthier men in London.[123]

Yet physicians dominated medical life at court. Jordan of Canterbury, who served Edward II and Edward III, is an early example.[124] A surgeon as well as an Oxford-trained physician, he was one of a select group of M.D.s who served on a military expedition. He accompanied Edward III on the Crecy campaign of 1346, and is alleged to have treated wounded soldiers and not just the king and his household, as was the custom for physicians.[125] Jordan was well paid for his efforts, drawing 109 shillings.[126] This was in addition to an annuity of twenty marks he had begun receiving since 1338, then a considerable sum for a doctor.[127] In 1340 he took a lifelong appointment at the court "on account of the expert skill which the king has found in him."[128] In the course of his career he was granted cash, property, benefices, and a pension of £20 a year.[129]

Jordan continued at court until his death in 1361. He became not only the principal royal physician, but a trusted general adviser. He was granted additional annuities in the 1350s, including cash and clothing, and became one of the first royal physicians to affect a livery.[130] Jordan, who had taken only minor clerical orders, had married, and his children, too, drank at the royal well. Sons William and Adam were placed on the king's payroll in 1352, while daughter Margaret got what might be de-

[122] N. H. Nicholas, ed., *Privy Purse Expenses of Henry VIII, 1529–1532* (London: William Pickering, 1827), pp. 41, 79, 124, 165, 203, 251.

[123] I have not been able to find his will. See Matthews, *Royal Apothecaries*, p. 66, and Plate 2, for his brass commemorative.

[124] In referring to all the physicians I will cite the *T&H* reference. *T&H* is best in dealing with famous doctors, especially physicians. It has excellent footnotes and is the starting place for research of any individual royal physician. For Jordan, see pp. 198–199. Also of use for Edward III's court doctors is George Gask, "The Medical Staff of Edward III," in his *Essays in the History of Medicine* (London: Butterworth and Co., 1950), pp. 77–93.

[125] Gask, "Medical Staff of Edward III," pp. 80–81.

[126] *Ibid.*

[127] CPR, 1340–1343, p. 114.

[128] *Ibid.*

[129] CCR, 1343–1346, p. 174.

[130] *Ibid.*

scribed as a royal dowry a year later.[131] Margaret's gift came with a testament; Edward granted it "for the good service done by the king's clerk, Master Jordan of Canterbury."[132]

Edward III had other court physicians. Master Pancius de Controne, called the king's "leech and clerk," served from 1327 to 1340.[133] A Lucchese, Pancius did more than practice medicine.[134] He was a merchant and financier, an important source of cash for Edward II and Edward III, and one of Edward III's principal backers at the beginning of the Hundred Years War.[135] By 1337, Edward owed him the considerable sum of £4,000, an amount that could be regained only from the rights to a royal tax farm.[136] Yet the size of the debt discouraged neither king nor physician. By 1340 it had grown to £6,000.[137] And the interest from the loan was just part of Controne's income. He received all the benefits of a royal physician—salary, livery, favors and exemptions, and property.[138]

Pancius was a fine physician. He was a medical author, and before coming to England had been physician to the pope. In the 1330s he was Edward's leading medical adviser, overshadowing even Jordan of Canterbury. When, for example, Edward went on his Scottish campaign in 1334, he started without his favorite physician.[139] But midway to Scotland he thought the better of it, and sent word that Pancius should join the army in due haste.[140] There was another facet to the polymathic Pancius. He was well versed in Roman and canon law, and picked up enough of English custom law to advise Edward on several legal matters.[141] By the time of his death in 1358, Pancius was one of the wealthiest and most influential men at the royal court.[142]

[131] CPR, 1345–1348, p. 61; CPR, 1350–1354, p. 357.

[132] CPR, 1350–1354, p. 501.

[133] T&H, pp. 234–237. This is one of the best entries.

[134] T&H, pp. 233–235.

[135] For the financing of the war, see, among many, H. J. Hewitt, *The Organisation of War Under Edward III, 1338–1362* (Manchester: University of Manchester Press, 1966). Rich individuals were obviously important, and lending money enhanced their positions.

[136] CCR, 1337–1339, pp. 192–193.

[137] T&H, pp. 234–237.

[138] *Ibid.*, p. 234.

[139] *Ibid.* The letter claims: "For Master Pancius de Controne and his men (presumably bodyguards), coming to the King in Scotland with some things of his."

[140] CCR, 1334–1338, p. 43.

[141] CCR, 1327–1330, p. 109.

[142] CPR, 1340–1343, p. 32.

Edward III had two other foreign physicians, the Frenchman William Radicis and the Italian Pascal of Bologna. A graduate of the University of Paris, Radicis came to Edward's attention late in the reign.[143] He was physician to the French royal party during the Battle of Poitiers, and accompanied Jean II in his captivity. Edward and his son, the Black Prince, were sufficiently impressed to offer him a position. Radicis continued to live some of the time in France, and was issued several royal safe-conduct passes across the Channel, traveling at various times with English and French parties.[144] Master Pascal of Bologna was styled as both physician and surgeon, and became doctor to Henry of Grosmont, the Duke of Lancaster and Edward's cousin.[145] He opened an ancillary practice in London, became physician to the king's second son, Lionel, Duke of Clarence, and in the 1360s began treating Edward himself.[146]

Other physicians at Edward's court included John of Glastonbury, who served from 1361 through the end of the reign, and into that of Richard II.[147] Walter of Gales was physician to Edward and the Black Prince, and accompanied the latter on his campaigns in Gascony.[148] In recompense, Gales was provided with Crown lands around Bordeaux. John Paladin treated Edward III from 1359 to 1367.[149] He may have been a foreigner, perhaps Italian, and also served during the French wars.[150] Paladin was provided with a lifetime annuity of £20. In 1367 he was permitted to travel abroad and, like Pancius de Controne and William Radicis, provided with a royal safe-conduct pass and a retinue. The retinue was considerable—six men-at-arms and seven horses, with £200 provided for expenses.[151] And there was Peter of Florence, primarily physician to Queen Isabella.[152] She paid him the handsome salary of £40 and helped him acquire several choice tenements in London, which he then rented out.[153]

The reign of Edward III was a landmark for court doctors. Edward

[143] *T&H*, pp. 411–412.
[144] Rymer, *Foedera*, p. 393 (Hiii,1,162); p. 402 (Riii,1,437); p. 405 (Hiii,11,79).
[145] *T&H*, p. 238.
[146] *Ibid.*, p. 238.
[147] *Ibid.*, p. 151.
[148] *Ibid.*, p. 367.
[149] *Ibid.*, pp. 147–175.
[150] Rymer, *Foedera*, p. 428 (Hiii,ii,79).
[151] CPR, 1367–1370, p. 58.
[152] *T&H*, p. 248.
[153] CPR, 1367–1370, p. 412.

was a lavish patron, and all his royal physicians left service far wealthier than when they had entered. He continued a tradition of bringing in foreign doctors, particularly Frenchmen and Italians, not surprising in light of the fact that Paris, Montpellier, Bologna, and Padua were the leading medical schools of the day. And he made his physicians go to war, a clinical experience which made them better doctors.

The reign of Richard II was not noteworthy. Richard was a reluctant soldier, diminishing that opportunity for all his practitioners. His doctors lacked the professional expertise of those of a generation earlier. Typical was John Leche, perhaps the most notorious doctor of the later middle ages, who, despite being trained as a surgeon, styled himself, among other affectations, as royal physician.[154] Leche was most noteworthy as a land speculator, and for all the documentation of his business life, there are few records of his medical practice. Richard's best physicians were Masters John Middleton and Geoffrey Melton. Middleton was a fellow at University College, Oxford; by 1392 he was treating the king.[155] He did well enough in three years to be granted a lifetime annuity of £40, followed by more gifts of cash and land.[156] He became Master of St. Nicholas' Hospital in York, and, given his interests, probably served as a physician as well as an administrator.[157]

Geoffrey Melton was "first heard of as Master of Arts at Oxford when he was forbidden to carry arms during the contention between the Artists and others in the University in 1377."[158] He was a cleric, and lived in Oxford for much of the 1370s and 1380s. Melton went to court in 1388, and with Middleton continued in royal service under Henry IV. He also treated several members of the nobility. And while, as is the case with most royal physicians, there is little record of his medical practice, there is evidence of his finances. He received several royal annuities, and "a benefice worth forty marks a year without cure, or 100 marks with cure."[159]

Richard's other physicians included the Neapolitan Anthony of Romanis.[160] Like other Italian royal physicians, Romanis branched out

---

[154] T&H, pp. 161–162.

[155] T&H, pp. 172–173; CPR, 1388–1392, p. 511.

[156] CPR, 1391–1396, p. 705; CPR, 1396–1399, pp. 258, 266; CPR, 1399–1401, p. 132.

[157] CPR, 1422–1429, p. 532.

[158] T&H, p. 53.

[159] Ibid., p. 54; CPR, 1396–1399, p. 577.

[160] T&H, p. 18.

from his medical practice to trade; unlike the others, he ran afoul of the law, and was jailed in 1394 for failing to pay his debts.[161] His was a good example of the advantages of royal patronage, for he was quickly freed and exonerated, probably the result of Richard's intervention.[162] John Bray was physician to John of Gaunt, the Duke of Lancaster, and perhaps to Edward III; he served Richard during the minority.[163] Bray succeeded in getting his wife on the royal payroll.[164] But he is most famous for his death. Bray was beaten and then hanged by the mob that plundered the Savoy Palace during the Peasants' Revolt of 1381, the victim of the unpopularity of his ducal employer.[165]

John Desphana, a Spaniard, and John Lounde, a Lincolnshireman, also served Richard.[166] In 1391, Lounde was given the lucrative position of royal searcher of the River Witham, in Lincoln.[167] John Wik was at court in the 1370s, and was still in Richard's employ in 1380, when he accompanied the soldiers of the Earl of March to Ireland.[168] Paul Gabriales was another Spaniard; he attended Richard in 1378.[169] Tideman de Winchcombe, a Cistercian and, in time, Bishop of Worcester, was called "the physician to King Richard II."[170] William Francis, a London leech, was in royal service at Berwick Castle when the king was in residence.[171] And there were the aforementioned William Holm, noted in Chapter Two for his progression from surgeon to physician; and Geoffrey Crook, physician turned pirate, both of whom served in the 1370s.[172] Both were symptomatic of Richard's court doctors: undistinguished but rich.

[161] CPR, 1392–1396, p. 259.

[162] He too served Henry IV. See CCR, 1405–1409, p. 273.

[163] T&H, p. 125.

[164] CCR, 1374–1377, p. 538.

[165] See Rodney H. Hilton, *Bond Men Made Free* (London: Temple Smith, 1973), pp. 192–193.

[166] T&H, pp. 141, 163.

[167] CPR, 1378–1392, p. 376.

[168] T&H, pp. 195–196. See too CPR, 1381–1385, p. 514.

[169] T&H, p. 240.

[170] B.M. Sloane Ms. 7; T&H, p. 362.

[171] T&H, pp. 394–395. He was the defendant in an infamous rape case. See CCR, 1396–1399, p. 117.

[172] T&H, p. 403; T&H, p. 52. They refer to him as "Creek." See too: CPR, 1391–1396, p. 330; Rymer, *Foedera*, p. 525 (Hiii,iv,92); London Guildhall, *Calendar of Hustings Deeds*, Rolls 130, m.3, 12.

Henry IV's physicians were more interesting and accomplished, and most of them were foreigners.[173] These included Elias de Sabboto, Anthony Romanis, Lorenco Gomes, Peter de Alkabasse, David Nigarellis, and Louis Recouches. So favored were they that Matthews has written, with justification:

> [Henry] staffed his household with French, Bretons, Lombards, and Milanese, thereby creating much suspicion in the minds of the Commons, that they decided these aliens must quit royal service. Some of Henry's annuitants were forced to surrender their current incomes.[174]

Sabboto has been discussed. He was replaced by another Italian, David Nigarellis of Lucca, a city that seems to have been a repository of Italian doctors bound for the British Isles. There are conflicting accounts of the length of his service at court.[175] But Nigarellis liked London, and remained there for several years before he was naturalized in 1412. Henry IV was a generous patron. Nigarellis was paid a salary of eighty marks a year, and had at his death a debt due him worth 300 marks.[176] A legacy of Richard II, Romanis received among other plums a place in the administration in Ireland.[177] Gomes was Portuguese.[178] He entered royal service about 1407, and was rewarded with a handsome benefice in Salisbury.[179] His success as a physician, however, was limited, and he lasted less than a year at the court. Yet even at the court of Henry IV this did not prevent him from becoming rich and having a successful church career.[180]

Louis Recouches probably served Henry during his exile, and may have accompanied him on his crusade in Baltic.[181] Spanish or French, he was made royal physician as soon as Henry took the throne, and was given land in Middlesex. He became warden of St. James Hospital in Westminster, a lucrative position and, more importantly, warden of the

---

[173] Talbot, *Medicine in Medieval England*, pp. 204–205; Matthews, *Royal Apothecaries*, pp. 38–39.

[174] Matthews, *Royal Apothecaries*, p. 39.

[175] Ironically, both come, at least in part, from Talbot. See *Medicine in Medieval England*, p. 205; and *T&H*, pp. 33–34.

[176] CPR, 1408–1413, p. 397.

[177] *T&H*, p. 18; CPR, 1385–1389, p. 232.

[178] *Ibid.*, pp. 201–202; CPR, 1405–1408, pp. 344, 348.

[179] CPR, 1405–1408, pp. 344, 348.

[180] *T&H*, p. 202.

[181] *Ibid.*, pp. 204–205.

King's mint in the Tower.[182] This was one of the best gifts a royal servant could get, and when Recouches disappeared from the records in 1408, his wardenship was assigned to David Nigarellis.[183] It paid an annual salary of £40, and offered, as did the job of keeper of the ports, considerable opportunities for corruption. The appointment suggests the high regard Henry IV had for his court doctors, and why members of the Commons so resented his foreigners.

Peter Dalcobace was, next to Elias de Sabbato, the most distinguished of Henry IV's physicians, and went on to serve Henry's son and grandson.[184] He was a Portuguese like Gomes; little is known about his education or practice, despite his considerable reputation.[185] But there are records of his business dealings. In 1412 Henry IV granted Dalcobace the first in a series of cash and landed gifts. These continued into the reign of Henry V, who had him naturalized and made him a citizen of London in 1420.[186] Dalcobace would receive cash, land, clothing, and other gifts until his death in 1427, and his will, proved in the Prerogative Court of Canterbury—in itself a sign of great wealth—shows the benefits of twenty years of royal service.[187] He gave his servants furs, silver, and a cash bequest of £20. He had, among many things, five horses, gave friends over £50, and requested burial in the Dominican church of London, a place reserved for the most prosperous citizens.

Henry IV even had a few English physicians.[188] One, John Malverne, an Oxford M.D., was a prominent medical author.[189] In all, Henry IV had a remarkable coterie of doctors in his short reign. He reestablished, albeit briefly, a tradition of earlier years by bringing in foreigners. More important and long-lasting, he sweetened the pot for court doctors. Frequently ill, or at least thinking he was, he kept his doctors busy. But he did not quibble about salaries or benefits, and in his reign, as in that of

[182] CPR, 1401–1405, p. 345.

[183] CPR, 1408–1413, p. 28.

[184] T&H, pp. 246–247.

[185] PRO, Issues of the Exchequer, Issue Roll 6 Henry V, pp. 355–356.

[186] CPR, 1416–1422, p. 311.

[187] PCC, "Luffenham," 1427, f. 8.

[188] Melton and Middleton have been mentioned. There was Richard Grisby, who in 1402 was granted a general royal safe-conduct pass. One John the Physician had accompanied the Earl of Derby on a military expedition in the 1390s; he remained in service when the earl became king. See T&H, pp. 111, 279.

[189] T&H, pp. 166–167.

Edward III, the position of royal physician became more attractive and lucrative than ever.

Henry V spent much of his reign on campaign and preferred surgeons. But he had court physicians, including Peter Dalcobace, and the Greek-born Demetrius de Cerno.[190] Demetrius practiced in England from 1413; he seems to have come to the kingdom on his own, caught the king's eye, and begun service around 1415.[191] Cerno married an English woman, had children, and was naturalized by 1424. In addition to his service at court, he became physician to the Countess of Kent, who was the daughter of Bernabo Visconti, Duke of Milan.[192] Yet his practice was undistinguished, especially when compared to those of Henry's surgeons. Indeed, the advisers of Henry VI rejected Demetrius as physician for the new king.[193] This set the tone for the later part of his career. When he left royal service, his fortunes faltered. The Countess of Kent left him a paltry five-mark legacy. And, after he was naturalized, Demetrius was made to pay the aliens' subsidy rate on trade goods, the sort of burden from which court physicians expected exemptions.[194]

The best of Henry V's physicians was Nicholas Colnet.[195] A fellow of Merton College, Colnet went to London in 1411, and was called to court by Henry IV as a clerk rather than as a doctor.[196] His medical star rose in 1413, when Henry V ascended the throne. Colnet was awarded a series of benefices, and was selected for the Agincourt army. Despite the considerable reputations of surgeons Thomas Morstede and William Bradwardine, Henry named him chief of the medical corps.[197] That ex-

[190] For Dalcobace, *T&H*, pp. 246–247; for Cerno, *T&H*, pp. 34–35.

[191] *Proceedings and Ordinance of the Privy Council of England*, ed. N. H. Nicholas (London: Eyre and Spottiswoode, 1835), iii, pp. 160–161.

[192] E. F. Jacob, *The Register of Henry Chichele, 1430–1447* (Oxford: Oxford University Press, 1937), ii, pp. 278–293.

[193] *T&H*, p. 34.

[194] *Ibid.*

[195] *Ibid.*, pp. 220–222; Gask, "Medical Staff of Edward III," pp. 84–93. Among the others were Thomas Feriby, who served at the outset of the reign and may also have treated Henry IV. See Rymer, *Foedera*, p. 579 (Hiv,ii,74). There was also John Barton, a distinguished Londoner, who dedicated a book to Henry V. See *T&H*, p. 121; *DNB*, iii, p. 346. And there was Peter Henewar, who like Colnet was distinguished by his service to Normandy in 1419. See *T&H*, p. 248. He must have been well regarded, for his salary was greater than that of any other doctor on the trip.

[196] *BRUO*, i, p. 469.

[197] Gask, "Medical Staff of Edward III," pp. 84–93.

pedition made Colnet's career. Before it, he was one of many physicians in London; afterward, as Talbot put it, "Henry's campaign to Agincourt . . . suddenly thrust him into prominence as the ranking physician."[198] It is likely that Colnet used the methods of his associates, the surgeons, in treating wounds. In any case, he was good enough to return to Normandy with Henry in 1417.[199]

Colnet's will, like that of Peter Dalcobace, was proved in the Prerogative Court of Canterbury. But Colnet was rich and important enough to have his testament included in an even more selective register, the book of Archbishop Henry Chichele.[200] Colnet had moveables worth more than £200, mainly in gold, silver, and jewelry. He had expensive clothing and extensive landholdings. He was a generous benefactor, devoted to education, the church, and his family. Among his more interesting legacies was the bequest of Bernard Gordon's *Lillium medicinae* to another Merton physician, John Mayhew.[201] He left £20 to Merton, cash to feed and clothe the poor of Oxford and London, and cash to the Hospital of St. Mary Bethlehem, in Bishopsgate, London.

Like the other Lancastrians, Henry VI preferred foreign physicians.[202] Francis Pamzonus (or Panizonus) of Alexandria was born in Greece.[203] He first came to court in the service of Queen Margaret of Anjou, who, by the late 1440s, was exerting an increasing influence over her weak-minded husband. There is no accounting of Pamzonus's medical skills. But in 1446 he was awarded an annuity of £100, to be drawn from the customs of the port of Southampton.[204] Among the other foreigners were: James of Milan, at court in the 1430s; John de Signorellis of Ferrara, the most noted of the aliens and, for a time, personal physician to Humphrey, Duke of Gloucester, also in the 1430s and 1440s; the Dutchman Gerald van Delft, who practiced in the 1440s; Michel Belwell, a Frenchman; Philibert Fournier, also a Frenchman and long-time physician to another of Henry V's brothers, John, Duke of Bedford; and

[198] *T&H*, p. 220.

[199] *Ibid.*

[200] Jacob, *Register of Henry Chichele*, ii, pp. 215–216.

[201] Mayhew, however, does not seem to have been a practitioner.

[202] An exception was the Englishman John Tiphanie, who served at court between 1421 and 1433. See *T&H*, p. 190; Rymer, *Foedera*, p. 625 (Hiv,iv,157).

[203] *T&H*, p. 49.

[204] CPR, 1441–1446, p. 406; CCR, 1441–1447, p. 336.

Thomas Frank, a Greek, who practiced in London in the 1450s.[205] None
was sufficiently distinguished or served long enough to make much of a
mark. But they benefited from their time at court, using their royal connections to secure naturalization, and practice medicine in London.[206]

Unlike his father and grandfather, Henry VI patronized a distinguished group of English physicians, the most prominent of whom was
Gilbert Kymer.[207] An Oxford M.D., Kymer had a multifaceted career,
serving the king as a royal serjeant as well as a physician. He was married, but when his wife died he began a long and successful ecclesiastical
career, ending up as the dean of Salisbury Cathedral.[208] He twice served
as chancellor of Oxford.[209] But it was as a physician that he achieved his
greatest prominence. Kymer's first connection with the royal family was
as chief doctor to Humphrey of Gloucester. This was important, and
helps explain his success. For Kymer, like Jordan of Canterbury and
Nicholas Colnet, had by an unusual combination of theoretical, university learning and practical military service. In Kymer's case the service
was with Gloucester during the Netherlands campaign of 1424.[210] The
connection with the duke was important for another reason; Kymer may
have convinced Humphrey to leave his library to Oxford, the beginning
of the famous Bodleian collection.[211]

Kymer was notable as a mediator. About the time he began service for
Gloucester he moved his practice from Oxford to London. He was soon
asked to adjudicate in some of the malpractice cases that filled London
courts early in the 1420s, serving as the referee in the most famous of
them, that involving the surgeon John Harrow.[212] This led, as noted in
Chapter One, to his role in the foundation of the College of Medicine in
1423. Kymer's reputation grew, and by the late 1420s he was called
"Professor of Medicine, Master of Arts and Physic."[213] He was too busy
to serve full time at the court, and may have acted as a consultant, trav-

---

[205] The *T&H* references are, respectively, pp. 55, 98, 182, 215, 253, 343–344.

[206] For example, see *ibid.*, p. 253.

[207] *Ibid.*, pp. 60–63; also *DNB*, 11, pp. 353–354.

[208] *T&H*, p. 60.

[209] *BRUO*, ii, pp. 1068–1069. See too L–B K, p. 5.

[210] *DNB*, ii, 353–354.

[211] Vern L. Bullough, "Duke Humphrey and His Medical Collections," *Renaissance News*, 14, 1961, pp. 87–91.

[212] *Cal. Plea Mem. Rolls*, 1413–1437, pp. 174–175.

[213] B.M. Sloane Ms. 4, ff. 63–104.

eling between Westminster, Windsor, Oxford, his London practice, Salisbury, and possibly even the court of the Duke of Gloucester. Ordinarily, this would have prevented a successful career as a royal physician, with the king merely choosing another practitioner. But Kymer was good enough to dictate his own terms.

Kymer's will, proved in the Prerogative Court of Canterbury, shows his success, both medically and financially.[214] He wrote a text called *Dietarium de sanitatis custodia*; and owned copies of Joannitius's *Isogogue*, a Galen, three commentaries on Hippocrates, a *Rosa medicinae* by John Gaddesden, a tract by Bernard Gordon. Among others were tracts by Avicenna and Peter Turisanus.[215] All were bequeathed to Oxford. He left twenty-five cash bequests and, like Peter Dalcobace and Nicholas Colnet, was one of the wealthiest doctors in late medieval England. Even the change from Lancastrian to Yorkist did not affect his fortunes, as it would those of other royal doctors. In 1462, Edward IV confirmed all the previous gifts to Kymer, and certified a land deal of questionable legality.[216]

John Arundell was a fellow of Exeter College, Oxford, scion of an eminent Cornish family that claimed uninterrupted nobility from the Conquest, and bishop of Chichester.[217] A 1449 summons from the Chancellor of Oxford addressed him as "the well-known personage, Master John Arundell, distinguished Doctor of Medicines, our dear colleague."[218] He was a don by the middle 1420s, a practicing doctor in the 1430s, and physician to many notables, including Henry Beauchamp, the Earl of Warwick, by the 1440s. Arundell began serving at court, where he was a chaplain as well as physician, in the 1450s, and was a member of the group that treated Henry after his first mental breakdown in 1454. But Arundell's general talents, like those of Gilbert Kymer, were such that by the late 1450s he found it hard to continue his medical practice. In 1457, while still a court physician, he was sent on a diplomatic mission to Scotland. This and his appointment as bishop in 1459 prevented him from practicing medicine full time, and his close identification with the Lancastrians ended his career at the royal court. Arundell did compile

[214] PCC, "Godyn," 1463, f. 1.

[215] *T&H*, p. 63, supply a more complete list. Also, see PCC, 1 Godyn.

[216] L–B K, pp. 17–18, 20.

[217] *T&H*, pp. 115–116; *DNB*, i, p. 618.

[218] *T&H*, p. 116.

two collections of medical recipes before his death in 1477, but after 1460 he directed his efforts to church and university.[219]

Master John Faceby was Henry VI's favorite physician.[220] With Arundell and William Hatclif, he was one of the physicians who treated the king in 1454. There is no record of a university education, but Faceby was a successful practitioner in Southwark when he was brought to Henry VI's attention. He began royal service in 1438; by 1444 he was receiving the staggering annuity of £100—equal, it will be recalled to that of Francis Pamzonus—plus £20 for his wife and a livery.[221] He also received annual salary supplements, and the Exchequer Rolls from 1456 show that in the nine preceding years Faceby had been paid another £150, taken from the customs of the port of London.[222] This was in addition to lands and other privileges and exemptions he received.[223] Since he was a layman, it is harder to follow his career than those of clerical doctors like Kymer and Arundell. Faceby too seems to have disappeared after 1461. But in the 1450s he was probably the richest and most prominent doctor in London.

William Hatclif was almost as rich and even more famous.[224] He was a scholar at Eton and King's College, fellow of Peterhouse, and for a time proctor at Cambridge.[225] More important, Hatclif was one of the first Englishmen to study the new medicine in Italy, in his case at the University of Padua, which had become Europe's finest medical school.[226] He received his licentiate in 1447, and was back in England and practicing at court by 1454.[227] Hatclif was paid £40 a year, and became keeper of the Fosse; in addition, he got six pence for every day he attended court.[228] Like Gilbert Kymer, Hatclif was good enough to survive the change in dynasties, becoming a favorite of Edward IV; when he was taken prisoner by French pirates in 1461, Edward ransomed him

[219] B.M. Sloane Ms. 7; O.U. Bod. Ashmole Ms. 1437.

[220] T&H, p. 143.

[221] CPR, 1441–1446, p. 271; CCR, 1441–1447, p. 179.

[222] PRO, Exchequer Accounts, E101/624/46.

[223] For example, CPR, 1452–1461, p. 398; Rymer, Foedera, p.688 (Hv,ii,82).

[224] T&H, pp. 398–399; DNB, 9, pp. 158–159.

[225] Rot. Parl., v, p. 87; Cambridge University Grace Book, F, p. xiii.

[226] T&H, p. 398; Rosamund J. Mitchell, "English Students at Padua," Transactions of the Royal Historical Society, 4th series, 19, 1936, pp. 101–117.

[227] CPR, 1452–1461, pp. 26, 147, 195, 235.

[228] Rymer, Foedera, p. 684 (Hv,11,55); p. 685 (Hv,11,66).

for £40.[229] He served as chief physician until his death in 1480, and was clever enough to be sent on embassies to Scotland, Brittany, and Burgundy. But Hatclif was primarily a medical man, an author as well as a practitioner, and judge in a famous leprosy malpractice case in 1468.[230] His will, proved like so many other court physicians in the Prerogative Court of Canterbury, gives additional evidence of the profitability of royal service.[231]

Henry VI had one more distinguished physician, John Somerset.[232] Somerset attended both universities, was a fellow at Pembroke College, Cambridge, and was master of the famous grammar school at Bury St. Edmunds.[233] He was one of the first supervisors of the College of Medicine in London, and in 1423 was taken into service for the infant Henry.[234] In 1430, he was part of the royal entourage that traveled to Rouen, drawing the basic wage of £40.[235] Somerset was twice married, and received a number of royal favors, including the wardonship of the royal mint in the Tower and a justiceship of the peace in Middlesex.[236] Oddly, having spent much of his early life in lucrative positions, he complained in old age of penury. Perhaps this was the result of his decision in 1447 to abjure his offices, end his medical practice, and retire to a more comfortable if less financially rewarding position at Oxford, where he wrote about medicine.[237] He donated a copy of an Avicenna to Pembroke, a Galen to Peterhouse, and two other medical books to the canons of St. Paul's in London.[238] He was also an author, compiling collections of *Materia medica*. Hence, whatever his financial situation, his fame as a doctor was undiminished at the time of his death in 1455.

Kymer, Arundell, Faceby, Hatclif, and Somerset constitute the most distinguished collection of court physicians in late medieval England.[239]

---

[229] *T&H*, p. 398.

[230] CCR, 1468–1476, p. 30.

[231] PCC, "Logge," 1480, p. 1.

[232] *T&H*, pp. 184–185; *DNB*, 18, pp. 653–654.

[233] B.M. Cotton Tiberius Ms. B, ix, f. 180; Robert S. Gottfried, *Bury St. Edmunds and the Urban Crisis, 1290–1539* (Princeton: Princeton University Press, 1982), pp. 207–214.

[234] L–B K, p. 41.

[235] CCR, 1435–1441, p. 146; CPR, 1436–1441, p. 299.

[236] CPR, 1436–1441, p. 418.

[237] *T&H*, p. 184; *Rot. Parl.*, v, f. 399a.

[238] *T&H*, p. 184.

[239] They were not Henry's only physicians. There was John Green of Bristol, a medical author. Green had an indifferent career, and his royal service may be explained by timing;

In one way or another, the Lancastrians were the keystones to the royal patronage of medical practitioners. Their courts were welcome places for physicians, and it will be argued in Chapter Four that their military expeditions were crucibles for surgeons. In either case, their doctors were well paid and, crucial in the history of both English medicine and the middle class, granted positions they could not otherwise have achieved.

Service at court remained the pinnacle of medical success under the Yorkists and the first two Tudors. Edward IV's household accounts have been discussed; they confirm the "arrival" of the royal physicians. Four of these physicians, William Hatclif, Gilbert Kymer, Dominic de Serego, and James Frise, have been mentioned.[240] The Italian Serego, along with Hatclif and the royal surgeon Roger Marshall, was asked in 1468 to examine an allegedly leprous woman and determine whether she ought to be isolated.[241] They made a clinical though somewhat inaccurate report stating that she was not, and should be allowed to remain at home. Perhaps this is what brought him to Edward IV's attention, for he entered royal service about 1469, and remained there until 1475. Serego was unfortunate in serving during the most turbulent part of Edward's reign, and in 1471 and 1472 had trouble collecting his salary. Moreover, in 1471 a ship carrying goods from whose sale he was to be paid was captured, just as he was to receive his salary. But this was made up. In 1472, with Edward once again firmly on the throne, Serego received £150 in lieu of payments in arrears; by 1475 he was drawing an annuity of £40 and received a bonus of £66.[242]

Frise served throughout Edward's reign, and continued as court physician to Edward V and Richard III.[243] A Frisian, he came to England to study at Cambridge, and must have been very good.[244] Within a year, Edward offered him a grant of £40, and took him in service. Frise

---

he served in 1471, during Henry's brief return to the throne. See *T&H*, p. 153. Sir Richard Bray was a member of a notable family from Worcestershire, and is best known for his service on Henry's Privy Council. By some accounts he was also a physician, and as such may have treated the king. See *T&H*, p. 275. And there was William Forest, physician to Henry V's widow, Queen Katherine, in the 1420s and 1430s. He treated Henry during the minority and was rewarded substantially for his efforts. See *T&H*, p. 394.

[240] For Serego, see *T&H*, p. 36. For the case, see Rymer, *Foedera*, p. 699 (Hv,ii,166).

[241] CPR, 1467–1477, p. 336.

[242] *Ibid.*, p. 512.

[243] *T&H*, pp. 296–298.

[244] Cambridge University Grace Book A, pp. 30, 33.

quickly accumulated property and began receiving cash grants; by 1467 he was given robes and a livery, an apartment in Windsor, and made a knight.[245] Two declarations of Parliament assured his position, and in 1473 he was given letters of denization.[246] Frise was a trusted servant of the House of York, acting in diplomatic and administrative as well as medical roles, and it was only with the accession of Henry VII that his career sputtered. He lost his position at court, and was deprived of some of his property. But even then, Frise fared relatively well; the new queen, after all, may well have been one of his old patients. He was allowed a corrody in the Priory of Christchurch in Aldgate, where he practiced as a private physician.[247]

The most prominent of Edward's physicians was Edmund Albon.[248] Like Frise, Albon was a product of Cambridge—Edward IV seems to have preferred them to Oxonians—and first appears in 1460, when he took his B.A.[249] But Albon had a more general education, read in the classics, and remained associated with the university for the rest of his life. He is of particular interest because of his place at Gonville Hall, to develop into Gonville and Caius, the Cambridge college with the best program in medicine. Albon was a cleric, and held at least a half dozen church offices, including a canonry at St. Paul's Cathedral. Perhaps this was the reason he accumulated less property and drew a smaller salary than the other court physicians. But perhaps too it was because he entered royal service late in Edward's reign, in 1479, and had fewer years to accumulate favors. Albon did hold several tenements in London, and his will, proved in the Prerogative Court of Canterbury, provided two houses and a cash bequest to Gonville.[250] He was physician to several prominent nobles as well as to the king, and the number of references to his services from 1480 suggest that Edward looked first to Albon when his health began to deteriorate.[251]

[245] CPR, 1461-1467, pp. 79, 188, 270.

[246] CPR, 1467–1477, p. 396.

[247] T&H, p. 98.

[248] T&H, pp. 38-39.

[249] Cambridge University Grace Book A, p. 31.

[250] PCC, 19 Logge.

[251] T&H, pp. 38–39. Edward had at least three other physicians. John Morton, like Albon, was physician to a number of aristocratic families, and served Edward in the late 1470s, perhaps just before Albon took his place at court. See T&H, p. 177. Thomas Bemmesley was referred to as the "doctor of the king's body" in 1483. He was receiving the traditional annuity of £40, and may have been a graduate of Oxford. Bemmesley also

Given the loyalty of the Yorkish physicians, it is not surprising that Henry VII would bring in a new group.[252] All of the old physicians save one, Thomas Bemmesley, were pensioned off.[253] Henry was a tight-wad, but still managed to assemble a capable medical staff. By 1485 the position of court doctor carried so much social prestige that financial gain was almost a second consideration. And even if the pay at court was just middling, the benefits that doctors accrued in the private practices more than made up for it.

The first of Henry's physicians was the Welshman Lewis Caer-lyon.[254] A Cambridge graduate, Caerlyon's initial contact at court came, ironically, as the physician to Queen Elizabeth, widow of Edward IV.[255] More important, he was physician to Margaret Beaufort, mother of the new king and a considerable power in her own right. Margaret introduced him to Henry, and Caerlyon may for a time have been physician to the exiled Earl of Richmond.[256] Stow believed that Caerlyon was in London in 1485, and was one of the principal conspirators in the overthrow of Richard III; he was alleged to be the conduit between Elizabeth, who was imprisoned in the Tower, and the Tudors.[257] Another account involves him in the Buckingham conspiracy, for which Richard III supposedly had him imprisoned.[258] With such impeccable Tudor credentials it is not surprising that he shared in the rewards of the victor after Bosworth Field. Caerlyon received cash gifts, annuities, and lands,

---

served Edward V and Richard III, and, as will be noted, Henry VIII. See *T&H*, p. 333. And there was the oft-mentioned William Hobbes, who had begun treating Edward when he was still the Earl of March. See below, pp. 153–156; and *T&H*, pp. 401–402. Hobbes was primarily a surgeon.

[252] Edward V and Richard III continued to use the physicians of Edward IV. Edward V was a sickly child, and it might be recalled that the household ordinances said that he should always be accompanied by a doctor. Frise, Hobbes, and Bemmesley served through his brief reign. Richard III may have employed a few more physicians, notably Thomas Cliff, a Cambridge M.D. See *T&H*, pp. 336–337. Cliff was married, had a general practice in London, and, as one of his perquisites, served as "overseer of the works of building" of Richard.

[253] *T&H*, p. 333.

[254] *Ibid.*, p. 203–204.

[255] Cambridge University Grace Book A, p. 52.

[256] Pearl Kibre, "Lewis Caerlyon, Doctor of Medicine, Astronomer and Mathematician," *Isis*, 43, 1952, pp. 100–108; Polydore Vergil, ed. Henry Ellis, *English History*, i (London: Camden Society, 1846), pp. 95–97.

[257] Stow, *Annals of England*, p. 465.

[258] *Ibid.*

and was made a Knight of the King's Alms for the Chapel of St. George at Windsor.[259] James Frise had also been awarded such a title, suggesting that, like the keepership of the mind in the Tower, the searcherships of the ports of London and Southampton, and the wardenship of Bedlam, the position had become reserved for court doctors.

As royal physician Caerlyon continued to treat the Queen Mother, the ex-queen, and Henry's wife, the new queen. He was the author of a series of recipes and perhaps an *Ars medica*. He was interested in mathematics and astronomy, and was considered an expert in both fields. It has been argued that he was an exponent of the new humanism, and wrote, annotated, translated, or transcribed at least a dozen texts.[260] Service to Margaret Beaufort proved fortunate for another royal physician, Thomas Denman.[261] Like Caerlyon, Denman was a Cambridge graduate, but was unusual in that he had taken both M.B. and M.D. degrees, and reportedly studied overseas.[262] Denman lived and practiced in Cambridge in the early 1480s, and may have kept his residence there and served at court only sporadically. But when Margaret fell ill in 1494 at Colly Weston, Northamptonshire, about a day's travel from Cambridge, Denman was called to attend her. He treated her successfully, won the king's gratitude, and was praised as a "doctor of good arts in medicine." More tangibly, he was rewarded with a cash payment, the wardenship of St. Mary Bethlehem, and more regular court service.[263] Denman continued his association with Cambridge, and in 1501 was nominated for the mastership of Peterhouse. His will is one of the most interesting of late medieval doctors because it contains a list of his private library.[264]

Like Henry IV, Henry VII was something of a hypochondriac and, for all his penury, surrounded himself with doctors. One of the best was Benedict Frutze.[265] A Dutchman or German, Frutze entered royal service soon after the accession in 1485; indeed, there is speculation that he, like Caerlyon, was with the Earl Richmond in Brittany and may even

---

[259] CPR, 1485–1494, pp. 75, 145, 219.
[260] Kibre, "Lewis of Caerlyon," pp. 100–108.
[261] *T&H*, pp. 339–340.
[262] *Ibid.*, p. 339.
[263] CPR, 1485–1494, p. 471.
[264] See below, p. 205; *T&H*, p. 340.
[265] *T&H*, pp. 24–25. As noted, he was also called Benet Fentre.

have attended the court of Richard III.[266] By late 1485 Frutze was given a lifetime appointment "to be one of the king's physicians," and was awarded cash gifts, an annuity of £40, property and privileges and exemptions.[267]

More prominent still were John Baptist Boerio, Robert Sherborn, and William Lynch. Boerio was Geneose, a member of that city's *Venerabile Collegium* of physicians. He had a considerable medical reputation, and was a long-time friend and correspondent of Erasmus, who educated Boerio's sons.[268] Boerio was invited to serve at court in 1500 where, because of his humanistic skills, he was sent on diplomatic missions. He even accompanied Henry VIII on the French campaign of 1513–1514, one of the few physicians to do so.[269] Boerio was well rewarded for his services and became rich. It is ironic that both his sons forsook careers in medicine, and turned instead to the law.[270]

Robert Sherborn, like Boerio, served Henry VII as a diplomat as well as a doctor.[271] This had become fairly common by the early sixteenth century, a reflection of the spread of humanism. There is more personal information for Sherborn than for most doctors. At age eleven he entered Winchester College, and at eighteen New College Oxford.[272] He held various positions at Oxford from the 1470s through the 1490s, and was associated with Merton College.[273] In all, he seems to have had a successful if uneventful career as a don, with few prospects for any

---

[266] *Materials for the History of the Reign of Henry VII*, ed. Henry Ellis (London: Rolls Series, i, 1858), pp. 67, 172, 223, 405.

[267] *T&H*, p. 266. Others include Ralph Sentiler, who in 1500 was physician to Elizabeth of York as well as to Henry. See Nicholas, *Privy Purse Expenses*, p. 215. And there was Thomas Forestier, a Norman, who also may have served Henry during his exile. He was the author of an influential text on dysentery, which he dedicated to Henry VII. He lived in England for much of the 1480s, and was given a royal pardon in 1488 for unmentioned offenses. Henry was paying him an annuity of £40 in 1488, and he probably treated the king between 1485 and 1488. See: *T&H*, p. 343; B.M. Add. Ms. 27582; B.M. Arundel Ms. 249; and CPR, 1485–1494, p. 202.

[268] B.M. Harley Ms. 433, f. 94; *T&H*, pp. 117–19; CCR, 1500–1509, p. 170; *LPFD*, i, i, #1477, p. 675; *ibid.*, i, i, #132, p. 69; *ibid.*, i, ii, #2223, p. 997; *ibid.*, i. ii. #2468, p. 1088; *ibid.*, i, ii, #2519, p. 1109.

[269] PRO, Exchequer Accounts, E101/56/10.

[270] *LPFD*, i, ii, #2847–48, p. 1238. Also, *T&H*, pp. 117–119.

[271] *T&H*, pp. 300–301.

[272] *BRUO*, iii, p. 1685.

[273] *Ibid.* Also, *Registrum Annalium Collegii Mertonensis, 1483–1521*, ed. H. E. Salter (Oxford: Oxford Historical Society, 76, 1923), p. 132.

changes. Then in the 1490s he became secretary to Cardinal Morton, and proved his mettle as a diplomat. In 1505 he was made Bishop of St. David's, and in 1508 was translated to the bishopric of Chichester.[274] He continued his career in the church until the Reformation, when, in 1534, ill and close to eighty, he transferred his allegiance from the pope to the king of England.[275]

Like Boerio, Sherborn distinguished himself in many academic fields, his interests ranging from literature to physical science. His medical career began around 1480. By 1496, probably on a good word from Morton, he was called to royal medical service; this he continued at intervals until his death in 1536.[276] Sherborn was also prominent as a medical author. He was a commentator on the Salernitan regiment, and many of his works were cited as authority in several sixteenth-century texts.[277] Sherborn became rich, partly from his church offices and partly from his medical practice. A testament to this wealth is the alabaster effigy which he commissioned for his tomb in Chichester Cathedral.[278]

William Lynch, a fellow of Oriel by 1477, was more exclusively a physician than Boerio or Sherborn.[279] He was at court by 1491, receiving the standard fee of £40.[280] Like Caerlyon and Sentiler, he backed into his role by first serving the queen, being in attendance in 1503 when she died. Lynch remained in royal favor throughout Henry VII's reign, and was one of three physicians who were at the king's funeral in 1509.[281] One of the other physicians was John Chamber. With Thomas Linacre, he was responsible for bringing the "new" Italian medicine to

---

[274] CPR, 1494–1509 p. 414. It will be remembered that John Arundell also served as bishop of Chichester.

[275] LPFD, Henry VIII, ii, ii, pp. 3336, 1341; ibid., iv, ii, p. 2081; ibid., iii, ii, p. 966; ibid., viii, 74, p. 368.

[276] Cal. State Papers, Venice, 1202–1509, pp. 237, 246, 247, 250.

[277] O.U. Bod. Ms. Lat. Misc., d 34.

[278] The effigy is still there. Sherborn's will is in PCC, "Hogan," 1536, f. 41.

[279] T&H, p. 407.

[280] CCR, 1485–1500, p. 182; CPR, 1485–1494, p. 379.

[281] LPFD, Henry VIII, i, i, p. 13. One of the others was Doctor Lacy, probably Walter Lacy. Lacy was a fellow of Peterhouse, and probably took his M.D. by 1489. He was a favorite of Catherine of Aragon, one of her first physicians when she arrived in England. Their ties remained strong, and he had a prominent place at the coronation of Henry VIII and Catherine, when he was styled "squire of the body." See: T&H, p. 369; Cambridge University Grace Books, B, i, p. 61; LPFD, Henry VIII, i, i, p. 13; and LPFD, Henry VIII, i, i, p. 13.

England and founding the Royal College of Physicians in 1518; as such, he will be discussed in Chapter Eight.

Chamber's friend and co-author, Sir William Butts, played a prominent role in the court of Henry VIII.[282] A contemporary of Chamber, Butts did not achieve medical prominence until the 1530s.[283] He was not, for example, a member of the College of Physicians until 1529.[284] He took his M.D. in 1518 from Gonville Hall, and by 1540 was receiving an annuity of £120 for his services. This was three times higher than the traditional fee, and set another standard to which the court doctors might aspire.[285] As Henry's personal favorite, Butts was almost always in attendance at court. He was knighted for royal service in 1540 and, with Chamber, looms large in the famous Holbein portrait of Henry VIII and his doctors.[286] Unlike Chamber, Butts was married. He had three sons, each of whom became a gentleman, and it goes without saying that by the time of his death in 1545 he was a very wealthy man.[287]

Henry VIII had a number of foreign physicians. There was Boerio, whom he inherited from his father, and Ferdinand de Vittoria, a Spaniard, who accompanied Catherine of Aragon to England.[288] Vittoria began serving Henry VIII in 1515, and made a quick and lasting impression. He became one of Henry's favorites, and in 1518 was one of the founding members of the Royal College of Physicians.[289] Vittoria was shrewd and ambitious, as well as being a good doctor. He asked that his Spanish M.D. be recognized by Oxford, and used his position at court to profitable ends, getting license to export "five hundred woolen cloths

---

[282] B.M. Sloane Ms. 1047.

[283] *DNB*, 3, pp. 555–556. *T&H* apparently felt he practiced too late to be included in their register.

[284] *DNB*, 3, pp. 555–556.

[285] *Ibid.*

[286] Holbein's wages for this famous portrait are discussed in Thomas Vicary, *The Anatomie of the Bodie of Man*, ed. F. J. and P. Furnivall (London: EETS, es, 53, 1886), pp. 238–239.

[287] *Ibid.* Henry VIII had other, less distinguished, physicians. One was Robert Yaxley, a Cambridge M.D., who had also incepted in law. Yaxley began his royal service around 1513 and continued to do so until 1531. Yaxley was a resident of London and had a profitable local practice resulting from his royal connection. He was a charter member of the Royal College of Physicians, had a wife, at least one son, and, like the other royal physicians, died a rich and famous man in 1540. See *T&H*, p. 306; PCC, "Alenger," 1540, f. 18.

[288] *T&H*, pp. 47–48.

[289] The others were Chambers, Linacre, Yaxley, and John Francis. See. pp. 297–298.

a year."[290] His wife was one of Queen Catherine's attendants at the meeting of the Field of the Cloth of Gold, and both husband and wife were among Catherine's early confidantes.[291] Vittoria continued to hold a position of prominence at the royal court in the 1520s, and wisely decided to cultivate Cardinal Wolsey. Yet he was clever enough to survive the downfalls of both Catherine and Wolsey, and stayed on as court physician until 1533, when he presumably returned to Spain.[292]

Henry VIII's other foreign physicians are more obscure. Philip de Karuges, "Doctor of Physic," was probably French.[293] He practiced in London from 1509 to 1533, and was a consultant on a number of occasions.[294] John Francis, another "Doctor of the Physic," was probably Italian.[295] He was personal physician to Cardinal Wolsey and like Vittoria a founder of the Royal College. It was under Wolsey's auspices, probably around 1526, that Francis began to attend the king, initially at Hampton Court and then at Windsor.[296] Like Boerio and Linacre, Francis was a scholar of wide-ranging skills, a friend of Erasmus, and had a European-wide reputation.[297]

Finally and in some ways most intriguingly there was John Argentine.[298] A Cambridge M.D. and provost of King's College, Argentine was one of the most prominent scholars and physicians of the late fifteenth and early sixteenth centuries. He may have studied at Padua—he was apparently Italian-born—and was a leading physician by 1475. He seems not to have been employed by Edward IV, but was involved with the disappearance of Edward's sons.[299] Argentine was a friend of the Tudor historian Mancini, who claimed that the physician treated Prince Edward when the latter was imprisoned in the Tower. Edward allegedly told Argentine that he and his brother were praying regularly, in anticipation of their death.[300] In any circumstance, his standing with the

---

[290] *LPFD*, ii, ii, p. 70.

[291] Jocelyne G. Russell, *The Field of the Cloth of Gold* (London: R.K.P., 1969), p. 204.

[292] *LPFD*, v, p. 714.

[293] *T&H*, pp. 252–257.

[294] *LPFD*, i, i, p. 59; PCC, "Hoen," 1533, f. 11.

[295] *T&H*, pp. 145–146.

[296] *LPFD*, iii, i, p. 2; *ibid.*, iii, ii, p. 1,532; *ibid.*, iv, ii, p. 1,069.

[297] *Ibid.*, iv, ii, p. 1,537.

[298] *T&H*, pp. 112–115; *DNB*, 1, p. 552.

[299] Dominic Mancini, *The Usurpation of Richard III*, ed. C.A.J. Armstrong, 2nd ed. (Oxford: Oxford University Press, 1969), pp. 88–89.

[300] *Ibid.* See too: D. E. Rhodes, "The Princes in the Tower and Their Doctor," *English*

Tudors was high. He became physician to Prince Arthur and perhaps Prince Henry at the same time that Thomas Linacre was their tutor.[301] He was a friend of another Tudor intimate, Cardinal Morton, who helped sponsor Argentine's university career. Argentine too benefited from his royal contacts, becoming rich and famous. But, given his high medical reputation, it is surprising that he did not spend more time at court.[302]

What, in summary, can be said about the court doctors? Virtually all of them were physicians. Whatever problems they may have had in the medical world they still picked the choicest fruits at court. And what fruits they were! The royal physicians were the social and financial elite of all the practitioners. They were, indeed, not part of the middle strata of the kingdom, but more—peers of gentlemen, and associates if not equals with members of the aristocracy. A few were bishops—which would in fact make them lords—while others were high officers in the universities. Court physicians were paid good wages and allowed to wear sumptuous liveries. And though many of them entered royal service rich and well known, all left richer and more famous, holders of large tracts of property, owners of gold and plate, recipients of fat annuities.

About a quarter of them were aliens. Indeed eighty-three percent of all alien physicians in England served at the court. Yet they occupied a strange position among the royal doctors. They served in large numbers only at particular points in time. Foreigners predominated in the fourteenth century, largely disappeared after the reign of Henry IV, and returned in large numbers with the accession of Henry VIII and his Spanish queen. During the "golden age" of late medieval medicine, the fifteenth century, most of the court physicians were Englishmen. Even in the early sixteenth century the most prominent physicians were denizens, albeit ones who had studied in Italy.

Many of the court physicians were famous scholars. By 1500 some had been trained in the new methods of humanism, and served in more than medical capacities. They were diplomats, lawyers, financiers, and general advisers. Indeed, this in some ways represents the most common strand. While the court physicians were a notable group, they did

---

*Historical Review*, 76, 1961, pp. 304–306; Charles Ross, *Richard III* (Berkeley, Cal.: University of California Press, 1981), p. 88; and Desmond Seward, *Richard III: England's Black Legend* (New York: Franklin Watts, 1984), p. 120.

[301] See, for example, CPR, 1494–1509, p. 158.

[302] See, for example, *BRUO*, iii, pp. 2106–2107.

not, with the exception of Colnet, Linacre, and a few others, distinguish themselves as doctors. Rather, they were men of style, wit, and grace, notable for their political skills—and, indeed, political skills were as important as those of physic in getting one to court in the first place. But just a handful wrote original medical tracts, and none seems to have devised new medical techniques. They examined, made diagnoses, and prognoses. Then, surgeons, apothecaries, and barbers applied the treatments.

Above all, royal physicians were rich and socially prominent. This was the principal reason for serving at court. Few doctors, even the most successful practitioners in London, could hope to rise much above the other bourgeoisie, either financially or socially. But at court the opportunities were unlimited. Kings did what they wanted. They could raise a doctor to the position of a lord. For physicians, struggling in an era of plague with a bad public image, the one sure way to success was to tend the king at court.

# 4

## SURGEONS AND WAR

Royal support was crucial for surgeons. By 1300 physicians had university educations, and in some cases church affiliations. They were the medical pace-setters, successful and respected; for them a position at court was a boon, but not the only path to success. Apothecaries were members of spicers' companies. While their medical role was circumscribed, they grew wealthy through the spice trade and rose to positions of prominence in their municipalities. But surgeons still carried the stigma of being craftsmen and the burden of violating the blood taboo.[1] They had neither the distinction of university degrees nor the advantage of ecclesiastical contacts. Few of them treated the wealthiest patients, and they lacked even the consolation of being rich. Hence, service to the king and the status and opportunities it brought offered surgeons their best chance to achieve fame and fortune.

Royal service also afforded the unique opportunity for the sharpening of old medical skills and the development of new ones. For late medieval monarchs took surgeons to war. Kings were expected to campaign regularly, and most did. France was the favorite battleground, with expeditions from 1294 to 1514. But there were other campaigns as well—seemingly unending struggles with the Welsh and Scots, forays to Ireland, expeditions to the Netherlands and Spain, the battles of the Wars of the Roses—in all, considerable opportunity for each generation of surgeons to serve on the battlefield. This brought two benefits. Since the kings who did the most fighting—Edward I, Edward III, Henry V, Edward IV—were astute and influential, their support was particularly effective. And, from a medical perspective, surgery on the battlefield presented an unparalleled opportunity to perform under pressure and on large numbers of patients; to compare, share, and learn techniques; and to experiment. This took on added importance because of the limitations in civilian practice on dissection and experimentation with cadavers. Indeed, the experience gained from war was central to the rise of surgery;

---

[1] Jacques Le Goff, "Licit and Illicit Trades in the Medieval West," in his *Time, Work and Culture in the Middle Ages*, trans. Arthur Goldhammer (Chicago: University of Chicago Press, 1980).

in combination with the changes caused by recurring epidemics it was the driving force behind late medieval English medicine.

War had another benefit. In 1300, English surgeons, like English physicians, were less skilled than their continental counterparts, especially those from Italy, Provence, and Iberia.[2] Hence, foreign surgeons, like foreign physicians, were brought to England to serve at court. But most foreigners refused to accompany military expeditions, and the Englishmen who served in their stead benefited accordingly. By the middle of the fourteenth century, even before the Black Death, the best English surgeons, such as John Arderne and Master Adam, were more effective than the best resident foreigners, and were probably the equals of any surgeons on the continent. By 1370 foreign surgeons were no longer coming to England. Natives would dominate surgery and clinical medicine for the rest of the middle ages.[3]

The reappearance of foreign surgeons during the reign of Henry VIII underscores the importance of war. Most of Henry's foreigners were Italians. They were trained in universities, and practiced a new surgery resulting from more accurate appraisals of anatomy and physiology, and integrated with physic.[4] If Henry wanted the best surgeons he had little choice but to seek them abroad. Despite his bellicosity and the campaign to France he undertook in 1513–1514, his army did little fighting.[5] By 1520 English surgeons, without the benefit of the university training of the Italians *or* the practical experience developed on the battlefield, had again fallen behind the best of the foreigners.

Military surgeons who served at court were peculiar to the later medieval centuries. Anglo-Saxon kings had court surgeons, but they generally did not take them to battle; the Normans and early Plantagenets had military surgeons but they seldom brought them to court.[6] The first king to combine the roles was, ironically, the placid Henry III. Henry had a "serjeant-surgeon," or chief surgeon, named Master William. Wil-

[2] Charles H. Talbot, "Medicine," in David C. Lindberg, ed., *Science in the Middle Ages* (Chicago: University of Chicago Press, 1978), pp. 409–423.

[3] See Chapter Eight for a discussion of the return of aliens.

[4] Nancy G. Siraisi, *Arts and Sciences at Padua: The Studium of Padua Before 1350* (Toronto: Pontifical Institute of Mediaeval Studies, 1973), pp. 269–302.

[5] C. G. Cruickshank, *Army Royal: Henry VIII's Invasion of France, 1513* (Oxford: Oxford University Press, 1969).

[6] *T&H*, p. 375: Edward J. Kealey, *Medieval Medicus: A Social History of Anglo-Norman Medicine* (Baltimore: Johns Hopkins University Press, 1981).

liam served in the field during several French campaigns, and treated Henry for two decades, beginning in 1233.[7] He was in the royal party in 1254 when Queen Eleanor traveled to Gascony to see the king.[8] This in itself was unusual. In the middle of the thirteenth century physicians and apothecaries rather than surgeons usually traveled with royal parties, and it speaks well for the confidence in which the king held him.[9] William was a cleric, albeit in minor orders.[10] But his position in the church never affected his medical practice, a fact which suggests that thirteenth-century doctors did not always adhere to church encyclicals.[11]

Henry III had another court surgeon, Henry of Saxeby.[12] Henry was born in Leicestershire, where he started his practice, moving to London around 1250. There he was brought to the king's attention, entered royal service as an assistant to William around 1251, became serjeant-surgeon at William's death in 1255, and retained the position until he died in 1271. Henry is notable for his financial success; he received the same gifts, gratuities, and salary—about £10—as the royal physicians did, and in 1254 was granted a house and thirteen shops in London, which together yielded an annual income of about fifty shillings.[13]

Beginning around 1260 Henry had an associate.[14] This was Thomas of Weseham, who came to court in 1252—hence, for a time Henry III had three surgeons—and lasted until the end of the reign. The most distinguished surgeon of his day, Thomas saved the king's life in 1257.[15] Like Saxeby, he traveled with Henry, and was with him when Saxeby and the queen joined the royal party in 1254. Weseham's skills made him rich, especially toward the end of the reign, when he seems to have forsaken medicine for making money. He took advantage of the plight of England's Jews, in the midst of the persecutions that would lead to their expulsion in 1290, by buying Jewish properties in London, Norwich,

[7] George E. Gask, "Vicary's Predecessors," in his *Essays in the History of Medicine* (London: Butterworth, 1950), p. 58.

[8] CPR, 1232–1247, p. 16.

[9] CPR, 1247–1258, p. 375.

[10] *T&H*, p. 375.

[11] Darrel W. Amundsen, "Medieval Canon Law on Medical and Surgical Practice by the Clergy," *BHM*, 52, 1978, pp. 22–44.

[12] *T&H*, pp. 82–83.

[13] CCR, 1251–1253, pp. 315, 395, 407; CCR, 1253–1254, pp. 29, 271, 273, 279.

[14] *T&H*, pp. 359–360.

[15] Gask, "Vicary's Predecessors," pp. 59–60.

and Oxford at well below their market value.[16] He received several annuities, was knighted, and made both a royal moneyer and forester.[17] As
Talbot and Hammond observed, all the references to Weseham toward
the end of his life deal with money and property.[18] The final record
treats Henry of Saxeby's son, Nicholas. A gentleman, Nicholas sued
Thomas Weseham over a tract of land the latter had apparently appropriated from Henry's estate.[19]

The position of the royal surgeons under Henry III, then, was improving. Some went to war, and their very presence at court and as part
of royal traveling parties was a triumph. They profited and prospered,
as royal physicians had for at least two hundred years. There was another development: the extension of peaceful contacts with France, and
especially Provence. Henry's queen was French, and so were many of
his advisers. The king spoke French as his first language, was a Franco-
phile, and traveled to France several times.[20] French surgery, particularly as taught at Montpellier, was more advanced than that in England.
Further, the surgeons there were in close contact with the even better
practitioners of northern Italy, men like William of Saliceto, who advocated the dynamic mix of physic and surgery that would begin to
transform first Italian and then European medicine.[21] Their successors
included such figures as Henri de Mondeville, whose *Chirurgie* changed
the way doctors diagnosed and treated wounds. Master William, Henry
of Saxeby, Thomas Weseham, and others must have had some exposure
and adopted some of the ideas of these men.

This set the stage for the doctors of Edward I. However exciting surgical theory might have been, it was no substitute for practice. With the
accession of Edward the opportunities for military practice became regular. He conquered most of Wales and tried to do the same to Scotland.
He opened the wars in France and was in the field virtually every year

---

[16] CCHR, 1257–1300, pp. 23, 24, 28; *Cal. Hustings Deeds*. London Roll 4, m.127, as cited
in *T&H*, p. 360.

[17] CPR, 1258–1266, p. 73; CCR, 1259–1261, pp. 54, 276, 249, 338, 427.

[18] *T&H*, p. 360.

[19] CPR, 1266–1272, p. 591.

[20] This is nicely described by Gask in "Vicary's Predecessors," pp. 58–61. See also
F. M. Powicke, *King Henry III and the Lord Edward*, vol. i (Oxford: Clarendon Press, 1947),
pp. 156–207.

[21] See below, pp. 281–286. Also see Vern L. Bullough, *The Development of Medicine as a
Profession* (New York: Hafner, 1966), pp. 46–73.

from 1293 until his death in 1307.[22] Furthermore, Edward was interested in medicine, especially surgery, and may have regarded proper medical care as a prerequisite for recruiting soldiers for future armies.[23] There is evidence from the Scottish campaign of 1298. The king took the physician Master John de Kenley for his private doctor.[24] But he also took his personal surgeon, Master Peter, probably Peter of Newcastle, to lead a group of surgeons who treated his troops.[25] Both John and Peter received wages of two shillings a day, equal to those of a knight; were allowed two assistants, a clothing allowance, and insurance for their horses.[26] Information survives for two other surgeons, recruited as part of the muster for London.[27] One, Gilbert the Surgeon, was a prominent citizen; his Hustings Court will mentions a wife, son, and daughter, and considerable property.[28] Less is known of the other, William the Surgeon, save that he was in trouble with authorities at least four times, twice for alleged assault, once for theft, and once for manslaughter.[29]

There is additional evidence about Peter of Newcastle. He served at court from 1298 until Edward's death in 1307, and continued on in the service of Edward II and Edward III.[30] His personal valet in 1298 was John Marshall, also a surgeon.[31] In addition to his surgical duties, Peter was commissioned to supply the royal court with medicines.[32] This must have been easy, for he operated a number of shops in London, where he dealt regularly with the pepperers; Peter may have been an

---

[22] R. Theodore Beck, *The Cutting Edge: The Early History of the Surgeons of London* (London: Lund Humphries, 1974), pp. 16–17. A general reference is Michael Prestwich, *The Three Edwards: War and the State in England, 1272–1377* (London: Faber, 1980).

[23] *Ibid.* But Beck is difficult to use, no less to cite, because he is imprecise about dates and does not use footnotes.

[24] *T&H*, pp. 158–159.

[25] *Ibid.*, pp. 251–252.

[26] *Ibid.* See too Gask, "Vicary's Predecessors," pp. 60–64. It might be remembered that a similar proviso was provided for Elias de Sabboto and his party. See above, p. 94.

[27] PRO, E101/13/39, membr. 3.

[28] *T&H*, p. 57; *Hustings Wills*, i, p. 234.

[29] *T&H*, p. 377; *Calendar of Early Mayor's Court Rolls in the City of London*, ed. A. H. Thomas (London: HMSO, 1924), p. 30; *Calendar of City Coroner's Rolls*, ed. R. R. Sharpe (London: HMSO, 1913), pp. 4, 24; PRO, Exchequer Accounts, E101/13/39, membr. 3.

[30] *T&H*, pp. 251–252.

[31] *Scotland in 1298: Documents Relating to the Campaign of King Edward the First*, ed. Henry Gough (London: A. Gardner and Paisley, 1888), p. 175.

[32] *T&H*, p. 251.

apothecary and perhaps even a member of the Pepperers' Company.[33]
As befitted a man of many talents, he served both Edward I and Edward
II on diplomatic missions. And, predictably, he became wealthy.[34]

Edward I's other surgeons included Henry the Leche, perhaps a physician but more likely a surgeon. He served in two Scottish campaigns,
and was left behind at Berwick Castle to tend the English wounded in
1302.[35] More famous were the father and son Simon and Philip of Beauvais, Frenchmen who came to England after being schooled in Italy and
Provence.[36] Simon was in royal service from 1276 until 1297. He was
Edward's most trusted doctor, physician or surgeon, and was first rewarded for "good service" in 1276.[37] He probably accompanied Edward
on the French campaign in 1293, and the Flemish expedition of 1297.[38]
Simon's son Philip was "one of the most eminent military surgeons of
the times."[39] He first accompanied Edward on the trip to France in
1286–1289, and then attended the king on every subsequent campaign
of the reign. He was the chief surgeon on these expeditions, and made
lasting friendships with members of the nobility—friendships that
would benefit him for the rest of his life.[40] Wealthy to begin with, probably from his private practices in Paris and London, Philip got richer
after entering royal service. He was awarded annuities, cash bonuses,
clothing and property, and inherited his father's entire estate. In 1304
he was called the king's serjeant, and in 1316 appeared before Edward II
to have his land and wealth confirmed.[41] Philip of Beauvais became a
courtier despite his status as a surgeon.

Martin de Vere, the last of Edward's military surgeons, began service
around 1305.[42] He was also the chief surgeon for most of Edward II's
campaigns, including Bannockburn and Boroughbridge. He was paid
forty shillings per campaign and, in addition to treating the wounded,

---

[33] For example, *Calendar of Hustings Deeds, London*, Roll 48, m.71, as quoted in *T&H*, p.
252.

[34] *Hustings Wills*, i, p. 350.

[35] *T&H*, p. 81.

[36] *T&H*, pp. 319–320; *ibid.*, pp. 254–256; Beck, *Cutting Edge*, pp. 21–26.

[37] cchR, 1257–1300, p. 202.

[38] Gask, "Vicary's Predecessors," pp. 61–62.

[39] *T&H*, p. 254.

[40] *Ibid.*, pp. 254–255.

[41] CCR, 1302–1307, p. 135; CPR, 1313–1317, p. 449.

[42] *T&H*, p. 211.

was responsible for laying in the medical stores.[43] These included between ten and twenty pounds of plasters and bandages, ointments,
balms, and salves, as well as equipment for amputation and the removal
of arrows and other missiles.

The reign of Edward II was notable for the growing role surgeons
played at court. They were not yet the fixtures that physicians and
apothecaries had become. But for the first time there were regulations
that described their role:

> The surgeon shall have his diet everyday in the hall, and if he is not hin-
> dered by some business certified by the steward and treasurer. And then
> he shall have his livery as a knight of the household, whether he be well or
> ill, that is to say, two drais of bread, one pitcher of wine, two messes of gros
> from the kitchen, and one mess of roast. And shall take everyday for his
> chamber one pitcher of wine, three candles, one tontes, litter all the year,
> fuel for dinner time, of the usher of the hall. He shall have twelve pence a
> day wages until he be advanced by the king and two robes yearly in cloth,
> or eight marks in money. For things medical he shall have forty shillings a
> year.[44]

This was a fine arrangement, especially for one considered a craftsman,
and offered opportunities for continuing advancement. But it was inferior to the arrangements of physicians. It was still only in war that the
surgeons could make real social and financial advances.

This is why the reign of Edward III was so important. Like that of
Edward I it was filled with war and the opportunities war brought. Edward or his sons were on campaign for most of the fifty-year kingship.
He and his eldest child, the Black Prince, were good generals and organ-
izers and, like the first Edward, realized that proper medical care was
important for recruiting.[45] And it was in his reign that that other storm-
cloud with a silver lining, plague, became epidemic. From these two disasters would evolve the finest medical care of the middle ages.

Edward first organized military surgeons for his expeditions in the
1330s and 1340s.[46] But his best work was done for the Crecy campaign

[43] Gask, "Vicary's Predecessors," p. 64.

[44] *Ibid.*, p. 64.

[45] This is nicely described by John Keegan in *The Face of Battle* (London: Jonathan Cape,
1976), pp. 78–116.

[46] These are the first records, in any case. See *Ordinances and Regulations for the Government of the Royal Household* (London: Society of Antiquaries, 1790), pp. 3–7. See too: Gask,
"Vicary's Predecessors," pp. 64–68; Gask, "The Medical Staff of Edward III," pp. 77–93,

of 1346.[47] Estimates of the size of the royal force vary.[48] Edward probably left England with an army of 15,000 and a fleet of 1,000, substantial
for Western Europe in the fourteenth century.[49] At the battle of Crecy
itself, Edward deployed about 11,000 fighting men—2,000 men-at-
arms, 500 light lancers, 7,000 English and Welsh bowmen, and 1,500
knifemen—probably the largest English army of the Hundred Years
War.[50] The Exchequer Rolls do not list all medical staff, as they do for
later battles.[51] But several chroniclers commented on the king's concern
for his wounded, and on the array of medical wagons drawn up behind
the English line.[52] The wagons carried medical stores, served as operating tables, and carried off the wounded. Impressive as this sounds,
Gask, an authority on military medicine, goes further in his assessment.
He claims that Edward III actually pensioned off his wounded after the
great victory.[53]

Records survive for a number of the individuals. One was the royal
physician Jordan of Canterbury, who, along with the surgeon Roger
Heyton, directed the medical team.[54] Jordan's career has been discussed. He was Edward's personal doctor, and at Crecy probably served
just the king, his son, and a few advisers.[55] Heyton entered royal service
late in the reign of Edward II, and was a reliable if unexceptional royal
servant throughout the 1330s and early 1340s.[56] He received the usual

also in his *Essays in the History of Medicine*; and J. J. Keevil, *Medicine and the Navy*, i (Edinburgh: E. & S. Livingstone, 1957), p. 20.

[47] A summary is A. H. Burne, *The Crecy War: A Military History of the Hundred Years War
from 1337 to the Peace of Bretigny, 1360* (London: Eyre and Spottiswode, 1956).

[48] In addition to Burne, *The Crecy War*, see: Gask, "Vicary's Predecessors," pp. 55–76;
and "The Medical Staff of Edward III," pp. 77–93; Desmond Seward, *The Hundred Years
War: The English in France, 1337–1453* (New York: Atheneum, 1978), pp. 41–75; Edouard
Perroy, *The Hundred Years War* (London: Eyre and Spottiswode, 1951), pp. 111–142; John
Barnie, *War in Medieval English Society: Social Values and the Hundred Years War, 1337–99*
(Ithaca, N.Y.: Cornell University Press, 1974); Mae McKissack, *The Fourteenth Century*
(Oxford: Oxford University Press, 1959), pp. 101–151.

[49] H. J. Hewitt, *The Organization of War Under Edward III, 1338–62*, (Manchester: Manchester University Press, 1966).

[50] Seward, *Hundred Years War*, pp. 50–53.

[51] C. T. Allmand, *Society at War: The Experience of England and France During the Hundred
Years War* (New York: Barnes and Noble, 1973).

[52] They are summarized by Gask, "The Medical Staff of Edward III," pp. 77–83.

[53] *Ibid.*

[54] *Ibid.*, pp. 82–83, 90–92.

[55] *T&H*, pp. 198–199.

[56] *Ibid.*, pp. 310–312.

gifts and annuities and did well enough.[57] Crecy provided a better opportunity. His skills in treating battlefield wounds proved him indispen-
sable, and by 1347 he was receiving a higher wage than even Jordan of
Canterbury. Heyton was allowed income from an entire manor in
Wales, which averaged about £50 a year, plus an annuity of £20. By the
late 1340s he held enough land to bring up the issue of whether he owed
the royal armies men from his estates.[58] Like Philip of Beauvais, Heyton
reached as grand a position at court and in the kingdom as a surgeon
could. Like Philip, he established a pattern for the future.

Of the others, there is some confusion over a Master Adam. One surgeon so named served Edward III and Queen Isabella from 1357 to the
end of the reign.[59] He probably accompanied the Black Prince on the
Poitiers campaign, had his annuities and gifts confirmed early in the
reign of Richard II, and treated Richard during the minority.[60] A certain
Adam de la Poultrie also served the Black Prince at Poitiers: hence the
speculation that he was one and the same with Master Adam.[61] In 1354,
he adjudicated a sticky malpractice case.[62] To further confuse identities,
one Adam Rous became Edward III's chief surgeon sometime in the
1350s.[63] Little is known of his training or background. Rous had a successful London practice, and beginning in 1359 received gifts and cor-
rodies from the king.[64] He too served on the battlefield, probably at
Poitiers, and continued as Richard II's principal surgeon. Rous's will,
proved in the Hustings Court in 1379, includes land in London and
throughout eastern England.[65]

John Arderne was the most famous doctor in medieval England, and
the best-known English surgeon on the continent.[66] He also acquired, or

---

[57] See, for example, CPR, 1327–1337, p. 220; CPR, 1338–1340, p. 307; *ibid.*, 1340–1343,
p. 295; CCR, 1341–1343, p. 308.

[58] For Heyton's holdings, see: PRO, *Register of the Black Prince*, i, p. 130; CCR, 1346–1349,
p. 66; CPR, 1334–1338, p. 556; CChR, 1341–1417, p. 134; *French Roll, 20 Edward III*, ed.
(London: William Salter Archaeological Society, 18, 1897), pp. 88, 100.

[59] *T&H*, p. 4.

[60] CPR, 1377–1381, p. 213.

[61] *T&H*, p. 6.

[62] L–B G, p. 21.

[63] *T&H*, pp. 7–8.

[64] CCR, 1354–1360, p. 618.

[65] *Hustings Wills*, ii, i, pp. 207–208.

[66] See *T&H*, pp. 111–112; *DNB*, ii, pp. 76–77; and Gerald N. Weiss, "John Arderne,

at least honed, his skills on the battlefield. It is not clear as to whether he was at Crecy, but he served the troops of Henry Plantagenet, Duke of Lancaster, in Antwerp in the 1330s, and in Spain in the 1340s, before attaching himself to the royal army.[67] About a quarter of his surgical and general medical manuals deal with military medicine, and his techniques and methods are inconceivable without experiences in battle.[68]

William Hamon was a Norman.[69] He was prior of the Benedictine cell of Cagges, Oxfordshire, and is another example of the gap between clerical prescription and actual practice.[70] Hamon served as royal surgeon from 1341 to 1367, and was the highest salaried of Edward III's doctors. From 1347—suggesting distinguished service at Crecy—he was paid a base salary of £30, supplemented by regular bonuses.[71] And in 1349:

> notwithstanding that he was born of the parts of Normandy . . . it is the king's will that he enjoys all lands and rents of the priory and be treated throughout England as a denizen and not as an alien, and that he be discharged of any amercements incurred in the Exchequer for non-appearance there to answer as an alien.[72]

Master Martin, William Swinbourne, William Holm, and William Blackwater were at Crecy.[73] Martin's tenure began before the battle, for in April, 1341, Edward ordered him paid wages of £13 for overseas duty with the army.[74] Swinbourne had a similar career.[75] He was excused a number of offenses in the general pardon of 1346, providing that he remained in service in France.[76] Holm was a court surgeon in the 1360s

Father of English Surgery," *Journal of the International College of Surgeons*, 25, 1956, pp. 247–256.

[67] See the introduction by D'Arcy Power to Arderne's *Treatise of Fistula in Ano* (London: EETS, 139, 1910), pp. xii–xiii; and Power, "English Medicine and Surgery in the Fourteenth Century," in his *Selected Essays*, 1877–1930, rept. (New York: Augustus Kelley, 1970), pp. 29–47.

[68] *Fistula in Ano*, pp. 1–36.

[69] *T&H*, p. 397.

[70] Beck, *Cutting Edge*, p. 51.

[71] CPR, 1345–1348, p. 447; CPR, 1348–1350, p. 394.

[72] CPR, 1348–1350, p. 407.

[73] *T&H*, p. 210.

[74] CCR, 1341–1343, p. 55. *T&H*, p. 211, hint that this might have been the same Martin de Vere who served Edward II. If so, he would have been quite old. See *French Roll, 20 Edward III*, p. 216.

[75] *T&H*, pp. 416–417.

[76] CPR, 1345–1348, p. 508.

and 1370s. He was one of the earliest royal doctors to be styled both
physician and surgeon, though the nature of his practice was essentially
surgical.[77] William Blackwater was doctor to both the king and the Black
Prince.[78] Like Holm, he was called both physician and surgeon, though
his methods were mostly those of physic.[79] Nevertheless, he served with
two royal armies led by Edward III, and with the Black Prince during
the Poitiers campaign.[80] At Poitiers, he was assisted by still another
prominent surgeon, Walter Gales.[81] Probably a Frenchman, Gales was
rewarded with property in Bordeaux.[82]

Several other doctors first came to prominence through service in the
army. Thomas Goldington was a royal surgeon from 1328 to 1348.[83]
There is evidence of his service in Scotland and France in the 1320s and
1330s; then, rich and well provided for, he became master of the Hospital of St. Leonard, Darby, from which he embezzled funds.[84] In 1359
the surgeon, Richard Wykens, was rewarded for "long service . . . as
well when absent from the household as present."[85] And Richard of Ireland and Peter Gymel both spent years in the royal household, and traveled throughout Britain with Edward III and his soldiers.[86] Each was
amply rewarded.[87] Given Edward III's fondness for old soldiers and his
continuing need to raise fresh troops, it could be argued that being a military surgeon was the best service a doctor could have.

Richard II and Henry IV provided fewer opportunities for service on
the battlefield than either Edward III or the Black Prince. There were
no prominent military surgeons in either reign, and most court surgeons
did not obtain the social and financial rewards their earlier counterparts
had acquired. Curiously, John Arderne, then at the height of his skills,
prestige, and influence, never seems to have been called to court. Rich-

---

[77] *T&H*, pp. 402–403.

[78] *Ibid.*, pp. 385–386.

[79] *Ibid.*, p. 385.

[80] PRO, *Register of the Black Prince*, iv, pp. 208, 270. See too H. J. Hewitt, *The Black Prince's Expedition of 1355–57* (Manchester: Manchester University Press, 1958).

[81] *T&H*, p. 367.

[82] Rymer, *Foedera*, p. 356 (Hiii,i,403).

[83] *T&H*, p. 367.

[84] CPR, 1327–1330, pp. 256, 306, 410, 461.

[85] *T&H*, p. 285; CPR, 1358–1361, p. 231.

[86] *T&H*, pp. 279–280; *T&H*, p. 248.

[87] CPR, 1361–1364, p. 251; CPR, 1367–1370, pp. 46, 402. For Gymel, see CPR, 1361–1364, p. 270.

ard II inherited many of his father's and grandfather's surgeons, including Adam Rous and William Holm. If, as suggested, they had military backgrounds, the young king would have benefited, for none of his other surgeons ever saw a battlefield. Chief among these was John de Bury.[88] Little evidence survives of his medical practice—a characteristic of court, as opposed to military, surgeons—though there is much about his business dealings.[89]

More characteristic was John Leche.[90] Leche served throughout Richard's reign, and into that of Henry IV. As with John de Bury, not much is known of his practice. At one point he styled himself a physician, but generally used the description surgeon.[91] Much is known, however, of his personal and financial affairs. In 1376 he was given large tracts of land in Ireland.[92] When in 1381 the estates were seized by the Earl of March, the king restored them, citing Leche's royal medical service.[93] Throughout his life, Leche collected annuities, one after another, each larger than its predecessor.[94] He was a schemer and raconteur, characteristics that are evident even from fragmentary evidence. In 1383 he claimed to be losing his vision; this, he said, and rightly so if it were true, was affecting his performance as a surgeon.[95] Consequently, he was pensioned off, though retained as a general adviser. But this must have been a ploy, for he was practicing again within a year. And he was getting into trouble. In 1385 a woman in Chester, where Leche had been given property, sued him, claiming that he had killed her husband on the operating table.[96] Richard II supported Leche, perhaps out of loyalty, or perhaps because he thought Leche was blind, and the case was dismissed. Yet Leche practiced for twenty more years.

Surgery was always a small part of the daily life of John Leche. For the rest of the reign of Richard II and into that of Henry IV, never interrupted by dynastic conflict or changeover, he continued to benefit from royal largesse. Indeed, few other practitioners of any stripe bene-

---

[88] *T&H*, p. 128.

[89] CPR, 1391–1396, p. 721.

[90] See above, p. 110. Also, see *T&H*, pp. 161–162.

[91] Beck, *Cutting Edge*, pp. 55–57, 73–74.

[92] CPR, 1374–1377, p. 402; CCR, 1377–1381, p. 178.

[93] CPR, 1381–1385, p. 182.

[94] For example, CCR, 1381–1385, pp. 283, 331.

[95] *Ibid.*, p. 324; CPR, 1381–1385, p. 578.

[96] CPR, 1381–1385, p. 182.

fited quite so much. He held offices in Chester, his principal residence, and continued to acquire land and annuities. His estates in Ireland grew, and he continued to get into trouble, rescued in the end by the king.[97] By 1410, just before his death, he had affected the title John Leche of Chester, esquire.[98]

The reign of Henry IV, so important for court physicians, especially aliens, was inconsequential for surgeons. But that of his son, Henry V, that most warlike and best-organized of late medieval English kings, was crucial. Henry was often at war, and always took surgeons with him. His first venture came during his 1405 campaign to Wales.[99] Among his surgeons were William Bradwardine, to be discussed, and John and Nicholas Bradmore, among the most prominent and notorious surgeons in London around the turn of the fifteenth century.[100] Their notoriety does not stem from faulty surgery; to the contrary, they were widely praised for their skills and recognized as pioneers in the development of surgical instruments.[101] But both had noses for trouble, and it was fortunate for them that they had the royal connections that allowed them to get out.

The first reference to John came in 1386, when he was pardoned by Richard II for counterfeiting.[102] Counterfeiting was a common offense among surgeons, who often held positions in the royal mints, and usually belonged to goldsmiths' guilds.[103] Indeed, the first reference to Nicholas, in 1389, accuses him of counterfeiting in Oxfordshire.[104] Both Bradmores associated with criminals, and were regularly sued and

[97] For example, CCR, 1389–1392, p. 207; CFR, 1383–1391, p. 306; CCR, 1392–1396, p. 238.

[98] CPR, 1405–1408, pp. 169–170; CPR, 1408–1413, p. 211. Richard's other surgeons included John Salesbury, John Swanlond, Richard le Leche, and William Bradwardine. Swanlond and Leche were prominent London surgeons, and were brought to court as consultants. John Salesbury may have begun service with Edward III. He treated Richard early in his reign. But little is known of his practice, except that he received several royal grants which provided him with an annual stipend of forty shillings. See: *T&H*, p. 423; *ibid.*, p. 188; *ibid.*, pp. 280–281; *ibid.*, pp. 387–388; CPR, 1388–1392, p. 453; CPR, 1391–1396, p. 398. For Le Leche, CPR, 1381–1385, p. 182. See too: Beck *Cutting Edge*, p. 55; CPR, 1377–1381, pp. 242, 244, 334, 603.

[99] Beck, *Cutting Edge*, pp. 55–56.

[100] *T&H*, pp. 123–124, 218–219.

[101] Beck, *Cutting Edge*, pp. 55–56, 76–78.

[102] CPR, 1385–1389, p. 215.

[103] South and Power, *Memorials of Surgery*, pp. 46–83; Beck, *Cutting Edge*, pp. 79–91.

[104] CPR, 1388–1392, p. 119.

counter-sued.[105] Three of these instances had medical overtones. As noted in Chapter Two, Nicholas sued a Southwark barber, who he alleged broke a service contract.[106] The barber filed a counter-suit, claiming that Bradmore never paid him. Nicholas also sued fellow surgeon Robert Fawkener, and was sued by and in turn counter-sued a Suffolk barber, all for breach of contract.[107] The latter suit was muddled when brother John became involved in a more serious case.[108] In 1408, he and another man were accused of smuggling 304 florins into the port of London without a license.[109]

Whatever their dark side, the Bradmores were first-class surgeons. The money they made as counterfeiters and smugglers was matched by their surgical incomes. Both held large tracts of land in and around London, and smatterings of property throughout the kingdom.[110] John was surgeon to the monks of Westminster Abbey.[111] The monks paid well and promptly, and had their choice of London surgeons; that they chose John Bradmore speaks well of him. John was also consulted by Henry IV, who rewarded him well. In 1408 he was made searcher of the port of London, an irony for a former smuggler.[112] The best testament to John's skills was his fame as a maker of surgical instruments. This was first noted in the 1380s, and explains his connection with the gold and silversmiths.[113] And this was what brought him to the attention of the Prince of Wales early in the fifteenth century, and convinced the Prince to include John in his retinue. According to Talbot: "Thomas Morstede reports that at the Battle of Shrewsbury he [John Brademore] extracted from the nose of Henry . . . the head of an arrow with an instrument of his own devising and healing took place in a matter of days."[114]

Yet this was just the beginning for Henry V. Henry was a superb

---

[105] For example, see CCR, 1396–1399, p. 209; CCR, 1399–1402, pp. 190, 419; CCR, 1402–1405, p. 182; CCR, 1409–1413, p. 99.

[106] CCR, 1405–1409, pp. 70, 81.

[107] CCR, 1409–1413, p. 134.

[108] CPR, 1408–1413, pp. 139, 154.

[109] *Ibid.* For similar instances, see CCR, 1399–1402, p. 199; CCR, 1392–1396, p. 488; CCR, 1402–1405, p. 182.

[110] These are summarized in *T&H*, pp. 123–124 and 218–219.

[111] E. A. Hammond, "The Westminster Abbey Infirmarers' Rolls as a Source of Medical History," *BHM*, 39, 1965, pp. 261–276.

[112] CCR, 1405–1409, p. 336; CPR, 1405–1408, p. 454.

[113] Beck, *Cutting Edge*, pp. 75–76. Also, see below, p. 234.

[114] *T&H*, p. 124.

quartermaster, and his campaigns to reconquer Normandy provided
him with the setting to show off his abilities.[115] He raised and equipped
a force of 8,000—2,000 men-at-arms, 6,000 archers and support personnel, and perhaps 1,500 ships to transport them.[116] Among the support-
ers were doctors, and when the subsidies he had got from Parliament
proved insufficient to pay them, he hocked the Crown jewels, leaving
some of them with Bradwardine and Morstede as security against payment of their wages.[117]

The records pertaining to the doctors are confusing.[118] Accounts in
Rymer suggest that Henry first raised a group of physicians, headed by
his personal doctor, Nicholas Colnet.[119] There is a detailed indenture
that lays out the conditions and payments of Colnet's service.[120] Colnet
was to have three archers to act as his bodyguard. If the expedition went
to Gascony, he was to receive a wage of forty marks a year, presumably
in addition to his normal wage as court physician.[121] If it went to northern France, a more dangerous prospect, he would get an additional shilling a day. Like Jordan of Canterbury two generations earlier, Colnet
was expected to treat just the king and his entourage. He seems to have
done well; Gask believes he "saved the lives of many English nobles,"
and Henry took him on campaign again in 1417.[122]

Chief surgeons Morstede and Bradwardine received pay equal to that
of Nicholas Colnet, an unusual scaling at a time when physicians were
considered superior practitioners, though explicable perhaps, given
Henry's pragmatism. Morstede, according to Rymer, got a "chariot"
and two sumpter horses to accompany his personal bodyguard of three

[115] For general reference see Gask, "Vicary's Predecessors," pp. 55–76; and Gask, "The
Medical Services of Henry the Fifth's Campaign of the Somme in 1415," pp. 94–102, in
his *Essays in the History of Medicine*; E. F. Jacob, *Henry V and the Invasion of France* (London:
Hodder and Stoughton, 1947); A. H. Burne, *The Agincourt War: A Military History of the
Latter Part of the Hundred Years War* (London: Eyre and Spottiswode, 1956); Keegan, *Face
of Battle*, pp. 78–116; Perroy, *Hundred Years War*, pp. 212–218; and Seward, *Hundred Years
War*, pp. 153–188.

[116] Jacob, *Henry V*, pp. 52–84.

[117] PRO, Exchequer Accounts, 101/48/3, membr. 2; CPR, 1441–1446, p. 394.

[118] Jacob, *Henry V*, pp. 52–84.

[119] *T&H*, pp. 220–222; Emden, *BRUO*, i, p. 469; Rymer, *Foedera*, p. 585 (Hiv,ii,116);
*ibid.*, p. 586 (Hiv,ii,127).

[120] Rymer, *Foedera*, p. 586 (Hiv,11,127).

[121] *Ibid.* See too *T&H*, pp. 387–388; Beck, *Cutting Edge*, pp. 58–60.

[122] Gask, "Medical Services," pp. 95–102.

archers.[123] How he raised his contingent, however, is not clear. It was his responsibility to recruit and assemble them at the general muster.[124] Further, Morstede was to receive his first quarter's wage in advance, with a few Crown jewels added as security. He seems to have used some of the jewels to hire his surgeons, but held the rest back. Like Henry, Morstede was a good organizer and leader. Henry wanted the best surgeons, and Morstede got them. We do not know just what argument he used, but he offered twelve pence a day and surely projected a picture of royal patronage if the expedition was successful.[125] Yet Morstede recognized that some of the best surgeons would still be reluctant to give up their safe and lucrative practices. He got royal authority to impress twelve surgeons, if necessary, and the power to fix their wages if they demanded more than he offered.[126]

Morstede convinced Henry to take apothecaries as well as physicians and surgeons.[127] All the doctors cooperated to lay in stores of medical supplies for the battlefield. In October, 1415, just before the fleet sailed, the physician Robert Benham was sent to Calais with part of the supplies.[128] They included forty pounds of verdigras, a balm for treating

[123] Rymer, *Foedera*, p. 586 (Hiv,11,116); (Hiv,11,123); (Hiv,11,127); p. 593 (Hiv,11,165).

[124] *T&H*, pp. 350–352; Beck, *Cutting Edge*, pp. 58–60.

[125] PRO, E101/48/3.

[126] Beck, *Cutting Edge*, p. 58. Morstede wrote: "To our most excellent and sovereign lord the king. Your humble, loyal and faithful servant, Thomas Morstede, surgeon, beseeches you that, of your benign grace, it may please you to grant letter under your private seal to your chancellor of England, to cause to be delivered to your said supplicant letters of commission, under your great seal, by virtue of which he may have permission to engage both from within and from outside franchises, twelve persons of his profession, at his own choice, to go in his company and to be of service to you, most sovereign lord, on your expedition.

"Again, it may please you, of your benign grace, to cause indentures to be drawn up, under your privy seal, between yourself, most sovereign lord, and the aforementioned Thomas, by virtue of which the said Thomas shall be obliged to serve you, most excellent lord, on the said expedition, as at men-of-arms, taking the same wages and rewards as are taken by others of his rank, with fifteen men in his retinue, of whom three shall be archers and others men of his profession, each of them receiving the same wages as are taken by other archers going on the same expedition; and the said indenture form as is drawn up for your esquires."

[127] Leslie G. Matthews, *The Royal Apothecaries* (London: The Wellcome Historical Medical Library, 1965), pp. 42–43. The petition is reprinted in its entirety in Allmand, *Society at War*, pp. 64–66.

[128] Matthews, *Royal Apothecaries*, pp. 42–43.

wounds, and forty pounds of *sal armouiac*, to act as a corrosive to keep
wounds open when that was deemed necessary.[129] It is significant that
the apothecaries acted mainly as procurers and dispensers of the drugs,
while the surgeons prescribed and applied them. Surgeons also did most
of the dressing of wounds, bandaging and wrapping. This, of course,
was in addition to their traditional and principal task: the extraction of
arrows and missiles and surgery on the wounded.[130]

As Thomas Morstede was to supply his team of twelve surgeons, so
William Bradwardine was to present nine.[131] There are no writs or petitions to or from Bradwardine, and we can only assume he went about
assembling his team in the same way as did Morstede. This is suggested
by a post-Agincourt writ to both men, which asks them once again to
raise surgeons for the 1417 French campaign:

> Know ye that we have appointed to you cojointly and severally surgeons
> and other workmen to take and provide without delay for the making of
> certain instruments necessary and fitting for your mystery [The London
> Fellowship of Surgeons] such as may be required for our present campaign
> beyond the sea, wherever they conveniently be found as well as within the
> city of London and elsewhere. And therefore we warn you that you may
> diligently attend to and execute these premises in the manner aforesaid.
> But we grant to all and every sheriff, mayor, constable and other officers,
> our servants and lieges, as well within the liberty as without, that they
> should consult and assist you as is fitting, according to the command which
> are to you and each of you entrusted.[132]

The individual surgeons of the Agincourt army are listed in two exchequer rolls.[133] Not much is known about most of them, though all
seem to have come from London.[134] Both arrays are listed in Table 4.1.
Bradwardine's were ranked, though it is not clear just what the rankings
represented. Philip Brichford was a prominent London surgeon, and
may have served at the court of Henry IV.[135] He was involved in a law-

---

[129] *Ibid.*

[130] Talbot, *Medicine in Medieval England*, pp. 206–207.

[131] PRO, Exchequer Accounts, E101/48/3; and E101/407/10; CPR, 1416–1422, p. 31. 145. PRO, Exchequer Accounts, E101/48/3; and E101/407/10.

[132] Talbot, in several references in *Medicine in Medieval England*, pp. 206–208, and in various biographical sketches in *T&H*, believes that some of the surgeons were conscripted.

[133] *T&H*, p. 256.

[134] Gask, "Vicary's Predecessor," pp. 70–72.

[135] *BRUO*, i, p. 469.

TABLE 4.1: Surgeons of the Agincourt Campaign

---

1. *The staff of Thomas Morstede—twelve surgeons and three archers*

| | |
|---|---|
| Reginald Axid | William Hinkley |
| Thomas Barber | Roger King |
| Philip Brichford | John Leche |
| Edward Broomfeld | Thomas London |
| Henry Butler | Richard Preston |
| Robert Hinkley | Thomas Ward |

2. *The staff of William Bradwardine—nine surgeons, ranked, possibly as a function of their skill*

| | |
|---|---|
| Matthew Bower (7) | Walter Hales (6) |
| Philip Buenles (3) | Stephan Lambe (4) |
| Richard Canterbury (8) | Richard Salesburgh (2) |
| Richard Cleobury (9) | John Smith (5) |
| Richard Dykes (1) | |

---

suit over some London property, and was important enough to be addressed as yeoman in 1410.[136] The Hinkleys were London citizens and probably brothers.[137] Richard Preston helped arrange a number of mainprises in the city.[138] Walter Hales continued in Henry's service after Agincourt, then became surgeon to the king of Scotland.[139] There is nothing on the others. But those who survived the battle—and apparently they all did—benefited from royal largesse, especially in the first flush of victory, and, of course, from their medical experiences. Most of them probably went on—if they were not already—to become surgeons in the London Fellowship, and participants in the foundation of the College of Medicine. And some of them returned to France in 1416 and 1417.[140]

There is evidence of non-royal doctors at Agincourt. William Bosan was commissioned by the Earl of Shrewsbury to serve as his personal surgeon.[141] He was paid forty marks a year, a wage equal to those of Colnet, Morstede, and Bradwardine, and was allowed to hire a bodyguard of two archers.[142] This was a traditional practice among the great lords,

---

[136] CCR, 1409–1413, p. 204; CPR, 1408–1413, p. 103; CPR, 1414–1416, p. 147.

[137] *T&H*, pp. 296–404.

[138] *Ibid.*, p. 282.

[139] *Ibid.*, p. 367.

[140] Beck, *Cutting Edge*, pp. 60–62.

[141] *T&H*, p. 387.

[142] *Ibid.*

and it is likely that many of Shrewsbury's peers had their own surgeons. Henry himself may have had personal doctors in addition to Colnet, for he usually traveled with a physician named Peter Henewar.[143] Henewar did accompany the king to Normandy in 1419. Later in the year he returned to England, only to be sent for once again.[144]

If the records on most of the Agincourt physicians are spotty, those for the chief surgeons, Morstede and Bradwardine, are quite full. Both were model doctors, and Morstede was, next to John Arderne, the most prominent English surgeon of the later middle ages. He began serving Henry IV in 1411, when he already had a thriving practice.[145] His personal fortune was discussed in Chapter Two.[146] Yet his financial success never impinged upon his surgical skills. He was such a good surgeon that the archival records, which often detail only the finances of doctors, have as much information on Morstede's professional life as they do his business dealings. He was a long-time master of the Fellowship of Surgeons and a founder of the College of Medicine.[147] He treated Henry V throughout the reign, and was retained by the advisers to Henry VI. When Henry VI came of age he kept Morstede.[148] Morstede trained dozens of apprentices, had a large library, books from which he lent out to other surgeons, and regularly made charitable donations to the sick, poor, and hospitals. His *A Fair Book of Surgery* remained the standard surgical text throughout the fifteenth century.[149] His career, even more than John Arderne's, is an example of how far a successful surgeon could go—a London practice, service at court and with the king's armies abroad, public office holder, teacher, author, and benefactor.

William Bradwardine's career was nearly as spectacular.[150] He began royal service two decades earlier, when Richard II included him in his

---

[143] *Ibid.*, p. 248.

[144] *Ibid.*

[145] See above, p. 66, and as an example, CCR, 1409–1413, p. 229.

[146] CFR, 1413–1422, p. 35. See too: H. L. Gray, "Incomes from Land in England," *English Historical Review*, 49, 1934, p. 637; and Sylvia L. Thrupp, *The Merchant Class of Medieval London* (Ann Arbor, Mich.: University of Michigan Press, 1962), pp. 260–261.

[147] L–B K, p. 30.

[148] CCR, 1447–1454, pp. 89–90.

[149] Beck, *Cutting Edge*, pp. 105–119, argues that the text survives in B.M. Harl. Ms. 1736, and reprints parts of it. Talbot, "Medicine," p. 426, n. 47, claims he was first. See below, pp. 230–235.

[150] *T&H*, pp. 387–388.

train to Ireland.[151] Bradwardine distinguished himself, was addressed subsequently as esquire, and by 1397 was receiving an annuity of over £30.[152] The change in dynasties did not affect his career at court or his London practice. He concentrated on the latter, which in the reign of Henry IV, with his preoccupation with foreign physicians, must have been a wise decision.[153] And, as noted, Bradwardine caught the eye of the Prince of Wales, who as king in 1415 made him surgeon serjeant.[154] He was granted land in London, throughout England, and in Ireland and received a number of royal offices and regular annuities. His only career failure seems to have come from his tenure at one of these posts, the wardenship of Marshalsea Prison.[155] Bradwardine was appointed in 1421, but apparently had no aptitude for it, for within a year twelve prisoners escaped. He did not go after them, as was the custom, and his appointment was revoked.[156]

By contrast, his medical career continued to be one success after another. In addition to royal service, he was a member of the Fellowship of Surgeons and the College of Medicine, and an expert witness in the alleged malpractice case of John Harrow, himself an important member of the Fellowship and the College.[157] With Morstede, he was entrusted by Henry V to hold some of the Crown jewels, pawned to help finance the Agincourt expedition. Indeed, the fact that Morstede and Bradwardine complied with Henry V got them in trouble with Henry VI, and in 1445 the two surgeons had to receive a royal pardon—Bradwardine's posthumous—to clear all suspicion of incorrect behavior thirty years earlier.[158] Like Morstede, Bradwardine was a model surgeon, in some ways the rule by the mid-fifteenth century rather than the exception.

Richard Wells and Simon Rolf also served Henry V.[159] Neither seems to have been at Agincourt or on subsequent expeditions, perhaps because they were barber-surgeons. But both were respected, had busy practices, and were appointed by London and royal authorities to adjudicate malpractice cases in the city. They were supervisors of the prac-

---

[151] CPR, 1391–1396, p. 473.
[152] CPR, 1396–1399, p. 204.
[153] See Gask, "Medical Services," pp. 94–102.
[154] T&H, p. 387.
[155] CCR, 1419–1422, p. 214.
[156] CCR, 1422–1429, pp. 83, 134.
[157] Cal. Plea Mem. Rolls, 1413–1437, pp. 174–175.
[158] CPR, 1441–1446, p. 394.
[159] T&H, pp. 283–284; ibid., pp. 325–326.

tice of barbery in London.[160] Wells and Rolf represent the best of the barber-surgeons, those who realized the importance of the quality of medical practice as well as corporate gain. While they were excluded from military service because of their affiliation, their success brought change. Two generations later most military surgeons came from the mystery of barber-surgeons.

Two other surgeons were prominent during Henry V's reign. William Stalworth was the chief surgeon during the early part of Henry VI's reign; he received his training and got his first taste of battlefield surgery under Henry V.[161] He may even have been at Agincourt as a last-minute replacement for Reginald Axid.[162] Stalworth's star rose throughout the 1420s, and his London practice grew. In 1430 he was given license to reside in Henry VI's household, and was put on the royal payroll at a fee of six pence a day.[163] Later in the year he was allowed £20 to hire four additional surgeons and collect medicines and supplies in order to accompany Henry VI to France.[164] He continued as royal surgeon until his death in 1446, benefitting in the usual ways.

Even more clearly in the royal, military, surgical tradition was John Harrow.[165] With Morstede and Bradwardine, Harrow ranks as one of the most accomplished surgeons of the fifteenth century. He was, as noted in Chapter Two, a long-time master of the Fellowship of Surgeons, a supervisor of the College of Medicine, a regular adjudicator of

---

[160] It read: "Well and faithfully [were Rolf and Wells] to watch over and oversee all manner of barbers practicing the art of surgery and within the liberty [of London] dwelling; to maintain and observe rule and ordinances of the craft or practice aforesaid; no one to spare, for love, favor, gain or hate; diligently without concealment to present unto the chamberlain of the said city, for the time being such defaults as they might find; at all times when duly required thereto, well and faithfully; to examine bruises, hurts and other infirmities, without asking anything for their trouble; and what they should find, at their discretion, when duly required thereto, distinctly to certify to the mayor and alderman of the said city, for the time being, as also faithfully to conduct themselves from thenceforth in the future; and all other things to do and perform which of right are befitted or requisite for the master or overseers of such practice to do." See Riley, *Memorials of London*, p. 606; L–B I, p. 135.

[161] *T&H*, pp. 415–416.

[162] *Ibid.*, p. 268; PRO, Various Acts, E101/48/3, membr. 2. Axid's name is crossed out in the muster.

[163] Rymer, *Foedera*, p. 648 (Hiv,iv,157).

[164] *Ibid.*

[165] *T&H*, pp. 154–155.

malpractice cases, and very rich.[166] It was fitting that in 1435 Henry's
advisers, asked him to recruit a medical staff to sail with an army going
to France:

> Commission to John Harrow, surgeon, to hire at a competent salary six
> surgeons or barbers, sufficiently erudite in the mystery, in the City of Lon-
> don and the suburbs thereof, or in the town of Southwark, for the relief of
> the King's lieges going with Humphrey, Duke of Gloucester, to the rescue
> of Calais.[167]

The army was raised, and the surgeons saw action. Henceforth, surgeons continued to be linked to the war in France, which in turn remained the key to their financial and professional success. And they continued to be recruited from London, a reflection of the dominant role
city practitioners played.

Henry VI was the least warlike of late medieval kings, and seldom
went on campaign. This did not, however, affect the quality of surgery.
By the mid-1430s, virtually all the London fellows had seen service with
Henry V or one of his brothers. The best practitioners of the 1430s,
1440s, and 1450s were experienced veterans with clinical backgrounds,
and the quality of medieval English surgery was never higher. In addition to Stalworth and Harrow, a few others stand out. One was Michel
Belwell, a Frenchman, who accompanied Henry VI on several trips to
the continent.[168] John Corby, exonerated with Harrow in the famous
1424 malpractice suit, was the third of the seventeen signatories of the
1435 regulations of the Fellowship, a prominent surgeon from an important family of surgeons.[169] He treated Henry VI, and remained a
consultant.[170] So too did John Hatfield, who appears second in the regulations, and Robert Wilton who was fifth.[171] Both may have been in
France with the Harrow expedition of 1435.[172]

[166] L-B K, p. 15; *ibid.*, p. 143; CPR, 1422–1429, p. 549. Harrow himself was accused of
malpractice. See *Cal. Plea Mem. Rolls*, 1413–1437, pp. 174–175.

[167] CPR, 1429–1436, p. 610.

[168] *T&H*, p. 215; Rymer, *Foedera*, p. 671 (Hv,i,117).

[169] *T&H*, p. 136; Guildhall Ms. 5244, f. 23v.

[170] *Cal. Plea Mem. Rolls*, 1413–1437, pp. 174–175.

[171] *T&H*, pp. 155–156; *ibid.*, p. 305; Guildhall Ms. 5244.

[172] CPR, 1429–1436, p. 610. Henry VI had three other important surgeons. Thomas Al-
denham served around 1450. See *T&H*, p. 32. Robert Warren and John Marshall were
part of the medical group called in to care for Henry at the time of his mental breakdown
in 1454. Marshall was the more prominent, addressed as yeoman surgeon to Warren's ser-

Like the reign of Henry V, that of Edward IV represents a milestone in the development of English surgery. But if Henry and his military surgeons represent an ascent, Edward's reign marks the beginning of a decline. Edward was bellicose enough, and spent much of the first ten years of his kingship in battle. But these were the battles of the Wars of the Roses, generally fought on a smaller scale with less-well-organized forces than those of the expeditions to France. Despite claims to the contrary, there is no evidence of medical corps in any of the armies at any of the battles, even the greatest of them, such as Towton.[173]

When his dynastic problems were behind him, Edward did reopen the French wars. In 1475 he organized an army after the model of Henry V, complete with a medical corps.[174] This expedition was crucial in the history of English medicine. In the 1430s and 1440s the best surgeons, members of the London Fellowship, had been war veterans. By 1470 these veterans were dead or retired. Increasingly, the new Fellows were less innovative and receptive to experiment and change. Edward's campaign offered the opportunity to gain the experience that had made earlier surgeons so skilled.

Edward IV was a good planner. He raised between 1,100 and 1,200 men-at-arms, 10,000–11,000 archers, and perhaps 1,000 technical and support personnel, including the doctors.[175] He got lavish financial support from Parliament, and set sail in July with what has been called "the finest, largest, best appointed force that had ever left England."[176] Like Henry V, Edward took along his personal physician, James Frise, and

jeant surgeon. Both apparently remained in Henry's service until he was dethroned. See: *T&H*, pp. 168, 305; and *Proceedings and Ordinances of the Privy Council*, ed. N. H. Nicholas (London: Eyre and Spottiswode, 1835), p. 146.

[173] Beck, *Cutting Edge*, pp. 14, 55, makes the claim. For an account of the armies and battles see: Charles Ross, *The Wars of the Roses* (London: Thames and Hudson, 1976), pp. 109–177; and John Gillingham, *The Wars of the Roses* (Baton Rouge, La.: University of Louisiana Press, 1981), pp. 32–50.

[174] F. A. Barnard, *Edward IV's French Expedition of 1475: The Leaders and Their Badges* (Dursley: Gloucester Reprints, 1975), pp. 15–46. This is a transcription of the College of Arms Ms. 2 M, 16.

[175] Charles Ross, *Edward IV* (Berkeley, Cal.: University of California Press, 1974), pp. 220–224; Barnard, *Edward IV's French Expedition*, pp. 145–146; J. R. Lander, "The Hundred Years War and Edward IV's 1475 Campaign in France," in Arthur J. Slavin, ed., *Tudor Men and Institutions: Studies in English Law and Government* (Baton Rouge, La.: Louisiana State University Press, 1972), pp. 70–100.

[176] Ross, *Edward IV*, p. 218.

paid him two shillings a day.[177] This was twice the wage he paid any of
his surgeons, even William Hobbes, in contrast with the equal-pay policy of Henry V. Frise's role was to care for the king and his entourage;
the surgeons would treat the troops. In the tradition of Henry V, two
teams were organized. The first was led by William Hobbes, and was
assigned to front-line duty (Table 4.2). All but Hobbes, who also got a
cash bonus, were paid a shilling a day.[178] The second, led by Richard
Feld, was to wait in reserve, and its members were paid six pence a day.
They were also designated as "assistants," and all save Feld, a barber-
surgeon, were barber-tonsors.[179] And everyone went eagerly; there is no
evidence of coercion, as there was in 1415.

But Edward's army, formidable as it was, did not fight. Edward and
Louis XI of France negotiated an agreement; Edward returned to England, and despite some later threats never sailed for France again. The
only affliction the English troops picked up was gonorrhea.[180] The doctors would enjoy royal favor and privilege as had their predecessors.
They had answered the assembly to muster and traveled with the king,
and Edward was quick to show his gratitude. They served at court and

TABLE 4.2: Surgeons of Edward IV's 1475 French Expedition

| Name | Position | Pay | Affiliation |
|------|----------|-----|-------------|
| Richard Brightmore | primary | 12d | Barbers |
| Richard Chamber | primary | 12d | Barbers |
| William Coke | secondary | 6d | Not known |
| Simon Cole | primary | 12d | Barbers |
| Thomas Collard | primary | 12d | Barbers |
| John Dennis | secondary | 6d | Not known |
| Richard Elstie | primary | 12d | Barbers |
| Richard Feld | primary | 12d | Barbers |
| William Hobbes | primary | 12d | Surg. & Barb. |
| Alexander Ledell | secondary | 6d | Not known |
| John Smith | primary | 12d | Barbers |
| Richard Smythys | secondary | 6d | Not known |
| John Stanley | secondary | 6d | Not known |

[177] *T&H*, pp. 96–98; Gask, "Vicary's Predecessors," pp. 71–75.

[178] Barnard, *Edward IV's French Expedition*, p. 145.

[179] *Ibid.*; *T&H*, p. 278.

[180] *The Brut: Chronicles of England*, ed. F.W.D. Brie (London: Oxford University Press,
1960), ii, p. 604.

became the leading surgeons in London. But they did not get the clinical experience of the battlefield that so distinguished the surgeons of the first part of the century. And, significantly, the only surgeon of the Fellowship willing to leave his practice and go to war was William Hobbes. The rest of Edward's surgeons were barbers. This came, too, at a time when the barbers were incorporating, and the king was a member of the barber-surgeons' mystery. In the past, the surgeons scoffed at the barbers' organization by flaunting their superior medical skills. By 1470 the professional gap between surgeons and barber-surgeons was disappearing.[181]

As for the individuals, some details of the career of William Hobbes have been discussed.[182] Hobbes, who ended his career as a royal physician, began it by following his father as a royal surgeon.[183] His techniques, even as a physician, remained those of the surgeon. Hobbes owned a copy of Guy de Chauliac's *Surgery*—he claimed the book "belonged to his art"—and followed its practice.[184] In 1470 he was styled "principal surgeon of the king's body"; and three years later as the "trusty and well beloved servant . . . surgeon of our body."[185] He had livery in the London Barber's Company and the Fellowship of Surgeons, and was an officer of both guilds. Hobbes studied at Oxford and Cambridge, was warden of St. Mary Bethlehem in London, served all three Yorkist kings, and by 1484 was drawing an annual salary of £40.[186] Contemporaries regarded him as the finest surgeon of his day.[187] But this must be placed in context. Hobbes's reputation was made in comparison with his colleagues. It is unlikely that he had the skills of Morstede, Bradwardine, Harrow, or Arderne.

Richard Feld, the other chief surgeon, first served the king when he

---

[181] This is, of course, a crucial point, and will be discussed subsequently. Perhaps the surgeons, not coerced as in 1415, did not want to go. Perhaps the wages were too low. Perhaps they forgot the professional uses of military surgery. Or perhaps Hobbes convinced the king of the merit of the barber-surgeons

[182] See above, p. 67. See too *T&H*, pp. 401–402.

[183] Father John Hobbes was distinguished in his own right, a royal surgeon from the 1440s. He owned a great deal of property in London. See: Guildhall Ms. 9171/5, "Sharp," f. 344; CCR, 1468–1476, p. 68; *T&H*, p. 156.

[184] He got this from his father. See Guildhall Ms. 9171/5, f. 344.

[185] CPR, 1467–1477, p. 211; *Rot. Parl.*, vi, f. 83b.

[186] CPR, 1476–1485, p. 166.

[187] Hence the praise, documented in note 185; and Myers, *Household of Edward IV*, pp. 124–125.

was still the Earl of March.[188] He began receiving annuities as soon as Edward took the throne, and was granted an apartment in the palace at Westminster.[189] He was appointed to the lucrative role of forester of King's Bere, near Winchester.[190] Yet there are no records that describe his medical skills; he had no military experience, did not go to a university, and was not an author. He was, at least initially, a barber, and his reputation, like Hobbes', was remarkable only in comparison with other barbers.

Of the others on the 1475 expedition, Richard Estie was the best known and perhaps, at least in the "bookish" sense, the best educated.[191] Estie, who styled himself as a "yeoman surgeon for the body of our sovereign lord," was Upper Warden of the Mystery of Barber-Surgeons of the London Barbers' Company in 1459, and again in 1463–1464.[192] He was well read, and left seven books of surgery to the barbers' library. He was a close friend of the Cambridge-educated Frise, was rich, and his son became a friar.[193] Richard Chamber was warden of the barber-surgeons in 1477–1478, 1482–1483, and 1486–1487.[194] He was good enough to continue serving Henry VII for twenty years.[195] And he was rich enough to have his will proved in the Prerogative Court of Canterbury.[196]

Richard Brightmore was also a warden of the barber-surgeons, in his case in 1467–1468[197]. Simon Cole held the same position in 1478 and 1487, while Thomas Collard did so in 1465 and perhaps 1485.[198] Collard, like Estie, was a scholar. He bequeathed to his son a number of books, two of which, Gaddesden's *Rosa Medicinae* and a surgery by Constantine the African, were important medical texts.[199] The son, who

---

[188] *T&H*, p. 278; Myers, *Household of Edward IV*, pp. 124–125, 245.

[189] CPR, 1461–1467, pp. 130, 176–177.

[190] CPR, 1476–1485, pp. 159, 251.

[191] *T&H*, pp. 277–278. He was also known as Richard Esty. See Beck, *Cutting Edge*, p. 165.

[192] Young, *Annals of the Barber-Surgeons*, p. 3.

[193] Guildhall Ms. 9171/6, "Wilde," f. 192[v]. *Ibid*. See Beck, *Cutting Edge*, p. 165, for a transaction.

[194] *T&H*, p. 276.

[195] *Ibid*.

[196] PRO, PCC, "Holgrave," f. 7.

[197] *T&H*, p. 275

[198] *Ibid*., p. 322; *ibid*., p. 337.

[199] Guildhall Ms. 9171/6, "Wilde," f. 326[v].

went on to become a surgeon, also received "all [his father's] instruments, be they of iron and steel" and other surgical equipment.[200] If the
son were to take up another profession, the books and tools were to go
to the Barbers' Company.[201] Hence, barber though he was, Thomas
Collard was distinguished among his colleagues for his interest in the
theoretical aspects of surgery and precision tools. So too were John
Smith and John Dennis, both of whom were authors.[202] But none had
battlefield experience.

What of the members of the Fellowship, of whom only Hobbes
served in 1475? A few served at court. There were the Dagvilles, father
John and sons John II and Thomas.[203] They were adept enough to develop a new surgical technique.[204] One of their fellows, Robert Ferbras—who like Hobbes and perhaps John Dagville II took livery in the
barber-surgeons' mystery—also pioneered new techniques.[205] Anthony
Lupayne treated both Edward IV and Richard III, and in 1483 was
granted a lifetime annuity worth one hundred shillings.[206] John Peerson
was granted an inspeximus and confirmation of privilege in 1512, which
stated that he had been surgeon to Edward and Richard.[207] Peerson was
a master surgeon and citizen of London by 1426, a fact which suggests
an extraordinarily long career.[208] And William Kirby, also a London citizen and master surgeon, served the Yorkists.[209] Like Peerson, he was
granted an inspeximus and confirmation of rights and privileges in 1512
that confirmed earlier rights.

Yet none of these most notables had military experience, or enough
clinical practice from other sources to provide them the skills a master
surgeon needed. The best of them, like Hobbes, Estie, and Collard,
were students of texts, like the physicians. Had the surgeons or, more
accurately, the barber-surgeons of the 1475 campaign, treated the battlefield wounded, they might have approached the skills of their prede-

[200] *Ibid*. The will is paraphrased in Beck, *Cutting Edge*, pp. 166–167.
[201] *Ibid*.
[202] *T&H*, pp. 140–141; *ibid*., p. 182.
[203] *T&H*, p. 139; *ibid*., pp. 139–140; *ibid*., pp. 337–338; Beck, *Cutting edge*, pp. 68–70, 90–91, 101–102, 124–126, 138–143, 160–161.
[204] Beck, *Cutting Edge*, p. 126.
[205] *T&H*, pp. 295–296; Young, *Annals of the Barber-Surgeons*, p. 61; Guildhall Ms. 9826.
[206] *T&H*, p. 18.
[207] *T&H*, pp. 175–176.
[208] *LPFD*, 1509–1517, p. 535.
[209] He was also known as William Kirkby; *T&H*, p. 405.

cessors. But they did not, and surgeons and surgery began a period of decline. Fewer members of the Fellowship achieved prominence, while more barber-surgeons made their way to court. Since all this coincided with the revival of physic, the consequences for surgery were disastrous.

Richard III was an active soldier; had he sat longer on the throne he might have revived the medical-military tradition. But he spent most of his short reign trying to hold it, and there is no evidence that surgeons played important roles in any of his expeditions. His successor, Henry VII, was uninterested in grandiose expeditions or spending money. He had several court surgeons, including carryovers John Peerson, William Kirby, and Richard Chamber, though he rejected the best of Edward's old surgeons, the ardent Yorkist William Hobbes.[210] The most interesting was William Altoftes, who came into service shortly after Henry's accession.[211] By 1487 he was receiving an annuity of over £26. He served Henry throughout the reign, and then continued, at least part-time, under Henry VIII. By the time of his death in 1521 Altoftes was living in the country and styling himself the king's gentleman and serjeant.[212] This was unusual. Most surgeons remained doctors throughout their lives, even when they became rich and landed. Most regarded themselves as bourgeois, and encouraged their sons to follow them. But Henry VII's surgeons were not like their predecessors; they served at court, not in the field.

Henry VIII again called surgeons to battle. J. J. Scarisbrick, claimed Henry wanted "the renewal of the Hundred Years War."[213] Whether or not this was the case, Henry did organize an expedition in 1512–1513, and did it well. Alliances were made with the Spanish and the Pope, and

[210] In 1482 Hobbes was sent by the king "to the north to attend upon the Duke of Gloucester." [*Issues of the Exchequer, Henry III—Henry VI*, as cited in *T&H*, p. 402n]. When Richard became king, he raised Hobbes's stipend to £40 a year. [CPR, 1476–1485, p. 374.]

[211] *T&H*, p. 276. Queen Elizabeth had her own surgeons, including the Londoner Richard Bullock. For Bullock, see *T&H*, pp. 380–381.

[212] PRO, PCC, "Maynwarying," f. 20. It is paraphrased in Beck, *Cutting Edge*, pp. 167–168.

[213] The sources for the expedition are mostly in the *LPFDs*, as will be cited, and Thomas Vicary, *Anatomie of the Bodie of Man*, eds. F. J. and P. Furnivall (London: EETS, e.s., 1888), pp. 236–237. Secondary sources are: Keevil, *Medicine in the Navy*, i, pp. 58–60; J. J. Scarisbrick, *Henry VIII* (Berkeley, Cal.: University of California Press, 1968), pp. 21–40; and C. G. Cruickshank, *Army Royal: Henry VIII's Invasion of France, 1513* (Oxford: Oxford University Press, 1969).

a joint Anglo-Spanish expeditionary force was landed in Acquitaine in 1512 as preparation for a larger invasion of northern France the following year. Thousands of suits of armor were ordered from Germany and Italy, and a dozen new cannon were cast.[214] An army of 40,000 was planned, and Henry set about building a fleet to transport it.[215] A drydock was enlarged at Plymouth, another repaired at Portsmouth, and dockyards built at Woolwich and Deptford.[216] Henry personally visited the yards several times in the spring of 1513 to check on progress, and the result was a fleet such "as was never seen in Christendom."[217] It consisted of sixty ships, some already the king's, others commandeered from merchants and privateers, others still newly repaired or built, each allegedly capable of carrying up to 250 fighting men, plus mariners.[218]

Henry outfitted his ships with surgeons, something of a departure from tradition.[219] Soldiers had been provided with surgeons since at least the thirteenth century, but sailors were expected to care for their own. There were doctors called sea-surgeons, who sometimes accompanied naval and merchants' vessels. These sea-surgeons generally came from or tried to affiliate with the London Barbers' Company, whence they were called "foreign brothers."[220] They could even practice in London if they paid an admissions fee and monthly taxes. But Edward I, Edward III, Henry V, and Edward IV did not take them when they crossed the Channel. As Keevil remarked:

> . . . the English traditional view was that a surgeon was only useful in battles; seamen were not fighting men and should not get wounded in the course of their proper duties; if soldiers were carried and a sea battle ensued, the provision of surgeons was their own concern.[221]

It is difficult to tell from the Exchequer Accounts how Henry's surgeons were hired or should be classified. On one hand, they were taken to treat the troops; on the other, some were called sea-surgeons. Perhaps they

[214] *LPFD*, i, #1046, p. 511.

[215] *Ibid.*, i, #2757, pp. 1,128–1,129.

[216] *Ibid.*, i, #1161, p. 547.

[217] *Ibid.*, i, ii, #2842, p. 1,235.

[218] *Ibid.* Also, see Keevil, *Medicine and the Navy*, i, p. 20.

[219] Keevil, *Medicine and the Navy*, i, p. 20.

[220] Young, *Annals of the Barber-Surgeons*, p. 258; Dobson and Walker, *Barbers and Barber-Surgeons*, pp. 47–48.

[221] Keevil, *Medicine in the Navy*, i, p. 20.

served in both capacities, but in any case English surgeons again had the chance to pick up battlefield experience.

The surviving accounts for twenty-five ships in the fleet show that they carried thirty-nine surgeons (Table 4.3).[222] This was just part of the medical staff, for records suggest that many lords and even captains commissioned private doctors to accompany them. Lord Bergevenny, for example, took John Yan, a barber-surgeon from Chelmsford.[223] William Barber, alias William Scarlett, a London barber, went to war in the company of captain Ralph Ascue.[224] These private commissions and service help explain a January, 1514, statute that protected the surgeons by carefully distinguishing them from the combatants.[225] It also extended another privilege: ". . . discharging surgeons from being constables, or taking any office requiring the bearing of arms, they being unharnessed in the field, according to the law of arms."[226] With this protection added to the prospect for spoils and royal favor should the expedition be successful, many surgeons must have been eager to go.

There is information about the surgeons and the practice of medicine in Henry's fleet. Some of it comes from the recent salvage of one of the ships, the *Mary Rose*, and identifies the surgeon's tools.[227] The *Mary Rose* was built for the 1513 expedition and successfully sailed the Channel. But it went down in 1545, either from French gunners, poor English sailors, or design defects, and remained submerged—and intact—for over four hundred years. In 1982 a barber-surgeon's chest was recovered. It contained sixty-four medical items, including jars of ointments; drug flasks; razors; a pewter bowl for bloodletting; a mortar and pestle; a chafing dish to hold lighted charcoal, used for cautery; the wooden handle of a surgical tool, probably a saw for amputation; a brass syringe with an eight-inch, hollow needle, probably used for extracting bladder stones or for treatment of gonorrhea; and a wooden mallet and metal helmet for anesthetizing the patient.[228]

[222] The tables have been assembled from PRO, Exchequer Accounts E101/56/10.

[223] *T&H*, p. 197; *LPFD*, i, #1836, pp. 838–839.

[224] *LPFD*, ii, #2863, p. 1247.

[225] *Ibid.*, #2590, p. 1135.

[226] *Ibid.*

[227] See the interesting and well-illustrated articles in *National Geographic*, May, 1983: Peter Miller, "Legacy from the Deep: Henry VIII's Lost Warship," pp. 647–652; and Margaret Ruler, "The Search for Mary Rose," pp. 654–675.

[228] *Ibid.*, pp. 654–675.

TABLE 4.3: Surgeons of Henry VIII's 1513–1514 French Expedition

*With the King:*
   1. John Veyrier
   2. Marcellus de la More (wage of 6d/day)
   3. William Forest

On the *Gabriell Riall*: 255 soldiers, 270 mariners, 30 gunners.
   4. William Brown (wage 10/ per day, later master surgeons 13/4)
   5. Thomas Morison, apprentice surgeon, (10/ per month)

On the *Henry Hampton*:
   6. Christopher Bird (10s)
   7. Christopher Prentice (10/)
   8. Henry Baldwin (10/)

On the *Lizard*: 40 soldiers, 75 mariners, 8 gunners.
   9. Christopher Dagnall (10/)

On the *Matthew Craddock*; 67 soldiers, 202 mariners, 10 gunners.
   10. Davy Johns (10/)

On the *Margaret Bonaventur*:
   11. Henry Browning (10/)

On the *Mary George*: 70 soldiers, 120 mariners, 20 gunners.
   12. Henry Capron (10/)
   13. Robert Hanson (10)

On the *Mary Brixham*:
   14. Henry Dickenson, called chief surgeon (10/)

On the *Katherine Fortaleza*: 160 soldiers, 200 mariners, 20 gunners.
   15. Henry Rippon (10/)
   16. John Knott, the Elder (13/4)
   17. John Knott, the Younger (10/)
   18. M. Symond (10/)
   19. William Ashwell (10/)

On the *Barbara of Greenwich*: 150 soldiers, 160 mariners, 20 gunners.
   20. Henry Woodcook (10/)

On the *Nicholas Draper*:
   21. Hugh Dyer (10/)

On the *Christ*: 61 soldiers, 90 mariners, 10 gunners.
   22. Jasper Adrian (10/)

On the *Peter Pomergarnett*: 143 soldiers, 160 mariners, 20 gunners.
   23. John Baker (10/)
   24. William Elvis (10/)

On the *Mary and John*: 70 soldiers, 80 mariners, 10 gunners.
   25. John Barber (10/)

On the *Mary James*: 70 soldiers, 120 mariners, 10 gunners.

26. John Canon, assistant surgeon (10/)
27. Robert Marshall (13/4)

On the *Christopher Davy*: 52 soldiers, 75 mariners, 5 gunners.

28. Lambert Mayre (10/)

On *Great Nicholas*: 130 soldiers, 150 mariners, 15 gunners.

29. Nicholas Grossen (10/)
30. Robert Smith (10/)

On the *John the Baptist*: 140 soldiers, 150 mariners, 15 gunners.

31. Robert Mestylden (13/4)
32. Rowland Clenell, Mestylden's servant, probably a surgeon to judge from the wages (10/)

On the *Antony Montrego*:

33. Robert Shene (10/)

On the *Mary Rose*: 150 soldiers, 200 mariners, 20 gunners.

34. Robert Simson, master surgeon (13/4)
35. Henry Young, assistant (10/)

On the *Trinity of Bristol*:

36. Robert Waterford (10/)

On the *Less Bark*: 171 soldiers, 80 mariners, 10 gunners.

37. Thomas Henbery (10/)

On the *Mary Toppesham*:

38. William Nowell (10/)

On the *Maudeline of Dover*:

9. Christopher Dagnall, who was transferred from the *Lizard*.

On the *Sancho de Gara*:

12. Henry Capron, who was transferred from the *Mary George*.

On the *Trinity Sovereign*: 299 soldiers, 260 mariners, 40 gunners.

39. Garet Ferrers (Ferris), master surgeon (13/4)

TOTALS:

25 ships
39 surgeons, 38 if Rowland Clenell is discounted.
2 surgeons served on two different ships.
1 ship had 5 surgeons.
1 ship had 3 surgeons.
7 ships had 2 surgeons, the rest one surgeon.

The surgeons, perhaps after the fashion of those of Edward IV and the 1475 expedition, were divided into two groups.[229] The members of one group were designated as "master surgeons"; they received wages of thirteen shillings, four pence, a month. The members of the second group were designated simply as surgeons, and received ten shillings. The accounts also show the number of men on some of the ships. On the royal ship *Gabrial Royal*, for example, there were two surgeons for 555 men.[230] On the smaller, hired ship, the *Christopher Davy*, there was a surgeon for 132 men. The average, as reflected by the data in Table 4.3 and including only those ships listing soldiers, mariners, gunners, and doctors, was about one surgeon for every 185 men.[231] Because the records are incomplete it is difficult to present other statistics. Nine of the ships from which surgeons are listed do not provide numbers of crewmen. Some of the ships did not seem to have sailed, and most probably did not have as many soldiers, sailors, or gunners as the muster record suggests. But the partial evidence is impressive. It suggests a greater surgical presence than in 1475, and perhaps greater even than that at Agincourt.

Had the surgeons of Henry VIII's army been blooded, the development of English medicine might have been very different. But they were not. Henry's campaign, whatever his original plan, turned sour.[232] There were a few skirmishes, and the English army besieged and took the town of Therouanne after a relatively easy and bloodless campaign. In August, 1514, a troop of French cavalry stumbled on the English and was scattered by cannon fire. The English called this the Battle of the Spurs, perhaps because in their haste to retreat spurs were the most lethal weapons the French used. And the town of Tournai was surrendered to the English. But through it all there were few casualties and virtually no need for the surgeons to work. Henry, his army, and its surgeons returned home triumphantly; while many of the surgeons were to enjoy royal favor, none gained field experience.

The quality and careers of Henry's personal surgeons, presumably

[229] PRO, Exchequer Accounts, E/101/56/10.

[230] *Ibid.*, membrs. 177a, 179, 180, 181.

[231] *Ibid.*, membr. 177a. This can be contrasted with the forces of the Spanish Armada in 1588. According to David Howarth, *The Voyage of the Armada* (New York: Viking, 1981), p. 17, it had almost 25,000 men, six physicians, six surgeons, and sixty-two medical orderlies.

[232] Scarisbrick, *Henry VII*, pp. 24–40.

the best in England, reflect this. It was, after all, during Henry's reign
and with his blessing, that the Royal College of Physicians was founded,
and the surgeons were joined with the barbers. Henry's surgeons were
clever and successful, but not distinguished as doctors. Among them
were four foreigners, John Veyrier, Marcellus de la More, Master Medicus, and Antony Ciabo, and their careers are illustrative of the
strengths and failings of early sixteenth-century surgery.

Veyrier was a Frenchman, and probably came to court late in the
reign of Henry VII.[233] By 1510 he was referred to as "the chief surgeon
of the king's body" and was receiving royal annuities.[234] He was made a
denizen in May, 1513, just before the French expedition, on which he
sailed on the flagship and served as Henry's personal surgeon.[235] Veyrier
was apparently Marcellus More's superior, and in theory the chief surgeon of the expedition, a post held in earlier campaigns by the likes of
Roger Heyton and Thomas Morstede. In 1514 he was receiving an annuity of forty marks.[236] But virtually nothing is known of his training or
background, or his skill as a surgeon. Most of the prominent surgeons of
the late fifteenth and early sixteenth centuries, like court physicians, left
extensive records of their financial and personal lives, but not much
about their professional careers. They left no tools, wrote little, and
rarely owned manuscripts. Some of this may be due to historical chance.
But some must also be a reflection of their preoccupations, of which surgery seems to have been less important than financial success.

John Veyrier may have been Marcellus de la More's superior in 1513,
but More's career lasted longer and he rose higher.[237] Information on his
personal service on the French expedition is extensive, and sheds more
light on the performance of the surgeons in the campaign. More was
provided with a wagon, presumably to ferry supplies, and perhaps later
to serve as an ambulance.[238] He was accompanied by an apothecary,
whose role was dispensing the drugs that More and the other surgeons
prescribed. The accounts show that the surgeons were paid a monthly
rate because some of them did not serve through the entire campaign. In
November, 1513, for example, More and the two other leading sur-

[233] *T&H*, p. 192; Beck, *Cutting Edge*, p. 168.
[234] *LPFD*, 1509–1513, p. 15.
[235] *LPFD*, 1509–1514, p. 1068.
[236] *LPFD*, 1515–1516, pp. 760, 875.
[237] *T&H*, pp. 207–208; Beck, *Cutting Edge*, pp. 168–169.
[238] *LPFD*, i, ii, #2404, p. 1068.

geons, Veyrier and William Forest, were allowed to return to London.[239] More later went back to France, when it appeared the campaign
was heating up.

In May, 1514, then called "the king's surgeon" in lieu of Veyrier,
More was put in charge of the entire medical corps.[240] He was also given
money to pay the staff of twenty-four surgeons. Four master surgeons
were paid thirteen shillings, four pence, a month, as agreed, and the
others, still called just "surgeons," ten shillings. It was an easy wage, for
the surgeons had only to treat the ailments they dealt with in their regular practices, and undertook no risks. More stayed in France for the rest
of the year, and in December submitted a new bill which included a fee
for treating a patient in Calais from June through November.[241] He also
requested the ten shillings wage for an unnamed surgeon who had
served on the ship *Lewes Southeron* for three months, claiming he had not
been paid since the preceding May.[242]

That the other surgeons allowed More to collect their wages—if in
fact they had a choice—shows a considerable degree of trust. But this
did not carry over when everyone returned to England. While he was
overseas More was sued for trespass by a London sherman, who alleged
that the king's surgeon had administered "medicines contrary to his [that
is, the sherman's] disease."[243] And he ran into trouble at higher levels.
More was able to get either the king or Cardinal Wolsey to obtain for his
son a prebend at the newly taken town of Tournai; the prebend was
granted as the expense of no less than Erasmus.[244] More's son proved to
be a cheat and a cad. He engendered little sympathy and no trust, and
Wolsey's vice-vicar, Dr. Sampson, claimed: "I think him not . . . so
good English that I should desire [such as he] in the Tournai church."[245]

Yet this ought not to besmirch More senior: a son's behavior is not
necessarily that of his father, and the sherman's malpractice case was
dismissed. More's career continued without a hitch. By 1515 he was receiving an annuity of forty marks, and given exemptions from customs
duties. And by 1516 he was allowed customs on trade with Florentine

[239] *Ibid.*
[240] *Ibid.*, i, ii, #3501, pp. 1,467–1,468.
[241] *Ibid.*, i, ii, #2479, pp. 1,093–1,098.
[242] *Ibid.*, i, ii, #3501, pp. 1,467–1,468.
[243] PRO, Chancery Proceedings, Bundle 340, no. 53.
[244] *LPFD*, ii, i, #889, p. 244.
[245] *Ibid.*, ii, i, #2066, pp. 616–617.

merchants that could have been worth up to £1,000 a year.[246] This grant was made in payment of a loan More had made to Henry in anticipation of the 1513–1514 French campaign. More had grown so rich that, like Pancius de Controne almost two centuries earlier, he was lending money to the king.[247] When Veyrier died in 1518 or 1519, More replaced him, as he had in France, as chief surgeon, but this time at court rather than on the battlefield.

More was chief surgeon until his death in 1530. He was replaced by Antony Ciabo (or Chabo). Little is known of Ciabo's medical career.[248] He was a Savoyard, and his naturalization in November, 1514, suggests that he was with Henry in France.[249] He was granted several large annuities, and by 1519 was probably getting about £60 a year.[250] To this was added another annuity in 1520—and others in 1521 and 1523.[251] In the 1530s, having the security of his position at court, Ciabo turned to land speculation and trade. In 1531 he was given license to import two hundred tuns of Gascon wine and an unspecified amount of Toulouse woad.[252] In 1534, he was given another license to import additional consignments of the same goods, and in 1538 was allowed, as noted in Chapter Two, to import six hundred tuns of Gascon wine.[253] He was still styled the king's surgeon, but he did not seem to be practicing medicine anymore. In 1542, the last reference to him, Ciabo was granted still another annuity.[254]

Master Medicus, Henry VIII's other foreign surgeon, was a Spaniard.[255] He too went on the French campaign of 1513–1514, in the retinue of Charles, Viscount Lisle.[256] Master Medicus may well have served in a private capacity, for his wages were different from those of the royal surgeons. He received from paymaster Sir John Daunce two shillings a

---

[246] *Ibid.*, ii, i, #1586, p. 439.

[247] *Ibid.* See too *ibid.*, iv, iii, #6383, p. 2,857.

[248] As far as I can tell, Ciabo is not in *T&H*. See Beck, *Cutting Edge*, p. 169.

[249] *Ibid.*

[250] *LPFD*, iii, i, #559, p. 192; *ibid.*, ii, i, #1263, p. 481; *ibid.*, iii, ii, #3677, p. 1521.

[251] Beck, *Cutting Edge*, p. 169.

[252] *LPFD*, v, #16, p. 365.

[253] *Ibid.*, vii, #1122, p. 443.

[254] *Ibid.*, xvii, #880, p. 478. Thomas Vicary is there too. This entry is also in Rymer, *Foedera*, p. 777 (Hvi,111,37).

[255] *T&H*, p. 215.

[256] *LPFD*, i, ii, #2575, pp. 1128–1129.

day for forty-nine days, and was given funds to pay five other surgeons, apparently assistants, eight pence *per diem*.[257]

Of the domestic surgeons in service to Henry VIII in the early part of the reign, a few achieved prominence. There was William Forest, already mentioned in connection with his service in France.[258] The Londoner Forest must have been well regarded, for he was the only Englishman to sail on Henry's flagship.[259] Daunce paid him a wage of a shilling a day.[260] Robert Marshall was also on the French campaign.[261] He was a master surgeon, and traveled with his own assistant. In 1513 Marshall was one of an elite group of surgeons mentioned in a Parliamentary inspeximus who were offered an exemption to military service, something he obviously declined.[262] This is of special interest. Marshall was a member of the Fellowship of Surgeons rather than the Barbers' Company, and most of his peers had refused to go to France. Surgeons, as noted in Chapter One, had gained exemptions from the army in 1493, 1513, and 1517. Apparently, Henry VIII thought barber-surgeons to be as competent as members of the Fellowship, and the Fellows no longer believed in the benefits of service with the royal armies.

Among Henry's other surgeons was Thomas Monford, another Fellow, who unlike Marshall did use his exemptions from the military.[263] Monford treated Henry only in Westminster. Thomas Martin and William Squires were prominent members of the barber-surgeons' mystery.[264] They were witnesses to the 1512 inspeximus that afforded the mystery greater medical powers, and guided the Barbers' Company through the 1510s and 1520s. Henry consulted them at court on both medical and administrative business, and granted them favors and annuities.[265] This was unheard of as late as 1490. Even Edward IV, who employed barber-surgeons to treat his troops, did not use them as court doctors. Edward always paid barbers lower wages than surgeons, and clearly relegated them to the bottom rung of the medical ladder.[266] Per-

---

[257] *Ibid.*

[258] *T&H*, p. 394.

[259] *Ibid.*

[260] *LPFD*, i, ii, #2480, pp. 1095–1097.

[261] *T&H*, p. 297.

[262] Vicary, *Anatomie of the Body*, i, p. 212.

[263] *T&H*, p. 250.

[264] *T&H*, p. 350; *ibid.*, p. 415.

[265] *Ibid.*

[266] Myer, *Household of Edward IV*, pp. 117, 121.

haps Henry VIII patronized them because his principal doctors were physicians, and he regarded all surgical practitioners as medical technicians, to be consulted only under special and generally trivial medical circumstances. But he brought barber-surgeons to court, where they squeezed out the members of the Fellowship.

Thomas Vicary represents the transition of surgery. Vicary, about whom more will be said in Chapter Eight, was a competent and trustworthy doctor.[267] But he was unlike John Arderne, Thomas Morstede, and even William Hobbes. Vicary was a barber, and rose through the ranks of the company and into the mystery as much on the basis of his administrative as his medical skills. He was of humble background, in itself a commendable feature, was a layman, and had no university training. In the fifteenth century these characteristics might have worked in his favor, making him flexible and open to new ideas. But in the sixteenth century, medicine was changing, and a university education was again becoming instructive as well as prestigious. And, like his peers, Vicary had no military experience and limited clinical training.

Vicary's shortcomings are apparent in his major work, *The Anatomie of Man's Body*.[268] It is a re-hash, and often an incorrect one, of earlier ideas, and is physic-like in its theoretical rather than practical approach to problems. *The Anatomie* is more valuable for its references to institutional developments than for its surgical or general medical ideas, and does not compare with Arderne's *Treatise on Fistula* or Morstede's *A Fair Book of Surgery*.[269] Vicary and all the other royal surgeons had become court doctors. This was a social and financial boon, but a medical disaster.

[267] See below, pp. 302–307; Beck, *Cutting Edge*, pp. 192–211.
[268] Vicary, *Anatomie of the Body*, i, pp. 11–86.
[269] See below, Chapter Six.

# 5

## TRADITIONAL PHYSIC

The institutional and social changes in late medieval English medicine were accompanied by changes in practice, concept, and method. But most of the changes were in surgery rather than in physic. The roles of physic and the physician were well defined by 1300, and in England progressed hardly at all in the next two hundred years. The corpus was essentially that developed by the Greeks, especially Hippocrates, Galen, and Dioscorides, and modified by their Islamic commentators, especially Avicenna. The educational and clinical aspects, such as they were, were locked into an ecclesiastical and university structure that was fully formed by 1250.[1] The system had the strengths of tradition, but also its weaknesses. Medieval physic was conservative and, as practiced in England, inflexible and resistant to change. These problems were compounded by the social and economic success of the physician. Secure atop the medical hierarchy, wealthy, and sometimes even respected, physicians had no reason to want, let alone effect, change.

Yet the Black Death brought problems. As the leading practitioners,

[1] A general discussion of Greek medicine is E. D. Phillips, *Greek Medicine* (London: Thames and Hudson, 1973). For Galen, see Owsei Tempkin, *Galenism: The Rise and Decline of a Medical Philosophy* (Ithaca, N.Y.: Cornell University Press, 1973). A good new edition of some of Galen's work is David J. Furley and J. S. Wilkie, eds., *Galen: On Respiration and the Arteries* (Princeton: Princeton University Press, 1983). Arabic medicine is discussed in: Donald Campbell, *Arabian Medicine and Its Influence on the Middle Ages*, 2 vols. (London: Kegan Paul, 1926); Max Meyerhof, *Studies in Medieval and Arabic Medicine: Theory and Practice*, ed. Penelope Johnstone; and Manfred Ullman, *Die Medizin im Islam* (Leiden: E. J. Brill, 1970). Two studies of Avicenna are: R. D. Clements, "Avicenna: the Prince of Physicians," *Minnesota Medicine*, i, 48, 1965, pp. 1,567–1,568; and ii, 49, 1966, pp. 187–192; and Mirko D. Grmek, "Influence of Avicenna on Western Medicine in the Middle Ages," *Salerno*, 4, 1967, pp. 7–21. A summary of medieval physic with a good bibliography is Charles H. Talbot, "Medicine," in David C. Lindberg, ed., *Science in the Middle Ages* (Chicago: University of Chicago Press, 1978), pp. 391–428. A survey of English medieval physic is Talbot, *Medicine in Medieval England*. For physic and the universities, see Pearl Kibre and Nancy G. Siraisi, "The Institutional Setting: Universities," in Lindberg, *Science in the Middle Ages*, pp. 120–144. A good biography of an important physician is Luke E. Demaitre, *Doctor Bernard de Gordon: Professor and Practitioner* (Toronto: Pontifical Institute of Mediaeval Studies, 1980). See too Katherine Park, *Doctors and Medicine in Early Renaissance Florence* (Princeton: Princeton University Press, 1985).

physicians were expected to find a remedy or at least provide relief for victims.[2] They did neither. Many refused to see the afflicted, or insisted on treating them, literally, at arms length.[3] Surgeons, by contrast, were innovative, and tried new approaches. A few prominent physicians did advocate change, and beseeched their colleagues to learn anatomy and practice surgery. But the reformers were a minority. Most physicians, secure in their social positions if not always in their practices, refused to consider new methods. The result was a century and a half of stagnation.

The dullness of physic began in medical school.[4] Most physicians attended Oxford or Cambridge.[5] Their curricula were based on that of the University of Paris.[6] This was unfortunate, for medicine was a minor subject at Paris, and its insignificance carried over to England. It was possible to take both a bachelors and a doctorate in medicine, but few students bothered.[7] Rather, the best, brightest, and most ambitious stu-

[2] Anna Montgomery Campbell, *The Black Death and Men of Learning* (New York: Columbia University Press, 1931); Robert S. Gottfried, *The Black Death* (New York: The Free Press, 1983). Carlo M. Cipolla, *Public Health and the Medical Profession in the Renaissance* (Cambridge: Cambridge University Press, 1976).

[3] Darrel. W. Amundsen, "Medical Deontology and Pestilential Disease in the Late Middle Ages," *JHM*, 32, 1977, pp. 403–421.

[4] See the works of Vern L. Bullough, as cited in the bibliography, below, p. 332 especially: *The Development of Medicine as a Profession: The Contribution of the Medieval University to Modern Medicine* (New York: Hafner, 1966); "The Mediaeval Medical School at Cambridge", *Mediaeval Studies*, 24, 1962, pp. 161–168; and "Medical Study at Oxford," *Speculum*, 36, 1961, pp. 600–612; and Humphrey D. Rolleston, *The Cambridge Medical School* (Cambridge: Cambridge University Press, 1932).

[5] Not all practitioners of physic matriculated. Rural empirics, like those discussed in Chapter Two, did not. But the medicine they practiced was a filtered-down version of that taught at the universities. For the education of an English empiric see James K. Mustain, "A Rural Medical Practitioner in Fifteenth Century England," *BHM*, 46, 1972, pp. 469–476; Talbot, *Medicine in Medieval England*, pp. 125–133. For fuller definitions of more formal medical education see Nancy Siraisi, *Taddeo Alderotti and His Pupils* (Princeton: Princeton University Press, 1981), pp. 96–146; and Siraisi, *Arts and Sciences at Padua: The Studium of Padua Before 1350* (Toronto: Pontifical Institute of Mediaeval Studies, 1973), pp. 143–171.

[6] Stephan D'Irsay, "Teachers and Textbooks of Medicine in the Mediaeval University of Paris," *Annals of Medical History*, 8, 1926, pp. 220–230; and Vern L. Bullough, "The Mediaeval Medical University at Paris," *BHM*, 31, 1957, pp. 197–211.

[7] The practicality of medieval students is discussed in Alan B. Cobban, "Medieval Student Power," *Past and Present*, 53, 1971, pp. 28–66. For English medical students see: Margaret Pelling and Charles Webster, "Medical Practitioners," in Charles Webster, ed.,

dents took degrees in the arts, law, or theology; and even some in medicine hedged by taking degrees in other fields.[8] This was explicable. Medicine could be lucrative, but so was law, and law and theology were more prestigious. Combined with the rigidity of the program and the mediocrity of the teachers, this was enough to drive most of the brightest students away.

The scholastic format of the medical program was problematic.[9] Teaching revolved around questions and disputations. Each word was analyzed and debated, its meaning expounded and amplified. Authorities were cited on both sides, and a conclusion reached. Then new questions were raised, and the procedure was continued. This method was useful for the study of many of the arts, and to some degree for law. It was good too for exegesis, and as a introduction to medical problems. But the seminal points of medicine, even theoretical physic, could not be proved by debate. They had to be tested clinically.

Scholastic medicine had another methodological shortcoming. Its proponents venerated authority and emphasized manipulation, especially by syllogism. Ideas, even those found to be incorrect, were juxtaposed but rarely replaced. Points were defended by citing Galen. New works, such as they were, tended to be commentaries or glosses, often just slightly changed from the original. There was little testing and no data, and even the most rational treatments were not empirically proved. Physicians may have despised surgeons and barbers for working with their hands, but practice was more essential to medicine than theory. University education allowed little opportunity even for observation, and provided few insights on how patients might react. It is ironic that the educations that made physicians a social elite condemned them to clinical failure.

The course of university medical study has been discussed elsewhere, and herein can be summarized.[10] Study for a bachelor's of medicine be-

---

*Health, Medicine and Mortality in the Sixteenth Century* (Cambridge: Cambridge University Press, 1979), pp. 189–204; Talbot, *Medicine in Medieval England*, pp. 64–71.

[8] Demaitre, *Doctor Bernard de Gordon*, pp. 23–24, claims that at Montpellier after 1340 the taking of joint degrees was proscribed.

[9] There is a good summary in Talbot, *English Medicine*, pp. 64–71.

[10] See, in addition to the works cited in notes 1, 4, and 5, Gordon Leff, *Paris and Oxford Universities in the Thirteenth and Fourteenth Centuries* (New York: John Wiley, 1968). Also helpful, especially as a starting point, is Hastings Rashdall, *The Universities of Europe in the*

gan with a series of ordinary, or morning lectures, usually twenty, on the *Isagoge in artem parvam Galeni* of Joannitius.[11] This was an overview of Greek humoral theory based on a close analysis of Galen's *Tegni*. Joannitius set an environmental framework to the humors, and explained how various aspects of daily life, such as exercise, diet, and bathing, affected them. Next came lectures on Hippocrates and other works by Galen or, more accurately, what medieval scholars thought were the ideas of the Greek masters, along with their commentators.[12] There were fifty lectures on Hippocrates's *Aphorisms*, twenty-six on his *Prognostics*, and thirty-eight to forty on *De regime acutorum*. This was followed by additional studies of Galen's *Tegni*, and of his commentaries on the Hippocratic corpus.

Noticeably absent were courses and even lectures on surgery. Some lectures were offered on anatomy, and a few surgeons did matriculate. In 1461 Peter Alcomlowe was admitted to Oxford to practice surgery; and in 1472 the surgeon John Stipse was said to be "using surgery within the University of Oxford."[13] But this was exceptional, and virtually unheard of at Cambridge.[14] And the absence of surgery and anatomy prevented the development of proper ideas of physiology.

The next phase stressed diagnosis, especially by uroscopy. Students learned uroscopy by studying treatises by Hippocrates, Theophilus, and Isaac Judeus. Pulse-taking was a second means to diagnosis; it was taught from texts by Theophilus and Philaretus. Isaac Judeus's works on fevers and diets, both taken largely from Galen, and Constantine the African's *Viaticum*, a general text of diagnosis, were also included. In the late middle ages, works from Arabic writers, especially Rhases, Avicenna, and their commentators, were added, along with better editions of Galen. There were also works from Christian authors. But they were

---

*Middle Ages*, 3 vols., eds. F. M. Powicke and A. B. Emden (Oxford: Oxford University Press, 1936).

[11] Joannitius was the Arab Hunain ibn Ishaq (d.c.877).

[12] Good tables of citations of medical authorities are in Demaitre, *Doctor Bernard de Gordon*, pp. 105–106, 111, 114. See too Margaret S. Ogdan, "Guy de Chauliac's Theory of the Humors," *JHM*, 24, 1969, pp. 272–291.

[13] *T&H*, pp. 244 and 187–188. The evidence of their Oxford careers is, respectively: *Registrum Cancellari Oxoniensis*, ed. H. E. Salter (Oxford: Oxford University Press, 1932), ii, p. 65; and B.M. Sloane Ms. 3866, f. 91v.

[14] For the exceptional case of William Hobbes see *The Cambridge University Grace Books*, ed. S. M. Leathers (Cambridge: Cambridge University Antiquarian Society, 1897), A, p. 33.

usually derivative, added little to the existing corpus, and were used primarily as tools to enlarge on particular points in traditional texts.

This period of textual study and debate took between four and seven years. Toward its end, the aspiring bachelor would take part in the *quodlibets*, a series of debates in which rhetorical ability counted as much as medical knowledge. Sometimes participation in the *quodlibets* could be avoided. There were so few masters of medicine teaching in the English universities that administrators often found it hard to raise the necessary quorum for debate.[15] A clever student might skip the details of his medical texts and concentrate on dialectic and rhetoric, which would better serve him in any case if he planned to make a career in the church or the university. At Paris, university officials tried to control this. Beginning in the 1340s students were supposed to take some time off from their textual studies, leave the university, and go out and practice medicine.[16] But there is little evidence that many students ever complied, and no record that the rule was applied at the English universities. Three-quarters of the English M.B.s and M.D.s did eventually practice, and a few students matriculated with some experience.[17] A few professors practiced too, including Nicholas Colnet, Henry V's physician at Agincourt.[18] But these were exceptions. It was possible to be a physician in late medieval England and rarely treat a patient; and it was typical to be a medical student and never see one.

This lack of clinical training helps explain why most bachelors of medicine continued for their M.D.s. But if they expected to pick up practical experience, they would have been disappointed. The path to a doctorate was more arduous than that to the baccalaureate. It took four to seven years, the texts were more complicated, the issues more involved, and students themselves had to do some lecturing. But the basic curriculum was unchanged. Ultimately, the tests of time and endurance were more important in determining whether a student got an M.D. than those of skill and knowledge. By the time he got his degree the newly graduated physician would be close to thirty—on the verge of middle-age in the middle ages. He would have spent his adult life in the university. Many M.D.s simply decided to remain in academe, often in

[15] Such was the case in Cambridge early in the fifteenth century. See Talbot, *Medicine in Medieval England*, p. 69.

[16] Among students with practical experience were: John Bilsden, William Hobbes and William Holm. See *T&H*, pp. 129, 401–403.

[17] Talbot, *Medicine in Medieval England*, p. 67–71.    [18] *T&H*, pp. 220–222.

other disciplines, rather than venture out into a wider world that they hardly knew.[19]

Those who remained became part of medical programs that were "small and undistinguished."[20] In 1414 Oxford had just one professor of medicine, and he was not English; Cambridge had none.[21] Continentals thought ill of the English system; the failure of Oxonian Thomas Brown to gain admission to Paris in 1396, described in Chapter One, is an example.[22] And there was little change, either in the quality of the program or the number of students, in the course of the fifteenth century. Between 1488 and 1511 just twenty-eight medical degrees were awarded by Cambridge, less than one percent of all those granted.[23]

The sorry state of Oxford and Cambridge can be contrasted with the progressive developments in Italian universities.[24] Medical programs at Bologna, Pavia, Padua, and Ferrara had the same Greco-Arabic bases as those at Oxford and Cambridge. But from the thirteenth century onward distinguished teachers like Taddeo Alderotti and his pupils were receptive to new ideas, and quick to change outmoded and incorrect concepts. They stressed the importance of anatomy and advocated the study and integration of surgery into physic. They allowed a larger role to Arabic authorities, especially Avicenna. When they studied Galen they used a wider range and better editions of his works.[25] The Italians were interested in physiology, a key to medical advance, and a subject that English medical professors rarely broached. Furthermore, the Italians stressed demonstration almost as much as textual study. When Mondino dei Luizzi wrote his *Anatomia* early in the fourteenth century, he assumed that its reading would be accompanied by dissection.[26] Dis-

---

[19] The example of the Mertonians, cited in Chapter One, is evidence.

[20] Talbot, *Medicine in Medieval England*, p. 68.

[21] *Ibid.*, pp. 68–71.

[22] See above, pp. 12–13. For Brown, see Heinrich Denifle, ed., *Chartularium Universitatis Parisiensis*, (Paris: Chatelain 1897), iv, 12–13. For French physicians there are two standards: Ernest Wickersheimer, *Dictionnaire biographique des medicins en France au Moyen Age*, 2 vols. (Paris: Droz, 1936); and Danielle Jacquart's *Supplement* (Geneva: Droz, 1979). See too Jacquart's *Le milieu medical en France du xiie au xve siecle* (Geneva: Droz, 1981).

[23] Pelling and Webster, "Medical Practitioners," p. 196. See too Bullough, "Mediaeval Medical School at Cambridge," pp. 161–168.

[24] Siraisi, *Taddeo Alderotti*, pp. 269–302.

[25] *Ibid.*, pp. 104–105.

[26] *Ibid.*, 66–112. Also, see Bullough, *Development of Medicine*, pp. 63–64. For an edition

section was begun at Bologna; the tradition passed to Padua, and perhaps to Montpellier, where early in the fourteenth century Guy de
Chauliac claimed to have dissected cadavers "many times."[27] This enlightened practice was not introduced into Oxford and Cambridge until
the middle of the sixteenth century, and had little impact until the seventeenth.

The best barometers of physic are the hundreds of medical tracts that
survive from late medieval England.[28] Some were written by Englishmen, and a few were original. But most were derivative of traditional
authorities, whose ideas went unchallenged and unchanged. Their appearance as well as their content is important, for they provide social and
cultural as well as medical information. The writing, study, and use of
texts set physicians apart from other doctors, and helped them maintain
their favored positions. More often than not and in contrast with surgical manuscripts, those of physic were large, expensively bound and
covered, and sealed with silver clasps.[29] The most elaborate of them provided the patient and other doctors with material evidence of the physician's financial and professional well-being, like the expensive auto-
mobiles that set off some twentieth-century doctors. Many of the
illustrations were only peripherally medical, with vaguely labelled and
imprecisely drawn zodiac men and anatomies or, more sublimely, illus-

of Mondino, see Ernest Wickersheimer, ed., *Anatomies de Mondino de' Liuzzi et de Guido da
Vigevano* (Paris: Droz, 1926).

[27] Margaret S. Ogdan, ed., *The Cyrurgie of Guy de Chauliac*, i (London: EETS, O.S., 265,
1971), in "The First Book."

[28] There are many guides and interpretive studies to late medieval English medical manuscripts. Among them are: D. W. Singer, "Survey of Medical Manuscripts in the British
Isles Dating Before the Sixteenth Century," *Proceedings of the Royal Medical Society*, 12,
1918–1919, pp. 96–107; Rossell Hope Robbins, "Medical Manuscripts in Middle English," *Speculum*, 45, 1970, pp. 393–415; Robbins, "A Note on the Singer Survey of Medical
Manuscripts in the British Isles," *Chaucer Review*, 4, 1970, pp. 66–70; Robbins, "The Physician's Authorities," *Studies in Language and Literature in Honour of Margaret Schlauch*, ed.
M. Brahmer et al. (Warsaw: Polish Scientific Publishers, 1966), pp. 335–341; Linda Ehrsam Voigts, "Editing Middle English Medical Texts: Needs and Issues," in Trevore Le-
vore, ed. *Editing Texts in the History of Science and Medicine* (New York: Garland Publishing
Company, 1982), pp. 40–68; and Voigts, "Medical Prose," in A.S.G. Edwards, ed. *Middle
English Prose: A Critical Guide to Major Authors and Genres* (New Brunswick, N.J.: Rutgers
University Press, 1984), pp. 315–336.

[29] A splendid book by Loren MacKinney, *Medical Illustrations in Medieval Manuscripts*
(London: Wellcome Historical Medical Library, 1965), describes manuscripts and illustrations. MacKinney also provides a concise statement of the practice of physicians.

trations of doctors at work. Their medical value might be limited. Yet there was little demand for new texts, and despite their expense the manuscripts remained popular throughout the middle ages.[30]

Most manuscripts followed one of two formats. The first was a combination of treatises, a contrast with surgeries, which tended to be individual tracts on particular topics, and the work of a single author. Because of their multifarious nature, physic manuscripts were used as general texts, often for teaching, and were passed from one physician to another through bequest or sale.[31] Sometimes they were combined with tracts on scientific subjects, which suggests ownership by dons who may not have practiced medicine, applied for a *licendi practicandi*, or, indeed, even taken a medical degree. The second format was also a combination, but a more practical and logical one. Tracts that discussed diagnosis and prognosis, such as those on urology, would be followed by those on treatments, such as bloodletting; they would be followed by pathologies and epidemiologies, and concluded with collections of remedies.[32] These manuscripts were most likely owned by practicing physicians.[33]

Some physic texts were designed for travel and quick reference. They were well indexed or had extensive tables of contents so that reference

---

[30] H. S. Bennett, *English Books and Readers, 1475–1557*, 2nd ed. (Cambridge: Cambridge University Press, 1970), pp. 97–109. See too H. E. Ussery, *Chaucer's Physician: Medicine and Literature in Fourteenth Century England* (New Orleans: Tulane Studies in English, 1971).

[31] A good example is C.U.L. Add. Ms. 6000. This is a curious combination, including an Henri de Mondeville surgery; a "Tractus," or collection of fragments from an Anglo-Saxon leechbook; and what appears to be an eighteenth-century Orthodox liturgy.

[32] C.U.L. Ms. Ff 2 6, Henry Daniel, "Urines," is an example.

[33] The difficult role of the copyist often affected the state and quality of the texts. The sheer drudgery of copying a manuscript of several hundred pages, probably by rote and with little understanding of the content or problems of the topic, must have induced the sort of boredom that prompted many scribes to take liberties. Odd bits of text might be highlighted, perhaps simply as a change of pace. Many manuscripts had marginalia of a non-medical, non-naturalistic bent. Sometimes, the marginalia were amusing, albeit in a sophomoric and immature way. There were little devils, invariably in monkish garb, along with monstrous and diabolical creatures. Editions of proctological manuals might be embellished with genitalia. Greatly enlarged penises and testicles were used as pointers to draw the reader to important sections. Or, inexplicably, large portions of text would be blocked or crossed out. At the very least, these impromptu additions must have proved distracting to the physicians and disconcerting to the patients. An example is B.M. Add. Ms. 29301.

would be facilitated. Chapter headings might be highlighted in red, a contrast with the black lettering of the texts, also facilitating reference. Many manuscripts had blank pages, often running to half the text. These were for additions, perhaps glosses on the effectiveness of particular treatments, additional remedies, or new works by later authorities.[34] There were also the marginalia added by doctors. Unlike the scribbling of the scribes, the doodling of the doctors usually had a medical purpose, recording information on cases and the effectiveness of cures. An example is a fifteenth-century version of a plague treatise by Bengt Knutson.[35] The manuscript has marginal comments on virtually every statement in the text. Another is a Cambridge miscellany in which the marginalia are combined with a physiology combining astrology, alchemy, and pathology.[36]

Utility was not always considered. Many physic texts were too bulky to be carried about, and could only have been used for reference. Even worse, most were impractical and rigid. There was seldom a logical ordering of medical topics, that is, a sequence that began with theory, moved to diagnosis, and ended with treatment and deontology. Even in the best indexed manuals these topics were usually presented higgledy-piggledy. As for the more portable ones, many were so general as to be useless and might best be described as commonplace books.[37] They were designed for layfolk as well as physicians, and physicians may have sold them to their patients.[38] After the Black Death, home-remedy or self-help books, as they might better be described, became increasingly popular.[39] They were utilitarian, almost always in English, and offered more than just medical advice. An example is a late-fifteenth-century manuscript belonging to a layman named David Garet.[40] In addition to receipts and a few sections on physic, it contained a dietary, several

---

[34] For example: B.M. Ms. Harl. 1735, "English Medical Texts"; C.U.L. Add. Ms. 6860.

[35] B.M. Ms. Sloane 404. Also good is B.M. Ms. Sloane 2276. The Knutson treatise was edited and printed as follows: Guthrie Vine, ed., Bengt Knutson, *A Little Book . . . for . . . the Pestilence* (Manchester: John Rylands Library, 1911).

[36] For example, C.U.L. Add. Ms. 6860.

[37] See B.M. Ms. Egerton 2724.

[38] For example, B.M. Ms. Harl. 5311.

[39] B.M. Arundel Ms. 249, edited and printed by William Nelson, *A Fifteenth Century School Book* (Oxford: Clarendon Press, 1956). See Laurel Braswell, "Utilitarian and Scientific Prose," in Edward, *Middle English Prose*, pp. 337–388.

[40] O.U. Bod. Ms. Ashmole 59, "Materia medica"; O.U. Bod. Ms. Ashmole 1444, "Ars medicinae."

poems, including some by John Lydgate, and a potpourri of other non-medical matters, all suggesting that Garet and its other owners used it as a general reference. Increasingly, cookbooks were included with medical tracts. Proper diet was central to Galenic medicine, making the inclusion of the cookbooks explicable. But the cookbooks themselves were concerned not with humors, nutrition, or even preparation so much as seasoning, flavor, and taste.

The method of physic manuals, such as it was, followed rough patterns.[41] The starting point was diagnosis and prognosis, accomplished in one or a combination of three methods: uroscopy, pulse reading, and astrology. The methods were a mix of the rational, usually derived from the Greeks, and the magical, drawn mostly folklore, but also from Christian sources and Pliny's nonsensical *Natural History*. The system was then meshed into the hierarchy of medical practice and the theory of what a physician ought and ought not to do. The discovery and description of an ailment was largely theoretical and speculative; there was little bodily contact with the patient. Then came reflection—the kind of problem and procedure that had been taught at the university. Treatment would be prescribed and usually carried out by an apothecary, surgeon, or barber. This gibed with the physician's vision of his role in the medical hierarchy.

Uroscopy was the principal diagnostic and prognostic tool. By the standards of the day it was logical and methodical. The key to analysis was the color, texture, odor, and sometimes even taste of the urine. The results were then fitted into the humoral scheme, with diagnosis and prognosis predicated upon variations of age, sex, and time of the patient's birth. Illuminations of physicians' offices show rows of urine flasks in varying hues, joined in a circle and running a gamut from white to red.[42] The physician would take the patient's sample and match it to the flasks. If office flasks were not available, or if they had turned color because of age or climate, there were examples in medical texts. The flasks were then linked to astral tables, much in the way that phlebotomies were connected with zodiac men (see Illus. 3, 9).[43]

More uroscopies have survived than any other type of physic manual,

---

[41] There is an excellent summary in MacKinney, *Medical Illustrations*, pp. 9–23.

[42] *Ibid.* p. 194.

[43] For two excellent fifteenth-century examples, see: O.U. Bod. Mss. Ashmole 391 and 789.

and it is easy to see why.[44] They were well indexed, and had *tabula* highlighted in red, to contrast with the black text. After 1400 they were usually written in English, the legacy of Henry Daniel, the fourteenth-century Dominican who popularized Isaac Judeus.[45] The Daniel version
was earthy and direct. His first chapter sets the tone for the rest of the
manuscript: "Here begins the first chapter of knowing the significance
of piss. What burn is where, and how it is made."[46] Many were covered
with wood, rather than leather or vellum, making them cheaper. That
they were heavily used is suggested by the cramped hands in which they
were written and the additions and scribblings of different physicians in
the margins.[47] So central had uroscopy become that by 1400 chapters on
it were often included in tracts on different topics.[48] And so popular was
it that many late medieval physicians translated the method to an analysis of blood samples. By 1400 the urine flask had replaced the traditional Hippocratic staff as the symbol of English physicians.[49]

Talbot has put uroscopy in perspective:

> . . . some of these ideas [that is, those about uroscopy] were already cur-
> rent in the ninth century, while the latter part [of a particular text under
> discussion] on urines is taken almost bodily from the treatise of Isaac Ju-
> deus, made available to the West by Constantine in the eleventh century.
> That they should still be current in the fifteenth century and form the
> stock-in-trade of most physicians, who presumably spent a number of
> years at a university studying medicine, is a devastating comment on the
> lack of enterprise shown by the medical profession of those days.[50]

I think he is right. For even if uroscopy were medically sound, a questionable premise at best, the colors of the urine flasks would have faded

[44] I have counted twenty-three uroscopies just among the Ashmolean manuscripts in the
Bodleian Library.

[45] See, for example: c.u.l. Ms. gg 3 29, "Liri tre unicrisiarum"; and c.u.l. Ms. ff 2 6,
"Book of Urines."

[46] b.m. Royal Ms. 17 d1, "Of the Domes of Urines."

[47] c.u.l. Ms. ii, 6 18, "Tractus urinaraum"; b.m. Ms. Egerton 1624, "Urines"; b.m. Ms.
Sloane 1721, "Urines."

[48] Wellcome Ms. 784, "Uroscopy". See too: o.u. Bod. Rawlinson Ms. d 1221, "judicum
urinarum"; c.u.l. Ms. gg 3 29; o.u. Bod. Ashmole Ms. 1517, "Urines"; and three o.u.
Bod. Rawlinson Mss.—d, 238, "Nota di iv temperamentia corpori"; d 247, "De coloribus
urinum"; and d 248, "Summula de urinis."

[49] Calvin Wells, "Fifteenth Century Wood Carvings in St. Mary's Church, Bury St.
Edmunds," *MH*, 9, 1965, pp. 286–288.

[50] Talbot, *Medicine in Medieval England*, pp. 133–135.

with time. In a generation of their composition physicians would have been hard-pressed to distinguish between "muddy red" and "frothy pale" urines. Hence, the best-intentioned and most learned urologist would have found it difficult to follow accurately the diagnoses and prognoses of the medical masters.

Pulse-reading was a second popular tool of diagnosis and prognosis.[51] The method of late medieval physicians was virtually unchanged from that of Galen and Avicenna, both of whom used it nearly as much as uroscopy. There are fewer texts which explicate it, however, and English doctors clearly seem to have preferred uroscopy. Pulse-readers argued that as uroscopy indicated the state of the liver so pulse-reading measured the state of the heart. This in turn led to the classification of the types of heartbeats, much in the manner of the urologist's examination of the color of urines. Various rhythms might be classified as "bounding," "formicant," "vermicular," or "gazelle-like."[52] Heartbeat and pulse-rates were also taken to indicate the stage which a particular ailment had reached. Finally, the whole analysis was considered, like uroscopy, in light of differences in age, gender, physical activity, season, and diet.

The third method of diagnosis and prognosis was astral and magical.[53] It was most common among leeches who had limited formal training. But many university-educated physicians used it too, and it was considered to be a legitimate tool for any doctor. Superstition, folklore, and magic were all accepted to one degree or another as an integral part of the healing process, and in many instances traditional folk cures were more effective than those taught in university classrooms.[54] Astral diagnosis enjoyed a special vogue after the Black Death, when methods of uroscopy and pulse-reading seemed particularly futile.[55]

The tenor of medical astrology was set in the seventh century by the encyclopedist Isidore of Seville. He wrote: "It is necessary for a medical

[51] MacKinney, *Medical Illustrations*, pp. 15–19.

[52] *Ibid.*, p. 15.

[53] *Ibid.*, pp. 20–23.

[54] Alan G. Debus takes this as one of his themes in *Man and Nature in the Renaissance* (Cambridge: Cambridge University Press, 1984), pp. 34–73. See too Wayne Shumaker, *The Occult Sciences in the Renaissance: A Study in Intellectual Patterns* (Berkeley, Calif.: University of California Press, 1983).

[55] Gottfried, *Black Death*, pp. 104–128. See too Campbell, *Black Death and Men of Learning*.

man to know . . . astronomy by which he may calculate the stars and change of seasons; for a physician has said that our bodies are affected by their qualities. . . ."[56] Isidore and others then linked the macrocosm, the stars, to the microcosm, the body's humors. The link was represented by the zodiac men so common in late medieval texts. Even the most practical doctors, such as the surgeons Guy de Chauliac and John Arderne, used them to guide their bloodletting. Their commonplace was exemplified by the many illuminations that depicted doctors wearing folded calendars at their waists.[57] Practitioners would take the patient's name, age, sex, and other vital statistics, give them a numerical value, line that up with the appropriate astral conditions, make a few arithmetic calculations and then a diagnosis.[58]

An example of these astral-medical texts is a calendar dating around 1462.[59] Small, compact, and portable, it would have fitted easily into the sort of pouch Chaucer's physician is sometimes depicted as wearing.[60] It was well-indexed and set up for easy and frequent reference. It was compiled in Latin, a clue perhaps that it was designed for a physician rather than a surgeon or empiric, and described treatment for the patient after diagnosis. This too was astral; various herbs and dietary strictures were applied to fit particular conditions, which in turn were dictated by movements of the planets and the stars. And while the manuscript was intended for a university-trained physician, it was a prototype for more general, simplified versions, usually in English, which could be used by other doctors, unlicensed practitioners, or even literate layfolk.

Most astral-medical manuals were organized by month. There was a table of movements of the sun, complete with illuminations and an astral man, a naked anatomical drawing, sometimes realistic, in which each part of the body was linked with its zodiac sign. The linkages are provided in Table 5.1. Treatment was predicated on a combination of humoral theory and astrology, along with tidbits of folklore and magic.

---

[56] As quoted in MacKinney, *Medical Illustrations*, p. 20. See too W. D. Sharpe, ed., Isidore of Seville, *The Medical Writings* (Philadelphia: Transactions of the American Philosophical Society, 1964).

[57] Ussery, *Chaucer's Physician*, pp. 5–31.

[58] Michael McVaugh, "Quantified Medical Theory and Practice at Fourteenth Century Montpellier," *BHM*, 43, 1969, pp. 397–413.

[59] B.M. Add. Ms. 28725, "Medical Calendar."

[60] Geoffrey Chaucer, *The Canterbury Tales*, trans. Nevill Coghill (New York: Penguin, 1977), pp. 30–31.

TABLE 5.1: Astral Man

| Sign | Body Part |
| --- | --- |
| Aries | Head |
| Taurus | Neck |
| Gemini | Chest |
| Cancer | Lungs |
| Leo | Stomach |
| Virgo | Abdomen |
| Libra | Lower Abdomen |
| Scorpio | Penis and Testicles |
| Sagittarius | Thighs |
| Capricorn | Knees |
| Aquarius | Calves |
| Pisces | Ankles |

Physicians were told when and how to let blood—or, more precisely, when to supervise its letting. It was not advisable, for example, to proceed on the body part whose sign was current, such as the lungs during Cancer. Blood flow was most vigorous then, and might not be stopped. But operations on other parts of the body were desirable since the blood flowed away. These procedures were ideal for the physician. They were complicated and could be understood and carried out only after long periods of training. They were setpieces that required little original thinking or creativity.

Occasionally a fourth, entirely magical, method of making diagnosis and prognosis was employed.[61] It revolved around the lore of the caladrius bird, or goldfinch, and was traditional from the fourth century B.C. The goldfinch was placed on the edge of the sickbed, facing the patient. Depending on the patient's state, the bird would look straight ahead, turn right, left, or away. Again depending on a variety of astral and personal circumstances, the bird's motion would determine diagnosis and prognosis. The use of the goldfinch was popular among the aristocracy, and could be found in the more lavishly illustrated texts and bestiaries of the fourteenth and fifteenth centuries.[62]

Among the most common texts were *Materia medica*. These collections

[61] MacKinney, *Medical Illustrations*, p. 22.

[62] Jerry Stannard, "Natural History," in Lindberg, *Science in the Middle Ages*, pp. 429–460; Beryl Rowland, "Bestiary," in Joseph R. Strayer, ed., *Dictionary of the Middle Ages*, ii (New York: Charles Scribner's Sons, 1983), pp. 203–207.

of tracts and recipes on various subjects—handbooks, in a sense—were
written at different levels but were used by doctors of all stripes. At
their heart was the notion that the best medium for healing was medication. This was the crucial link between physicians and apothecaries.
Drugs were used by all doctors, even surgeons, who for all their innovations generally began surgery after prescribed drugs had failed. Drugs
were taken internally and externally, as pills, potions, mixes with confectionaries and sweetened wines, powders, balms, salves, and ointments.[63] The prescriptions were generally based on classical compilations, especially Theophrastus's *Medical Botany* and Dioscorides's *De
materia medica*, both written in the first century A.D.[64] Their corpus was
constantly being added to and amended. One source was folklore. Another was Avicenna, whose texts on pharmacy were the product of a culture with different customs and better access to the spice markets of
south Asia.

The *Materia* were designed for frequent reference and were well indexed.[65] Their format was usually a variation of Dioscorides' original.
This had five books: spices, salves, and oils; animal products and a few
select plants thought to have a close affinity to animals; most plants;
trees; and wines and stones. In each section treatments were suggested
for particular ailments and conditions, often with directions for compounding concoctions. A fifteenth-century English version offers this
remedy for "the bloody flux," a term used for stomach ailments, but
often applied specifically to intestinal dysentery: "For the blood flux.
Take a yarrow and weybread and stamp them in a mortar, and take the
juices of them and fair flour of wheat and temper them together and
make a cake and bake it in ashes and make the sick eat it as hot as he may
suffer it. *Probatum est*."[66] And one for impotence: "For palsy in a man's
privy member. Seeth caster in wine and wash him therewith around the

[63] Stannard, "Natural History," pp. 429–460.

[64] Talbot, "Medicine," in Lindberg, *Science in the Middle Ages*, pp. 391–428.

[65] They were very common. To use the Ashmolean collection again, I have looked at
241 Ashmolean manuscripts which are entirely or partially on medical topics. They break
down as follows: *Materia medica*, specifically pharmacy, 100 manuscripts; *Ars medica*, 50;
uroscopies, 23; phlebotomies, 18; gynaecologies, 10; astral medicines, 9; surgeries, 8; anatomies, 7; and "quakeries," 6.

[66] W. R. Dawson, ed., *A Leechbook, or Collection of Medical Recipes of the Fifteenth Century*
(London: Macmillan, 1934), pp. 46–47. Other edited leechbooks include: Margaret S. Ogdan, ed. *Liber de diversis medicinis* (London: EETS, O.S., 207, 1969); and George Henslow,
ed., *Medical Works of the Fourteenth Century* (London: Chapman and Hall, 1938).

share [that is, the pubic area] and wet the cloth therein upon the pyntell [the penis] in a manner of a plaster."[67]

Galen had shed doubt on such remedy compilations.[68] But his reservations were countermanded in the sixth century by Cassiodorus, who was to become an authority for medieval thinkers simply because he preserved so many classical ideas. Cassiodorus praised the pharmaceutical method, particularly that of Dioscorides. The *Materia* had other advantages. Many were pictorial and colorful, which added to their appeal. Each page had detailed illustrations, followed by simple directions and descriptions. Lynn Thorndike argued that the Dioscorides's *Materia* remained the most popular text and method among physicians until the sixteenth century.[69] For many physicians it was the only text they needed.

Some *Materia*, called *antidotarii* or *receptaria*, were used mainly by apothecaries.[70] The remedies were drawn from Theophrastus and Dioscorides, but were usually shortened or excerpted. One format for the *antidotarii* was the *parvum*, brief compilations containing about five hundred remedies taken from the *Salernitan Regiment*, itself drawn from Theophrastus and Dioscorides, with additions made by Nicholas of Salerno and others of his school.[71] A second was the *Magnum*, containing 2,500 remedies, and drawing on Arabic as well as Greek sources.[72] Both were common in late medieval England. Indeed, the use of pharmaceuticals was general. By the middle of the fourteenth century virtually every physic manual and some of surgery had at least a partial list of remedies. An example is the surgery of Guy de Chauliac. Guy wrote:

> Often it is necessary and very useful for physicians and especially surgeons to know how to find and compound, as well as to administer medicines to patients, since often they practice in places were there are no apothecaries, or if they are not trustworthy or well supplied with [*Materia medica*].[73]

[67] Dawson, *Leechbook*, p. 234–235.

[68] Henry E. Sigerist, "Materia Medica in the Middle Ages: A Review," *BHM*, 7, 1939, pp. 417–423.

[69] Lynn Thorndike, "When Medicine Was in Flower," *BHM*, 33, 1959, pp. 110–115.

[70] MacKinney, *Medical Illustrations*, pp. 24–29.

[71] Brian Lawn, *The Salernitan Question* (Oxford: Oxford University Press, 1973).

[72] *Ibid.* See also Edward J. Kealey, *Medieval Medicus: A Social History of Anglo-Norman Medicine* (Baltimore: Johns Hopkins University Press, 1981), pp. 1–56; and Bullough, *Development of Medicine*, pp. 40–45.

[73] Ogdan, *Cyrurgie*, "The Seventh Book." See also to articles by Ogdan: "Galen's Works

In some manuscripts this description was accompanied by an illumination showing the doctor preparing drugs with the traditional tools of
mortar, pestle, and jars, like the urine flask the symbols of physic.[74]

A general treatment suggested by the *Materia* was the use of purgatives. Stomach troubles were common enough. Food spoiled easily,
and, given the state of medieval mill wheels, loaves of bread probably
contained a high percentage of chalk and even stones. Digestive problems that did not respond to drugs were treated with clysters or enemas.
A fifteenth-century version of Galen's *De usus farmacorum* suggested that:

> clysters are often applied in diseases for which other remedies are impos-
> sible. They can be prepared in various ways, harsh or mild; if mild, they
> are made with warm water mixed with oil or milk. . . . Mild clysters are
> applied when hard feces press the intestines. . . . Clysters are useful for
> ailments of the lowest intestines, for dry choler . . . for flux, for constant
> lustful desires, etc. Sometimes we prepare a clyster of salt water, to elimi-
> nate putrid ulcers in dysentery. . . .[75]

Salt-water enemas were much favored as a general remedy, and were
used to treat other ailments. Among these was the disgorging of leeches
which, during bleeding, burrowed into the patient's body.

*Materia medica*, then, were a staple of the physician's practice, and
there are, literally, hundreds of surviving copies. Typical was the aforementioned fifteenth-century version, probably commissioned by John
Beaufort, Duke of Somerset.[76] It was comprehensive, even exhaustive,
in its treatment, with remedies presented alphabetically by ailment.
They were similar to those in other leechbooks—indeed, the content
varied little from one to another. But there was considerable variation in
length, number, and organization. Further, they came in all shapes,
sizes, bindings, and styles, and with and without illustrations and indexes. *Materia* were written for different kinds of readers, and suggest
the large market that must have existed, not just among professional
practitioners, but also among literate laymen.[77]

---

Cited in Guy de Chauliac," *JHM*, 28, 1973, pp. 24–33; and "Guy de Chauliac's Theory of
the Humors," pp. 272–291.

[74] MacKinney, *Medical Illustrations*, pp. 196, 219.

[75] *Ibid.*, p. 42.

[76] Dawson, *Leechbook*.

[77] There were also physical variations among the *materia* that compounded the distinctions of *parvum* and *magna*. Some were grossly simplified, even for *parva*. They were often
worn and tattered, and may well have belonged to empirics or layfolk. See for example

The poetic form of some of them made for pleasant reading, and it has been argued that the *Materia medica* were among the most popular forms of vernacular literature of the later middle ages.[78] Verse made prescriptions easier to remember. For example:

> Of humble herbs now I
> Will tell you by and by
> As I have found written in a book
> That is borrowing I betook
> Of a great lady's priest and company.
> It drives aways all foul mysteries
> And destroys venom and wicked humors
> It destroys the morfew
> And despoiling the leper.[79]

And:

> For the health of the body, cover the cold of the head.
> Eat no meat and take to bed.
> There to drink wholesome wine, seed and bread.[80]

Some of the best *Materia medica* began with verse.[81] A fifteenth-century version commenced with a poem distinguishing the social and medical roles between physicians and surgeons.

> That men will of leechcraft learn
> Read one this book and you may hear
> Many a medicine both good and true
> To heal sores, both old and new.[82]

It was a comprehensive text, with tracts on surgery, gynecology, physiology, and uroscopy as well as remedies. It was large, had colored chapter headings, and must have been expensive; it may have been a bit too modest for a king, magnate, or even a royal physician, but only a pros-

---

C.U.L. Add. Ms. 4407, "Collectionea"; C.U.L. Ms. DD 5 66, "Medical Recipes." Others were thick and comprehensive, even for *magna*; they had illustrations, some in color, of zodiac men and calendars, with indexes and chapter headings highlighted in red. Yet often they were cheaply made and portable, and may have belonged to physicians and leeches who traveled a circuit to see patients. See, for example, C.U.L. Ms. DD 6 29, "Medica."

[78] Bennett, *English Books*, pp. 97–109.

[79] C.U.L. Ms. DD 10 49, "Collection of Medical Works," f. 123.

[80] O.U. Bod. Add Ms. V 60, 122v.

[81] O.U. Bod. Ashmole Ms. 1477III, f. 1.

[82] *Ibid.*

perous practitioner could have afforded it. Poetry, then, explicated physic. John Lydgate wrote a dietary.[83] And less talented and prominent writers authors rhymed phlebotomies, zodiacs, astrologies, and deontologies.[84]

By the beginning of the fifteenth century general texts called *Ars medica* were built around the *Materia*.[85] A Cambridge manuscript provides a good example.[86] Written in English, it had the Greek, Galenic base of most physic manuscripts, and was divided, in addition to its *Materia*, into treatises of uroscopy, midwifery, botany, and alchemy. Others of the genre include: compendia that are in English, Latin, or a combination of both; those with botanies; those with treatises about particular diseases, usually plague; and those with tracts attributed to famous doctors.[87] Some *Ars medica* were notable for their lavish illustrations, large folios, leather bindings—and highly simplified texts. An example is the famous Apocalypse manuscript.[88] It had large and graphic if not entirely accurate illustrations of anatomy, which must have cost a great deal to produce. And Apocalypse, like many of the grander *Materia*, was more than a medical manuscript. It was filled with theological and literary allusions, and its tone was allegorical. It was as much an object of art as a medical book, and its owner must have been wealthy.

Other *Ars medica* were written in Latin and included in broader scientific manuscripts.[89] Medical recipes might be integrated into collections on botany or alchemy, and occasionally complete tracts were meshed into works on alchemy, astrology, or aspects of technology, such as the preparation of gunpowder.[90] Such manuscripts were favored

[83] o.u. Bod. Musaeo Ms. 52 (Bodley Ms. 3510), "Medical Pieces." See too Charles F. Mullett, "John Lydgate: A Mirror of Medieval Medicine," *BHM*, 22, 1948, pp.403–415.

[84] See, for example: o.u. Bod. Rawlinson Ms. D 251, "The Knowing of Veins"; o.u. Bod. Ashmole Ms. 1481, "The Knowing of Veins," virtually identical with Rawlinson Ms. D 251; o.u. Bod. Wood Ms e, pt. 24, "Who so Will Be His Leech's Soul"; o.u. Bod. Ashmole Ms. 1444, "Ye man it will of leechcraft lere"; o.u. Bod. Douce Ms. 78 (Bodley Ms. 21652), unnamed verse, f. 14.

[85] o.u. Bod. Ashmole Ms. 1477. This is so for 47 of the 72 leaves that deal with medieval medicine. The rest of the tracts in the manuscript deal with sixteenth and seventeenth century medicine.

[86] c.u.l. Ee I 13, "Medica et Alchemica."

[87] See, for example: c.u.l. Kk 6 30; and c.u. Gonville and Caius College Ms. 336.

[88] Wellcome Ms. 49.

[89] o.u. Bod. Ms. 181 (Bodley 2081), "Ars medicinae."

[90] *Ibid.* Also, see o.u. Bod. Lyell Ms. 36, "Scientific Miscellany"; and c.u.l. Add Ms. 6860, "Imago Mundi."

by Oxford and Cambridge dons, perhaps trained as physicians—though more likely not—who maintained a general, often theoretical, interest in science.

Because they were central to physic, *Ars medica* often passed through generations of practitioners. This was the case with a Cambridge manuscript that was used and continually amended from the thirteenth through the early sixteenth century.[91] Updating was common and necessary for working physicians, despite the slow pace of medical change. The Cambridge manuscript was kept current enough so that in 1553 a Master Dunn was able to deliver from it a lecture on anatomy to the Royal College of Physicians.[92] Like many of the comprehensive *Materia*, it had a manual of surgery, in this case, drawn from Henri de Mondeville, including the detailed and graphic illustrations that most Mondevilles' had. A second example is a Cambridge manuscript owned by several authors, whose detailed marginalia adorn the manuscript.[93]

A few *Ars medica* were written just for general audiences. An example, mostly in English, was part of a collection including a cookbook, two agronomies, and an herbal entitled "The Virtues of Rosemary to the Queen of England."[94] These non and quasi-medical topics notwithstanding, the manuscript provided comprehensive coverage of physic. Among its medical treatises were a text, two herbals, two surgeries, four uroscopies, two phlebotomies, and a complete copy of John of Bordeaux's treatise on plague. The same can be said for a London manuscript of about the same date.[95] It combined general scientific texts with those on a range of medical topics. But this manuscript was unusual in that it contained the names of some of its owners, including two very distinguished royal physicians, John Somerset and Roger Marshall. Its author acknowledged the authorities whose ideas he appropriated, including Arnold of Villanova, Roger of Salerno, Bernard Gordon, and John Malverne.[96]

---

[91] c.u. Trinity College Ms. 1148, "Medica."

[92] *Ibid.*, ff. 1, 20.

[93] b.m. Add Ms 8928, "Medical Miscellany." See too b.m. Royal Ms. 18vi, which portrays the internal organs like a bunch of grapes.

[94] b.m. Sloane Ms. 7, "Medical Miscellany."

[95] b.m. Sloane Ms. 59, attributed to John Somerset. See *T&H*, pp. 184–185, and 314–315.

[96] b.m. Sloane Ms. 7, ff. 1, 106, 155, 181, 185. See too b.m. Sloane Ms. 2463, "Medical Miscellany"; Wellcome Ms. 542, "Collective Leechbooks"; o.u. Bod. Ashmole Ms. 59, "Materia medica"; o.u. Bod. Add. Ms. (Bodley 29179), "Medical Recipes," o.u. Bod.

Other *Ars medica*—in this case, more properly *Materia medica*—were notable for their pharmacy, and were probably written explicitly for apothecaries. One, written mostly in English, short and compact, had the usual recipes and general tracts on singular medical topics, all simplified.[97] But in a hand similar to that which wrote most of the text was a section entitled "For to read and understand the writings of leeches in physic and the writing for their making of medicines which it be in English or Latin. . . ."[98] There followed a list that might best be described as a code deciphering physicians' shorthands for pharmaceuticals.[99] This was followed by a preparatory table to a list of herbals, written in different hands, that gave weights and prices for many of the prescribed drugs of the late middle ages.

Apothecaries' manuscripts often followed this pattern.[100] They were designed to help the apothecary understand the treatments prescribed by physicians, hence enabling them to fill their traditional role. But since pharmaceuticals were so central to treatment many patients went directly to apothecaries and asked for advice. This in turn was the watered-down physic of their *Materia materia*. Since apothecaries also drew on traditional remedies, Germanic and Celtic as well as Greco-Christian, many pharmacy manuscripts contained botanies. An example is an Oxford manuscript composed around 1500, one of whose owners was the London apothecary William Aderston.[101] It had recipes in English, a medical glossary—just the sort of thing an apothecary would find essential—and a range of treatments to be applied after diagnosis.

Another fifteenth-century manuscript, once belonging to Dr. Bernard Serle, was small, beautifully made, comprehensive, and well indexed.[102] It included medical tracts, but was mostly devoted to pharmacy. Drugs were discussed in Latin and English; each herb was

---

Ashmole Ms. 1481, "Medical Miscellany"; O.U. Bod. Douce Ms. 78 (Bodley 21652), "Medical Recipes."

[97] O.U. Bod. Rawlinson Ms. c381, "Ars medicinae."

[98] *Ibid.*, f. 12b.

[99] *Ibid.*, f. 100. By these I refer to those manuscripts that have only pharmaceuticals, or those that deal with just pharmacological problems.

[100] Matthews, *Royal Apothecaries*, 36–56.

[101] O.U. Bod. Ashmole Ms. 1389, "Materia medica," f. 2. Interesting too are its table of weights, f. 284.

[102] B.M. Harl. Ms. 5294, "Herbarium." See also L. E. Voigt, "One Anglo-Saxon View of the Gods," *Studies in Iconography*, University of Kentucky, 3, 1977, pp. 3–16.

explicated; and many plants were illustrated. There were marginalia, both professional and doodling.[103] One illustration depicted a combination hospital and apothecary shop, with patients, customers, and the usual collections of bottles, mortars, and pestles, mixing bowls and other compounding equipment.[104] The apothecary running the shop was shown with a physician, thus suggesting their common if unequal practice.

One of the best pharmacies was a combination manual and inventory of the shop of John Hexham, like Aderston a London apothecary.[105] The inventory was taken when Hexham was arrested for counterfeiting. The total value of his professional goods was £5, 3 shillings; of this, £4, 4/7 was for the contents of his shop, that is, the drugs and equipment, including a still; and 19/ for household furnishing. Of the drugs themselves, twenty-five were taken from vegetable bases, three from animals, and one from lead oxide. If Hexham was typical—and it has been argued that he was—then alchemy, though popular among university physicians, had not yet made headway among most apothecaries.[106] They relied on organic materials and, by implication, a traditional as well as a Greek corpus.

After the all-purpose *Ars* and *Materia medica*, the most widely used physic manuals were calendars and almanacs. Mention has been made of their practicality; they could be folded and worn from a belt. Since they were based on astral medicine and were used primarily for diagnosis and prognosis, they were perfectly suited to the physician. Most popular was that by the English Carmelite Nicholas of Lynn, a good copy of which is a fifteenth-century English language version.[107] It had the omnipresent zodiac man, was well indexed and convenient to use, and was so general that it could have been understood by an empiric or educated laymen. Indeed, parts of it were religious rather than medical, and there was a cover sketch of Christ and the Virgin Mary. Other Lynns, such as a fourteenth-century manuscript, written in Latin and

---

[103] A doodle on f. 12 appears to be Cosmas and Damian.

[104] MacKinney, *Medical Illustrations*, pp. 196, 211, 220–221.

[105] B.M. Add. Ms. 24453. See also Geoffrey E. Trease and J. H. Hudson, "The Inventory of John Hexham, a Fifteenth Century Apothecary," *MH*, 9, 1965, pp. 76–81. They reproduce the PRO document.

[106] Trease and Hudson, "The Inventory of John Hexham," p. 77.

[107] A new edition is Sigmund Eisner, ed. *The Kalendarium of Nicholas of Lynn* (Athens, Ga.: University of Georgia Press, 1980). See too O.U. Bod. Ashmole Ms 8, "Calendar."

English, were more detailed.[108] Like the London manuscript, it had a
zodiac man, folded conveniently, and could have been easily carried
about at the waist. But it drew on the more detailed parts of the original
tract. More importantly, it had a logical and orderly structure, unified
by a physiology, and a phlebotomy which allowed for some treatment
after diagnosis and prognosis.

Other influential almanacs include a late-fourteenth-century Oxford
copy that was attributed to the famous though enigmatic thirteenth-century Englishman, Ricardus Anglicus.[109] In 1386, it belonged to Richard
Thorpe, a physician, astronomer, and Austin Friar.[110] Like most calendars it was small, thin, and portable, could be worn at the belt, and explained illness by cosmology. But it recommended treatments based on
pharmaceuticals and had a slightly different medical theory, credited to
Hippocrates and the English physician John Mirapiece.[111] It also had a
clear and beautifully made astral wheel and is notable for its combination of style, elaboration, portability, and practicality. Its form, in effect, was that of Nicholas of Lynn, but its substance was more varied
and original.[112]

Another type was a *calendarium ecclesiasticum et astronicum*. Bigger and
more elaborate than most calendars, this genre included non-medical
tracts, and its medical segments often had religious overtones. One fifteenth-century Oxford version was written entirely in Latin, unusual
among practical medical books, and parts of it were highlighted in gilt-
edge.[113] This made reference easier, but its price dearer. It was probably
designed for a physician; this copy had a uroscopy and a physiology
based on cosmology, as well as the calendars. A third variation was
fuller and more detailed still, but plainer and cheaper than the gilt-edged
versions. An example is another fourteenth-century manuscript, also in
Oxford.[114] In addition to the calendar, in this case clearly based on

[108] o.u. Bod. Ashmole Ms. 210ii, "Calendar."

[109] o.u. Bod. Ashmole Ms. 2101.

[110] *Ibid.*, f. 1.

[111] *Ibid.*, f. 10.

[112] o.u. Bod. Ashmole Ms. 210ii is similar to Ashmole Ms. 2101. The former has attached a sixteenth-seventeenth century tract on mathematics.

[113] o.u. Bod. Ashmole Ms. 789 vii.

[114] o.u. Digby Ms. 176. Other astrological calendars include: o.u. Bod. Ashmole Ms.
391v, "Astrological/Medical"; o.u. Bod. Digby Ms. 57, "Fragmentum ex. tract. de medicinae"; o.u. Bod. Rawlinson Ms. d251, "Astrological Miscellany," which includes a poem
entitled "Knowing the Veins."

Lynn, this tract had that distinct characteristic of post-Black Death medicine, a series of plague treatises that divided diseases into etiological types.

But most calendars were strict copies of Nicholas Lynn.[115] The *Kalendarium* was written about 1386 and dedicated to John of Gaunt, Duke of Lancaster and uncle to Richard II. Lynn was well known, and there has been speculation about his relationship with Geoffrey Chaucer, who was interested in astrolabes.[116] Lynn was also known as a mathematician, and may have been associated with Merton College.[117] This helps explain the *Kalendarium's*—and indeed, virtually all other almanacs' and calendars'—preoccupation with saints' days, sun and moon rises, eclipses and other astral phenomena. Its—and their—medical importance lay in giving the most propitious times for phlebotomy and other purgative treatments. This accounts for the zodiac men and *volvelle*, or spinning wheels, found in *Kalendarium* and almanacs, such as that composed around 1380 by John Somers.[118]

Lynn's *Kalendarium* was so popular that by the 1470s a cheaper, abridged version containing only the medical parts was put together. The abridgement centered on the ninth and eleventh canons of the full edition. The ninth canon dealt with the zodiac signs of the moon. Since the moon facilitated phlebotomy, bloodletting was to be avoided at all costs. The eleventh canon, by contrast, told of "the apt time for letting blood," the second and fourth phases of the moon.[119] Then the humors were least conducive to blood flow, for, like the tides, the flow of blood was dependent on such things. In the first and third quarters of the moon, the humors flowed from the interior out; this, obviously, was a bad time to bleed. But in the second and fourth they flowed from the exterior, and this was the right time. Overlaying the influences of the moon were the zodiac signs for the parts of the body, and the roles of the instruments used in bleeding. A hot iron, for example, changed the nature of the humors, and required additional strictures.

The twelfth canon of the *Kalendarium* was also medical. It explained the dispensing of medicines, and operated under the theory that the giving and receiving of medicines, especially laxatives, was also influenced

---

[115] Eisner, *Kalendarium*, pp. 34–35.

[116] *Ibid.*, pp. 2–5, 29–34.

[117] For a list of the medical Mertonians, see above, p. 14.

[118] Eisner, *Kalendarium*, p. 8.

[119] *Ibid.*, pp. 206–207.

by the movements of the heavenly bodies. This was due, at least in part, to the four powers—attractions, retentions, digestion, and expulsion—that went hand in hand with the humors. Each power related to a humor, and each humor to a zodiac sign. In turn, each power was considered strong or weak at particular times in the year. For if bloodletting or any other treatment were tendered at an inauspicious time, the patient could suffer an adverse reaction, and in some cases die.

The Bodleian Library has several good manuscript copies of the *Kalendarium*.[120] One version, dating from about 1400, was small—just forty-two vellum leaves with a parchment cover—and neatly written.[121] Yet despite its small size it contained all the essential elements, including a fine zodiac man and a sketch of an astrolabe. A second manuscript, dating from about 1450, is even shorter, with just twenty-nine leaves.[122] But it too had all the basic medical ingredients, including the omnipresent zodiac man. Both are good examples of the shorter, cheaper versions of the *Kalendarium* that became common during the fifteenth century. A third manuscript, also dating from the fifteenth century, was more elaborate.[123] In addition to a zodiac man it had a complete phlebotomy and an astral-based urology. All aspects of physic were closely tied to the movements of the heavenly bodies. This marked something of a departure or at least a variation from the strict interpretation of Galen, who stressed the independence of the humors and pneuma, or oxygen. It too was a result of the Black Death and the medical response to plague by the doctors of the Universities of Paris and Montpellier, and their search for a solution to the new diseases.

Gynecology and pathology were physic's other focal points. Gynecology was drawn from traditional authorities like Galen and Avicenna, from Soranus, a leading member of the Roman Methodist school, and the Trotula manuscripts.[124] English authors preferred the Trotula. The Dame Trot allegedly lived in eleventh-century Italy; in fact, the au-

---

[120] O.U. Bod. Ashmole Ms. 5, "Kalendarium"; O.U. Bod. Ashmole Ms. 370, "Kalendarium"; O.U. Bod. Ashmole Ms. 391v, "Astrological Medicine"; Mss. Ashmole 5 and 370 are just the Lynn texts, and acknowledge his authorship; as noted above, Ms. 390v is more in the tradition of the *Materia medica*, and contains other tracts.

[121] O.U. Bod. Ashmole Ms. 5.

[122] O.U. Bod. Ashmole Ms. 370.

[123] O.U. Bod. Ashmole Ms. 391v.

[124] Beryl Rowland, ed. *Medieval Woman's Guide to Health: The First English Gynecological Handbook* (Kent, Ohio: Kent State University Press, 1981).

thor—or, more likely, authors—were men who were associated with the medical faculty at Salerno.[125] This was unfortunate. For while parts of the Trotula suggest clinical practice, most of it bespeaks ignorance. Real experience, born of extensive personal contact, was prevented by prudery and the general reluctance of physicians to deal directly with patients. Further, many women took their gynecological problems to female empirics or midwives.[126] This too was unfortunate since female doctors were ridiculed by male physicians.[127] Hence there was little professional work on gynecology or obstetrics. The *Trotula*, by default, remained the major text. To make matters worse, this essentially inaccurate manual was further diluted in the fourteenth and fifteenth centuries in the rush to produce "how-to" books.[128]

The *Trotulas* were based on humoral theory and astrology.[129] Many came with *volvelle*, like the calendars, and used a kind of cosmological urology to determine gynecological problems and their treatment. The manuscripts opened with praise and sympathy for women and their medical problems. Women, the author claimed, had unique ailments, many fatal, and were often too embarrassed to discuss them with male doctors. This was wrong, a sin against God.[130] Women were hotter than men, and had more moisture: this explained menstruation. Disease was generally explained by the combination of three humors in the uterus: phlegm, yellow and black bile. Proper health, as usual, came from proper balance. Balance in turn came from diet, bloodletting, and drugs, the general solution for most medical problems. Using this base, the Trotula discussed a variety of ailments, especially those of the uterus. These ranged from the profound—rawness, aching, and inflammation—to the sublime—wind and its precipitation.

One part of the Trotula, that on childbearing, its strains and dangers, was good. It began with a clear and cogent segment on delivery, includ-

---

[125] Edward F. Tuttle, "The *Trotula* and Old Dame Trot: A Note on the Lady of Salerno," *BHM*, 50, 1976, pp. 61–72.

[126] Lucille B. Pinto, "The Folk Practice of Gynecology and Obstetrics in the Middle Ages," *BHM*, 48, 1973, pp. 513–523.

[127] See above, pp. 86–89.

[128] Braswell, "Utilitarian Literature," pp. 337–387. Also see: Suzanne W. Hill, *Chaste, Silent and Obedient: English Books for Women* (San Marino, Calif.: Huntington Library, 1982); and John Stanbridge, *A Fifteenth Century Schoolbook*, ed. William Nelson (Oxford: Clarendon Press, 1956).

[129] Rowland, *Medieval Woman's Guide*, p. 2–48.

[130] *Ibid.*, p. 58–59.

ing that by Caesarean section. Then it took the practical tone of the surgeon. There were graphic and accurate sketches of the positions the fetus could take during pregnancy, and how delivery might be affected. Fifteen types of "unnatural" births were discussed, along with special treatments in case of difficulties.[131] All this was exceptional to the general tradition of physic manuals. It described direct and practical treatments, and showed concern and compassion for the patient.

Trotula had rivals. Gilbertus Anglicus, one of the most prominent late medieval English physicians, wrote a general text which contained a section called *De passionibus mulierum*.[132] Some parts of it were culled from the Trotula. But others were original, more detailed, and sometimes more accurate. Illustrative were six sketches, adapted from but by no means identical to those of the Trotula, which showed the various ailments that affected women. The first was the retention of fluids during menstruation, and the second suffocation of the matrix. The third illustrated the method the physicians ought to use in discerning whether a woman is afflicted with either ailment: "Place a little vessel full of water on her breast; if it moves, she is alive, but if not, she is dead."[133] The fourth showed the kinds of women most likely to suffer from suffocation of the matrix, namely virgins and widows, "whose natural instincts had no outlets."[134] The fifth showed uroscopy as a tool for gynecological analysis during pregnancy, while the last showed dissection, though not always of women.

Together, the Trotula and the *De passionibus mulierum* formed the basis and showed the strengths and weaknesses of gynecology. More than the other branches of physic, its theory, diagnosis, and prognosis were conducted by doctors with a minimum of practical experience. Further, gynecology was even more impervious to change than the other medical specialties. From the eleventh through the fifteenth centuries methods developed hardly at all. But its practice was sometimes effective, primarily because of the skills of female empirics and midwives. They may have seemed ignorant to physicians, and they lacked formal training, but they had clinical experience, which was more important. A woman in labor probably had a better chance of receiving proper care than a man with kidney stones.

[131] *Ibid.*
[132] It is excerpted in Talbot, *Medicine in Medieval England*, pp. 80–83.
[133] *Ibid.*, p. 82.
[134] *Ibid.*

Among the best manuscript examples of gynecologies was a fifteenth-century tract called "Diseases of Women," in a general *Ars medica*.[135] Written in English, it was based primarily on the work of Gilbertus Anglicus, though it has mistakenly been attributed to that of Gilbert Kymer, the most prominent English physician of the fifteenth century.[136] Its theory was like that of the Trotula, based on the humors and claiming that women had less heat and more moisture than men. Hence they had periodic expulsions, that is, menstruation, and their treatment was to be adjusted accordingly.[137]

An Oxford manuscript, dating about 1500, abandoned humoral theory.[138] Rather, it presented recipes, some of which followed the treatment of the Trotulas, others of which were typical of general remedy books, and a few more of which were based on folk traditions. A London tract, compiled in English around 1510, was similar in format, sources, and order.[139] It was brief, running to just thirty folio pages, had no illustrations and limited marginalia. The author's justification for writing was that women were weaker than men and suffered doubly from the burden of childbirth. He then described the difficulties of childbirth, and offered practical and traditional as well as Trotulan cures. But different is not always better, and the recipe approach was also ineffective. Good intentions did not make effective medicine.

Like gynecology, pathology changed little in late medieval England. Given the depredations of plague, this is surprising. Pathology was based on urology, and was more clinical in approach than the other fields of physic. But pathologists were hampered by the lack of iatrochemistry and proper measuring devices. Further, the treatment of disease, a major part of late medieval pathology, was encumbered by humoral theory, making it dependent on Greek medicine, especially Hippocrates and Galen, neither of whom had seen plague nor most of the diseases of the late middle ages.[140]

---

[135] B.M. Royal Ms. 18A, ff. 35–57. This would appear to be an abbreviated version of B.M. Ms. Sloane 5.

[136] Talbot, *Medicine in Medieval England*, p. 80.

[137] O.U. Bod. Digby Ms. 79, "De morbis mulierum"; O.U. Bod. Ashmole Ms. 1416, "Midwifery."

[138] O.U. Bod. Rawlinson Ms. D 678, "Midwifery."

[139] B.M. Sloane Ms. 421A, "Diseases of Women."

[140] Phillips, *Greek Medicine*, is especially good on this.

A fourteenth-century manuscript shows this.[141] The manuscript was a general *Materia*, with a pathology and astrology linked by the newly popular astral physiology. It was derived almost entirely from Galen. A second example is a fifteenth-century pathology, large and well indexed, and comprehensive in its coverage of medical topics.[142] It too was Galenic, but related its various medical topics to pathology. Two other fifteenth-century Oxford manuscripts had good pathologies. One contained general tracts, including a plague treatise derived from John of Burgundy, remedies, and some nonmedical topics such as poems attributed to John Lydgate.[143] The other was more narrowly focused on pathology, and went into considerable detail.[144] But both were Galen derivatives. Pathology, then, showed physic at its worst. Ideas of entrenched authorities were glossed, but rarely rejected.

Some physic tracts were based on the work of individuals rather than subjects. The principal authorities in later medieval England were Richard Anglicus, Gilbert Anglicus, Bernard Gordon, John Gaddesden, Simon Bredon, Roger Marshall, and Richard Fournival. Richard lived in the twelfth century.[145] He has been described as a physician and professor at, variously, Salerno, Montpellier, and Paris. Nothing can be proved, but Montpellier was most likely. A number of texts have been attributed to him, particularly the first five sections of the *Micrologus*.[146] The first section was called the *Practica*, and concentrated on diagnosis and prognosis. The second was a urology, the third an anatomy, the fourth dealt with purgatives, and the fifth with prognosis once again. Richard's work was neither original nor particularly sound, which brings up the question of why anyone would use it. Perhaps the answer lay in his delivery; the *Micrologus* was written in clear, correct, and expository Latin. But it was drawn from classical sources, especially Hippocrates's *Aphorisms*; and was unusual only in that Aristotle was cited more often than in most medical texts, perhaps a reflection of the excite-

---

[141] o.u. Bod. Ashmole Ms. 345, "Pathology." In the seventeenth century it was owned by Kenelm Digby.

[142] o.u. Bod. Ashmole Ms. 1468, "Pathology." It also contains several non-medical tracts, including a *Piers the Ploughman*.

[143] o.u. Bod. Laud Ms. 598, "Pathology."

[144] o.u. Bod. Laud Ms. 685.

[145] *T&H*, pp. 270–271; Talbot, *Medicine in Medieval England*, pp. 58–61.

[146] Talbot, *Medicine in Medieval England*, pp. 158–161.

ment of twelfth-century scholars at getting the bulk of the Aristotelian corpus.

Sometimes, sections of the *Micrologus* were copied separately and used as texts. This was especially so with the *Practica*, which became common as a working guide for practitioners. One fourteenth-century edition discussed the body from head to toe, albeit in brief and rather incomplete fashion.[147] The author explained:

> Let the reader note that I do not deal with certain afflictions, such as epilepsy, chronic toothache, paralysis, apoplexy, etc., because I think they are incurable and I could find nothing certain or the fruit of experience in the authors I have read, though there are some quacks who vainly try to cure them.[148]

Also popular and often produced on its own was Richard's *Anatomy*. Richard divided the body into four principal organs: the brain, liver, heart, and testicles. This marked something of a departure from traditional humoral theory, and Richard made his case in great detail, setting up a scholastic debate between Hippocrates and Aristotle, arguing, among other things, on the role of the testicles and the origins of sperm.[149] But interesting though this might have been, Richard's format was old hat—that is, theoretical—and had little medical value.

Gilbert, who wrote in the thirteenth century, was more influential.[150] He is credited with compiling the *Compendium Medicinae*, one of the standard references for physicians until the seventeenth century, and was cited by Chaucer as a model physician.[151] Yet this renown is hard to explain. The *Compendium* was unoriginal, and, unlike the *Practica* of Ricardus Anglicus, was dull. It derived mainly from the *Aphorisms*, and to a lesser extent on Richard and Arabic physicians.[152] It might have been written by a doctor who had never seen a patient, which is of course pos-

---

[147] C.U.L. Ms. Ii 1 16.

[148] *Ibid.*, f. 51.

[149] Talbot, *Medicine in Medieval England*, pp. 60–61.

[150] *T&H*, pp. 58–60. Talbot, *Medicine in Medieval England*, p. 213, mentions H. F. Handerson, *Gilbertus Anglicus: Medicine of the Thirteenth Century* (Cleveland, 1918). I have not found it.

[151] Talbot, *Medicine in Medieval England*, pp. 76–77. It seems to have first been printed in Lyons in 1510. See Elizabeth Eisenstein, *The Printing Press as an Agent of Change* (Cambridge: Cambridge University Press, 1980), pp. 538–539. The reference in *Canterbury Tales* is pp. 30–35.

[152] Talbot, *Medicine in Medieval England*, pp. 76–77.

sible. Gilbert accepts without question the opinion of earlier authorities, and provides cures through exegesis and syllogism.

The *Compendium* has its strong points, as shown in a fine fourteenth-century version that survives in the Cambridge University Library.[153] This is a beautiful manuscript, with gilt edges, capitals in color, and a comprehensive table of contents. It was written in Latin in a clear hand, and had the names of two owners, physicians who practiced in the fourteenth and sixteenth centuries.[154] It had strengths of content as well as presentation, being rational and straightforward, and lacking the superstitious overtones that permeated Richard's *Practica*. In one section, that on leprosy, the explication might even be called pathbreaking.[155] Following the Salernitan tradition, it presented sound arguments for good hygiene and a balanced diet. There was a fine discussion of smallpox, one that in certain ways was better than the more famous analysis of Gaddesden, who has been credited with being the first Englishman to distinguish the disease from measles.[156] When this is considered with his analysis of leprosy, Gilbert appears as a first-rate epidemiologist. Further, he was more interested in surgery than were most physicians.

But it would be misleading to play too much on these strengths. The *Compendium*, as noted, was generally unoriginal; it is unlikely that Gilbert ever practiced medicine—and certain that he was not a surgeon.[157] It is in the surgery that Gilbert is most revealing. He claimed that the physician ought to keep his distance. His role was supervisory: "the main job of the physician is to know certain that obstruction to the passage of urine is due to no other cause than stone or the presence of blood clots."[158]

For years, historians thought Bernard Gordon was a Scot or an Englishman; it is more likely, however, that he was French.[159] National origins notwithstanding, Gordon was a major authority for physicians in late medieval England and, like Gilbert and John Gaddesden, was cited in *The Canterbury Tales* as a model doctor. A professor in the med-

---

[153] C.U.L. Ms. Ff 2 37, "Compendium."

[154] This is one of the manuscripts that belonged to Thomas Denman. See above, p. 123.

[155] Talbot, *Medicine in Medieval England*, p. 75.

[156] *Ibid.*, pp. 107–115.

[157] *Ibid.*, p. 79.

[158] C.U.L. Ms. Ff 2 37.

[159] *T&H*, p. 25; Talbot, *Medicine in Medieval England*, pp. 104–106. Other studies have been superseded by Demaitre, *Doctor Bernard de Gordon*.

ical school at Montpellier, he wrote his most influential text, the *Lillium medicinae*, between 1303 and 1305.[160] Two good versions survive in Cambridge and London.[161] The Cambridge tract was in a general manuscript called *De Astronomica mediocre* that, as the title suggests, had treatises dealing with other sciences, including astronomy and astrology. Appropriately, the aspect of the *Lillium* that was emphasized was the link between movements of the heavenly bodies, diagnosis and treatment. The London manuscript, by contrast, stressed another of Gordon's concerns, surgery. Indeed, so concerned with it was he that many contemporaries and a few modern scholars have treated him as a surgeon, despite his training and professorship.[162] The surgery in the London manuscript was written in Latin and was well indexed and organized; its only shortcoming was its length, which would have made it a cumbersome guide in actual practice.

The *Lillium*—innovative yet down-to-earth, suggestive yet always inclusive of traditional theories and treatments—proved extremely popular.[163] Originally written in Latin, by 1440 it had been translated into English, French, Spanish, German, and Hebrew.[164] But, like most other manuals of physic, its strengths sank in a sea of shortcomings. Gordon did not practice surgery—indeed, he may not even have practiced physic—and the *Lillium* lacked the direct, succinct descriptions of a practicing doctor.[165] When his rational theories were proved inadequate, he resorted to other ideas, especially superstition. An example was his treatment of skin diseases, ranging from leprosy and acne to scrofula. If they could not be cured by medication, he recommended the "king's magical touch."[166] And more than most other authors of physic manuals, Gordon was a moralizer. He told, for instance, of a Montpellier bachelor of medicine who first treated and then made love to a count-

---

[160] Demaitre, *Doctor Bernard de Gordon*, pp. 37–70. See too the discussion in Talbot, *Medicine in Medieval England*, pp. 104-106, 111–116.

[161] C.U.L. Ii I 13, "De astronomica mediocre"; B.M. Sloane Ms. 418.

[162] Talbot, *Medicine in Medieval England*, p. 97.

[163] *Ibid.*, p. 166. See Lynn Thorndike and Pearl Kibre, *A Catalogue of Incipits of Medieval Scientific Writings in Latin* (Cambridge: Medieval Academy of America, 1963); and Demaitre, *Doctor Bernard de Gordon*, pp. 37–70.

[164] Demaitre, *Doctor Bernard de Gordon*, p. 26.

[165] Demaitre is vague on this. He argues for practicality, but never really proves his point, and often hedges. See *Doctor Bernard de Gordon*, pp. 133–155.

[166] There is the famous book by Marc Bloch, *The Royal Touch: Sacred Monarchy and Scrofula in England and France*, trans. J. E. Anderson (London: R.K.P. 1973).

ess. As a result, the physician developed leprosy.[167] He argued, too, that "the Jews generally suffer from bleeding hemorrhoids," and that epilepsy could be cured by magic.[168]

Gordon's mix of knowledge and nonsense is further reflected in a passage about the relationship of medicine and the environment:

> But if the physician is in an army, then the King's tent and the tents of the physicians and surgeons should be on higher ground, facing a favorable wind; on no account should the tent be at a lower level where all the refuse gathers. Good fresh air, without any stench of corpses or any other things should be chosen. In summer, the tent should face south and the physicians should carefully take into account everything that might bring sickness on the army and eliminate it as far as possible; such things are heat, rain, rotting corpses, diseases, nuts, cabbages, trees, plants, reptiles, swamps, and such like.[169]

There is sound advice here. Even some of the more foolish statements were, in late medieval context, scientific, since they drew on the complex and logical Aristotelian-Galenic system. But his superstition and prejudices were also true to form. Hence, to cite another example, Gordon's explanation of an epileptic seizure: "My own opinion is that [the patient] became ill through too much roasted chicken given him by a woman; but no one can follow a decent diet when women are in charge."[170]

John Gaddesden was the most famous English physician of the late middle ages.[171] His masterpiece, the *Rosa anglica*, was copied over and over, and he too was lionized in *The Canterbury Tales*.[172] Gaddesden was born late in the thirteenth century, and died in 1349, probably a victim of the Black Death.[173] But little else is known of his life. One biographer believed he had studied at Montpellier, perhaps with Bernard Gordon and the eminent surgeon Henri de Mondeville.[174] Much of the *Rosa* was taken from their works, and the very title seems an English play on

---

[167] Demaitre, *Doctor Bernard de Gordon*, pp. 51–52.

[168] *Ibid.*, pp. 9, 158.

[169] As quoted in Talbot, *Medicine in Medieval England*, p. 105.

[170] *Ibid.*, p. 106.

[171] H. P. Cholmeley, *John Gaddesden and the Rosa Medicinae* (Oxford: Oxford University Press, 1912); *T&H*, pp. 148–150.

[172] Chaucer, *Canterbury Tales*, pp. 30–31.

[173] Cholmeley, *John Gaddesden*, pp. 9–21.

[174] *Ibid.*, pp. 12–19.

words from that of Gordon's in French. But there is no conclusive evidence, and Gaddesden's M.D. was probably from Oxford. He did more than practice medicine, serving both Edward II and Edward III as an administrator as well as a physician.[175] He was also a cleric and active theologian, and held several choice preferments.[176] His worldly success helps explain why he was so bitterly criticized by other doctors, an unusual circumstance among the cliquish physicians of late medieval England.[177] But the *Rosa* proved popular and influential throughout Europe, and in 1492 was printed at Pavia.[178]

The *Rosa anglica* was a compendium.[179] It drew from folk as well as Greek traditions, and had religious overtones. The practical, folk-based parts were the best. There was, for example, a section on scrofula that described the symptoms, suggested ointments for cures, and did not invoke the king's touch. Gaddesden occasionally called on charms and incantations, but only after more rational attempts had failed. There was a good section on surgery, and perhaps the best available collection on dentistry, though the latter might have been taken from Gaddesden's contemporary, Robert Sidestern.[180] Gaddesden also provided good advice on phlebotomy and the dispensing of drugs, particularly their overuse:

> I saw a man to whom the physician had given a sneezing powder made of pepper and ginger, not knowing the patient suffered from nose bleeding, and when he had taken it he lost so much blood that he swooned and bled for three days, so that he was thought to be dead.[181]

This led Talbot to conclude that Gaddesden occasionally performed surgery—a remarkable accomplishment if it were true.[182]

But as with the other authorities, it would be an error to overestimate

[175] *T&H*, pp. 148–150.

[176] *Ibid.*

[177] Guy de Chauliac, for example, regarded Gaddesden as a second-rate copyist. See *Chirurgie*, pp. 3–10.

[178] *T&H*, pp. 148–150.

[179] Two fifteenth-century copies are: B.M. Sloane Ms. 75; O.U. Bod. Bodley Ms, 608 (2059), "Rosa medicinae." The Oxford manuscript had inscribed the name of the physician Christopher Matteras, who in the sixteenth century was responsible for updating the *Rosa*. Parts of it are transcribed and analyzed in Cholmeley, *John Gaddesden*, pp. 22–74.

[180] Talbot, *Medicine in Medieval England*, p. 107.

[181] *Ibid.*

[182] *Ibid.*

the medical value of the *Rosa*. Most of Gaddesden's recipes sound like quackery; to excuse them, as Talbot did, as mere copying, does not make the *Rosa* more useful or its author more original or creative.[183] Further, whatever his interest in surgery, Gaddesden was bitterly critical of the best surgeons of his day, including Lanfranc of Milan and Bruno Longoburgo, for their innovative suggestions. At least when other surgeons, such as Henri de Mondeville, criticized their peers, they did so from a technical perspective.[184] Gaddesden also made some rather miraculous claims. He described his cure of a kidney stone by using a combination of scarabs and grasshoppers.[185] And parts of the *Rosa* seem to have been written for amateurs. Perhaps this helps to explain its popularity, for it was popularity rather than sound medical knowledge that distinguished its author. And if simplicity were in fact the key to the *Rosa*'s popularity it does not do credit to late medieval physicians.

Simon Bredon, a fellow of Merton College, Oxford, was the author of at least fourteen treatises on science.[186] One of these, the *Trifolium*, was primarily about medicine, and became both popular and influential early in the fourteenth century.[187] Divided in thirds, as the name implies, the first part dealt with problems of general health, in the Salernitan fashion, and the second with infectious diseases. The second part was composed before the Black Death, and drew mainly on classical sources. The third, called prophylaxis, presented cures drawn from Avicenna's *Canon*, and was traditional and conservative, even in the context of late medieval English physic. There is no mention of surgery, just pharmacy.

In all the *Trifolium* was comprehensive, methodical, predictable, unexciting, unoriginal, derivative, and ineffective. As with the *Rosa* it is hard to explain its popularity and influence, save perhaps from the author's affinity with the prestigious Mertonians.[188] Bredon was a successful scientist, and an authority on astronomy and the astrolabe. He was a priestly pluralist, was a hospital warden in Maidstone, and became

---

[183] *Ibid.*, pp. 110–112.

[184] See below, pp. 218–219.

[185] Cholmeley, *John Gaddesden*, pp. 48–52.

[186] *T&H*, pp. 320–322. See also Charles H. Talbot, "Simon Bredon (c. 1300–1372), Physician, Mathematician and Astronomer," *British Journal for the History of Science*, 1, 1962–1963, pp. 19–30.

[187] Talbot, *Medicine in Medieval England*, pp. 198–199.

[188] *T&H*, pp. 320–322.

quite wealthy. And he had a large library, which he bequeathed to Balliol, Merton, Oriel, and Queen's Colleges.[189] Bredon was also lucky. The survival of so many fragments of the *Trifolium*—to the best of my knowledge, there are no complete copies—made him well known. Availability may be the real reason for his popularity.

Most popular authors of physic manuscripts wrote before the plague. But one, Roger Marshall, wrote after.[190] Marshall was a fellow of Peterhouse Cambridge, and, as noted in Chapter Three, was a royal physician and the arbiter in a famous leprosy case in 1468. Like Bredon, he had a large personal library, which he bequeathed to Peterhouse College, and Gonville Hall, and perhaps to Pembroke and King's Colleges. Marshall was an active writer; glosses attributed to him can be found in at least a half dozen manuscripts.[191] He probably owned and wrote parts of another manuscript, now in the British Library, which contained tracts written or copied in the thirteenth and fourteenth centuries.[192] The manuscript itself is a fine example of a practicing physician's text: it was small and thick, well indexed, with clear, schematic diagrams, red *tabula*, and the kind of cramped marginalia that suggest frequent and continuous additions. Talbot attributes to Marshall another text, the *Lantern of Physicians and Surgeons*.[193] Be this as it may, the *Lantern* was unexceptional, and seldom cited as an authority. Rather, like Simon Bredon, Roger Marshall was best known for his glosses, his royal service, and the books he bequeathed. His physic was conservative and uninspired, and, given most physicians' veneration for older authorities, there would have been little to recommend his works over earlier authorities.

Also influential were the works of Richard Fournival.[194] A Frenchman, Fournival lived in the thirteenth century.[195] His father Roger was royal physician to the king of France, a position to which Richard succeeded; indeed, there is speculation that the son also served Hen-

---

[189] Breden's will is printed in F. M. Powicke, *Medieval Books of Merton College* (Oxford: Clarendon Press, 1931), pp. 82–86.

[190] *T&H*, pp. 314–315.

[191] *Ibid.* p. 315; B.M. Harl. Ms. 531; B.M. Egerton Ms. 889; O.U. Bod. Bodley Ms., 141; O.U. Bod. Laud Ms. 594; O.U. Magdelene College Ms. 174.

[192] B.M. Sloane Ms. 420.

[193] *T&H*, p. 315.

[194] Wickersheimer, *Dictionnaire*, p. 700.

[195] *Ibid.*

ry III.[196] What makes Richard so interesting is that his *magnum opus*, the *Liber alchyme*, became popular in England in the fourteenth and fifteenth centuries.

As the title implies, the *Liber* dealt with science as well as medicine. A fourteenth-century version, written in Latin and English, places medicine in the context of natural science.[197] The medical parts were, for the most part, derivative, drawing from Greek and Arabic sources. But Fournival added a new twist by using iatrochemistry to explain physiology, and made uroscopy the key to understanding medicine. Cure was effected through drugs, mostly of Greek rather than folk origin. The *Liber* was also interesting because it was more scientific than most physic texts. Fournival stressed mathematics and its role in both diagnosis and treatment.[198] But this novelty was obscured by the usual shortcomings. The iatrochemistry was that of theory, not the lab. As a royal physician—assuming, in fact, that he was—Fournival must have had some practical experience. But this was not apparent in the *Liber*, which was as impractical and in some ways more abstract than other manuals.

This raises an interesting question. If Fournival's scientific interests were atypical, what were most physicians reading once they came down from the universities? It is almost impossible to know. But there is evidence from the library of Thomas Denman. Denman, as noted, was a royal physician, a Cambridge M.D., and a fellow of Peterhouse College.[199] In his will, proved in 1502, he left Peterhouse several manuscripts, including seven on medicine. These were: *Medica quondam*, a general miscellany; Bernard Gordon's *Lillium medicinae*; a version of Avicenna's *Canon* from Jacobus de Partibus's *Super Avicennum*; William Holm's *De Simplicibus Medicinis*; a miscellany entitled *Medica magnini*; an *Astrologica*; and Gilbertus Anglicus's *Compendium medicinae*. Denman was a competent but by no means distinguished physician. He was wealthy, but not more so than most physicians. His royal and university careers were successful, but by no means exceptional. In effect, his library was probably typical of those of many late medieval physicians. If

---

[196] *Ibid.*, pp. 700, 721; C.U.L. Add. Ms. 4087, "Liber alchyme."

[197] C.U.L. Add. Ms. 4087, "Liber alchyme."

[198] Though like the work of some of the Montpellierans. See McVaugh, "Quantified Medical Theory," pp. 397–413.

[199] *T&H*, pp. 339–340; Eric Sangwine, "Private Libraries of Tudor Doctors," *JHM*, 23, 1978, pp. 167–184.

so, they were learning the same things physicians had a thousand years earlier.

Were there other tracts, perhaps anonymous, which were more original and creative? Two texts from the fifteenth century suggest not. One was a general workbook, dating from about 1450.[200] Perhaps belonging to a Cambridge don and entitled *De diversis et medicinsis*, it was a medical miscellany, drawing from Galen and Aristotle in content and method, but generally at second-hand.[201] It was small and compact, meant for use, and, despite its title, written mostly in English. It was indexed, had distinct chapter headings and clearly marked subjects. But as with manuscripts attributed to famous physicians the workbook was unexceptional and uninspiring. Diagnosis and prognosis were based on uroscopy and the treatment of herbals. Indeed, what distinguished it was a memorandum of expenditure stuck in the middle called "The Book of Costs."[202] Four physicians, Drs. Lang, Smith, Barnsley, and Walker, were listed, along with their fee schedules.[203] Unfortunately, the fees stand alone, with no reference to the ailment, the success of the treatment, or the financial situation of the patient. They range from eleven shillings, four pence, to four pence, with twelve pence the average.[204] It was, in essence, another commonplace book, seemingly typical of medieval physic texts.

A second fifteenth-century commonplace book combined treatises on astronomy, astrology, and cookery as well as medicine.[205] For a time it belonged to John Crophill, the East Anglian empiric discussed in Chapter Two. The manuscript was designed for practical use; it contained all the essentials of physic—uroscopy, gynecology, phlebotomy, what might be described as a marriage manual, and an herbal. Most of these segments were a distillation of more complicated and theoretical texts so that any physician and most empirics might understand them. The manuscript had a great many marginalia, both as text and graffiti, the latter including a woman with long, wavy hair, a gallows, and many phallic symbols.[206] Like the Cambridge commonplace book, that of

---

[200] C.U.L. Ms. Dd 5 76, "De diversis et medicines."

[201] *Ibid.*, ff. 12–24.

[202] *Ibid.*, ff. 25–27.

[203] *Ibid.*

[204] *Ibid.*, ff. 27-27b.

[205] B.M. Harl. Ms. 1735, "English Medical Texts."

[206] There are lots of bodies, men and animals, ships, urine flasks, monks and praying

Crophill had a list of patients and what appear to have been fees.[207] In general, the fees were low, even in towns and when treating the local gentry. Perhaps this was because of his part-time status. But it is important to note that the sick, even the sick poor, were treated by practitioners of physic like Crophill as well as by barbers and quacks. The ideas of Galen may have been misplaced and ineffective, but they remained popular even after the plague.

By means of conclusion, there is the workbook of Philip Allen, a physician who practiced in the mid-sixteenth century.[208] It was a general miscellany of the kind that late medieval general practitioners relied on, a series of recipes and selected manuscripts on topics like urology and gynecology.[209] The presentation was medical scholastic, the theory humoral, and the text in Latin and English. There was much about deontology, and in this it differed from most fifteenth-century texts, especially commonplace books. But, basically, a generation after Thomas Linacre, the foundation of the Royal College of Physicians and the advent of the "new" physic, the Allen manuscript proved more of the same. It was more sophisticated than the Crophill but it was a sophistication that reflected additional knowledge of old methods rather than a new approach. Allen may have come closer than most to comprehending fully the theories of Galen and his learned commentators, but he made no real attempt to break new ground.

This, of course, was the problem with traditional physic. Despite the new medical conditions of the later middle ages, its practice and nature did not change. Rather, it just got more complicated. When venerable methods failed, they were changed, but rarely scrapped. The format, practice, and mode of education remained stagnant. All this might—indeed, probably would—have been overcome, at least to some degree, had physicians undertaken clinical training and treatment. But the system of physic was moribund and, with physicians' social and financial positions never in jeopardy, there was little incentive to change.

---

devils. The cookery segments have splendid illustrations of the animals to be cooked, including rabbits, chickens, sheep, and pigs.

[207] There is controversy over this. See: Mustain, "Rural Medical Practitioner"; Rossell Hope Robbins, "John Crophill's Ale-Pots," *Review of English Studies*, N.S., 20, 1969, pp. 182–189; E. W. Talbert, "The Notebook of a Fifteenth Century Practising Physician," *Studies in English*, 22, 1942, pp. 5–30.

[208] Wellcome Ms. 38, "Medical Notebook."

[209] It is possible that C.U.L. Ms. DD 5 76 also belonged to Allen.

# 6

## CHANGING SURGERY

Like physic, surgery drew on a Greek corpus, particularly the works of Hippocrates.[1] The surgeon's concerns were with the bones and tissues rather than what Hippocrates referred to as "the soft parts."[2] Hippocrates regarded surgery as a last resort. Concerned with the difficulties of stopping bleeding and the high rate of post-operative infection, he argued that it ought to be attempted only when all other procedures had failed.[3] Further, Hippocrates recommended preceding surgery with phlebotomy, then following up in a few days with a purgation in order to avoid inflammation. The wound was dried with a sponge, and then coated with a linen cloth soaked in wine or vinegar. Hippocrates also advocated suppuration, the festering or "maturation" of a wound by covering it with corrosives to keep it open. Suppuration was practiced with few exceptions throughout the middle ages, usually to disastrous effect. It enhanced the prospect for infection, and probably killed many of the patients who survived the surgery.

Other classical authorities were no more helpful. Celsus, who wrote in the first century A.D., generally followed Hippocrates. He added some new procedures, including the use of sutures to help guard against hemorrhaging during phlebotomy.[4] But he was an advocate of suppur-

---

[1] A general reference to Greek surgery is E. D. Phillips, *Greek Medicine* (London: Thames and Hudson, 1973). See too W. A. Heidel, *Hippocratic Medicine: Its Spirit and Method* (New York: 1941); Ludwig Edelstein, *Ancient Medicine* (Baltimore: Johns Hopkins University Press, 1967); and George Sarton, *A History of Science*, 2 vols. (London, 1953–1959). References on medieval English surgery include: R. Theodore Beck, *The Cutting Edge: Early History of the Surgeons of London* (London: Lund Humphries, 1974); W. J. Bishop, *The Early History of Surgery* (London: Robert Hale, 1960); Jessie Dobson and R. Milnes Walker, *Barbers and Barber-Surgeons of London* (London: Blackwell, 1979); George Gask, *Essays in the History of Medicine* (London: Butterworth and Co., 1950); Geoffrey Parker, *The Early History of Surgery in Great Britain* (London: A. C. Black, 1920); John Flint South and D'Arcy Power, *Memorials of the Craft of Surgery in England* (London: Cassell and Co., 1886); Charles H. Talbot, *Medicine in Medieval England* (London: Oldbourne, 1967; and Young, *Annals of the Barber-Surgeons*.

[2] *Hippocrates*, vol. 3, trans. E. T. Withington (London: Loeb Classics, 1938).

[3] *Ibid.* There is a good abridgment in G.E.R. Lloyd, ed., *Hippocratic Writing* (New York: Penguin Books, 1983), pp. 277–314.

[4] For Celsus, see *De medicina*, trans. W. G. Spencer, 3 vols. (London: 1935–1938).

ation and corrosives, and recommended surgery only when other procedures had failed. As for Galen, he was less influential in surgery than
in other fields of medicine.[5] He accepted and passed on the Hippocratic
tradition with little modification.

Until 1150, most surgeons accepted classical procedures without
much question. The majority of operations were performed on the
limbs. Even successful surgery could be followed by post-operative infection. Within these constraints, surgeons could be effective. They set
bones and did lancing and bloodletting. Occasionally, they tried more
ambitious operations, such as trephining, a procedure for removing
bone fragments from the head.[6] Holes were bored into the base of the
skull, whence the surgeon set to work with his probes. But trephining
was unusual, and attempted only by the most skilled practitioners. For
most surgeons the normal role was that of craftsmen; they were the doctors who carried out the plans formulated by the physicians.

Change began in the middle of the twelfth century, starting in the
medical schools of Salerno and Bologna.[7] The faculty at Salerno benefited from traditional ties with Arabic doctors and medicine. Like the
Greeks, most Arabic doctors, including Avicenna, frowned on surgery.[8] But the Arabs placed more emphasis on anatomy and its integration into medicine.[9] A proper knowledge of anatomy was, obviously,
crucial to successful surgery. Just as important, Arabic medicine pro-

---

[5] For Galen and surgery see *On Anatomical Procedures*, trans. Charles Singer (London:
1956).

[6] There is a good description of the operation based on John Arderne's technique and
including illustrations in Sir D'Arcy Power, "English Medicine and Surgery in the Fourteenth Century," in his *Selected Essays*, rept. (New York: Augustus M. Kelley, 1970), pp.
29–47.

[7] An introduction to the medical faculties including a bibliography is provided in Vern
Bullough, *The Development of Medicine as a Profession* (New York: Hafner, 1967). Bullough
has written separate articles about the schools in Bologna, Paris, Montpellier, Oxford,
and Cambridge. See below, p. 332. See too Paul Oskar Kristeller, "The School at Salerno," *BHM*, 17, 1945, pp. 138–194; and Pearl Kibre and Nancy G. Siraisi, "The Institutional Setting: Universities," in David Lindberg, ed. (Chicago: University of Chicago
Press, 1978), pp. 120–144.

[8] For Avicenna, see: *The First Book of the Canon*, trans. O. C. Gruner (London: Luzac and
Co.: 1930); and sources, *Poem on Medicine*, ed. Haven C. Krueger (Springfield: Charles C.
Thomas, 1963).

[9] For Arabic medicine, see: Donald Campbell, *Arabian Medicine and Its Influence on the
Middle Ages*, 2 vols. (London: Kegan Paul, 1926); and Manfred Ullman, *Die Medizin im Islam* (Leiden: E. J. Brill, 1970).

1. Satirical illumination of an ape-physician treating a human.

2. In this surgical exploration of a fractured cranium, an incision in the shape of a cross—standard procedure—has been made in order to determine the extent of the wound and the internal condition. The doctor may be a physician, since he is wearing a stylish turban and a long robe.

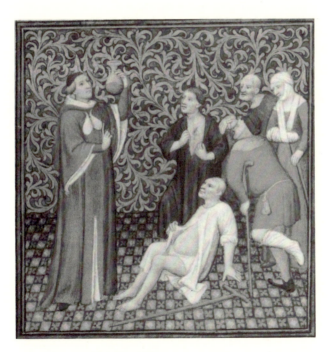

3. A physician examining a urine flask in a clinic.

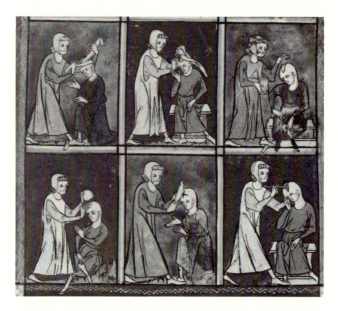

4. *A surgeon treating head wounds, probably fractures. The panels are of interest for the variety of treatments shown: in the first, a bandage, possibly a compress; second, a cleansing cloth; third and fourth, administration of a balm, called in the text* apostolicon chirurgicon; *fifth and sixth, exploration of the fracture, using the characteristic cross incision for probing; sixth, the probing itself. Note that medication comes before surgery. The surgeon wears a long, sleeveless outer garment over a short robe, and a tight-fitting bonnet. He has placed his foot on the patient's, perhaps to hold him down.*

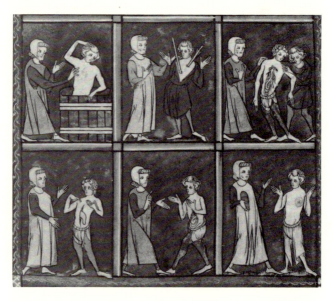

5. *This is another of the series of panels that runs for several pages, showing the surgeon performing a variety of medical treatments. In the third panel he has an assistant, dressed in a short gown. Here the surgeon is treating wounds to the body rather than the head, a rarity in the later middle ages.*

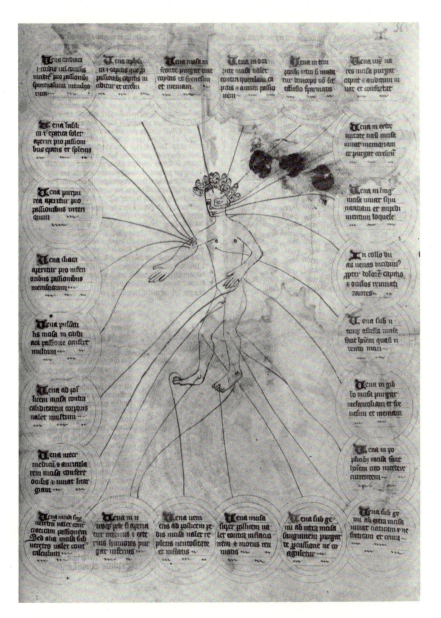

6. *This drawing depicts the appropriate times and places for letting blood. Each part of the body is linked to a condition and a time for bleeding. The bleeding points are colored red.*

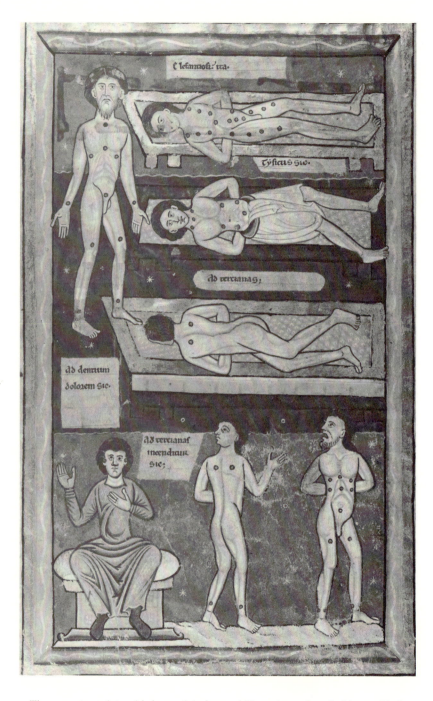

*7. These are cautery points, with characteristic charts and illustrations to show physicians, cookbook fashion, when and where to apply the iron.*

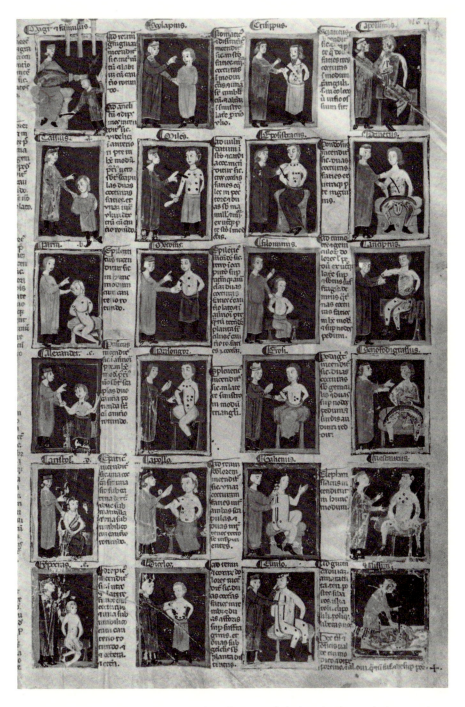

8. *This chart of cautery points shows twenty-four ailments, methods of treating them, and where to apply the iron. It is interesting, too, because it depicts famous doctors in each scene. Galen, for example, is treating kidney problems in scene 19, while Hippocrates is treating an eye condition in scene 21.*

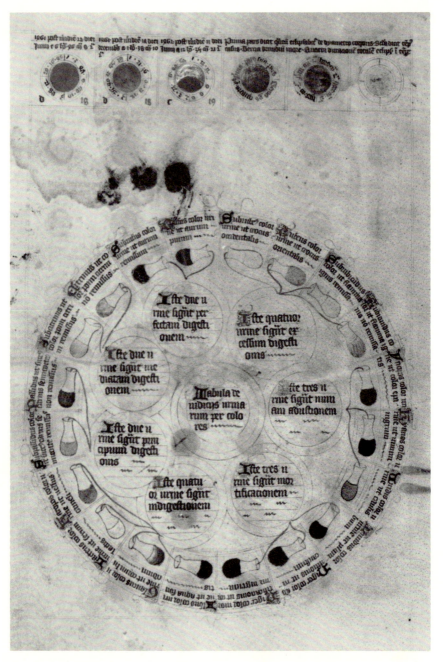

9. *This uroscopy chart, used in diagnosis, shows twenty different-colored flasks, divided into seven groups, each representing a condition of digestion. The colors range from ruddy red to green to milk white.*

10. *In one of the most famous of all medical illustrations, John Arderne is here ready to perform a proctological examination. Bearded and splendidly attired in turban and long-flowing robe, the great surgeon sits in a beautifully carved chair.*

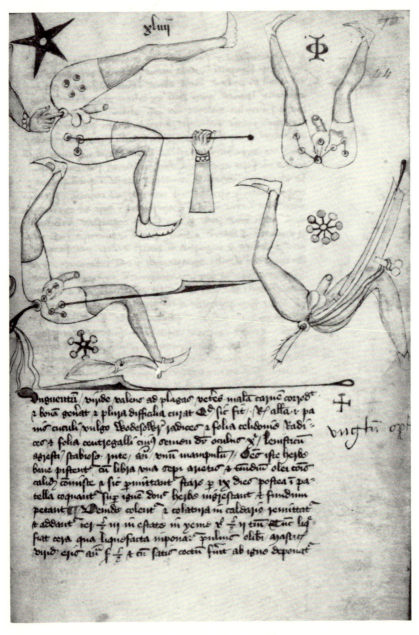

*11. Here Arderne, presumably having found the cancer, shows four steps in the operation. The incision marks, strings, and probes are clearly shown and graphically described.*

*Another key figure.*

duced several influential surgical writers, notably Albucasis.[10] Writing in the tenth century, Albucasis accepted the basics of the Hippocratic system, adding a list of ointments and medications that might be used as corrosives. But he was interested in the mechanics of surgery—that is, the instruments and the techniques of operation—and added a great deal about both. These became standards for medieval surgeons until the fourteenth century.[11]

Albucasis's influence appeared in the *Chirurgia* of Roger of Salerno.[12] Written around 1150, the *Chirurgia* was practical and didactic, eschewing much of the theory that cluttered earlier manuals, especially those of Galen and his commentators. It could be followed in a kind of cookbook fashion, a format which helped account for its popularity for over four hundred years, even after much of its theory had been discounted. The *Chirurgia* was divided into four books, all of which dealt with what might loosely be described as wounds. The first treated those of the hand, mostly from war. Incongruously, a potpourri of other ailments was discussed, including scrofula, toothache, and a variety of upsets of the stomach. The second book dealt with wounds of the neck, again mostly from war, and, again incongruously, with scrofula. The third dealt with potentially fatal wounds, primarily to the trunk, the part of the body that surgeons were reluctant to operate on; while the fourth treated wounds to the limbs, especially the legs.

Roger was especially interested in head injuries. For example:

> If the skin and cranium are cut open by a blow with a sword or a similar weapon, or by a blow with a rock or some such object, so that the skin hangs down or is cut, excise the hanging skin through the middle [of the wound] down to the fractured cranium with a rasp and suture from both sides.[13]

The wound was cleaned and medication applied, and if necessary, trephining would begin. A second procedure went like this:

> Concerning cranial fracture in the shape of a fissure. Sometimes it chances that the cranium is fractured like a fissure and is split so that neither side

---

[10] M. S. Spink and G. L. Lewis, eds., *Albucasis on Surgery and Instruments* (London; Wellcome Historical Medical Library, 1975).

[11] In some ways, they were more complex. See *ibid.*, pp. 127, 129, 131, 135, 349, 487, 623, for good examples.

[12] Roger of Salerno, *Chirurgia*, as quoted in Loren MacKinney, *Medical Manuscripts in Medieval Manuscripts* (London: Wellcome Historical Medical Library, 1965), pp. 66–67.

[13] *Ibid.*

seems higher than the other; also, it is uncertain whether the fracture extends inside the cranium. To find out, have the patient hold his mouth and his nostrils shut, then blow vigorously; if any breath comes out of the cleft, you know the cranium is fractured unto the cerebrum. Treat as follows. If the wound is narrow, enlarge it, and unless prevented by bleeding immediately trephin with an iron instrument, very cautiously on both sides of the fissures. Make as many holes as seems wise, then cut the cranium from one hole to another with a bistoury, so that the incision extends to the edges of the fissure. Carefully remove pus oozing from above the cerebrum with a silk or fine linen cloth, introduced sideways between the cerebrum and the cranium by means of fissures.[14]

The area to be operated on was cleansed, the surgery performed, and an ointment applied.

Another common operation was for scrofula, an enlarged lymph gland.[15] Initial treatment was offered by physicians—application of an ointment designed to shrink the gland. If this failed—and given the nature of these ointments it must have failed frequently—surgery was undertaken. Roger advised:

Scrofulas are threefold, arising in the throat, under the shoulder joints, and in the groins. . . . When they come to a head, incise them according to the nature of their location, so that pus exudes. If they harden and swell for a month or half a year, or if the patient is a boy, use this [prescription]. At the waning of the moon . . . take two poultices of fetid iris and wild radish; use one on the tenth day, another on the ninth, and so on to the end of the moon. On this, or some other day, bleed him once. If this medication is not sufficient, surgery must be resorted to . . . [the patient's throat] should be held firmly with one hand while the epidermis is cut longitudinally, then scraped and [the scrofula] caught with a hook and drawn out. . . .[16]

The contrast between physic and surgery is striking. (See Illus. 4, 5.)

Roger's treatment of war wounds was followed by subsequent authors. He described the extraction of an arrow:

If a wound is made by a barbed arrow we extract it as follows. If it is possible to use larger forceps we carefully grasp the barbs with the forceps and, bending them back to the stem of the arrow, retract it. But if this is difficult, we work a small iron or bronze tube into one of the barbs, retracing that barb into the tube, doing the same to the other barb. Thus with

---

[14] *Ibid.*

[15] The familiar skin condition is the manifestation of the glandular disease.

[16] Roger of Salerno, *Chirurgia*, as quoted in MacKinney, *Medical Manuscripts*, p. 73.

much care and diligence we skillfully extract the arrow. We can do this also with two goose quills.[17]

Two other operations reveal the skills of medieval surgeons. Hernia, like scrofula, was first treated by medication, and then with a truss. If these failed, surgery was performed. Roger recommended the following:

> Concerning the rupture of the peritoneum. The peritoneum is the membrane that prevents the intestine from falling into the scrotum; and often it is loose or only partly ruptured. If the aperture is small, only wind will escape, inflating [the scrotum] like a nut, or if large like an egg. The intestine may descend through the inguinal canal and press the peritoneum into the testicles, then creating a hernia. If the aperture is small and of brief duration, and if the patient is a boy, press a ligature over it and apply a poultice made of anagallis and the yolks of eleven eggs.[18]

If this was ineffective, a scrotal hernia operation was performed.

> If the intestines descend into the scrotum, first restore them to their proper place. If this cannot be done easily, clyster or purge, then apply mollificants and replace the intestines as we have said. Have an assistant place a finger on the rupture while the *medicus* cuts into the thin skin above the testicle at this point. Having extracted the testicle [from the peritoneum], scrape the inguinal canal even to the top with an instrument. If there is wind in the canal, decompress it internally. Suture [the top end of the inguinal canal] well with thread, and bind with thread, leaving it detached at each end so that it hangs an inch outside the suture. Placing the patient on a plank, burn the inguinal canal with cauteries three times, up to the thread. Then apply tow and egg and put the patient to bed for nine days, applying egg and oil as we have said. When the heat and the thread are gone from the wound, after nine days, foment with water in which bears' paws, vitriola, absinth, etc., has been cooked. Then treat as directed. . . .[19]

This was a serious procedure, and was rarely attempted.

Surgery for bladder stones and hemorrhoids was also risky, and generally used only when there was no other means of relief. But Roger was confident, as always. He wrote:

> If there is a stone in the bladder make sure of it as follows: have a strong person sit on a bench, his feet on a stool; the patient sits on his lap, legs

[17] *Ibid.*, p. 74.
[18] *Ibid.*, p. 78.
[19] *Ibid.*, p. 79.

bound to his neck with a bandage, or steadied on the shoulders of his assistants. The *medicus* stands before the patient and inserts two fingers of his
right hand into his anus, pressing with the left fist above the patient's
pubes. With his fingers engaging the bladder from above, let him work
over all of it. If he finds a hard, firm pellet, it is a stone in the bladder,
which [the bladder] is soft and fleshy; thus you find what impedes urina-
tion. . . . If you want to extract the stone, proceed it with light diet and
fasting for two days beforehand. On the third day, having done everything
beforehand, as we have said, to find whether there is a stone, bring it to the
neck of the bladder; there, at the entrance, with two fingers above the anus,
incise lengthwise with an instrument and extract the stone.[20]

Though it drew on Arabic medicine, much of Roger of Salerno's *Chirurgia* was original.[21] His expertise is shown in that most difficult of operations, trephining. Those surgeons who could perform it were an
elite, and Roger's procedure was different from Galen's. He bored a series of small holes rather than one or two larger ones; this meant greater
risk of bleeding and infection, but more space to clear away bone fragments without damaging the meninges. And Roger advocated—here as
well as for other procedures—the use of the sophoric sponge as an an-
esthetic.[22] The sponge was soaked in a solution derived from opium,
hyosciamers, mandrake, ivy, lettuce, and hemlock, and applied broadly
across the area to be operated on, and over the patient's nose and mouth.

Although the *Chirurgia* was didactic, it was too complicated for begin-
ners. Apprentices and even university students without extensive practical or clinical experience would have found the procedures difficult to
follow. It was designed as a guide for experienced surgeons, and it was
with these masters in mind that Roger came to the same conclusion as
the ancients. Surgery of any kind, however skilled the surgeon, was
dangerous, and the chances of a post-operative infection high. Hence,
the surgeon had to consider alternate treatments before going to his scalpel. This helps to account for the inclusion of potions and other cures of
physic in the otherwise quintessentially practical descriptions of surgical procedures.

There are several late medieval English versions of the *Chirurgia*.[23] All
were well indexed and easy to consult. The surgical and anatomical il-

---

[20] *Ibid.*, pp. 80–81.
[21] Talbot, *Medicine in Medieval England*, pp. 88–91.
[22] *Ibid.*, p. 90. Also, Bullough. *Development of Medicine*, p. 61.
[23] For example, see B.M. Sloane Ms. 1977, "Book of Surgery."

lustrations were good, though not quite so graphic and detailed as those in fifteenth-century copies of Henri de Mondeville, Guy de Chauliac, or John Arderne.[24] Perhaps this was a reflection of Roger's conservatism. For, despite its merits, the *Chirurgia* was not so innovative and daring as those of the best authors of the post-plague period, Chauliac and Arderne. This explains why the *Chirurgia* lost some of its appeal in the late fourteenth century. But Roger's practical, forthright, and detailed approach represented the initial breakthrough for surgeons from the text-bound surgery that was available in physic compendiums.

About 1200 William of Congenis wrote the next important surgical manual.[25] A professor at Montpellier, Congenis followed the example of Roger of Salerno in stressing the practical aspects of surgery. He was a teacher as well as a practitioner, a tradition at Montpellier, even among physicians—witness Bernard de Gordon—and one of the reasons it produced good surgeons. Students, William claimed, were taught: ". . . not merely listening but watching, because only in this way can the student obtain full comprehension of operating, and besides, this way he gets courage, because boldness is essential."[26] Congenis was important for his detailed descriptions and step-by-step directions for complicated operations, like trephining and removing tumors from other parts of the body, the removal of cataracts, and the repair of hernias. In essence, then, Congenis and his peers at Montpellier picked up in the thirteenth century where Roger of Salerno and his colleagues had begun in the twelfth, emphasizing the importance of practical skills and clinical experience. This was the seed of the superiority over physicians that English surgeons would achieve by the fourteenth century. For, as with Roger's *Chirurgia*, Congenis's manual was well copied and circulated in England.[27]

[24] See, for example, B.M. Sloane Ms. 3844.

[25] For a brief summary on William of Congenis, see Talbot, *Medicine in Medieval England*, pp. 93–95.

[26] As quoted in Talbot, *Medicine in Medieval England*, p. 93. See too Vern L. Bullough, "Teaching of Surgery at the University of Montpellier in the Thirteenth Century," *JHM*, 15, 1960, pp. 202–204.

[27] A good manuscript example is O.U. Bod. Ms. Bodley 553. In the mid-thirteenth century Bruno Longoburgo, a professor of medicine at Bologna and then Padua, broke with the Salerno-Montpellier tradition and placed greater emphasis on the works of the Greeks. This was unfortunate, for it meant playing down the practical surgery and stressing the theoretical. The influence of Longoburgo can be seen in the example of another influential Bolognese professor of medicine, Theodore of Lucca. Theodore's father Hugh had been a

William of Saliceto was a surgeon and a physician.[28] In Italy, as noted, the distinction between surgery and physic was less pronounced than in England. Physicians were still considered socially superior, but many surgeons were trained in universities, and most physicians were given some schooling in anatomy and at least the rudiments of surgery. William of Saliceto took advantage of this dual background in assembling his manual, the next important influence on English surgery. Not all of it was original; he combined elements from Roger of Salerno, William of Congenis, and the Arabs, especially Albucasis. But the text included descriptions of military surgery, suggesting that Saliceto, like Roger and the most distinguished English surgeons of the fourteenth and fifteenth centuries, polished his skills on the battlefield. And, like Roger, William of Saliceto was a master of the particular. Each procedure was described in minute detail, allowing a skilled surgeon to follow along, step-by-step.

A good edition of William's *Surgery* is a late-fourteenth-century copy in Latin.[29] It was well organized, clear, and logical, with an exhaustive index and excellent illustrations. One of these showed a surgeon lancing an arm, while his assistants held down a grimacing patient.[30] Such assistants, apprentices, or perhaps what in craft guilds were referred to as journeymen, were expected to learn by watching and participating in the more mundane parts of the operations. Be this as it may, the illustration suggests how difficult this and most other procedures were. The patient appears to have been in great pain. Holding him down must have been difficult and required a great deal of energy; indeed, their physical

---

practicing and practical surgeon in Bologna early in the thirteenth century. But Theodore rejected out of hand his father's kind of surgery, and stressed theory. He became a Dominican, further limiting the kinds of surgery he could perform, and toward the end of his life was often referred to as a physician. To air his perspective, he compiled his *Chirurgia magna*. Some parts of his work do give practical advice—the use, for example, of alcohol-based liquids as a disinfectant. But its tenor is theoretical, and it is difficult to distinguish it from texts of physic. This did not affect English surgeons. See Eldridge Campbell and James Coltan, eds., *The Surgery of Theodoric*, 2 vols. (New York: Appleton Century Crofts, 1955–1960); Vern L. Bullough, "Medieval Bologna and the Development of Medical Education," *BHM*, 32, 1958, pp. 201–215; Bullough *Development of Medicine*, pp. 61–62; and Siraisi, *Taddeo Alderotti*, pp. 15–18.

[28] For William, see Talbot, *Medicine in Medieval England*, pp. 99–101; Bullough, *Development of Medicine*, pp. 61–62. Bullough regards him as seminal.

[29] B.M. Add. Ms. 17810, "Chirurgia."

[30] *Ibid.*, f. 1.

exertions probably kept the assistants from watching as much of the surgery as they would have liked. The master performed in a characteristic long gown, to distinguish him from short-gowned barber-surgeons, and a skullcap. And the operation was performed before a gallery, presumably of masters and, if there were room and they were not otherwise occupied, assistants and students. (See Illus. 2.)

William of Saliceto was outdone by his student, Lanfranc of Milan.[31] Although not as famous on the continent as two later writers, Henri de Mondeville and Guy de Chauliac, Lanfranc was influential in England, and wrote one of the best surgical manuals of the middle ages. John Arderne, for one, seems to have been influenced more by him than by any other writer, including Henri and Guy. Lanfranc's principal texts, *The Major Surgery* and *The Minor Surgery*, follow the themes of his mentor and the Salerno-Montpellier tradition. Two good editions, both combinations of his major texts, survive from around 1400.[32] Their format divided the combined surgeries into thirds. The first third defined the goals and limits of surgery and included a deontology and a discussion of the surgeon's role. The second had an anatomy, and the third an "acts," that is, the procedures for operating. Both manuscripts had exhaustive tables of content, allowing for easy and quick reference. Like virtually all the other copies of Lanfranc's surgery they were small and compact, and relatively cheaply produced, which made them portable and affordable. They could have been carried into an operating room, or in the bags of a surgeon traveling his circuit.

Lanfranc's work was more comprehensive than that of his predecessors. He treated everything from brain tumors to baldness, but never recommended surgery casually.[33] Rather, he recounted the problems of stemming the blood flow and the high rate of infection.[34] He wrote of the difficult conditions and the physical demands on the surgeon. But once committed he proceeded with a rare combination of innovation and bravado. He was, for example, one of the few surgeons who described procedures on the trunk of the body as well as those on the head and

[31] Lanfranc of Milan, *The Science of Chirurgie*, ed., Robert von Fleishhacken (London: EETS, cii, 1894).

[32] o.u. Bod. Ashmole Ms. 1396, "Science of Cirurgie"; b.m. Add. Ms. 10440, "Anatomy and Surgery."

[33] Lanfranc, *Science of Cirurgie*, pp. 3–21.

[34] *Ibid.*, pp. 64, 98, 111–113.

appendages.[35] Yet despite this break with the past traditions, Lanfranc had a keen interest in classical medicine. Describing what he called the "science of surgery," he explained the Greek etymology of the word and proclaimed a unity of all the medical sciences. These he defined as having the bases of "cutting, healing and removing excrescences."[36] But Lanfranc broke with the medieval interpretation of the classical tradition in his advocacy of clinical practice.[37] Indeed, his surgeries were in large part given over to descriptions of war wounds, which suggests the customary military background.

Lanfranc was also concerned with deontology.[38] The surgeon must be temperate, balanced, and a "well-made" man, both in appearance and outlook. Ugly surgeons scared off patients and probably had bad manners.[39] A surgeon should have a broad, general education; otherwise, he might be mistaken for a craftsman. He should know philosophy, grammar, and rhetoric as well as the subjects of the quadrivium. He must be generous and pleasant with his patients; he could not be gluttonous or niggardly. Bedside manner was important. The surgeon should always tell the patient that he would recover, no matter how gloomy the prognostication. But at times he must be honest; he should tell the family and friends of the patient the truth. Money was an important consideration. Rich surgeons were happier and more effective than poor ones, and likelier to obtain high social standing; furthermore, riches freed the surgeons for things like charity work. The surgeon should be modest. Too much self-praise was not becoming. He should never denigrate his colleagues, and never give advice contrary to theirs.

Lanfranc's deontology is similar to that found in other surgical manuscripts.[40] But he went beyond other authors in urging that surgeons learn physic and become familiar with the "science of mixture," that is, pharmacy.[41] Accordingly, a section of the manual was given over, not surprisingly for an individual who so venerated the Greeks, to a discus-

---

[35] *Ibid.*, pp. 161–176.

[36] *Ibid.*, p. 8.

[37] Talbot, "Medicine," pp. 391–396, argues that classical surgery was indeed practical. Be this as it may, the medieval perception was that ancient doctors stressed theory.

[38] Lanfranc, *Science of Cirurgie*, p. 8.

[39] *Ibid.*

[40] Deontology was rare, however, in physic manuals. Physicians apparently did not feel the need to list professional and ethical characteristics.

[41] Lanfranc, *Science of Chirurgie*, pp. 9, 346–55.

sion of physic designed for surgeons.[42] It was unoriginal and based on humoral theory, and good physicians would have found it boring, pretentious, and simplistic. But it was important because it points out the retrograde aspects of even the best pre-plague, pre-Hundred Years War surgeries. Practical though they might have been, surgical authors still revered physicians. Lanfranc based many of his procedures on physic and the humors, and linked successful surgical procedures, especially bleeding, with the behavior of the heavenly bodies.[43] This explains the almanacs and calendars that surgeons and barbers as well as physicians and university dons carried about.

It would be misleading, however, to leave Lanfranc on a sour note. After describing physic and its effect on surgery he proceeded apace to the task of the surgeon. The surgeon performed three major tasks.[44] He: "undoes that which is whole, as when he bleeds, scarifies or cauterizes. He heals wounds; and he removes the aforementioned excrescences, like cataracts or polyps."[45] Lanfranc stressed the importance of a proper knowledge of anatomy. He described in detail the parts of the body, their characteristics, and how to treat them under a bewildering array of conditions. An example, perhaps learned on the battlefield, was Lanfranc's account of wounds in the sinews, by which he meant the nerves. A wound cutting the nerve was treated lengthwise. This afforded less opportunity for damaging the nerve, and was the easiest such operation to perform. If the nerve was cut, the limb would lose all feeling, and hang loosely. If the nerve was punctured, the result would be muscle cramps. In both cases, the first step in treatment—a partial reflection of Lanfranc's preoccupation with physic—was to open the skin, provide an ointment, hot oil, and, if there was considerable pain, opium.[46] Then, if necessary, the surgeon operated.

Lanfranc was notable in another respect. Toward the end of his career, he moved from Italy to the University of Paris.[47] His presence there helped to bring to northern universities, including Oxford and Cambridge, the more advanced ideas and techniques of Italian and Provençal surgery and anatomy. It was probably from Paris rather than It-

---

[42] *Ibid.*, pp. 18–20.
[43] *Ibid.*, p. 201–209.
[44] *Ibid.*, pp. 18–19.
[45] *Ibid.*
[46] *Ibid.*, pp. 39–42.
[47] *Ibid.* For details on Lanfranc, see Talbot, *Medicine in Medieval England*, pp. 97–102.

aly that the first copies of Lanfranc's surgeries came to England late in the thirteenth century. And at Paris Lanfranc paved the way for the two leading continental surgeons of the fourteenth century: Henri de Mondeville and Guy de Chauliac.

Henri de Mondeville met Lanfranc in Paris and was directly influenced by him.[48] Mondeville was educated at Montpellier, exposed to the work of Roger of Salerno and William of Congenis, and taught there before moving to Paris. Montpellier may have had a better medical school, but Paris was more prestigious, and because of its location offered better opportunities. One of these opportunities was royal service, which Mondeville took up at the court of Philip the Fair. Mondeville was direct and brusque. He was a cleric and a theologian, and his text is presented in scholastic fashion. But neither philosophy nor theology entered his argument; Mondeville was above all practical, and his *Chirurgie* was designed for teaching.

Three things distinguish Mondeville's surgery. First, like Lanfranc, he stressed deontology: between them they began a trend that later authors followed. Second, in its original if not always copied forms the *Chirurgue* contained thirteen graphic anatomical drawings, complete with descriptions.[49] And, third, he was very well read. He quoted fifty-nine established authorities, from Hippocrates to Lanfranc. In a sense, Mondeville even more than Lanfranc combined his surgical experience, which included military service, with bibliophilia in writing his manual. Perhaps this was why he became the single major authority early in the fourteenth century.[50]

Book I is the most interesting part of his surgery, covering anatomy, deontology, and general professional problems. Mondeville was careful to separate surgery from physic. But instead of praising physic, as did most surgical writers, he excoriated it. He praised surgery, raising it to a position of equal authority and at times implied that it was superior. Mondeville ridiculed physicians who refused to consider any aspect of

[48] See: Louis Dulieu, *La Chirurgie a Montpellier de ses origines au debut du xixe siecle* (Avignon: Les Presses Universelles, 1975); Talbot, *Medicine in Medieval England*, pp. 101–104; and Bullough, *Development of Medicine*, pp. 57–59. Edited versions of his surgery are: E. Nicaise, *Chirurgie*, 2 vols. (Paris: Feliz Alcan, 1893); and A. Bos, ed., *La Chirurgie*, 2 vols. (Paris: Librairie de Firmin Didot Et Cie: 1896). I have used Nicaise.

[49] Mondeville's drawings are in Charles Singer, *The Evolution of Anatomy* (London: Kegan Paul, 1925).

[50] Talbot, *Medicine in Medieval England*, p. 103.

surgery and in some instances even anatomy, and who looked down on most skilled master surgeons. And he condemned those physicians, mostly Parisians, who bypassed surgeons when they did prescribe surgery, and called instead on "ignorant" barbers.[51]

Book II discussed wounds, ulcers, and hemorrhages. It was more detailed than its predecessors, but its content was substantially the same. Book III was more original. It dealt with particular surgical problems, such as incision, cautery, phlebotomy, amputation, embalming, and abscesses. Here Mondeville made some of his most perceptive points. He believed that a wound was best treated by applying salves or balms and then letting it heal, or, if the bleeding was especially bad, using ligatures.[52] This ran contrary to conventional theory, which argued that wounds ought to be kept open, if necessary with caustics.[53] For a few decades in the fourteenth century, many surgeons followed Mondeville. But when the even more influential Guy de Chauliac stressed caustics, the Mondeville argument was pushed aside.[54] It was not until the eighteenth century that the ligature argument finally and completely won out. Book IV was planned but never written. Mondeville fell sick and never even began it. But there was a Book V, apparently started earlier. It treated medicines for surgical procedures. It was drawn largely from Avicenna, and presented no new ideas.

A good English language copy of Mondeville was made in 1392.[55] It was large, passed through several owners, had a good tabula, albeit without colored headings, and must have been easy to use. Further, in addition to the standard illustrations that distinguish the Mondeville manuscripts, it included drawings of surgical instruments.[56] It was, in all, a practical manuscript, and probably belonged to a practicing surgeon. Clarity and practicality were characteristics of Mondeville and

[51] Mondeville, *Chirurgie*, ed. Nicaise, pp. 95–119.

[52] *Ibid.*, pp. 513–575.

[53] Among the few who agreed with Mondeville was Theodore of Lucca. See Siraisi, *Taddeo Alderotti*, pp. 16–18. Occasionally, so did John Arderne.

[54] Margaret S. Odgan, ed., *The Cyrurgie of Guy de Chauliac*, 2 vols. (London: EETS, 265, 1971). See too Bjorn Wallner, *The Middle English Translation of Guy de Chauliac's Treatise on Wounds* (Stockholm, Almqvist and Wiksell, 1979), which is Book II of the surgery, and deals primarily with wounds; and W. A. Brennan, trans., *On Wounds and Fractures* (Chicago: University of Chicago Press, 1923).

[55] Wellcome Ms. 564, "Chirurgia."

[56] *Ibid.*, f. 163.

Lanfranc, and explain why their surgeries were more popular than those of Roger of Salerno, William Congenis, or William of Saliceto.

Lanfranc and Mondeville were superseded in the middle of the fourteenth century by Guy de Chauliac's *Cyrurgie*.[57] Guy remained the most popular surgical authority in England and northern Europe through the fifteenth century, and his manual was used in some places until the 1720s.[58] Dozens of late medieval copies have survived.[59] They were big, well organized, straightforward, and easy to follow, even for an inexperienced surgeon.[60] They were written in English and Latin, were profusely illustrated, and must have been expensive. With their wide margins for glosses and colored section headings, both kinds of *Cyrurgie* hint at the reason for Guy's enduring popularity.

Guy de Chauliac was also popular because of his ideas. He wrote after the Black Death, when many people were disillusioned with physic; furthermore, his ideas sometimes broke from surgical traditions.[61] Guy was a scathing critic, contemptuous of just about all of his predecessors save Galen.[62] He was a good anatomist. And he emphasized clinical training to a greater degree than most surgical writers before him. There is no evidence that he had military experience, as Lanfranc and Mondeville seem to have had, but he spent a great deal of time in practice in addition to writing and teaching.[63] And the practice prospered, for Guy included among his patients several popes and the king of France.[64]

[57] In addition to editing Guy, Margaret S. Odgan has written two articles. See her: "Galenic Works Cited in Guy de Chauliac," *JHM*, 28, 1973, pp. 24–33; and "Guy de Chauliac's Theory of the Humors," *JHM*, 24, 1969, pp. 272–292. See too Talbot, *Medicine in Medieval England*, pp. 116–17, 191–195; and Bullough, *Development of Medicine*, p. 58.

[58] Fernand Braudel, *Civilization and Capitalism*, i, trans. Sian Reynolds (New York: Harper and Row, 1979), p. 80, claims Guy went through sixty-nine editions between 1478 and 1895. In most cases, however, his work was replaced in the sixteenth century by the works of Ambroise Pare. See: Geoffrey Keynes, ed., *The Apologee and Treatise of Ambroise Pare* (London: Falcon Educating Books, 1951); D. W. Singer, trans., *A Selection from the Works of Ambroise Pare* (London: Macmillan, 1924); W. B. Hamby, *Ambroise Pare, Surgeon of the Renaissance* (St. Louis: Green, 1967); and Hamby, "Ambroise Pare," *Dictionary of Scientific Biography*, 10, 1974, pp. 314–317.

[59] For example, see C.U.L. Ms. Dd 3 52, "Antidotary."

[60] For example, see C.U.L. Gonville and Caius Ms. 336, "Medical Miscellany."

[61] Robert S. Gottfried, *The Black Death* (New York: The Free Press, 1983), pp. 104–128.

[62] *The Cyrurgie*, pp. 2–16.

[63] See Lynn Thorndike, *A History of Magic and Experimental Sciences*, iii (New York: Columbia University Press, 1934), pp. 518–524.

[64] *The Cyrurgie*, p. 9.

For all this, Guy's *Cyrurgie* was less original than Mondeville's, and much of it was taken from Lanfranc.[65] And for all the debunking, much of the *Cyrurgie* was retrogressive. As noted, Guy insisted on treating wounds with cautery and suppuration rather than with salves and balms and, if necessary, ligatures, as Mondeville advised.[66] Guy's method led to infection, and in the view of some historians of medicine set surgery back for three hundred years.[67] But the force of his personality, his reputation, the comprehensiveness and fine organization of his manuscript, his thoroughness as an anatomist, and the very size of his manual—the modern transcription runs to 639 pages—combined to make him the principal surgical authority of the later middle ages.

These were the continental authorities whose works were copied and circulated among Englishmen. Their influence was considerable, and probably prevented more Englishmen from writing. They especially inhibited the compiling of general texts. Even so accomplished a surgeon as John Arderne, in his specialties far better than Chauliac, was tentative and unoriginal in his general *Practica*, which he took largely from Guy.[68] But when they dealt with particular problems English surgeons were unmatched—precise, decisive, and authoritative.

John Mirfield, John Arderne, and Thomas Morstede were the most widely read English authors. Mirfield, who died in 1407, was an unlikely authority.[69] Trained as a physician, he was a cleric, and may never have practiced medicine.[70] But he treated surgery in the ninth section of

---

[65] *Ibid.*, especially Books I, II, and IV, and particularly the parts in IV on ulcers, which is also similar to the work of Roger Salerno. Guy does acknowledge other surgeons, even when he defames them. Some authors took credit for every idea in their texts.

[66] *Ibid.*, especially Books I and II.

[67] See, for example. Erwin N. Ackerknecht, *A Short History of Medicine* (Baltimore: Johns Hopkins University Press, 1982), pp. 89–90.

[68] John Arderne, *Treatise of Fistula in Ano*, ed. D'Arcy Power (London: EETS, 139, 1910). I am unaware of a translation or transcription of the entire *Liber medicinarium sive receptorum liber medicinalium*. Excerpts are in D'Arcy Power, trans., *De Arte Phisicale* (London: J. Bale and Co., 1922). Good manuscript versions are B.M. Ms. 335; and Sloane Ms. 962. Arderne wrote or is credited with three other texts. They are a commentary on Isaac Judeus's *De judiciis urinarium phlebotomiae*, in English; University Library, Glasgow, Ms. 328; *Hoc est speculum phlebotomaie*, B.M. Sloane Ms. 56; and *Scala sanitatis*, B.M. Add. Ms. 1080. Unlike the *Fistula*, they are not original or particularly interesting.

[69] See Sir. Percival Horton-Smith Hartley and Harold Richard Aldridge, eds., *Johannes de Mirfield: His Life and Works* (Cambridge: Cambridge University Press, 1936), pp. 2–34.

[70] Ironically, Talbot and Hammond present this as the reason for not covering him in *T&H*, p. 422.

a fifteen-part compendium called the *Breviarium Bartholome*, a reference to St. Bartholomew's Hospital in London, with which he was associated.[71] Most of the *Breviarium* was derivative, drawing from Galen and Greek physic; and most of the surgery was culled from Lanfranc of Milan.[72] Yet the *Breviarium* proved to be a practical and highly usable tract, the result perhaps of Mirfield's friendship and even collaboration with Adam Rous, surgeon to Edward III and the Black Prince, and companion to the prince in his Poitiers campaign.[73] Mirfield may also have known John Arderne and John Gaddesden.[74] In any case, he, like Henri de Mondeville, read extensively. If he had never seen a battlefield, he must have talked with participants or read the accounts of those who had. And Mirfield went beyond discussion of the usual kinds of war wounds caused by lance, sword, and arrow to discuss a new kind, that caused by gunshot.[75] Herein he was a pioneer, whose work served as a starting point for later authors.

Mirfield made another contribution. He played down, even belittled, the differences between physic and surgery.[76] The distinction, he claimed, was the result of physicians' arrogance. In the past, physicians, like surgeons and barbers, had learned anatomy, let blood, and even shaved. But then they got rich, and disdained working with their hands. This was bad, for: "the distinction was rather artificial. To be a good physician one had to be a good surgeon. A physician must know how to bleed and shave, and much of the distinction between the practices was due to the arrogance of the physicians."[77]

The *Surgery* was divided into eight parts. The first dealt with the general treatment of the wounds. It had six short chapters, a listing of which gives the flavor of Mirfield's approach: 1. On some categories. 2. On simple wounds in the flesh only. 3. On the methods of bandaging wounds. 4. On the methods of suturing wounds. 5. On the methods of washing wounds. 6. On diet of the wounded. None of the chapters was as concise as it might have been. Admonitions to Jesus and Christian

[71] John Mirfield, *Surgery*, ed. James B. Coltan (New York: Hafner, 1969).

[72] Mirfield also wrote a second medical text, called the *Florarium Bartholomei*. This had religious overtones, and long sections on the proper role of the Christian healer.

[73] Mirfield, *Surgery*, p. ix. See above, p. 138, for Rous.

[74] *Ibid.*, pp. ix, 143.

[75] *Ibid.*, p. 14.

[76] *Ibid.*, pp. 5–6.

[77] *Ibid.*

physicians, so overwhelming in his other text, the *Florarium*, ran throughout this one as well. But as the chapter headings suggest, the business of surgery was dealt with in its most essential terms, and the importance of a clerical physician praising surgery and belittling physic ought not to be overlooked. Mirfield's advice was almost always sound. He emphasized keeping wounds clean and the patient calm and rested. And he knew when the surgeon could no longer help: "But you should know that every wound, after it persists beyond four or five months, is incurable; for it is not called a wound but a cancer. . . ."[78]

So went the next seven chapters. Chapter Two "treated wounds and blows, particularly those which can occur in any part of the head, neck and throat."[79] It had sixteen subdivisions, dealing with wounds to the eyes, and wounds from "arrows or weapons of the like."[80] Mirfield continued to encourage sanitation and cleanliness, advising surgeons not only to keep the wound clean but to wash their hands before operating. The surgeons should shave as well, and scrub down, using balms, salves, rose oil, egg yolks, and warm water. Mirfield was cautious. He discussed trephining, but discouraged it as too risky.[81] The surgeon's basic job was to work with fractures and wounds.

Chapter Three dealt with "wounds involving the anterior clavicle as far as the last vertebra next to the arms, and wounds of the arms, the hands and the like."[82] Mirfield described how to take stitches and sutures, and how to treat damaged nerves. He discussed the dangers of a punctured stomach, a recurring challenge for a military surgeon, problems in dealing with damage to the intestines, and general injuries to the spine. And in an allusion to Galen and classical authorities, he recommended the use of Armenian clay as a poultice.[83]

Beginning with Chapter Four, Mirfield's sections got shorter, and the surgery less useful. He seemed to have run out of things to say, and his comments became less succinct and clear. Perhaps clerical modesty came to play, for Chapter Four discussed "wounds which can occur

---

[78] *Ibid.*, p. 21.

[79] *Ibid.*, p. 27.

[80] *Ibid.*

[81] *Ibid.*, p. 51.

[82] *Ibid.*, p. 81.

[83] *Ibid.*, p. 123. Armenian clay is rich in iron oxide. Galen recommended it first as an astringent, and then as a remedy for pestilence.

from the anus and genitals down as far as the foot."[84] The fifth chapter
dealt with wounds and bites from puncture, including subsections entitled: "The Wounded Man: Will He Live?" "Bites of Men and Horses";
and "Punctures of the Muscles in Phlebotomy," once again problems
confronted by military surgeons.[85] To the modern eye, this is Mirfield's
weakest segment. He quoted the work of John Gaddesden and the Salernitans, but relied mainly on that kind of folk medicine furthest re-
moved from clinical practice. The dangers of coitus were expounded on,
and doctors were cautioned about operating too near the menstrual
cycle. Most of the treatments for wounds were herbal. But even here,
Mirfield showed good sense. Surgeons were advised to keep themselves
and their patients as clean as possible in order to avoid infection, always
to be receptive to advice, and to realize that no doctor can save every patient.

Chapter Six was drawn mainly from the works of Avicenna, and dealt
with concussions, excoriations, and ulcers. Excoriations were those
wounds resulting from religious excesses. Chapter Seven concerned
phlebotomy and the symptoms of wounds. It drew on Lanfranc, and
made humble comments about the propensity of all men, even doctors,
to err. Finally, Chapter Eight covered medications, most of which were
herbal. This was followed by a postscript with a general discussion
about the shortcomings of physicians and, lest they too become arrogant, a caution to surgeons to learn the skills of physic.

John Mirfield has been dismissed as a compiler.[86] This is unfair. He
was a popularizer. He was superstitious, and may never have practiced
medicine. But he was well read and knowledgeable, and his advice on
the bread-and-butter topics of pre-plague surgery could usually be followed with success. If the sections of the *Breviarum Bartholomei* that dealt
with physic were of middling quality, Book IX on surgery was specific
and concise. It might even have been used by a master surgeon.

Mirfield pales, however, in comparison with John Arderne, the most
original and best known of all late medieval English surgeons.[87] His treatises, especially the *Practica* and the *Fistula in Ano*, often combined into
a single text, have survived in large numbers, and were the fourth most

[84] *Ibid.*, p. 125.
[85] *Ibid.*, p. 139.
[86] *T&H*, p. 422; Talbot, *Medicine in Medieval England*, pp. 200–201.
[87] The most extensive work has been done by D'Arcy Power. See his introduction to
*Fistula*, pp. ix–xxxiii; and *Selected Writings*, pp. 29–42. See too the citations in note 68.

commonly held text among those doctors in the file who held books.[88] Most copies of Arderne were illustrated, as befitted a surgery, but usually in ink rather than in colors, perhaps to hold down costs. Further, most of the manuscripts were relatively small, suggesting that surgeons could have carried them about.[89] Copies survive in English, Latin, and combinations of the two, and were often bound up with anatomies and collections of medical recipes.[90] Many had illustrations of surgical instruments.[91] Taken together, they made the ideal handbook for working surgeons, a compendium of the essentials they needed in their operations.

Arderne was born in 1307, according to Power, of a noble north country family.[92] There were Ardernes who had made their way in high society in the thirteenth and fourteenth centuries, but there is no evidence, most tellingly from John himself, that he was a member of the famous family. Talbot doubts the connection because Arderne was a surgeon, and he is probably correct.[93] Power also suggests that Arderne was trained in Montpellier, primarily because of the authorities he cites in his texts.[94] Talbot doubts this too, and again is probably correct.[95] But it does not matter. Arderne did serve, as noted in Chapter Four, in the armies of Henry, Duke of Lancaster, Edward the Black Prince, and perhaps Edward III during the Crecy campaign, and it was on these expeditions that he acquired his surgical skills.[96] Even if he did not attend university, he could read English, Latin, and probably French and had mastered the works of the most important medical authorities, physicians and surgeons, including these were Roger of Salerno, Lanfranc, Guy de Chauliac, Gilbertus Anglicus, Roger Bacon, Isaac Judeus,

[88] I have looked through sixty-four copies. For a list, see below, pp. 314–321.

[89] See, for example: B.M. Mss. Sloane 6; Sloane 56; Sloane 76; Sloane 335; Sloane 795; Sloane 2002; Sloane 3844; and Add. Ms. 29301.

[90] See, for example: C.U.L. Ms. DD 5 53; and C.U. Gonville and Caius, Ms. 69.

[91] See, for example C.U.L. Trinity College Ms. 1153.

[92] *Fistula*, pp. 1–4, has autobiographical information. See too D'Arcy Power, "English Medicine and Surgery in the Fourteenth Century," in his *Selected Essays*, pp. 30–35. See too *DNB*, 1, pp. 548–549.

[93] Talbot, *Medicine in Medieval England*, p. 121.

[94] *Fistula*, p. xii.

[95] Talbot, *Medicine in Medieval England*, p. 121.

[96] *Fistula*, pp. xi–xiv. See too *T&H*, pp. 111–12; and *DNB*, 1, pp. 548–549. Power, in his introduction to *Fistula*, p. xii, doubts that Arderne was at Crecy.

Henry Daniel, Avicenna, Hippocrates, and Galen.[97] Talbot claimed that Arderne's "reading was as wide as that of Gaddesden."[98] It was, and unlike Gaddesden, Arderne understood what he read.

Arderne's military service ran from the mid-1330s to the mid-1340s, and again, briefly, in the 1350s.[99] After the Black Death he settled in Newark, in Nottinghamshire, which seems to have been something of a center for surgeons in the later middle ages, presumably because of its three hospitals.[100] He probably lived there between 1350 and 1370, service in France excepted, and around 1370 went to London.[101] Perhaps he was attracted to the capital by the opportunities it offered, or perhaps he tired of provincial life. In any case, he cut back his number of patients, which afforded him the time to write down what he had learned in thirty-five years of practice. The treatise on fistula first appeared in 1376, when his old patron, the Black Prince, "that strong and warlike lord," died.[102] Arderne may have been a member of the Fellowship of Surgeons, helping the Fellows gain ascendance over the barber-surgeons in the early years of their struggle.[103] He probably died in 1390, an octogenarian at a time when life expectancy even for those who survived childhood was barely over forty years.[104]

Though some of his methods derived from Albucasis, Arderne's work was generally original and always innovative. Before Arderne, cancerous tumors were thought to be inoperable. William of Saliceto, himself an innovator, said surgery should be attempted only as a last resort; Mirfield, the synthesizer, believed that it could not be done.[105] Arderne

---

[97] *Fistula*, pp. 52–63; Power, "English Medicine," pp. 29–47.

[98] Talbot, *Medicine in Medieval England*, p. 121.

[99] The sources for this surgery are provided in *T&H*, pp. 111–112.

[100] A Hamilton Thompson, *Newark Hospitals and Colleges* (Leicester: E. Backus, 1937).

[101] There is evidence that Arderne lived briefly in London in the 1340s, when he first returned home from France, and bought land in Surry with his war money. But his wife apparently died there during the Black Death, and Arderne did not return until the end of Edward III's reign. See *T&H*, pp. 111–112.

[102] *Fistula*, p. xii.

[103] *T&H*, pp. 111–112.

[104] In a curious contradiction, Talbot, in *Medicine in Medieval England*, p. 124, gives the later date, which Power subscribes to. But *T&H*, p. 112—perhaps written by Hammond—gives 1376. In *Fistula*, p. 1, Arderne comments on a patient who lived until 1387, so he must have been alive until then. Beck, *Cutting Edge*, p. 50, claims to have found Arderne's *Inquisitione post mortem*, dating from 1392.

[105] Power, "English Medicine," pp. 33–34; *Fistula*, pp. xiv–xxviii.

proved them wrong. He described many such operations, most of them successful. He secured the patient; a probe was passed through the fistula and, if it were in the anus, out through the rectum.[106] The incision was secured with ligatures, which were tightened; then the fistula was lanced. A balm was applied, much in the fashion of Henri de Mondeville, and the corrosives advised by Guy de Chauliac and virtually all other surgeons ignored. Arderne listed some of his most famous patients, beginning in 1346 with Sir Adam of Everingham, and followed by a host of knights, friars, merchants, and priests.[107] Testimony to his success was the fee he charged, £40, plus a suit of clothing annually and an annuity of one hundred marks for as long as the patient lived.[108]

Fistula was Arderne's speciality, but he dealt with other ailments. He provided case histories of treatments for diseases of the eyes, ears, nose and throat, chest, lungs, stomach, liver, spleen, and genitals. This is a case of kidney stone:

> I saw a young man with a stone as big as a bean so lodged in his penis that it could not escape through the eye, neither could it be pushed back, but it remained in the middle of the organ. . . . I cured him easily with an incision for I put him on his back and tied his member with linen threads on each side of his stone to prevent it from shifting, and after making a small cut with a lancet over the stone I squeezed it out. I then sutured the skin with a needle and thread over the whole, and dressed it with white of egg and finely ground flour, and having wrapped up the penis in a piece of old and thin linen I let him go in peace for three days. I cut and removed the thread at the next dressing, and in less than a fortnight I had cured him completely. There is no need for alarm in these cases, even though the urine escapes from the wound for three or four days after such an operation, for the patient will certainly be cured.[109]

And another case history:

> I cured a man from Northampton who had three holes in the left buttock and three in the scrotum. . . . The blood escaped freely after the rectum was divided, because the fistula had tracked deeply. I put a [probably sophoric] sponge into the bowel and made him sit on a chair. The bleeding

---

[106] *Fistula*, pp. 22–26.
[107] *Ibid.*, p. 1.
[108] *Ibid.*, p. 6.
[109] This is transcribed in Power, "English Medicine," p. 33.

stopped directly, and as soon as the patient had eaten a meal and had been put to bed he slept well all night without further hemorrhage.[110]

This was the best advice a fourteenth-century urologist or proctologist could give.[111] (See Illus. 10, 11.)

Arderne, like Lanfranc of Milan and Henri de Mondeville, was concerned with deontology.[112] He advised on fees, appearance, and behavior. The surgeon should offer his fee in advance of surgery, and make it high—up to £100.[113] If the patient was taken aback, the surgeon should add that while the quoted fee was what the operation was worth, he would in fact take less. Further, the doctor should soak the rich and treat the poor as charity cases. This had the advantage of providing happiness on earth and in heaven. The surgeon should never take advantage of female patients, and never steal. He should be confident, but also modest and self-effacing. Surgeons should be pious and charitable, yet wary— "not every patient can be cured."[114]

The surgeon should be sober and studious, not gluttonous or cynical, and courteous and continent. He should not be jealous of the success of other leeches. He should be chaste and friendly to servants, easy of address, and neither too rough nor too familiar. When he undertook a cure he should be ready to see the case through to completion. He should never be foul-mouthed and, indeed, should cultivate silence. He should have a store of merry tales and comfortable sayings and appreciate the psychological aspects of healing. And he should keep mum on the patient's condition.

Successful operations, obviously, were more profitable than failed

---

[110] *Ibid.*, pp. 33–34.

[111] It caught the fancy of most of the scribes who copied the manuscripts, as well as the surgeons who used them. Many Arderne manuscripts were splendidly illustrated, with schematics of the surgery, anatomies, and drawings of instruments. The drawings were graphic and included the genetalia. Whether from a sense of humor or boredom or immaturity many Arderne's were filled with phallic doodles. Penises rather than pointers were used to indicate key parts of the texts. Most patients were provided with enormous sexual organs, and many were tied down to their beds; indeed, some of the doctor-patient sketches look more like acts of sodomy than surgery. One Arderne, filled with penises, women, and marginalia, had written across it, "Lord's Torture Chamber." See B.M. Sloane Ms. 56, ff. 22, 33, 85b.

[112] *Fistula*, pp. 2–9. A good manuscript copy is B.M. Sloane Ms. 2002, "Fistula in Ano"; "Practica."

[113] *Ibid.*, pp. 5–6.

[114] *Ibid.*, p. 4.

ones, when the surgeon had trouble collecting any payment at all. Surgeons had to have confidence in their abilities, more so than the physicians. For a surgeon's failure was liable to die on the operating table, or,
if he survived, soon thereafter; while the physician's patient, even if maltreated, might linger on. And, unlike physicians, surgeons often faced
pay-if-you survive fee schedules.[115]

The Arderne manuscripts provide information on surgical instruments.[116] This is important; few instruments have survived into the
twentieth century because most were made from precious metals, and
there was always the temptation to melt them down and use them for
other purposes.[117] One manuscript had, in addition to graphic gynecological sketches, twenty-five different kinds of tools.[118] Medieval surgeons were skilled craftsmen, and, as noted in Chapter Three, many
members of the Fellowship were also members of London's gold and
silversmiths' company. Instruments were among the surgeons' most
valuable possessions, and those that did survive would be treated as heirlooms, to be passed from one generation to the next.[119]

Arderne described the basic instruments recommended by Albucasis,
Henri de Mondeville, and Guy de Chauliac. These included scalpels,
tweezers, hooks, clamps, or weights. In addition to their silver heads,
they probably had ivory rather than wooden handles.[120] Arderne followed Mondeville in devising four basic categories: hooks, arrows, scalpels, and hammers.[121] But he also added seven new instruments designed
to perform the fistula operation. These were the probe (*sequere me*); the
snouted needle (*acus rostrata*); the dilator (*tendiculum*); the strong thread
(*Fraenum Caesaris*); the vertical peg, which fitted into the hole in the wide
part of the dilator; a syringe with lateral openings; and a syringe with
only a terminal opening.[122] He may have added others. One fifteenth-
century manuscript showed instruments used for surgery on the

[115] Power, "The Fees of Our Ancestors," in *Selected Writings*, pp. 95–102.

[116] See B.M. Sloane Ms. 2002, ff. 24–24b; *Fistula*, pp. 10–11 copies them.

[117] Beck, *Cutting Edge*, pp. 89-90, is good on this.

[118] B.M. Sloane Ms. 6, ff. 174–177b; Sloane Ms. 56, ff. 33–58b; Add Ms. 29301, f. 10b.

[119] This can be seen in wills. See: John Dagville I, PCC 31 Wattys; John Dagville II, London Com. Court, vii, Lichfield f. 91; and John Dalton, London Com. Court, v, Sharpe f.
271v.

[120] There are excellent illustrations in Margaret Ruler, "The Search for Mary Rose,"
*National Geographic*, May, 1983, pp. 654–675.

[121] Wellcome Ms. 564, Henri de Mondeville, "Chirurgia," f. 163.

[122] B.M. Sloane Ms. 2002, f. 24. See too *Fistula*, p. 2.

joints.[123] These included drills for boring and trephining, and saws, presumably for amputation. Curiously, the patients in these illustrations were often depicted as awake and observant.[124] Most were naked, the copyists detailing the genitalia. They were tied down, but this appears as much for the surgeon's benefit as it does for the patient's pain, which must have been considerable, even with the use of the sophoric sponge. And dangerous too, for after discussing instruments, Arderne admits that even after successful surgery many patients died.[125]

This high rate of fatality figured in Arderne's procedures. While he recommended surgery for fistula, a cancer or ulcer that could not be dried up, he argued that apostemes or abscesses might be cured without surgery. They were to be desiccated with balms and ointments. They should not be allowed to burst, but should be opened after the ointments had softened them. Like Mondeville, Arderne presented an alternative to corrosives, at least to some degree, and a successful one. He described thrombosis, other circulatory problems, and the proper way to straighten, stretch, and set broken bones. He recommended enemas, and claimed that his purgations were better than any of those offered by the "Lombards who practiced in London."[126]

Arderne had weaknesses. He was a master gynecologist by four-teenth-century standards, but his recipes were little different from and more effective than those of the physicians or apothecaries. He had a number of prejudices common to his peers. He believed, for example, in the curative power of charms and amulets. He felt that menstruating women, garlic and onions were dangerous to the sick, and that humoral theory was proper physiology.[127] Most of his treatises came with astral charts, which recommended where and when to bleed. But these shortcomings were overshadowed by his strengths. His surgical skills and experiences were the result of a combination of theoretical textual learning and practical clinical experience, much of the latter from the battlefield. His texts were clear and lucid, and became the most influential works of surgery in late medieval England. And he wrote in English, as did most

[123] Wellcome Ms. 49, "Apocalypse," ff. 12–13, though not an Arderne, is a good example.

[124] MacKinney, *Medical Illustrations*, pp. 205–209.

[125] *Fistula*, pp. 9–12.

[126] *Ibid.*, p. 76.

[127] *Ibid.*, p. 88.

surgeons, making his ideas available to a wider number of practition-ers.[128]

Thomas Morstede was the third influential surgical author. A great deal is known about him, some of which has already been presented.[129] He was the leader of one of the surgical teams at Agincourt, a co-founder in 1423 of the College of Medicine, and a warden of the Fellowship of Surgeons.[130] He was alleged to have been the richest man in London in the 1430s.[131] He was a royal surgeon, and sometime in the 1440s gath-ered his ideas in a text called *A Fair Book of Surgery*.[132] *A Fair Book* was prefaced by a long and detailed table of contents, assuring easy use.[133] It had the basic threefold division of surgical manuals—anatomy, wounds, and recipes—and was not original in the sense that it followed a tradi-tional form and borrowed from established authorities. But it was im-portant in that most of the treatments and all the operations were colored by Morstede's own experiences. And all the procedures were brief, to the point, accurate, and of great help to a surgeon about to perform an operation.

An example is the description of the surgeon's qualities. Morstede ar-

[128] The rise in surgery coincided with the spread of vernacular medical texts. See Tal-bot, *Medicine in Medieval England*, pp. 186–197; Linda Ehrsam Voigts, "Editing Middle English Medical Texts: Needs and Issues," in Trevor H. Levore, ed., *Editing Texts in the History of Science and Medicine* (New York: Garland Publishing Co., 1982), pp. 39–68; Voigts, "Medical Prose", in A.S.G. Edwards, ed., *Middle English Prose: A Critical Guide to Major Authors and Genres* (New Brunswick, N.J.: Rutgers University Press, 1984), pp. 315–336.

[129] See above, pp. 21–22, 66–67, 144–148. Also, see *T&H*, pp. 350–352; Beck, *Cutting Edge*, pp. 79–120; Talbot, *Medicine in Medieval England*, pp. 193–203. His will was proved in the PCC, 12 Rous. Beck summarizes it, pp. 95–97.

[130] *T&H*, pp. 350–52; Beck, *Cutting Edge*, pp. 79–120.

[131] Sylvia L. Thrupp, *The Merchant Class of Medieval London, 1300–1500* (Ann Arbor, Mich.:, University of Michigan Press, 1962), p. 260; H. L. Gray, "Incomes from Land in England," *English Historical Review*, 49, 1934, p. 637.

[132] B.M. Harl. Ms. 1736, "Old English Medical." A few historians questions whether this is really *A Fair Book*. Others, including Talbot, *Medicine in Medieval England*, pp. 193–196; and Beck, *Cutting Edge*, pp. 82–83, both claim to have been the first to "identify" it. Talbot simply "identifies" it, while Beck argues for the coincidence of time and place. But, in a sense, the argument is moot. At the very least the tract in question was surely based on *The Fair Book*, and may well have been the product of one of Morstede's disciples or colleagues in the Fellowship of Surgeons.

[133] Beck, *Cutting Edge*, pp. 105–119, has transcribed parts of B.M. Ms. 1736. I will refer to Beck's transcription, in this case, pp. 106–107.

gued that the surgeon ought to be eloquent and lettered in both theory and practice, a reiteration of the old theme voiced by Mirfield, Arderne, and others.[134] He should be well-mannered and of good countenance, shapely of body, have small fingers and steadfast hands that never trembled, and have clear sight. The surgeon should be bold, hearty, and gracious to the sick, merciful to the poor, and reasonable rather than covetous toward the rich.[135] These were the hallmarks of a successful and experienced surgeon who had made a financial as well as medical success.

Morstede's experience shows in the surgical as well as the deontological parts of the treatise. This was particularly so when he dealt with war wounds; much of *The Fair Book* was given over to the problems of extracting arrows and other missiles, and the instruments used in their operations. Morstede railed against those surgeons—presumably barber-surgeons—who had no military experience, calling them ignorant, pretentious, and overly cautious.[136] Yet, ironically, Morstede was more conservative than John Arderne. He argued that surgeons ought to avoid operating on the body cavity, and should restrict their work to the limbs unless absolutely necessary. Operations on "the soft parts" rarely succeeded. Their treatment, consequently, should be limited to the medications of physicians; if they failed, physicians would have to take the blame.[137]

They must have failed often because Morstede did not think well of physicians. In contrast, he believed surgeons were craftsmen—and very good ones at that—who ought to take pride in their work and their high rate of success.[138] Yet while surgeons used instruments instead of drugs to work their cures, they still ought to know about pharmacy. They should be literate, well read, and masters of anatomy. Consequently, large segments of *The Fair Book* were given over to anatomy.[139] Morstede made what he considered an important distinction. Surgery was the particular or "natural part" of medicine. Physic was the abstract, universal part. Physicians diagnosed; surgeons treated. This was why anatomy

[134] *Ibid.*, p. 108.
[135] *Ibid.*
[136] B.M. Harl. 1736, ff. 6–14.
[137] *Ibid.*
[138] *Ibid.*
[139] *Ibid.*, ff. 16–41.

was so important, for it would serve as the bridge between the two principal branches of medicine.

Morstede was concerned with how doctors learned. Here again, he trumpeted the importance of anatomy. And he argued that, while it was necessary to study texts, it was also crucial to perform dissections. He described how to get the bodies and perform the procedure.

> Therefore, it is needful to have sight of anatomy written in letter. [But] the second manner of anatomy and expertise is dead men's bodies, for leeches may be expert through sight of newly dead men's bodies. As of them whose heads have been smitten off or hanged [that is, executed criminals] by the which may be made anatomy of the members and offices inward of the flesh and brain and skin of many veins and arteries and sinews. . . . Do the body be laid on a bank, the one part upward, and the nether part downward, and do not make there of four lessons after when the body is opened and every hollow part longing thereto.[140]

He noted the proper procedures, and in doing so criticized Galen, whose knowledge of anatomy came from the dissection of animals rather than humans.

> In the first part shall be treated nutritive members, as the stomach, with what that belongs thereto. In the second part shall be treated of the nutritive members and that that belongs thereto. In the third part *solely* members. And the fourth part the extremities of the body as arms and legs and that that belongs thereto. Of the which four parts members are to be considered things, that is to say: (1) setting; (2) substance; (3) complexion; (4) quantity; (5) number; (6) figure; (7) colygens; (8) the genderings; (9) the acts, deeds, utilities and profits. . . . And anatomy must be had of dead men's bodies set on [the] gibbet in summer time, and dried in the sun. Be how may be had knowledge of bones, gristles, nerves, joints. . . . And be these manner of ways. Galen in men's bodies appraises swine and in many other beasts, come to the truth of the knowledge of anatomy.[141]

Hence, Morstede made his case for practical rather than abstract medicine. This was the echo of a military surgeon who had surely dissected dozens of bodies. Yet it is worth reiterating that Morstede valued books and abstractions. His next section, on physiology, was lifted from Galen.[142] Here he was approving and uncritical, perhaps the result of a

[140] Beck, *Cutting Edge*, p. 83.
[141] *Ibid.*, p. 110.
[142] *Ibid.*, pp. 79–81.

lack of experience or original thinking. Here too were the principal shortcomings of surgeons: their lack of theory and conception. Even the best surgeons ignored what might be called an holistic approach.

Once finished with physiology, Morstede returned to what he knew first-hand. He discussed accurately and comprehensively the properties of the body—the skin, muscles, bones, and tendons. In Chapter Nine, he included a guide for the setting of broken bones. Like Arderne, Morstede was interested in surgical instruments. But Morstede was more daring. He took special pride in developing his own tools, and singled out five that he felt were especially novel and useful. He illustrated each:[143]

A *rugyne*: to draw out bits of bone, alien matter in the wound.

A lever: as above, for more difficult and larger pieces:

A trephin: sharp, for making and boring holes:

A separatory: to pick out pieces after the trephin makes a hole.

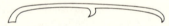

A lenticulare: also for removing bits:

Morstede described how the instruments should be made. And he depicted a relatively new tool designed by the surgeon John Bradwardine, supposedly used to extract an arrow from the nose of Prince Hal after the Battle of Shrewsbury:[144]

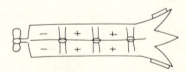

This, he claimed, was a modified but razor-sharp tweezer.

[143] B.M. Harl. 1736, ff. 41–52.
[144] See above, pp. 142–143.

Morstede was the last important English surgical writer of the middle ages. Generally, there were fewer writers of surgical manuals than there were those of physic. For one, there was more of a market for physic texts. There were more physicians, and they were more dependent on texts.[145] There were plenty of barbers, but not all of them were literate, and many could not afford to buy texts. Further, surgical manuals were usually of high quality, and were more direct and straightforward than those of physic. It was easier to describe a surgical procedure than to debate medical theory. Hence, the available surgeries proved adequate and uncontroversial, and there was not much call to replace them.

But while Morstede was the last notable author, around 1450 segments on surgery began to appear in *Ars medica*. Surgery was becoming more respectable, if not yet in the universities then at least among the practicing physicians of London and the county towns. And surgical manuals themselves, that is, copies of Lanfranc, Chauliac, Mondeville, Mirfield, Arderne, and Morstede were expanded to include topics of physic. Some fifteenth-century versions of John Arderne, for example, had inserts of medical miscellanies.[146] Even the manuals owned by provincial barbers suggested this broader if not yet comprehensive practice.[147]

The general fifteenth-century surgical manuscripts dealt with a standard litany—cautery, phlebotomy, surgical technique, and instruments. Cautery had been popular with Roman surgeons, and was extolled by the Salernitans.[148] The theory guiding its use was the destruction of aberrant tissues; when properly done, it was thought to eliminate corrupt matter, prevent the spread of infection, stop the flow of blood, and, with phlebotomy and various corrosive ointments, help restore harmony and balance the humors by removing the noxious materials in the wound. This general concept, coupled with the idea of suppuration and endorsed by such influential writers as the Salernitans and Guy de Chauliac, was of course disastrous. Only a few enlightened surgeons, notably Mondeville and Arderne, opposed it, and even Arderne waffled on occasion.[149]

[145] See below, pp. 260–263.

[146] b.m. Sloane Ms. 335, John Arderne, *Liber medicinae*, ff. 79–82.

[147] o.u. Bod. Ms. Ashmole 1434 i, John Arderne, *Practica*. John Whelan, a Norwich barber, was credited with the section called "Alumen, a way to make alum water. . . ."

[148] MacKinney, *Medical Illuminations*, pp. 48–54, has an excellent summary and, as usual, illustrations.

[149] Arderne, *Fistula in Ano*, pp. 26–28.

Cautery was usually done with a hot or cold iron. There were several types, differing primarily in length and the number of prongs and types of serrations. The wound was kept open for some days, usually with caustics, even after the aberrations were considered destroyed. This allowed for drainage, the length of time of which was determined by charts linked to particular kinds of wounds.[150] Then a scab was allowed to form, and the wound healed. Cautery was generally performed by a surgeon or a barber-surgeon. Occasionally, however, it would be done by a physician.[151] Some mystery surrounded the process, and a few authorities believed that only a physician could do it properly.[152]

Bloodletting, or phlebotomy, was even more popular. By 1450 it was applied to just about every kind of medical problem, from toothaches and melancholy to fevers. Its theory was Galenic; bleeding would purge the body, rectifying the humoral imbalance called *Dyskrasia*, and restore it to the perfect state of *Eukrasia*. Because of this association, physicians sometimes supervised the operation. But this did not dissuade surgeons, who along with barber-surgeons and barber-tonsors did the actual cutting. Guy de Chauliac even more some changes in the Galenic theory, suggesting that surgeons thought of phlebotomy as their own treatment.[153]

Calendars, almanacs, and zodiac men were used as practical guides. Each vein and organ had to be let at a particular time for a particular ailment. For a patient suffering from liver-trouble blood was let between the middle and the ring finger, since those veins were believed to lead to the liver.[154] Virtually all the surgical manuscripts which had illustrations also had zodiac men.[155] Zodiac men were often inaccurate and hastily drawn. But they were clearly marked and labelled and after some initial training must have proved easy to use. Standard procedures were followed before the operation. The practitioner washed himself, his scalpels, and razors in hot oil and rose water. The patient was tied down

[150] There were fifteen ailments to a chart. See MacKinney, *Medical Illumination*, pp. 49–50.

[151] *Ibid.*, p. 51.

[152] *Ibid.*, pp. 51–52.

[153] Guy de Chauliac, *Chirurgie*, pp. 7–13.

[154] See, for example: B.M. Add. Ms. 28725; and B.M. Add Ms. 29301, which is an Arderne, *Practica Chirurgia*.

[155] Charles Talbot, "A Medieval Physician's *Vade Mecum*," *JHM*, 16, 1961, pp. 213–233.

or held by assistants. The incisions were made and the blood allowed to flow freely and "darkly." The patient's pulse was checked regularly, and if it dropped too quickly the bloodletting was stopped. If after the first session the patient did not improve, the phlebotomy would continue, if necessary for several days or even weeks. And when the cure was finally effected, future afflictions were to be prevented the physician's ways, through changes in diet designed to keep the humors in balance.

Surgeons also performed cupping, the placement of heated cups over shallow incisions. Leeching too was common. Both were specialized but less rigorous, demanding, and dangerous operations than bleeding, and were usually performed by barber-surgeons or barber-tonsors, often in bathhouses as part of a cleaning and purifying process. The leeches were carefully selected and graded, and the process could be expensive.[156] Green or lime-colored leeches from frog ponds were preferred. They were starved for a day, and the wound or spot to be leeched was rubbed raw. The patient placed his feet in a tub of hot water to facilitate the flow of blood, and the leech was attached. Occasionally a leech would suck itself right into the patient's body. Then a saltwater enema would be used to expel it.

Despite the increasing use in the late middle ages of alcohol-based anesthetics, sophoric sponges, sedative drinks, ointments, and opium, surgery must have been excruciatingly painful. Most illustrations show the patient writhing in agony.[157] The whole process was brutal, and medieval patients must have viewed any visit to the surgeons as modern patients look at a trip to the dentist. There are no records that allow for precise measurements, but the rate of post-operative infection must have been very high—John Arderne suggested close to fifty percent.[158] This was the major reason that he, the boldest of surgeons, was reluctant to operate.

Most of these fifteenth-century surgical miscellanies were small, for easy carrying and quick reference. Talbot has shown how *vade mecum* were folded and carried in the omnipresent pouches depicted in illustrations of doctors.[159] Surgical manuscripts must have been cheaper than

---

[156] MacKinney, *Medical Illustrations*, pp. 60, 203.

[157] *Ibid.*, pp. 235, 242.

[158] Arderne, *Fistula in Ano*, p. 3.

[159] Talbot, *Medicine in Medieval England*, pp. 126–27; and Talbot, "A Medieval Physician's *Vade Mecum*," *JHM*, 16, 1961, pp. 213–233.

those of physic. Though illustrations were more essential to surgeons, surgical books had fewer of them. And those they did have were usually simple sketches rather than illuminations. But it is important to emphasize that they were practical, well conceived and laid out, and easy to follow. They were informative and functional. Most had either tables of content, often running to several pages, or indexes for easy reference. They had broad margins so that addenda and glosses could be added. In some manuscripts there were markers in the margins to point out special places in the texts. Many had marginalia, often in different hands. Most were highly abbreviated, no doubt to keep copying costs down. But this and the lack of colored illustrations and fancy bindings notwithstanding, surgical manuscripts were far better for practicing doctors than those of physic.

One example of these general fifteenth century manuals was drawn primarily from Lanfranc of Milan.[160] Its convenient, effective layout read as follows:

Chapter 1: Head, neck, shoulders, connection to the hands
Chapter 2: Shoulders, arms, hands, fingers
Chapter 3: Ribs, arms, hands, fingers
Chapter 4: Uterus, womb, stomach
Chapter 5: Haunches, feet

Each chapter was then subdivided, and provided with a kind of cross-reference of ailments. In the first chapter, for example, there was a sub-section entitled "Simple Wounds." There followed these descriptions:

Wounds in the bones
Simple wounds
Ever more complex bones
Wounds from wood
Phlegm
Melancholy
All sorts of pustules
Burns
Carbuncles
Ulcers

[160] B.M. Add. Ms. 10440, Lanfranc, "Anatomy and Surgery." Much of it was taken from William of Saliceto.

In dividing his topics even further the author dealt not only with the particulars of a specific wound, such as carbuncles, but with anything else that might affect treatment. Thus there was a section on algebra, since the author thought that to understand it "is to understand the breaking of bones."[161]

Because formulas were used, the copyists played a key role in the presentation of the surgeries. Lengthy segments were lifted from one treatise and placed in another. This could be problematic, as it allowed for additional opportunities for error. If a surgeon did the copying, some of the mistakes might be caught and identified. When a scrivenor did it, the opportunity for corrections was slim. An example of a manuscript "gone bad" is a *Chirurgia* of Roger of Salerno.[162] It was a summary, which was constantly being amended. With each amendment came a series of errors, often compounding older errors until the finished copy was barely recognizable as Roger's.

Sometimes, the copyists planned and arranged poorly. The recipes, for example, might be so close together that it was barely possible to add new ones or even gloss the old. It would have been difficult, too, to write up those case histories so important to surgeons, one of the things that gave them their medical edge. Patients' responses to physicians' drugs varied little; hence, a few comments after the drug treatment would usually suffice. But reaction to a surgical procedure was more varied. It was important to note the nuances of response to a particular technique, for this was the only way to develop an effective treatment.

A second example is a manuscript that belonged to the London barber-surgeons Richard Dod and Robert Sands.[163] Little is known about either, though Dod was an officer in the Barbers' Company.[164] The manuscript might best be identified as a *Materia medica* and, for a time, was thought by historians to be a poorly translated version of Macer's *Liber Floribus*.[165] In addition to the surgery, it had recipes and advice on phlebotomy, both rather common in surgeons' manuals by 1450. But it

---

[161] *Ibid.*, f. 1.

[162] B.M. Sloane Ms. 1977, "Surgical Operations."

[163] B.M. Sloane Ms. 5; B.M. Egerton Ms. 2572.

[164] Young, *Annals of the Barber Surgeons*, p. 3. Dod is not listed in *T&H*. See too Talbot, *Medicine in Medieval England*, p. 187.

[165] This has been edited by Margaret S. Ogdan, *Liber de Diversis Medicinis* (London: EETS, 25, 1936).

also contained an English version of Galen's *De sectis*, a gynecology, a copy of Daniel's *Domes of Urine*, and other tidbits of physic. The margins were filled with annotations, some in Latin but most in English. In effect, the Dod manuscript may have been designed originally for a barber-surgeon whose "speciality" was bloodletting and simple surgery, but its scope was such as to serve later owners in the practice of general medicine. Barber-surgeons in the county towns were usually the principal medical practitioners; because of their modest fee schedule, they may have been forced to apply more general medical treatments. The Dod manuscript, a simple yet concise guide to the sort of problems ordinary practitioners encountered every day, must have been more useful to barber-surgeons than copies of John Arderne.

Another example was the guild book of the barber-surgeons of York.[166] It contained most of the guild's records, as noted in Chapter One, but also served as a kind of communal reference. There was a large coverpiece illustration of Ss. Cosmas and Damian, who were identified as "the tone a Physician, and the toder a Surgeon."[167] This was followed by a number of pretentious allusions to the role of doctors, and a kind of deontology. But its purely medical parts were useful. It had a fine drawing of a zodiac man, with an explanation of when and where to bleed for special medical problems, in essence, just the sort of thing most barber-surgeons had to deal with. Three more zodiac figures appeared later in the text, along with a calendar for "helping things, zodiac influence, power of men, etc."[168] There was a version of John of Burgundy's popular treatise against the plague, a poem on bloodletting, and a series of medical recipes—in sum, precisely the kinds of things found in the Dod manuscript, and just the sort of problems that provincial general practitioners met every day. Further, much of the manuscript had blank pages, room to add not only the names of new members or changes in guild regulations, but also new medical ideas.[169]

Finally, there is the question of what surgeons were taught and how

---

[166] See above, pp. 42–44. For additional discussion see: G. A. Auden, "The Gild of the Barber-Surgeons of the City of York," *Proceedings of the Royal Society of Medicine*, 21, 1927, pp. 70–76; and Margaret C. Barnet, "The Barber-Surgeons of York," *MH*, 12, 1968, pp. 19–30.

[167] B.M. Egerton Ms. 2572, ff. 51–54.

[168] *Ibid.*

[169] *Ibid.*

they were trained. Lanfranc, Mondeville, Arderne, and others stressed the importance of manual dexterity and anatomy.[170] They conceded that surgery was a craft. It will be argued in Chapter Seven that surgeons were professionals, and comfortable members of a "middle class." But they were also, in the purely vocational sense of the word, craftsmen. Their success depended on their skills with their hands, a salient feature touched on by Arderne and Morstede. Since most surgeons made their own tools, manual dexterity was doubly important. A first step, then, was the learning of mechanical skills.

After dexterity came knowledge of anatomy. This was best learned through a combination of texts and dissection. But while the texts were readily available, the bodies were not. Further, there was considerable prejudice against dissection on the part of both Roman philosophers and Christian theologians.[171] In northern Italy and southern France, many of these obstacles were overcome late in the thirteenth century, and dissections occurred regularly, even at the universities.[172] English university authorities were more rigid, believing that dissections should take place just a few times each year—if that often.[173]

Most English surgeons were not trained at a university; they had to look elsewhere for opportunities to dissect. There is evidence that the London barbers were allowed one cadaver a year; this presupposes a similar and perhaps better arrangement for the surgeons of the Fellowship, though there are no records to prove it.[174] Thomas Morstede, as noted, wrote about dissections and claimed they were "not uncommon."[175] And Thomas Vicary implied that they occurred regularly by the 1530s.[176] But there is no other evidence of the practice, underscoring again the importance of military service. Away from normal domestic constraints, surgeons did as they pleased.

[170] Vern L. Bullough, "The Training of Non-university Educated Medical Practitioners in the Later Middle Ages," *JHM*, 14, 1959, pp. 446–458.

[171] Darrel W. Amundsen, "Medieval Canon Law on Medical and Surgical Practice by the Clergy," *BHM*, 52, 1978, pp. 22–44. There is a more general discussion in Daniel Boorstin, *The Discoverers* (New York: Random House, 1983), pp. 351–60.

[172] Siraisi, *Taddeo Alderotti*, pp. 111–112, 297–298.

[173] Talbot, *Medicine in Medieval England*, p. 83.

[174] Young, *Annals of the Barber-Surgeons*, pp. 361–62; Beck, *Cutting Edge*, pp. 82–91; Bullough, *Development of Medicine*, pp. 86–87.

[175] Beck, *Cutting Edge*, p. 110; Talbot, *Medicine in Medieval England*, p. 195.

[176] Vicary, *Anatomie of the Bodie*, p. 124.

There were other difficulties. Cadavers had to be obtained. Generally
these were of executed criminals, but criminals were often hanged and
left for days, or mutilated, so that a body cut down from the gibbet
might not have all the right things in the right places. There was a problem of decomposition. Most dissections were done outside during the
summer, over a period of three or four days. In that time, especially in
hot, humid weather there would be considerable decay. Thomas
Morstede recognized these problems, and suggested that cadavers be
first dried out.[177] But even then the dissection was performed in haste,
sometimes sloppily. Further, many students could not get a close look,
and fewer still could participate. Hence, for young surgeons in particular, military experience was often the only way to learn anatomy properly.

The course of English surgical training, like that of physic, followed
a Parisian model.[178] Paris—like London—had an elite corps of surgeons,
distinguished from the barber-surgeons and barber-tonsors. Organized
by 1258, they were allowed long robes to mark their rank, and may have
attended classes in the university even if they did not matriculate.[179]
Barbers, by contrast, were trained in their corporations. In France, the
barber-surgeons' guild was chartered by 1371.[180] A master practitioner
was allowed four or five apprentices for a term of seven to ten years. As
in other guilds, the master provided room and board in addition to education, and in return got unpaid and increasingly useful help. The key
to this as an educational system, obviously, was the quality of instruction provided by the master. After apprenticeship the budding barber-
surgeon became a journeyman.[181] He was allowed to assist in virtually
all procedures, and sometimes performed simple operations under the
master's supervision. The road to mastership was difficult, and not always dependent on professional skills. It required time, money, and
luck, and some barber-surgeons labored their entire lives without practicing on their own.

Training in England was essentially the same, save for a greater em-

---

[177] Beck, *Cutting Edge*, pp. 108–109.

[178] Bullough, *Development of Medicine*, pp. 82–85.

[179] Bullough, "The Training of Non-University Educated Medical Practitioners," pp.
451–456.

[180] Bullough, *Development of Medicine*, pp. 89–91.

[181] Bullough, "The Training of Non-University Educated Practitioners," pp. 451–456.

phasis on textual learning even among the barber-tonsors.[182] By 1370 Barbers' Hall in London was said to have had a library, and by 1400 there were public lectures on surgery and anatomy.[183] From 1376 barbers—mostly barber-surgeons but also some barber-tonsors—began bequeathing books in their wills, usually to other barbers, or to the company library.[184] One of the reasons, no doubt, were the changes brought by the Black Death. But another was the increase in vernacular medical texts. By 1520 virtually all barber-surgeons read English.[185] Barbers still acquired most of their training in practice, which, as has been stressed, was most important in any case. They used texts far less than the surgeons of the Fellowship, to say nothing of the physicians. But their growing literary perspective was important, and would serve the barbers well when they started to challenge surgeons' control over certain kinds of operations.

The best way to sum up the dynamic character of surgery in late medieval England is to reiterate what was most important in their rise: their experience on the battlefield. There, surgeons suffered no restraints. They could dissect or perform as they wished, subject only to the scrutiny of their peers. This too was important, for a kind of surgical method developed from war. The sheer volume of cases allowed for the evolution of a standard surgical method that was constantly being tested and refined. From their success on the battlefield, confidence grew. It was no coincidence that the veterans of Agincourt had the verve and wherewithal to approach the king, Parliament, and the physicians in founding

---

[182] Young, *Annals of the Barber-Surgeons*, pp. 361–364. A. R. Myer, *London in the Age of Chaucer* (Norman, Okla: University of Oklahoma Press, 1972), pp. 188–190, claims that by 1470 "forty percent of male Londoners could read Latin, and many more English." Hence the decision in 1422 by the brewers to keep their records in English "For there are many of our craft . . . who have the knowledge of writing and reading in the said English idiom."

[183] Young, *Annals of the Barber Surgeons*, pp. 361–364.

[184] See, for example, the following wills: John Dagville I, PCC, 31 Wattys f. 246; John Dagville II, London Com. Court, vii, Lich-field f. 91; John Queldrick, London Com. Court, v, Sharpe f. 13v; John Hobbes, London Com. Court, v Sharpe f. 344; Hugh Hert, London Com. Court, vi, Wilde f. 11; Thomas Colard, London Com. Court, vi, Wilde f. 326.

[185] Evidence of literacy comes from the 1513–1514 expedition to France. Of thirty-nine surgeons for whom records survive, thirty-six were barbers. Of these, *at least* twenty-five were able to sign their names to contracts of service.

the College of Medicine. And when this college failed, the associations begun in war carried over. The surgeons turned back to their Fellowship, had its regulations chartered and confirmed, and used their hall as a meeting place. In this way, military service functioned as a kind of second school. But military surgeons were not untried students. They were master surgeons thrown together at the peak of their careers, able to compare notes and select the best treatments.

The result was the superior surgery accounted in the texts of John Arderne and Thomas Morstede. They did not practice "modern" surgery. Their knowledge of anatomy was incomplete, and the discovery of the microbes that caused disease was centuries away. But they were not bound by tradition, and were eager to try new techniques. As physic stagnated, surgery moved ahead and became the most effective kind of medical treatment. The ideas of English surgeons rather than those of physicians spread to Europe.[186]

[186] *T&H*, p. 111, on John Arderne, puts it nicely.

# 7

## PROSPEROUS AND
## MIDDLE-CLASS

Virtually all the physicians, most of the surgeons, and perhaps half the barber-surgeons in late medieval England were prosperous and bourgeois.[1] It might even be argued that they were "middle class." This is contentious and dangerous ground; historians have been debating the composition, timing, and importance of the "rising" bourgeoisie for over one hundred years.[2] The debate is old and hackneyed, yet crucial for a proper understanding not just of English medicine but of late medieval and modern society. Despite this importance, it seems no closer to resolution now than it was seventy-five years ago when Max Weber and Werner Sombart were writing.[3] And the entire argument has taken on added significance in light of the many new studies about the emergence of capitalism in the early modern period, and the central place of the bourgeoisie in the process.[4] Prominent scholars such as Richard Tawney, Louis Wright, and A. F. Pollard have seen the middle class as the *deus ex machina* of modernization, linking it with the continued develop-

---

[1] Early drafts of this chapter were read before meetings of the Social History Group and West European Studies Center, both of Rutgers University. Some of the ideas and data have been published from a slightly smaller pool of 2,153 cases as "English Medical Practitioners, 1340–1530," *BHM*, 58, 1984, pp. 164–182.

[2] It is hard to figure precisely where, when, and how the debate began. As near as I can tell, it was in the sixteenth century. For more recent arguments see: Richard H. Tawney, *Religion and the Rise of Capitalism* (London: Pelican Books, 1947); and J. G. Hexter, "The Myth of the Middle Class in Tudor England," in his *Reappraisals in History* (New York: Harper and Row, 1961), pp. 71–116. Georges Duby, *The Early Growth of the European Economy* (Ithaca, N.Y.: Cornell University Press, 1974), p. 238, claims that bourgeois was "the term used [to describe townsfolk] since c. 1000."

[3] Both Weber and Sombart were, to say the least, prolific. For Weber, see *The Protestant Ethic and the Spirit of Capitalism*, trans. Talcott Parsons (New York: Scribners, 1958). For Sombart, see *Luxus und Kapitalismus* (Munich: Duncker & Humbolt, 1913).

[4] Four stand out: Fernand Braudel, *Civilization and Capitalism*, 3 vols., trans. Sian Reynolds (New York: Harper and Row, 1979–1984); Carlo Cipolla, *Before the Industrial Revolution*, 2nd ed. (New York: Norton: 1980); Immanuel Wallerstein, *The Modern World System*, 2 vols. (New York: Academic Press, 1974–1980), with a third volume projected; and Eric Wolf, *Europe and the People Without History* (Berkeley, Cal.: University of California Press, 1982).

ment of commerce, Protestantism, the discovery of a America, and the progress of English monarchy.[5] Few historians now working would go this far. And a few seem to doubt the role of the middle class altogether.[6]

If there is a consensus view on the rise of the middle class, it is that expressed by J. H. Hexter.[7] Hexter wrote: "The Middle Class [is] as fluid as water. A concept that at a distance seems solid gold turns out on closer inspection to be mere melted butter."[8] Hexter did not deny that there was a middle class. Rather, he was concerned with restricting its definition, in getting the middle class, such as it was, out of the country-side, and disassociating it from the gentry and the yeomanry. Hexter accepted the definition offered by the sixteenth-century essayist Claude Seyssel—"merchants, financiers, industrialists, town rich, the bourgeoisie."[9]

A number of studies give substance to Hexter's definition of a limited, urban middle class. Lauro Martines argued that he "found bourgeois values" among lawyers and notaries in fourteenth- and fifteenth-century Florence.[10] These values encompassed a mind set that concentrated on urban life, resources, and spatial perceptions. The world was seen in terms of cities; the countryside was to be exploited for the benefit of the town—exploited, that is, for its food, raw materials, and cheap man-power. The closely defined perimeters of the town gave the bourgeoisie a new sense of personal relations, one based more on a stem than an extended family. Economic life was closely wedded to social and personal relations. And one's role in public affairs was affected by the corpora-

---

[5] Tawney, *Religion and the Rise of Capitalism*; Louis B. Wright, *Middle Class Culture in Elizabethan England* (Chapel Hill, N.C.: University of North Carolina Press, 1935); A. F. Pollard, "The Advent of the Middle Class," in his *Factors in Modern History* (London: Macmillan, 1907).

[6] See, for example, Peter Laslett, *The World We have Lost*, 3rd. ed. (New York: Scribners, 1984), pp. 23–54.

[7] Hexter, "The Myth of the Middle Class," p. 72.

[8] *Ibid.*

[9] As quoted by Hexter, "The Myth of the Middle Class," p. 75.

[10] Two studies by Martines are: *The Social World of the Florentine Humanists* (Princeton: Princeton University Press, 1963); and *Lawyers and Statecraft in Renaissance Florence* (Princeton: Princeton University Press, 1969). His views are synthesized in his *Power and Imagination: City-States in Renaissance Italy* (New York: Knopf, 1979). Braudel, in the third volume of *Civilization and Capitalism, The Perspective of the World*, pp. 546–547, notes the rise during the High Middle Ages "in the number of lawyers, notaries, doctors and university professors," citing as his source Carlo Cipolla, "The Professions, The Long View," in *The Journal of European Economic History*, Spring, 1973, p. 41.

tism upon which medieval urban life was based, and by the seemingly endless layers of guilds, societies, fraternities, neighborhood and church groups, one atop and cutting across the other, all governing different phases of life. In this bourgeois society, money took on new importance. It became one of the most important measures of worth, success, and achievement. And bourgeois values allowed greater play for mobility, both social and geographic. It was easier to be a parvenu in a town than in the countryside because most of the important folk in towns were themselves relatively recent arrivals.

Italian towns and their inhabitants, like Italian medicine and doctors, were better developed and more sophisticated than their English counterparts.[11] It is hard to imagine a prosperous, well-defined, and self-perpetuating middle class in England until the fourteenth century, and even then only in London and the larger county towns. But in late medieval London, Sylvia Thrupp argued for, if not exactly a middle class, then at least what she felt comfortable calling "the middle strata of the nation."[12] Thrupp was cautious in her assessment. She added that high mortality and a propensity to buy land and become a gentleman prevented the development of anything like class identity.[13] This was noted as late as 1510 by Edmund Dudley in his *Tree of the Commonwealth*.[14] Dudley followed the traditional tripartite scheme and divided English society into three segments, or functions. He placed all townsmen—

---

[11] See Robert S. Lopez, "Hard Times and Investment in Culture," reprinted in Wallace K. Ferguson et al., *The Renaissance: Six Essays* (New York: Harper and Row, 1962), pp. 29–54.

[12] Sylvia L. Thrupp, *The Merchant Class of Medieval London* (Ann Arbor, Mich.: University of Michigan Press, 1962), p. 288.

[13] Several readers have expressed reservations about the use of the terms "middle class" and "bourgeois." They point out—correctly—that these terms were not used until he eighteenth and nineteenth centuries. Yet I found myself in a quandary that I felt was terminological. There is no good English word, like the Dutch *burgerklasse*, to express what I, obviously, feel is a bourgeois middle class. Middle strata, which Thrupp uses, seems awkward and unexpressive. Further, as pointed out in note 1, Georges Duby claims that bourgeois was "the term used since c. 1000." As for the concept of class and its use in analyzing medieval social structure, see Zvi Razi, "Struggles Between the Abbots of Halesown and Their Tenants in the 13th and 14th Centuries," in T. H. Aston et al., *Social Relations and Ideas: Essays in Honour of R. H. Hilton* (Cambridge: Cambridge University Press, 1983), pp. 151–167.

[14] Edmund Dudley, *The Tree of the Commonwealth*, ed. D. M. Brodie (Cambridge: Cambridge University Press, 1948).

bankers as well as bakers—in the third function, along with peasants and manual laborers.

But Dudley was unusual, perhaps unique by the sixteenth century. Most late medieval writers did give the bourgeoisie a separate and substantial place in the social hierarchy.[15] As early as the middle of the fourteenth century, the authors of the *Cursor Mundi* and *The Book of St. Albans* had divided society into the three functions.[16] But these were not the traditional functions of cleric, warrior, and worker. Rather, they were those who held land; those who worked in towns, mostly in trade; and those who worked the land. And within a generation first Chaucer and then Lydgate wrote about the *mediocres*, a free, middle-strata group that played an ever-growing role in daily affairs.[17] Most interesting of all, John Russell, in his *Book of Nurture* written about 1450, presented a close analysis of the middle class.[18] He described them as "worshipful merchants and rich artisans—they are to be given a parallel rank at banquets to members of the gentle class."[19]

John Russell and not Edmund Dudley was typical of late medieval social thinkers. They believed in the emergence of a well-heeled middle class, and so too do many, perhaps most, modern historians.[20] But the extent, importance, and precise role of the bourgeoisie is by no means agreed upon. To this fire has been added the incendiary fuel of Fernand Braudel's recent argument for bourgeois primacy in the sixteenth and seventeenth centuries.[21] Such a debate cannot be settled by the analysis of a single group from a particular kingdom. But the evidence respecting the doctors, from both literary sources and the data of the computer file, is such that it is possible to make the case that at least some late medieval English medical practitioners had the characteristics that most histori-

[15] For a collection of views, see V. J. Scattergood, *Politics and Poetics in the Fifteenth Century* (London: Blandisford, 1971).

[16] *Cursor Mundi*, ed. Richard Morris (London: EETS, 8 texts, 1961–1966); *The Book of St. Albans*, ed. William Blades (London: Macmillan, 1981).

[17] Geoffrey Chaucer, *The Canterbury Tales*, trans. Nevill Coghill (New York: Penguin, 1977); John Lydgate, *Minor Poems*, ed. N. N. MacCracken (London: EETS, 192, 1962).

[18] John Russell, *Book of Nurture*, in *Early English Meals and Manners*, ed. F. J. Furnivall (London: EETS, 32, 1868).

[19] *Ibid.*, p. 72.

[20] See Wallerstein, *The Modern World System*, i, pp. 224–298, for a good general study; and P. R. Coss, "Literature and Social Terminology: The Vavasour in England," in Aston et al., ed., *Social Relations*, pp. 109–150, for a good particular study.

[21] Braudel, *Civilization and Capitalism*, ii, pp. 459–600.

ans would judge bourgeois and "middle class." And by the middle of the fifteenth century English doctors ranked among the richer and, in a few cases, more powerful men in the kingdom.

It is necessary to explain briefly the makeup of the data bank. It contains information on 2,282 physicians, leeches, surgeons, barber-surgeons, barber-tonsors, apothecaries, and medical authors who practiced in England between 1340 and 1530.[22] Each doctor was treated as a "case," and each case could have up to fifty-three different kinds of information. This includes names; dates and type of practice; residence; royal service; legal and social standing; education; family information; occupations of other family members; manuscripts or books owned; manuscripts or books authored; property owned; whether they were educated or practiced abroad; whether they were clerics; gender; religion; and variations of these variables.

In the interests of comprehensiveness I have counted as medical practitioners anyone calling himself or herself physician, leech, *medicus*, surgeon, barber-surgeon, barber-tonsor, apothecary, barber plus another craft occupation; anyone who received an M.B. or M.D. from a university; or anyone who could be identified as a medical author or unlicensed practitioner. Practitioners were then divided into six groups: those who practiced physic, further distinguishing between physicians with a university education and leeches; surgeons; barber-surgeons; barber-tonsors; apothecaries, and unlicensed and non-professional practitioners.[23]

[22] The nature of the file is discussed in more detail in Robert S. Gottfried, "Medieval Medical Practitioners," *Bulletin of the History of Medicine*, 57, 1983, p. 577; Gottfried, "English Medical Practitioners, 1340–1530," pp. 164–182. I have added over a hundred cases since the publication of these articles; but while the precise numbers have changed somewhat, the general trends remain the same.

[23] As demonstrated in Chapters One and Two, these distinctions were made by the practitioners themselves, and there were rules and regulations and customs that sustained and perpetuated the divisions. But such distinctions could be artificial. Again it might be remembered that universities, the training ground for physicians, also educated a few surgeons. Further, many surgeons were authors of medical texts. Some barber-surgeons attended university lectures, and after 1493 were virtually indistinguishable from the surgeons. Barber-tonsors were generally accounted inferior to the other surgical practitioners, but they were organized into the same companies as barber-surgeons, and formed the well from which the latter were often drawn. In provincial towns there was often little distinction. And the apothecaries, as noted in Chapter Two, whatever their medical station, were often wealthier than any of the other practitioners. Hence, the social and professional distinctions among the different kinds of doctors, while real enough in

The file is representative of late medieval English medical practition-ers, but it is not complete. Information from each category is not avail-able for every doctor. More importantly, many and possibly even most late medieval doctors failed to leave any record of their practice. Hence, the data are more thorough in some areas than in others. They are fairly comprehensive for university-trained physicians, medical authors, and surgeons, most of whom can be traced through the records of Oxford and Cambridge, surviving manuscripts, the archives of the London-based Fellowship of Surgeons, military campaign archives, and royal writs and annuities. The file includes a sizeable segment of barber-sur-geons, apothecaries, and barber-tonsors. They can be identified through town, corporation, and guild records. No town has complete mu-nicipal archives covering the entire two centuries of the later middle, and many lack the best records, such as guild memberships and contin-uing series of freemen's rolls. But all have some records which allow for the identification of doctors for at least a brief time span. There are also geographic factors affecting the quality of the sample. About half the practitioners lived in or around London. In part, this was owing to the splendid opportunities for fame and fortune that London offered. But, in part, it bespeaks the city's excellent records. For similar reasons there are large numbers of practitioners from Oxford, Cambridge, and the dozen or so largest county towns.

The file's weakness is in the countryside. There are fewer institu-tional records for English villages and hamlets, and more part-time, un-licensed doctors. In a kingdom in which perhaps ninety percent of the population lived in communities with a population of less than one thou-sand this is a problem. An extensive and comprehensive search of ma-norial records might turn up more village leeches. But I have looked through three such collections, including a 300-year span of the Bacon records, among the best accounts, and found reference to just three doc-tors.[24] Unlicensed, non-professional practitioners clearly played an im-portant role in medical care, particularly in rural areas. To judge from sixteenth-century evidence, they charged the lowest rates and operated where more formally trained doctors cared neither to venture nor to

---

their late medieval context and generally followed in this book, were often blurred and should not be overplayed. For a definition of the term doctor see Vern L. Bullough, "The Term 'Doctor,' "*JHM*, 18, 1963, pp. 284–287.

[24] The Bacon Collection, the Regenstein Library, the University of Chicago, covering estates in East Anglia, especially Suffolk, mostly held by the Abbey of St. Edmundsbury.

practice.[25] Keith Thomas has shown how what he calls "cunning men," part of the counter-culture of magic in rural areas, also practiced a kind of medicine.[26] Furthermore, many scholars believe that women played an important role in medieval medicine, especially in rural environs.[27] In one speciality, obstetrics, they may have been the principal practitioners. Yet women rarely appear in the records. Less than one percent of the sample is female, a clear and obvious shortcoming (Table 7.11).

But the sample is large—almost 2,300 individuals, with up to fifty bits of information for each one. At the very least it represents a broad cross-section of late medieval medical practitioners. It is not possible, even in a long book, to present all the evidence of the sample. Bits of information have already been used to shore up other parts of my argument. Herein I will present data which suggest that many practitioners constituted a prosperous bourgeoisie, certainly by 1500 and probably by 1400.

First, there was a steady increase in the number of licensed practitioners until the end of the fifteenth century. More particularly, of the five principal kinds of doctors practicing medicine in late medieval England—physicians, surgeons, barber-surgeons, barber-tonsors, and apothecaries—growth was greatest among the most skilled practitioners, that is, the physicians, surgeons, and barber-surgeons (Table 7.1). Clearly not all doctors were middle class. Virtually all the barber-tonsors, for example, might better be classified as artisans.[28] But all the physicians and surgeons and many of the barber-surgeons were indeed members of the middle strata. In 1400, university-trained physicians, surgeons, and barber-surgeons constituted about a third of the licensed practitioners. By 1500 this was close to half—and they served a population about three-quarters the size of that of a century earlier.[29] Putting

[25] Margaret Pelling and Charles Webster, "Medical Practitioners," in Webster, es., *Health, Medicine and Mortality in the Sixteenth Century* (Cambridge University Press, 1979), pp. 165–235.

[26] Keith Thomas, *Religion and the Decline of Magic* (London: Pelican Books, 1982), pp. 252–300.

[27] See, for example, Lucille Pinto, "The Folk Practice of Gynaecology and Obstetrics in the Middle Ages," *Bulletin of the History of Medicine*, 47, 1973, pp. 513–523.

[28] Because of considerable wealth, apothecaries are difficult to classify. See S. L. Thrupp, "The Grocers of London, a Study of Distributive Trade," in Eileen Power and M. M. Postan, eds., *Studies in English Trade in the Fifteenth Century* (London: Methuen, 1933), pp. 247–292.

[29] For estimates of population in the fifteenth century, see: J. C. Russell, *British Medieval Population* (Albuquerque, N.M.; University of New Mexico Press, 1948); Alan R. H.

TABLE 7.1: Types of Practitioners Through Time.

| Dates | N* | P/L | Sur. | B-S | Barb. | Apoth. | Barb+ |
|---|---|---|---|---|---|---|---|
| | | | | All in % of the total (N) | | | |
| 1340–1530 | 2,282 | 19.8 | 12.1 | 6.5 | 55.4 | 5.5 | .7 |
| To 1360 | 65 | 38.5 | 12.3 | 4.6 | 16.9 | 26.2 | — |
| 1361–1390 | 197 | 28.9 | 11.7 | 1.0 | 43.1 | 15.2 | — |
| 1391–1420 | 355 | 20.3 | 11.0 | 3.1 | 60.6 | 5.1 | — |
| 1421–1450 | 435 | 18.6 | 9.4 | 3.7 | 64.4 | 3.2 | .7 |
| 1451–1480 | 446 | 18.3 | 9.2 | 3.8 | 65.5 | 2.2 | .7 |
| 1481–1511 | 361 | 23.8 | 11.9 | 8.6 | 48.5 | 6.1 | 1.1 |
| 1511–1530 | 450 | 12.0 | 11.0 | 22.5 | 48.7 | 4.7 | 1.1 |

Physicians/leeches who attended university: 41.4% (178 of 430). Clerics who were physician/leeches and who attended university: 47.2% (84 of 178).

CODE: P/L = Physicians and leeches; Sur. = Surgeons; B-S = Barber surgeons; Barb. = Barbers; Apoth. = Apothecaries; Barb+ = Barbers who were also members of another craft.

* In this and the other tables, not all the data were complete for all the categories. Hence, some of the subtotals add up to less than the totals, and some of the percentages to less than 100 percent. Or sometimes, as in this table, a few practitioners were listed twice, making the total greater than 2,282.

it another way, at the beginning of the sixteenth century Oxford, Cambridge, and the elite fellowships and mysteries of surgeons and barber-surgeons were producing half again as many doctors as they were at any other time in the later middle ages—and for fewer people.

Given the quality of medical care provided by some physicians, this increase in numbers may not necessarily have been beneficial.[30] But even their most questionable treatments were more effective than those of the apothecaries, barber-tonsors, unlicensed practitioners, and quacks. And in cultural and socio-economic terms, the things that counted most for being prosperous and bourgeois, they were more influential and far richer than most other doctors, including surgeons.

The rise of the surgeons and barber-surgeons is notable. Between 1480 and 1520 their proportion of all doctors practicing medicine doubled, the percentage gains coming at the expense of the less skilled bar-

Baker, "Changes in the Later Middle Ages," in H. C. Darby, ed., *New Historical Geography of England* (Cambridge: Cambridge University Press, 1973), pp. 186–247; and Robert S. Gottfried, *Epidemic Disease in Fifteenth Century England* (New Brunswick, N.J.; Rutgers University Press, 1978).

[30] Allen G. Debus, *The English Paracelsians* (London: Oldbourne, 1965); Charles Webster, *The Great Instauration: Science, Medicine and Reform* (New York Holmes and Meier, 1976).

ber-tonsors. In 1514, for instance, there were seventy-two surgeons practicing in London who had the skills to pass a qualifying examination.[31] Early-sixteenth-century London had a population of between 50,000 and 60,000. This made for a surgeon/patient ratio—as opposed to a general ratio of all doctors to patients—of about 1/700. In 1980, by comparison, the surgeon/patient ratio in London was 1/2,000.[32] This surfeit was known at the royal court. As noted in Chapter Four, when Henry VIII organized his expedition to France in 1513 he gathered a fleet to transport his army.[33] Twenty-five ships sailed with about 5,000 men, and had thirty-nine surgeons, at least one and in most cases two per ship, a ratio even greater than that in civilian London.[34] To put the growing numbers of both physicians and surgeons in modern perspective once again, the overall ratio of doctors to patients in early-sixteenth-century London was three times greater than the corresponding figure for 1980.

Well trained, elite, favored by the Crown—the case made in Chapters One, Four, and Six—surgeons, who in the past had been condemned by some social critics as mere craftsmen, began to associate with the university-trained physicians. This was important socially as well as medically since the physicians, whatever their medical skills, were considered "middle strata" by dint of their university educations. Indeed, barber-tonsors and apothecaries who wished to make money and improve their social position, at least as doctors, had to study to become barber-surgeons, surgeons, or physicians. Some, like Thomas Vicary and Andrew Boorde, did, and moved into the middle strata.[35] Others,

[31] R. R. James, "The Earliest List of Surgeons to be Licensed," *Janus*, xli, 1927, pp. 255–60.

[32] For the population of London, see Thrupp, *Merchant Class*, pp. 1–14; and Roger Finlay, *Population and Metropolis: The Demography of London* (Cambridge: Cambridge University Press, 1981). For figures for the rest of England see Pelling and Webster, "Medical Practitioners," pp. 187–188. According to *The World Health Statistics Annual, 1978*, iii (Geneva: W.H.O, 179), pp. 51–52, 62, 65, 69, England and Wales had a population of 49,195,000. It had 64,000 physicians, 14,200 dentists, and 16,626 pharmacists.

[33] *Letter and Papers, Foreign and Domestic, Henry VIII, 1514* (London: HMSO, 1920), #2757, pp. 1128–1129.

[34] The data are summarized in Thomas Vicary, *Anatomy of the Body*, i (London: EETS, 53, 1888), pp. 236–237. Also, see above, pp. 157–167.

[35] Both are covered in the *Dictionary of National Biography*. For Boorde, see *DNB*, ii, pp., 833–835; for Vicary, *DNB*, xx, pp. 300–301. Beck discusses Vicary in *Cutting Edge*, pp. 192–211. See also Sidney Young, *Annals of the Barber-Surgeons of London* (London: Blades, East and Blades, 1890), pp. 522–524.

probably most of the barber-tonsors and all those apothecaries who were not also spice merchants, did not, and remained artisans. At its upper level, medicine had become professionalized, and its members a bastion of the bourgeoisie.[36]

The concept of the middle class must be qualified. The triumph of physicians and surgeons did not take place throughout all of England. Rather, it was restricted to London, the university towns, and the twenty and perhaps thirty largest provincial centers (Tables 7.2 and 7.3). Most of these towns were in the southeastern part of England. In the northwest and more remote rural areas, barber-tonsors, village leeches, and other unlicensed practitioners continued to predominate. Some of the barber-tonsors might have aspired to middle-class status, but they must have been few in number. A general medical rule of thumb was that the better educated the doctor the more likely he was to practice in an urban area, especially greater London. It was the larger

TABLE 7.2: Regional Distribution of Doctors

1. By location and date:

| Dates | N | London | County Towns* | Oxford/Cam | Rural |
|---|---|---|---|---|---|
| 1340–1530 | 2,282 | 54.3 | 35.5 | 6.5 | 3.7 |
| To 1360 | 65 | 60.0 | 16.9 | 16.9 | 6.2 |
| 1361–1390 | 197 | 58.4 | 32.5 | 7.1 | 2.0 |
| 1391–1420 | 355 | 54.1 | 39.2 | 3.1 | 3.7 |
| 1420–1450 | 435 | 44.8 | 42.3 | 6.2 | 6.7 |
| 1451–1480 | 446 | 53.6 | 32.3 | 9.2 | 4.9 |
| 1481–1511 | 361 | 52.1 | 36.3 | 8.9 | 2.8 |
| 1511–1530 | 450 | 62.9 | 33.4 | 3.0 | .7 |

2. By kinds of practitioner:

| | N† | P/L | Sur. | B–S | B–T | Apoths. | Barb+ |
|---|---|---|---|---|---|---|---|
| London | 1,239 | 15.0 | 19.8 | 8.0 | 51.0 | 6.1 | .1 |
| County Towns | 810 | 12.8 | 3.5 | 3.4 | 75.1 | 3.3 | 1.8 |
| Oxford/Cam. | 148 | 86.9 | 6.2 | — | 6.2 | .7 | .7 |
| Rural areas | 85 | 33.3 | 8.6 | 1.2 | 56.8 | — | — |

* County towns have been defined as any town ranking among the top twenty in the lay subsidy assessments of 1334 or 1523/24.
† Not all the practitioners could be classified for all categories.

[36] For a general discussion of the professionalization of medicine, see Vern L. Bullough, *The Development of Medicine as a Profession* (New York: Hafner, 1966). For a general theory of the rise of the professions, see Cipolla, "The Professions," pp. 37–52.

TABLE 7.3: Practitioners in Selected Communities

1. By type

| Community | N | In %<br>Phys. | Surg. | B–S | B–T | Apoth. | B+ |
|---|---|---|---|---|---|---|---|
| London | 1,108 | 14.4 | 19.2 | 11.1 | 49.3 | 5.9 | .1 |
| Bury St. Edmunds | 21 | 14.3 | — | — | 85.7 | — | — |
| Bristol | 47 | 6.4 | — | 12.8 | 68.1 | 6.4 | 6.4 |
| Cambridge | 49 | 93.9 | — | — | 6.1 | — | — |
| Canterbury | 168 | 4.8 | 6.0 | 3.0 | 78.0 | — | — |
| Coventry | 31 | 12.9 | — | — | 87.1 | — | — |
| Exeter | 30 | 33.3 | 3.3 | — | 53.3 | 6.7 | 3.3 |
| King's Lynn | 16 | — | 6.3 | 6.3 | 75.0 | 12.5 | — |
| Leicester | 20 | 20.0 | — | — | 80.0 | — | — |
| Oxford | 92 | 90.2 | 8.7 | — | 1.1 | — | — |
| Norwich | 110 | 12.7 | 3.6 | — | 80.9 | .9 | 1.8 |
| Shrewsbury | 20 | — | — | — | 100.0 | — | — |
| York | 225 | 9.8 | 2.7 | 4.9 | 77.3 | 1.8 | 3.6 |

2. By proportion of aliens and clerical practitioners

| | N | Aliens | Clerics |
|---|---|---|---|
| London | 1,108 | 6.0 | 2.9 |
| Bury St. Edmunds | 21 | — | 4.8 |
| Bristol | 47 | — | 2.1 |
| Cambridge | 49 | 2.0 | 30.6 |
| Canterbury | 168 | — | — |
| Coventry | 31 | — | — |
| Exeter | 30 | — | — |
| King's Lynn | 16 | — | — |
| Leicester | 20 | — | — |
| Oxford | 92 | 1.0 | 39.1 |
| Norwich | 118 | 2.7 | 0.4 |
| Shrewsbury | 20 | — | — |
| York | 225 | 0.1 | 2.2 |

towns, after all, that offered the opportunities for practice and fat fees that could be translated into the influence and riches of middle-class status.[37]

Two additional, important characteristics of middle-class doctors in England were that, increasingly in the later middle ages, they were den-

[37] Braudel has cautioned not to equate too directly the middle class and the bourgeoisie, at least in the strict sense of the latter word. Surely he is correct. Middle-class doctors in England were a phenomenon of the larger towns. See *Civilization and Capitalism*, ii, p. 460.

izens and laymen. Traditional interpretations of medieval English medicine ascribe a major role to foreign and clerical doctors.[38] While this
may have been so in 1200, it was not by 1300. Foreigners, or aliens as
the natives called them, comprised less than four percent of all the doctors practicing in the kingdom between 1340 and 1530 (Tables 7.4 and
7.5). Further, this proportion diminished through the course of the later
middle ages. These aliens, despite their small numbers, did have influence. Over ninety percent of them lived in London, and eighty-three
percent, as noted in Chapter Three, were at one time or another in royal
service. But virtually all were physicians and, as has been stressed, physicians made less an impact on medical practice than did surgeons. Further, most of the aliens practiced before 1410 or after 1510.[39] It was in
the fifteenth century that doctors in general and surgeons in particular—
virtually all natives—made their greatest medical and social gains. Only
in the early sixteenth century, when Italian practitioners brought new
concepts of anatomy from Padua and Bologna to the English universities
and the Royal College of Physicians, did foreigners make a real impact
on medicine and benefit enough from their contributions to make their
marks socially.[40] It might even be argued that English students such as
John Free, John Chamber, and Thomas Linacre, who had studied medicine in Italy and then returned home, were just as important in dissem-
inating the new ideas.[41] Once again, these medical advances were translated into social and economic gains. Chamber and Linacre, to take two
examples, ended up at the royal court.[42] Neither was armigerous and,

[38] See, for example, Benjamin Lee Gordon, *Medieval and Renaissance Medicine* (New
York: Philosophical Library, 1955), pp. 30–83; and David Riesman, *The Story of Medicine
in the Middle Ages* (New York: Hoeber, 1935), pp. 17–27.

[39] The exact figures are in Table 7.4.

[40] Pelling and Webster, "Medical Practitioners," pp. 165–210.

[41] *Ibid*. See too, Roberto Weiss, *Humanism in England During the Fifteenth Century*, 3rd
ed. (Oxford: Blackwell, 1967); and R. J. Mitchell, "English Students at Padua," *Transactions of the Royal Historical Society*, 4th series, xix, 1936, pp. 101–117. See below, pp. 281–
286.

[42] For Argentine and Chamber, see Charles Talbot and E. A. Hammond, *Medical Practitioners in Medieval England* (London: Wellcome Historical Library, 1965), pp. 112–115;
and 131–133. For Free, see R. J. Mitchell, *John Free: From Bristol to Rome in the Fifteenth
Century* (New York: Longmans, 1955). For Linacre, see, among many things, Talbot and
Hammond, *Medical Practitioners*, pp. 348–350; *DNB*, xi, pp. 1,145–1,150; and Francis R.
Maddison, Margaret Pelling, and Charles Webster, eds., *Linacre Studies: Essays on the Life
and Work of Thomas Linacre, 1460–1524* (Oxford: Clarendon Press, 1977).

TABLE 7.4: Foreign Doctors Practicing in England

**1. By country of origin**

| | N* | % of all doctors | % all Aliens |
|---|---|---|---|
| Denizens | 2,204 | 96.6 | — |
| Italians | 35 | 1.5 | 43.2 |
| Frenchmen | 14 | .6 | 17.3 |
| Spaniards | 10 | .4 | 12.3 |
| Portuguese | 6 | .3 | 7.4 |
| Dutch/Frisians | 5 | .2 | 6.2 |
| Brabantines | 4 | .2 | 5.0 |
| Greeks | 3 | .1 | 3.7 |
| Flemings | 2 | .1 | 2.5 |
| Germans | 2 | .1 | 2.5 |

**2. By time**

| | N | % of all doctors in period* |
|---|---|---|
| To 1360 | 9 | 16.4 |
| 1361–1390 | 9 | 5.2 |
| 1391–1420 | 11 | 3.2 |
| 1421–1450 | 10 | 2.4 |
| 1451–1480 | 6 | 1.4 |
| 1481–1511 | 8 | 2.4 |
| 1511–1530 | 19 | 4.4 |

**3. By settlement**

| | | |
|---|---|---|
| London | 64 | 90.1 |
| County Towns | 5 | 7.0 |
| Oxford/Cambridge | 2 | 2.8 |
| Rural Areas | — | — |

**4. By practice**

| | N | % of aliens |
|---|---|---|
| Physicians | 53 | 74.7 |
| Surgeons | 9 | 12.7 |
| Barbers | 4 | 5.6 |
| Apothecaries | 5 | 7.0 |

**5. By ecclesiastical affiliation**

| | | |
|---|---|---|
| Laics | 64 | 90.1 |
| Priests | 3 | 4.2 |
| Deacons | 3 | 4.2 |
| Friars | 1 | 1.4 |

* Not all practitioners could be classified for all categories.

TABLE 7.5: Clerical Doctors

|  | N* | % of all doctors |
|---|---|---|
| 1. By order |  |  |
| Non-clerics | 2,161 | 94.7 |
| Priests | 63 | 2.8 |
| Deacons | 45 | 2.0 |
| Franciscans | 3 | .1 |
| Dominicans | 3 | .1 |
| Benedictines | 2 | .1 |
| Austin Friars | 2 | .1 |
| Carthusians | 1 | — |
| Carmelites | 1 | — |
| Cistercians | 1 | — |
| 2. By time |  |  |
| To 1360 | 7 | 12.7 |
| 1361–1390 | 21 | 12.1 |
| 1391–1420 | 21 | 6.2 |
| 1421–1340 | 14 | 3.4 |
| 1451–1480 | 21 | 4.9 |
| 1481–1511 | 21 | 6.3 |
| 1511–1530 | 13 | 3.0 |
| 3. By practice |  |  |
| Physicians | 115 |  |
| Surgeons | 2 |  |
| Barbers | 4 |  |
| Apothecaries | 0 |  |

* Not all practitioners could be classified for each category.

despite becoming wealthy, both continued to practice medicine until their deaths. Both were seemingly content to live in comfortable but ordinary houses in London and Oxford—and yet each had the ear of the king and his councillors.

Nor did clerics dominate English medicine.[43] Clerics comprised but five percent of the doctors' sample, a figure lower than their proportion of the general adult male population (Table 7.5). Virtually none were surgeons. And to lay to rest still another misconception: less than half the physicians trained at a university bothered to take anything more

[43] See the citations in note 47. But I should add that Chamber was a canon and prebendiary, and that Linacre had a large number of benefices, beginning in 1509, and was ordained as a priest two years before his death.

than lower orders. There were relatively few prominent clerical doctors in the fifteenth century, in contrast with the many of the twelfth, thirteenth, and early fourteenth centuries.[44] After 1452, physicians were allowed to marry, and most did.[45] Only a handful of clerical physicians served at the royal court, another contrast with their presence during the high middle ages. In effect, clerical doctors either practiced in seclusion and obscurity in monasteries, or stayed at a university and pursued other academic careers. Medicine was a secular profession by 1450.

The process of professionalization, crucial in solidifying the middle-class position of the doctors, is evident in many ways. One was their increasing association with hospitals. Before the Black Death the file contains records of just five doctors who were connected in any way with hospitals. Pre-plague hospitals were primarily pensionaries or hostels, and very few even had medical facilities (Table 7.6).[46] It is likely that these doctors, all of whom were clerics, simply used hospital estates as

TABLE 7.6: Hospitals with Affiliated Practitioners

| Hospital | N of practitioners | Hospital | N of practitioners |
|---|---|---|---|
| St. John, Oxford | 5 | St. John, Dorchester | 1 |
| St. Katherine, Exeter | 1 | St. John, Beds. | 1 |
| St. Barts, Hythe | 1 | St. Katherine, Worcester | 2 |
| St. Nicholas, Salisbury | 3 | St. Katherine Tower, London | 1 |
| St. Anthony, London | 1 | St. Mary Beth., London | 3 |
| St. Nicholas, Bury | 3 | St. Mary Mag., Preston | 1 |
| St. Barts, London | 9 | New Work, Maidstone | 1 |
| St. Barts, Playden-Rye | 1 | St. Nicholas, Carlisle | 1 |
| St. Cross Winchester | 1 | St. Nicholas, Pontefract | 1 |
| St. Edmund, Helmswell, Lincs. | 1 | St. Nicholas, York | 1 |
| Greatham, Durham | 1 | Pammatone, Geona | 1 |
| Holy Trinity, Rome | 1 | St. Thomas, Acon. | 1 |
| St. James, Westminster | 1 | St. Thomas Martyr, Bolton | 1 |
| St. John, Cambridge | 3 | | |

[44] For high medieval medicine, see Edward J. Kealey, *Medieval Medicus: A Social History of Anglo-Norman Medicine* (Baltimore: Johns Hopkins University Press, 1981).

[45] *Calendar of Papal Registers, ix, 1431–1447*, ed. J. A. Tremlow (London: HMSO, 1912), pp. 227–228; *C. Papal R.-Petitions, i, 1342–1419*, ed. W. H. Bliss (London: HMSO, 1896), p. 7; Beck, *Cutting Edge*, pp. 120–144; Erwin H. Ackerknecht, *A Short History of Medicine*, rev. ed. (Baltimore: Johns Hopkins University Press, 1982), p. 85.

[46] The best work is still Rotha Mary Clay, *Medieval Hospitals of England*, 2nd ed. (London: Frank Cass, 1966).

sources of income. After the Black Death, for reasons I have discussed elsewhere, the functions of hospitals became more medical.[47] Between 1349 and 1530 there are records of fifty doctors associating with hospitals. This is still a tiny percentage of the practitioners in the sample. But all of them were physicians or surgeons, and only ten were clerics who had taken higher orders. Since a few of the hospital doctors kept commonplace books, there is evidence that they practiced medicine as well as drawing an income.[48] Some even seem to have been resident doctors. And a few hospitals, such as St. Nicholas in Bury St. Edmunds, seem to have arranged what might be called training programs. Young M.B.s from Cambridge seem to have come to Bury and served a kind of internship.[49]

Another sign of professionalization was the increasing emphasis on education, a general characteristic of the middle strata. Education was not new to one group of doctors, the university-trained physicians; they had to be literate to matriculate, and their training was based on reading. But it became general among surgeons and barber-surgeons in the fifteenth century. The members of the Fellowship of Surgeons, as noted, spent a good portion of their apprenticeships studying from books. They had a library which occupied parts of two townhouses near the London Guildhall, and a fund to buy books for it.[50] The barber-surgeons also had a library, and there is evidence that the barber-tonsors subscribed to its upkeep.[51] More impressive is that ten percent of all doctors and forty-five percent of the physicians owned manuscripts or books in an age when an illustrated medical text might cost half a year's income (Table 7.7).[52] And eight percent of the doctors—and forty percent of the physicians—were themselves authors of medical texts (Table 7.9). The figure for "published" physicians in the late middle ages is, in fact, twice the percentage of British physicians who were medical au-

[47] Gottfried, *Black Death*, pp. 104–128.

[48] See, for example, B.M. Mss. Egerton 2724, Sloane 5; Harl. 1735; and O.U. Bod. Mss. Ashmole 1477; and Ashmole 1481.

[49] Robert S. Gottfried, *Bury St. Edmunds and the Urban Crisis, 1290–1539* (Princeton: Princeton University Press, 1982), pp. 192–207.

[50] Power and South, *Memorials of the Craft of Surgery*; Beck, *Cutting Edge*.

[51] Young, *Annals of the Barber-Surgeons*; Jessie Dobson and R. Milnes Walker, *The Barbers and Barber-Surgeons of London* (Oxford: Blackwell 1979).

[52] H. S. Bennett, *English Books and Readers, 1475–1557*, 2nd ed. (Cambridge: Cambridge University Press, 1970), pp. 97–109; E. A. Hammond, "Incomes of Medieval English Doctors," *JHM*, 15, 1960, pp. 154–169.

TABLE 7.7: Named Medical Works Owned by the Practitioners
(N = 321)

| 1. Authors/Titles | N | % of named works |
|---|---|---|
| Materia medica | 52 | 15.9 |
| Isaac Judeus/Henry Daniel | 31 | 9.7 |
| Guy de Chauliac | 27 | 8.4 |
| Nicholas of Lynn | 19 | 5.9 |
| John Arderne | 18 | 5.6 |
| Lanfranc of Milan | 17 | 5.3 |
| Galen | 16 | 5.0 |
| Avicenna | 15 | 4.7 |
| John Mirfield | 14 | 4.4 |
| Salerno Regimen | 14 | 4.4 |
| Hippocrates | 13 | 4.0 |
| John Gaddesden | 11 | 3.4 |
| Rhazes | 10 | 3.2 |
| Bernard Gordon | 9 | 2.8 |
| Henri de Mondeville | 9 | 2.8 |
| Thomas Morstede | 7 | 2.2 |
| Gilbertus Anglicus | 6 | 1.9 |
| Roger of Salerno | 6 | 1.9 |
| William Saliceto | 5 | 1.6 |
| Theodore of Lucca | 5 | 1.6 |
| Ricardus Anglicus | 4 | 1.2 |
| Albertus Magnus | 3 | 0.9 |
| Arnald of Villanova | 1 | — |
| Mondino de' Liuzzi | 1 | |
| Averroes | 1 | |
| Bruno Longoburgo | 1 | |
| Isidore of Seville | 1 | |
| Serapion | 1 | |
| Haly Abbas | 1 | |
| Peter Turisanus | 1 | |
| Roger Bacon | 1 | |
| Robert Grosseteste | 1 | |
| (Unnamed works) | (203) | |

2. Practitioners Holding Books

| | N | % of all prs. (N = 2,193) |
|---|---|---|
| One | 206 | 9.3 |
| Two | 102 | 4.7 |
| Three | 59 | 2.7 |
| Four or more | 42 | 1.9 |

TABLE 7.8 Characteristics of Oxbridge Graduates (% of N)

|  | Oxford (N = 123) | Cambridge (N = 66) |
|---|---|---|
| Clerics | 49.7 | 40.9 |
| Priests | 26.8 | 24.2 |
| Physicians | 99.5 | 98.5 |
| Surgeons | 3.3 | 1.5 |
| Apothecaries | .8 | — |
| Aliens | .8 | 1.5 |
| Settlements |  |  |
| London | 20.3 | 22.7 |
| County Towns | 13.8 | 12.1 |
| Ox. and Cam. | 61.8 | 62.1 |
| Rural Areas | 4.1 | 3.0 |
| Marrieds | 5.7 | 18.2 |

TABLE 7.9: Characteristics of Medical Authors (N = 177)

|  | N | % of all authors |
|---|---|---|
| Physician/Leeches | 131 | 74.0 |
| Surgeons | 35 | 19.7 |
| Barber-surgeons | 7 | 4.0 |
| Barber-tonsors | 1 | 0.5 |
| Apothecaries | 3 | 1.6 |
| Aliens | 4 | 2.3 |
| Clergy | 39 | 22.0 |
| Settlements |  |  |
| London | 70 | 39.4 |
| County Towns | 20 | 11.2 |
| Oxbridge | 81 | 45.7 |
| Countryside | 6 | 3.4 |
| Married | 19 | 10.7 |

thors in 1980.[53] Once again, there is a caveat. This literary proclivity
was a regional phenomenon. Three-quarters of the medical authors
lived in either London or one of the university towns, while the rest re-
sided in one of the larger county towns (Table 7.9).

There are other important characteristics of the authors and the books

[53] I.J.T. Davies, "Summing Up," British Medical Journal, 1, 1979, p. 320, claims that
there are currently about 3,000 medical authors in Britain. Using the figures cited in note
32, medieval doctors come out ahead.

Table 7.10: Characteristics of Englishmen Who Studied Abroad (N = 16)

| | N |
|---|---|
| 1. Residence | |
| London | 6 |
| Oxford/Cambridge | 5 |
| County Towns | 4 |
| Rural Areas | 1 |
| 2. Kind of Practice | |
| Physicians | 16 |
| 3. Clerics | 6 |
| 4. University attended | |
| Bologna | 3 |
| Padua | 8 |
| Montpellier | 2 |
| Paris | 5 |
| 5. Married | 6 |

Table 7.11: Women Practitioners (N = 28)

| | N | % of all women |
|---|---|---|
| Leeches | 8 | 28.6 |
| Barbers | 16 | 57.1 |
| Apothecaries | 4 | 14.3 |
| Aliens | 0 | — |
| Settlement | | |
| London | 10 | 35.7 |
| County Towns | 4 | 14.3 |
| Countryside | 14 | 50.0 |
| Married | 12 | 42.9 |

they owned. Three-quarters of the authors were physicians. But virtually all of the rest were surgeons, and their proportion of the sample rose to close to thirty percent by 1500 (Table 7.9). About forty percent of the authors lived in London; this proportion also rose—to 49 percent—by 1500. And over ten percent of them were married, another figure which rose—to 21 percent—by the end of the fifteenth century. All this points toward the secularization and *embourgeoisment* of professional medical practitioners.[54]

[54] There were two hundred additional references in the wills that could not be figured into tables because authors or titles were not mentioned—that is, they were simply re-

Of the titles and authors that were named, there was a preponderance of the practical (Table 7.7). The most popular titles were, respectively: versions of *Materia medica*; Isaac Judeus's and Henry Daniel's *Domes of Urines*; the surgery of Guy de Chauliac; the *Kalendarium* of Nicholas of Lynn; and the surgeries of John Arderne and Lanfranc of Milan. All of these stressed practice and not theory; all were more appropriate for and more probably owned by active physicians than by university dons or even physicians whose concern was natural philosophy rather than clinical medicine. The numbers of books owners, too, is significant. Almost ten percent of the doctors in the sample owned texts. When it is considered that about 1,200 of the doctors came from lists, that is, freemen's rolls, guild enrollments, and the like, in which there was no opportunity to mention possessions of any kind, this becomes more impressive. Close to five percent of the doctors had two books, three percent three books, and two percent four books or more.

Moreover, the evidence of the Oxford and Cambridge practitioners suggests that they two were becoming more prosperous and middle class (Table 7.8). The number of clerics among them diminished steadily after the 1450s, when physicians began to marry in greater numbers. Throughout the two hundred years measured in the sample, the proportion of Oxbridge practitioners was about a quarter. But their proportion was around sixty percent in 1350, and less than twenty percent in 1530. Virtually all of them were physicians, both in the beginning and the end; there would be no widespread acceptance of surgery in late medieval England, as there was in northern Italian and southern French universities.[55] Neither English university had a program diverse or innovative enough to attract many foreign students. But more and more of the graduates were leaving the university towns for lucrative practices throughout the kingdom. Over twenty percent from both went to London, and over ten percent to the largest county towns. Here too the numbers increased through time. By 1530, thirty percent of the Oxford practitioners and thirty-five percent of those from Cambridge were

---

ferred to as books, texts, or manuals. If they could be figured into the sample the proportion of book owners would more than double.

[55] For Italy, see: Carlo M. Cipolla, *Public Health and the Medical Profession* (Cambridge: Cambridge University Press, 1976), pp. 1–66; Nancy G. Siraisi, *Arts and Sciences at Padua: The Studium of Padua Before 1350* (Toronto: Pontifical Institute of Mediaeval Studies, 1973), pp. 143–171; and Siraisi, *Taddeo Alderotti and His Pupils: Two Generations of Italian Medical Learning* (Princeton: Princeton University Press, 1981), pp. 269–302.

going to London; while fifteen percent of the Oxonians and nineteen percent of those from Cambridge were going to the county towns. There they could make more money and play a greater role in civic affairs than they could in the university towns, and their connections and probably interests in academic medicine would have of necessity have diminished.

The evidence from the file shows how rich doctors could become. This was especially so among the physicians, surgeons, and those apothecaries who were members of the London Grocers' Company. There are references to this, as noted in Chapter Two in the literary and narrative sources.[56] And there are many outstanding individual cases. Thomas Morstede, it is worth repeating, was thought to be the richest man in London during the 1430s and 1440s.[57] In the 1442 assessment of the city's elite, which included long-distance traders, financiers, mercers, drapers, and grocers, he was indeed the wealthiest.[58] Such prosperity was still evident in the sixteenth century, and in the countryside as well as London. The 1523–1524 Lay Subsidy was a general, relatively comprehensive tax of the wealthier folk in England.[59] To take one example, in Suffolk, there were more doctors assessed in the anticipation than there were members of any other occupational group save clothiers.[60]

Further evidence of the doctors' wealth comes from the data file. Several quantitative measures of wealth were set up. A general scale, using a multiple regression analysis, was constructed, taking data for movables, cash on hand, gifts to friends, charity, and the extent of landholding.[61] These results for medical practitioners were then compared with those from an earlier measure taken from 223 other occupational groups from fifteenth-century London, St. Albans, Ipswich, Bury St. Ed-

[56] See above, pp. 52–60. Chaucer, *Canterbury Tales*, p. 31; and William Langland, *Piers the Ploughman*, ed. J. F. Goodridge (New York: Penguin Books, 1966), p. 88, are especially notable.

[57] Thrupp, *Merchant Class*, pp. 260–261. For Morstede, see Talbot and Hammond, *Medical Practitioners*, pp. 350–352; and Beck, *Cutting Edge*, pp. 79–120.

[58] For an additional perspective see H. L. Gray, "Incomes from Land in England," *English Historical Review*, 49, 1934, pp. 607–639.

[59] John Sheail, *The Regional Distribution of Wealth in England as Indicated in the Lay Subsidy Return of 1524* (London: London University Ph.D. thesis, 1968).

[60] *Suffolk in 1524. Being the Return for a Subsidy Granted in 1523*, Suffolk Green Books, x (Woodbridge, Suffolk: Booth, 1910).

[61] For a detailed explanation of regression see Hubert M. Blalock, Jr., *Social Statistics* (New York: McGraw-Hill, 1972), pp. 219–508.

munds, and Norwich (Table 7.12).[62] In all, the doctors, defined as physicians, surgeons, barbers, and apothecaries, ranked fifth, behind gentlemen, mercers, drapers, and grocers. They ranked ahead of their fellow professionals, lawyers and notaries, and such wealthy guildsmen as goldsmiths and skinners. To put it another way: doctors' wealth was fifty-seven percent of that of the gentlemen, while millers' was ten percent. The other occupational groups measured less than ten percent (Table 7.12).

This wealth ranking is especially impressive since it included the barber-tonsors, who were poorer than the rest of the practitioners. In fact, the wealth of the doctors was well distributed among the different kinds of doctors. To assess more accurately this distribution an Index of Concentration, using a Lorenz Curve was constructed.[63] A figure of 1 on this

TABLE 7.12: Wealth of Selected Occupational Groups

| Group | N | As a % of the wealthiest occupation |
|---|---|---|
| Gentlemen | 55 | 100 |
| Mercers | 79 | 77 |
| Drapers | 53 | 62 |
| Grocers | 109 | 61 |
| Doctors | 339 | 57 |
| Lawyers | 21 | 54 |
| Goldsmiths | 34 | 47 |
| Butchers | 78 | 34 |
| Stationers | 7 | 34 |
| Scriveners | 14 | 29 |
| Bakers | 84 | 22 |
| Weavers | 224 | 21 |
| Corvisers | 119 | 18 |
| Tailors | 93 | 17 |
| Smiths | 31 | 17 |
| Masons | 27 | 17 |
| Tanners | 59 | 14 |
| Chandlers | 34 | 13 |
| Cookshop owners | 11 | 13 |
| Fullers | 68 | 12 |
| Millers | 32 | 10 |

[62] Gottfried, *Epidemic Disease*, pp. 162–175.

[63] For a more detailed explanation and historical applications of Lorenz Curves, see

index indicates a perfect equality of distribution among the members of
the sample, while a figure of 100 would mean that all the wealth was concentrated among the richest one percent. Indices were run for all 224 occupational groups, for the ten wealthiest, and for the doctors. The first
index, that for all occupations, came to seventy-one percent, which suggests a general skew toward the wealthier groups. The second, for the
ten wealthiest, came to fifty-five percent, which suggests that wealth
was reasonably well distributed among the more prosperous bourgeoisie. And the third index, just for doctors, came to fifty-nine percent,
suggesting too a relatively even distribution of wealth among members
of a well-heeled group.

There are other indications of wealth. Almost a quarter of all the practitioners in the file held at least one piece of property (Table 7.13). Of
these, twenty percent held property in and around London, the largest
and busiest of England's markets. Yet those practitioners who held more
than one piece of property—albeit less than seven percent of the sample
did—tended to hold them in provincial towns or the countryside. About
three percent of the doctors held two or more tracts in the county towns,
and close to four percent two or more in the countryside. And a large
proportion of doctors held special status in their towns, London and

TABLE 7.13: Practitioners and Property

|  | N | % of the sample |
|---|---|---|
| 1. Holding one piece. | | |
|    In London | 422 | 20.0 |
|    In provincial towns | 76 | 3.6 |
|    In rural areas | 25 | 1.2 |
| 2. Holding two pieces. | | |
|    In London | 4 | 0.2 |
|    In county towns | 57 | 2.7 |
|    In rural areas | 77 | 3.6 |
| 3. Holding three or more. | | |
|    In London | 1 | — |
|    In county towns | 1 | — |
|    In rural areas | 37 | 1.7 |

Gottfried, *Bury St. Edmunds and the Urban Crisis*, p. 130; and David Herlihy, "Family and
Property in Renaissance Florence," in Harry A. Miskimin, David Herlihy, A. L. Udovitch, eds., *The Medieval City* (New Haven, Conn.: Yale University Press, 1977), pp. 6–9.

otherwise (Table 7.14). Over half were described as citizens, burgesses, or freemen. Of these, close to eighteen percent were citizens in London, the most prestigious designation an English bourgeois could attain.

To sum up: professional medical practitioners tended to live in England's larger towns. Their numbers and influence, by comparison with all practitioners of medicine throughout the kingdom, increased in the course of the later middle ages. Doctors were rigorously trained and were generally laymen. They were well educated; many of them invested in expensive reference texts, and even more took an active part in their continual revision. They were rich and apparently happy as "middle strata" professionals. This is an important distinction, because the prosperous merchants studied by Wolff, Heers, Mandrou, and, to a lesser extent, Thrupp, did not always share this contentment.[64] By contrast, many doctors wanted their sons to be doctors.[65]

Further evidence that many practitioners were content to be bourgeois doctors comes from their family histories (Table 7.15). In those cases where there is evidence—that is, where doctors had children and

TABLE 7.14: Practitioners Holding Burghal Status (N = 1,264)

| Status | N | % of all practitioners (2,293) |
|--------|---|-------------------------------|
| Citizen | 391 | 17.1 |
| Freeman/Master | 831 | 38.9 |
| Burgess | 77 | 3.4 |
| Esquire | 21 | 0.9 |
| Yeomen | 12 | 0.5 |

[64] Phillipe Wolff, *Commerces et marchands de Toulouse* (Paris: SEVPEN, 1954); Jacques Heers, *Genes au xvᵉ Siecle* (Paris: SEVPEN, 1961); Robert Mandrou, *Introduction to Modern France, 1500–1640*, trans. R. E. Hallmark (New York: Harper and Row, 1975); Thrupp, *Merchant Class*, pp. 234–287. Thrupp is guarded in her assessment and figuring from the data in her appendix, "Aldermanic Families," pp. 321–377, less than twenty percent of the merchants did become gentlemen. Lawrence Stone has found fewer cases of such mobility form the sixteenth through the eighteenth centuries. See Lawrence Stone and Jeanne C. Fawtier Stone, *An Open Elite? England, 1540–1880* (Oxford: Clarendon Press, 1984), particularly pp. 211–255.

[65] It should be noted that many doctors invested in urban property, particularly tenements in London, which they sometimes rented out. About fifteen percent of the doctors so invested, including close to half the doctors and surgeons who lived in London. I do not wish to make more of this because doctors' use of these tenements is not often made clear, and my data, mostly from wills, is probably incomplete.

TABLE 7.15: Families of Practitioners Who Left Wills

|  | N | % of total |
|---|---|---|
| 1. All Practitioners (N = 322) | | |
| Married | 272 | 84.4 |
| Married more than once | 21 | 6.5 |
| Sons | 110 | 34.2 |
| Daughter | 55 | 17.1 |
| Children of Age | 23 | 7.1 |
| 2. Surgeons (N = 85) | | |
| Married | 81 | 95.3 |
| Remarried | 7 | 8.7 |
| Sons | 49 | 57.6 |
| Daughters | 13 | 15.3 |
| Children of Age | 10 | 12.3 |
| 3. Londoners (N = 205) | | |
| Married | 174 | 84.8 |
| Remarried | 17 | 8.3 |
| Sons | 95 | 46.3 |
| Daughters | 41 | 20.0 |
| Children of Age | 16 | 7.8 |

left records about them—over sixty percent of the children followed their fathers.[66] This was true irrespective of gender, type of medical practice, or time in my broader period of the late middle ages. And it was even more the case for surgeons than physicians, and for Londoners, those archetypically prosperous bourgeoisie, than for practitioners living anywhere else in England. A practitioners' son, be it in 1340 or 1520, was more likely than not to become a doctor. So too was the daughter of an apothecary if she did not marry.[67] In this sense, doctors and other professionals were probably the most stable members of the bourgeoisie.

But rich and prosperous though they might have been, were medical

[66] Again, there is a problem with the data, which makes me reluctant to develop this point any more. Most of the information about children come from wills, which only about fifteen percent of the doctors left. And, of course, not all doctors who made wills mentioned their families.

[67] It was even true for barbers. Walter Serjeant, a citizen and barber of London, told in his will, proved in 1375 in the London Com. Court, Courtney, f. 25v, that his wife and two sons were barbers. In 1448, Thomas Ingham was also a member of a barbering family. See London Com. Court, Prowet, f. 240v.

TABLE 7.16: Medical Families

1. Family Occupations: Fathers of Practitioners

|              | N      | %    |
|--------------|--------|------|
| No listing   | 2,059  | 98.4 |
| Physicians   | 3      | .1   |
| Surgeons     | 8      | .4   |
| Barbers      | 20     | .9   |
| Merchants    | 1      | —    |
| Gentlemen    | 1      | —    |
| Craftsmen    | 22     | 1.0  |

2. Family Occupations: Sons of Practitioners

|              | N      | %    |
|--------------|--------|------|
| No listing   | 2,081  | 98.4 |
| Physicians   | 1      | —    |
| Surgeons     | 5      | .2   |
| Barbers      | 17     | .8   |
| Merchants    | 1      | —    |
| Gentlemen    | 1      | —    |
| Craftsmen    | 9      | .4   |

practitioners—or at least some of them—"middle class"? This depends on the definition of middle class. Thrupp, as noted, was reluctant to use the term, preferring the expression "middle strata."[68] Other scholars have been more explicit. Robert Mandrou claimed that to be a middle class meant "to share in a mentality, a way of thinking."[69] It included "forethought, thrift, a sense of profit and expenditure."[70] For Fernand Braudel, it encompassed patriotism.[71] For Joseph Strayer it was exemplified by secularism; like Braudel and his patriotism Strayer felt that secularism first appeared on a general level among the bourgeoisie.[72] All of these were characteristic of many medical practitioners by 1450.

There were other characteristics, as well. One was a changing perception of work. The theorists of the eleventh century who developed the

[68] Thrupp, *Merchant Class*, pp. 234–287. See too A. R. Myers, *London in the Age of Chaucer* (Norman, Oklahoma: University of Oklahoma Press, 1971), pp. 85–143.

[69] Mandrou, *Introduction to Modern France*, pp. 109–110.

[70] *Ibid.*, p. 110.

[71] Braudel, *Civilization and Capitalism*, ii, pp. 515–559.

[72] Joseph R. Strayer, "The Laicization of French and English Society in the Thirteenth Century," in his *Medieval Statecraft and Perspectives in History* (Princeton: Princeton University Press, 1971), pp. 251–265.

concept of trifunctionalism allowed that, generally, manual labor and even trade was the function of the third order, the *laboratores*: hence the name.[73] This was Biblically ordained.[74] Japhet and Shem, the two eldest sons of Noah, had received their father's blessing; their descendants were clerics and gentlemen. But Ham had been cursed, and his descendants were forced to work. This ordering, as noted in Chapter Two, carried over into medicine. Traditionally, physicians, often clerics and university students, stood atop the medical heap. But surgeons were workmen—operatives or craftsmen, as physicians and social critics from the eleventh through the fourteenth centuries were wont to remind them. Indeed, critics argued that the very name *chirurgia* came from the Greek *chir*, meaning hand, and *gios*, operate.[75] Surgery was *manua operatio* by definition. This explains the perspectives of many early-fourteenth-century physic texts, which excoriated surgeons as laboratores.[76] It was those who worked *manua operatio* who caused public dissatisfaction with medicine.

Yet attitudes were different by the fifteenth century. Jacques LeGoff has discussed changing ideas about work, arguing for a decline in the old blood taboo.[77] This affected medicine, and helped the surgeons. Increasingly, critics advised doctors a "hands-on" policy in dealing with their patients. Physicians and surgeons were urged to cooperate and share their secrets and skills so that "they can heal and help all."[78] Authors called for a common practice.[79] At the same time, those authors who were condemning physicians were praising surgeons, and doing so

[73] Georges Dumezil, *Mythe et Epopees*, 3 vols. (Paris: Bibliotheque des sciences humaines, 1968–1993); Georges Duby, *The Three Orders: Feudal Society Imagined*, trans. Arthur Goldhammer (Chicago: University of Chicago Press, 1978).

[74] Denys Hay, *Europe: The Emergence of An Idea* (Edinburgh: University of Edinburgh Press, 1957).

[75] *LFPD*, iii, ii, Appendix 5, p. 1562.

[76] See, for example: O.U. Bod. Add. Ms. B 60, f. 1; *Ibid.*, Ms. Ashmole 1443, f. 401; *Ibid.*, Ms. Ashmole, 1477, III, ff. 1–47. Quotations from these texts are excerpted above, pp. 62–72.

[77] Jacques LeGoff, "Licit and Illicit Trade in the Medieval West," in his *Time Work and Culture in the Middle Ages*, trans. Arthur Goldhammer (Chicago: University of Chicago, 1977), pp. 58–70.

[78] O.U. Bod. Ms. Ashmole 1477, III, f. 2.

[79] See, for example: *The Knight de la Tour Landry*, ed. Thomas Wright (London: EETS, 33, 1868), Chap. 103; *Caxton's Dialogues, English and French*, ed. Henry Bradley (London: EETS, es, 79, 1900), p. 25; John Mirfield, *Surgery*, ed. James B. Coltan (New York: Hafner, 1969), pp. 4–5. The quotations are discussed in Chapter Two.

because they did use direct methods of treatment. Chaucer's surgeons "by license and assent of switch as were wise as a rose."[80] And Langland praised the surgeon for taking the initiative and treating the sick when physicians shrank back.[81] Indeed, by early in the sixteenth century things had reached the point where, in a lawsuit between an English and Italian surgeon, the Englishman defended his practice by arguing for the spiritual goodness and high social position of those who, like himself, worked with their hands.[82] Laborers and artisans might still be despised, especially by the nobility. But among those middle-class folk living in towns and working *manua operatio*, like surgeons or goldsmiths, or working with money or commodities, like bankers and clothiers, the stigma of the *laboratores* had all but vanished by 1500.

A second characteristic of late medieval doctors that seems to have been common to the middle classes was their social mobility. Social theorists, most of them clerics, had traditionally argued the virtues of meekness and contentment with one's lot. What counted, after all, was salvation; the next life was eternal, and the tribulations of a brief stay on earth were mere trials for better things to come.[83] Competition was discouraged. Hence the verse that urged children to follow in their parents' occupations and lifestyles:

> And if their father were servants or husbandmen
> Let them go seek work in the fields.[84]

As for townsmen: *si laboratores sunt, faciant quod volunt*. Ambition was to be discounted.

This too was changing in the later middle ages, especially among the bourgeoisie. This was the time of the "world upside down," and, whatever the admonitions of social critics and people in authority, competition and ambition were regarded as virtues.[85] But herein an important distinction must be made. For the wealthy merchant or even govern-

---

[80] This is quoted in full in Ida B. Jones, "Popular Medical Knowledge in Fourteenth Century English Literature," *BHM*, 5, 1937, p. 415.

[81] *Ibid.*, p. 419.

[82] *LPFD*, 3, ii, p. 1562.

[83] Jacques LeGoff, *The Birth of Purgatory*, trans. Arthur Goldhammer (Chicago: University of Chicago Press, 1984), pp. 133–153.

[84] *Middle English Sermons from MS Roy. 18B*, ed. W. O. Ross (London: EETS, 208, 1938), p. 32.

[85] R. H. Robbins, *Historical Poems of the Fourteenth and Fifteenth Centuries* (New York: Columbia University Press, 1959), p. 63.

ment official social mobility often meant upward movement into the ranks of the gentry. The circumstance of Thomas More and his family—merchant, lawyer, chancellor of England—is a good case in point.[86] Such movement could not have helped the stability of a nascent middle class.

The case of doctors, however, was different. As noted, they were generally happy with what they were. There was considerable social mobility among them, but it was within the medical ranks. Each kind of doctor wanted the privileges, status, and wealth of his colleagues just above him in the pecking order. There is much evidence for this. To take the barber-tonsors as an example: until the early fourteenth century they were pretty well locked into their occupations.[87] Barbering provided a decent living but a limited social position, and an ambitious barber who wished a broader medical practice was constrained by custom and, in some instances, law.[88] By 1400 things were different. *Mutatis mutandis*—the discrediting of physicians, the rise of surgery, the incorporation of the barbers' companies—social mobility was possible. Barber-surgeons and barber-tonsors usually belonged to the same company. The companies were controlled in every way by the barber-surgeons. Yet the barber-surgeons inevitably recruited members for their elite mysteries within the larger companies from among the barber-tonsors. Indeed, by 1450 it was expected that the most talented barber-tonsors would in time rise to the top of the larger company.[89]

Nor did social mobility stop there. The best barber-surgeons wanted to become surgeons. Those in London petitioned and sometimes fought with the surgeons of the Fellowship throughout the fifteenth century, until by 1490, as noted in Chapter One, they had won an administrative if not quite medical parity. By 1500 they could treat the same kinds of patients and use the same methods as the surgeons. Mention has been made of the large number of doctors who qualified for surgical licenses in 1514.[90] Of the seventy-two, at least sixty can be identified as members of the London Barbers' Company.[91] And as a final example of social mobility, most surgeons wanted medical parity if not a commonality of

---

[86] Richard Marius, *Thomas More* (New York: Alfred A. Knopf, 1984), pp. 3–33.

[87] Young, *Annals of the Barber-Surgeons* pp. 39–90.

[88] *Ibid.*, pp. 261–260.

[89] *Ibid.*

[90] James, "Earliest List of Surgeons," pp. 255–260.

[91] *Ibid.*

practice with the physicians. The surgeons increased the amount of theoretical training they gave to their apprentices, and even began attending the university. In a few cases, surgeons petitioned successfully the chancellor of Oxford to allow them advanced academic standing in M.D. programs on the basis of their years as practicing surgeons.[92]

A few physicians and surgeons did, of course, become gentlemen and abandon medicine.[93] But they were a minority. Most doctors were happy with medicine; they just wanted the highest rewards the profession could offer. And, as suggested, while these rewards were high, wealth was generally well distributed. This contrasts with the doctors' fellow professionals, lawyers, a few of whom did become enormously rich and so were able to buy large estates and acquire a county seat of some sort.[94] This is important to the rising middle class. Since few doctors could afford large estates, they were, in effect, forced to cultivate a bourgeois mentality.

A third middle-class characteristic exemplified by doctors was their preoccupation with courtesy and manners. This was a trait shared with and no doubt picked up from the aristocracy. Indeed, from the twelfth century onward, good manners, etiquette, and appropriate dress and grooming had begun to supplement and in some cases replace the older martial values of the *bellatores*. By the fourteenth century such habits were being aped by the gentry, and by the fifteenth by the bourgeoisie. But the bourgeois manner was a bit different. It concentrated less on material things like dress and more on comportment. And the medium through which it spread was books.[95]

Among doctors the new courtesy took the form of deontology. Sections on ethics were inserted into medical books. Guy de Chauliac's *Cy-*

---

[92] These included William Hobbes, John Leche and William Holme. See *T&H*, pp. 161–162; and 401–403.

[93] A good example is the Italian Antony Ciabo. A royal surgeon he was given license to import wine. By 1540, Ciabo had abandoned medicine for commerce. See Beck, *Cutting Edge*, pp. 156, 169.

[94] Hexter, "Myth of the Middle Class," p. 75n.; Lawrence Stone, *Crisis of the Aristocracy* (Oxford University Press, 1965), especially chapters 3 and 8.

[95] Suzanne W. Hill, *Chaste, Silent and Obedient: English Books for Women* (San Marino, Cal.: Huntington Library, 1982), is a general guide. A fine specific example is John Stanbridge, *A Fifteenth Century Schoolbook*, ed. William Nelson (Oxford: Clarendon Press, 1956). See too Laurel Braswell, "Utilitarian Prose," in Anthony S. G. Edwards, *Middle English Prose: A Critical Guide to Major Authors and Genres* (New Brunswick, N.J.: Rutgers University Press, pp. 337–388.

*rurgie* was probably the most widely imitated text of its kind in the late middle ages.[96] Following the principles of courtesy, Guy described the ideal surgeon:

[He] should be well mannered, bold in many ways, fearful of dangers, that he should abhor the false cures or practices. He should be affable to the sick, kindhearted to his colleagues, wise in his prognostications. He should be chaste, sober, compassionate and merciful: he should not be covetous, grasping in money matters, and then he will receive a salary commensurate with his labors, the financial ability of the treatment, and his own dignity.[97]

John Arderne also wrote about deportment.

In clothes and other apparel he should be honest, and not liken himself in apparel and bearing to minstrels, but in clothing and bearing he should show the manner of clerks. For why? It seems that any discreet man clad in clerk's garb may occupy the boards of gentlemen. And be he courteous at the lord's table, and be he not displeasing in words or deeds to the guests sitting near by, hear he many things but let him speak few. . . . And when he shall speak, let the words be short, and as far as possible, fair and reasonable and without swearing. Beware that there never be found double words in his mouth for then none will believe him.[98]

And there were cautions about liaisons with female patients and bedside manner.

[Never] broach any other subject than that which concerns the treatment; neither may he chat with the mistress of the house, the daughter or the maidservant, nor look at them with leering eyes. For people are soon suspicious, and by such things he is apt to incur their enmity, while the doctor had better keep on friendly terms with them.[99]

And:

[The doctor should] never reveal the confidences of his patients, neither those of men or women, nor set one person against another. For if a person

---

[96] Guy de Chauliac, *Surgery*, ed. Margaret S. Ogdan, 2 vols. (London: EETS, 265, 1971), is very much an autobiography as well as a medical manual. There are discussions of deontology in Talbot, *Medicine in Medieval England*, pp. 134–145, in which the author points out the similarities between late medieval and Hippocratic ethics; and Bullough, *Development of Medicine*, pp. 93–111.

[97] *Ibid.*, p. 19.

[98] Arderne, *Treatise of Fistula*, p. 5.

[99] Jan Yperman, *De cyryrgie*, as quoted in Bullough, *Development of Medicine*, p. 96.

sees that the physician keeps another man's counsel he will trust him no more.[100]

Courtesy was not the only characteristic the bourgeoisie shared with members of other social groups. There were ambitious magnates, generous gentlemen (in theory, by definition), upwardly mobile artisans, and thrifty peasants. But it was the combination of these and no doubt many other traits which distinguished the middle-class mentality. A key word, to add yet another characteristic, is dynamism. By 1500 the bourgeoisie, as exemplified by doctors, were disinclined to acquiesce and do what they were told. Bourgeois customs and institutions were more flexible than those of the lords, the church, and the peasantry, perhaps because they were less old. It was this dynamism which, in the changing world of late medieval and early modern Europe, facilitated the spread of the middle-class mindset into high society.

It can be argued that everything that has been written applies to conditions in the seventeenth and eighteenth as well as the fourteenth and fifteenth centuries. Things changed slowly before the eighteenth century, and this is one reason why so many perceptive historians have claimed that the middle class was rising in their era. Surely, Braudel is correct in his distinction between material and economic life; since he argues that economic life was developing by 1400 but not developed until 1800, and that the bourgeoisie were the only group to partake fully of both lives, then perhaps the middle class did take four hundred years to rise, as some critics of the concept suggest.[101] But it is possible to be more precise. There was no middle class in the early or high middle ages, at least outside a few Italian and Flemish cities. There was an English middle class by 1450. Merchants formed an important part of it. Yet many merchants, for a variety of reasons summed up nicely by Mandrou, seemed unhappy and insecure in their middling position.[102] In England by 1400 they were associating with the gentry in the House of Commons; by 1500 they were often called *generosi*, and the term *mediocre* was applied to those below great merchant but above artisanal rank.[103]

A final example, the case of lawyers in late medieval England, might help shore up this argument. Recent work has shown how diverse a

[100] Arderne, *Treatise of Fistula*, p. 8.
[101] See, for example, Laslett, *World We Have Lost*, pp. 22–52.
[102] Mandrou, *Introduction to Modern France*, pp. 109–114.
[103] As quoted in Thrupp, *Merchant Class*, pp. 292–294.

group they were.[104] A few had a common bond drawn from their schooling at one of the inns of court. But there were also many local practitioners with no formal legal training. Some were notaries or stationers, or
other intelligent, literate men like the village leech John Crophill, who
managed to get hold of a law book or a few statutes, and still others akin
to Keith Thomas's cunning men. Apparently, there were no lawyers'
guilds. But, these caveats notwithstanding, the lawyers, even in the
broadest sense, were like the doctors. They were rich, well read, ambitious, and, by and large, bourgeois. And if the wealthiest of them often
became gentlemen, the majority aimed to achieve and remain members
of the middle strata.[105]

To return to medical practitioners: perhaps social mobility is the most
crucial bourgeois characteristic. Doctors, to reiterate, were content to
remain what they were, and encouraged their children to follow them.
Along with other professionals, middling-level merchants, and the more
prosperous artisans they formed the stable core of the bourgeoisie. They
were tied to towns; indeed, professionals, the middle class, and urban
life were inexorably linked. The professionalization of medicine was
crucial to the rise of the middle class.[106] Today everyone wants to be
called "professional," but historically this was not the case. Status was
still generally tied to the land and the hereditary titles that went with it.
This is why many wealthy merchants wanted to become gentlemen.
While the doctors compared favorably with the great merchants, they
did less well against the gentry, to say nothing of the great magnates. In

---

[104] The most detailed study of lawyers is Eric W. Ives, *The Common Lawyers of Pre-Reformation England, Thomas Kebell: A Case Study* (Cambridge: Cambridge University Press,
1983); Others include: Robert C. Palmer, *The County Courts of Medieval England, 1150–1350*
(Princeton: Princeton University Press, 1982); Wilfred R. Prest, *Inns of Court Under Eliz-
abeth I and the Early Stuarts* (Totowa, N.J.: Rowman & Littlefield, 1977); Eric W. Ives,
*Faction in Tudor England* (London Historical Association, 1979); Ives, *Wealth and Power in
Tudor England* (Atlantic Highlands, N.J.: Humanities Press, 1978); Ives, "The Common
Lawyers," in Cecil Clough, ed., *Profession, Vocation and Culture in Late Medieval England:
Essays Dedicated to the Memory of A. R. Myers* (Liverpool: Liverpool University Press, 1982),
pp. 181–208; John H. Baker, *Introduction to English Legal History* (London: Butterworths,
1979); and C. T. Allmand, "The Civil Lawyers," in Clough, *Profession, Vocation and Culture*, pp. 155–171. Hexter, "Myth of the Middle Class," p. 75n., expresses reservations.
[105] Cipolla, "The Professions," pp. 37–52; Bullough, *Development of Medicine*, pp. 93–
111.
[106] Ives, *The Common Lawyers*, pp. 7–22, 308–309, 394–421. See the data for lawyers,
scriveners, and stationers in Table 7.12.

the fifteenth and indeed the eighteenth centuries the bourgeoisie were, quite simply, less prosperous and prestigious than the aristocracy. But by 1400 the doctors seemed wedded to and generally satisfied with their urban digs and situation. They, professionals like them, and the more modest merchants were the backbone of the middle class.

Supposing all this were so; what then was the role of the middle class? It is not necessary, as Weber, Pollard, Wright, and others have done to link them directly to all the great movements and events of the early modern period. Obviously, the middle class was important to the Reformation and the discovery of America, but so were many other factors. Nor is it necessary to argue, as Mandrou has about France, that in the early modern period the bourgeoisie were "the most active and enterprising of all sections of . . . society."[107] It is enough to claim, as has Braudel, that the middle class was most important in the development of capitalism and a world economy, or, in the case of England, a national economy.[108] And it is enough to claim that the bourgeois mentality first gained ground among members of high society in the late middle ages, and that this mentality would increasingly become the norm. It was unfortunate that in early-sixteenth-century England, most of the surgeons and apothecaries and all of the barber-surgeons were cut out of this "middle class."

[107] Mandrou, *Introduction to Modern France*, p. 110.
[108] Braudel, *Civilization and Capitalism*, ii, pp. 461–513.

# 8

## THE FAILURE OF ENGLISH
## MEDICINE

It has been argued that surgery was the most dynamic branch of medicine in England during the later middle ages. Toward the end of the fifteenth century the surgeons of the London Fellowship were joined in their practice by the increasingly well-trained barber-surgeons. Taken together, as shown in Chapter Seven, the two groups showed the greatest growth in the numbers of practitioners. Physicians continued to revel in their social status and high incomes. But their practice remained moribund and ineffective.[1] By the 1490s, then, surgeons and barber-surgeons seemed on the verge of bringing about a transformation in which surgery, anatomy, and a new and more accurate physiology would be incorporated into physic. Most important, the "new" medicine would encompass clinical training, the hands-on practice that physicians had forsworn. English medicine seemed ready for the sort of cultural enlightenment that had transformed Italian medicine two centuries earlier.[2]

The new medicine was part and parcel of the larger cultural renaissance that was shaking England. Thomas More wrote in *Utopia*:

> My friend . . . had also brought some medical textbooks with him, a few short works by Hippocrates, and Galen's *Handbook* (the *Microtechne*). The Utopians think very highly of them, for, though nobody in the world needs medicine less than they do, nobody has more respect for it. They consider it one of the most interesting and important developments of science—and

[1] Ironically, and rather out of character with the rest of the book, this is what Charles Talbot argues in *Medicine in Medieval England* (London: Oldbourne, 1967), pp. 198–211. See too: Margaret Pelling and Charles Webster, "Medical Practitioners"; and Paul Slack, "Mortality Crises and Epidemic Disease in England, 1485–1610," both in Charles Webster, ed., *Health, Medicine and Mortality in the Sixteenth Century* (Cambridge: Cambridge University Press, 1979), pp. 165–235, 9–59.

[2] Roberto Weiss, *Humanism in England During the Fifteenth Century* (Oxford: Blackwell, 1967); Antonia McLain, *Humanism and the Rise of Science in Tudor England* (New York: Neale Watson, 1972).

as they see it, the scientific investigation of nature is not only a most enjoy-able process, but also the best possible method of pleasing the Creator.[3]

This medical "revolution" did not, of course, take place. Rather, be-tween 1510 and 1540 the indigenous English parts, especially surgery and anatomy, were scrapped. The Royal College of Physicians was founded, and the barber-surgeons and surgeons were placed more firmly than ever as second-class medical citizens. Finally, in 1540, sur-geons and barber-surgeons alike were absorbed by the mass of the bar-ber-tonsors. The gains of a century and a half would be dissipated in a generation, and it would be another two hundred years before English medicine became effective.

One cause of this decline has already been indicated; indeed, it began in the halcyon years of the last third of the fifteenth century. English kings stopped their foreign wars. In 1513 Henry VIII did assemble an expedition in 1513 for the invasion of France. It was well organized, and sailed for France the following year.[4] But Henry's army did not do much fighting, and his surgeons never gained the techniques, experience, or subsequent royal support that their predecessors enjoyed. This fol-lowed the non-combative expedition of Edward IV in 1475. Edward's surgeons, too, never had the opportunity of battlefield practice. But in 1475 some of his surgeons had seen action during the last years of the French wars and possibly during the most active phases of the Wars of the Roses.[5] By the sixteenth century, with the possible exceptions of two or three who had spent time in the Netherlands, none of Henry's surgeons had wartime experience. Hence, they did not have the oppor-tunities of surgeons a century earlier to perfect their skills in the harrow-ing yet ideal circumstance of battle. Henry VIII, unlike Henry V, never supported surgery, thus eliminating one of the bulwarks earlier sur-geons had against the established power of university-trained physi-cians.

There were other reasons for the demise of surgery and the triumph of physic. There was the introduction into England of new ideas of med-

---

[3] Thomas More, *Utopia*, Book II, ed. Paul Turner (London: Penguin Books, 1965), p. 100.

[4] *LPFD*, i, #2757, pp. 1128–1129; Thomas Vicary, *The Anatomie of the Bodie of Man*, i, ed. Frederick J. Furnivall (London: EETS, 53, 1888), pp. 236–237; C. G. Cruickshank, *Army Royal: Henry VIII's Invasion of France, 1513* (Oxford: Oxford University Press, 1969).

[5] See above, pp. 157–167, also, Francis Pierrepont Barnard, *Edward IV's French Expedition of 1475: The Leaders and Their Badges* (Dursley: Gloucester Reprints, 1975), pp. 145–146.

icine from Italy, particularly from the school at Padua, and the foundation of the Royal College of Physicians. It has been shown how, from
the thirteenth century, northern Italian physicians had incorporated
ideas of anatomy and surgery into their practices and university curricula.[6] Surgeons attended a university, and taught as members of the faculties. They did not enjoy equal status or pay with physicians. Further,
the spirit of Renaissance Italy was not always friendly; the barbs of Petrarch and other humanists will be remembered from Chapter Two.[7]
But surgeons' ideas and practical successes kept Italian physic dynamic
and open to new ideas. And it has been shown how Italian cities and
towns, often as early as the thirteenth century, employed both physicians and surgeons as municipal doctors.[8] This was the result of recurring plague epidemics, and evolved into a kind of civic medicine that included hospitals, boards of public health, and free medical care for the
indigent.

Englishmen were increasingly conscious of the Italian system. Merchants had begun to venture to Italy in growing numbers by 1450; soon
after went students.[9] They went to Italy primarily to learn more of the
new ideas espoused by the humanists and Platonists of Florence and
Rome, or to take courses in canon and civil law at the Italian universities.[10] But a few went to study medicine, and at least four took M.D.s
by 1500.[11] They were: William Hatclif, who was graduated in March,

[6] Nancy G. Siraisi, *Taddeo Alderotti and His Pupils* (Princeton: Princeton University
Press, 1981), pp. 269–302. See too Katherine Park, *Doctors and Medicine in Early Renaissance
Florence* (Princeton: Princeton University Press, 1985).

[7] See above, p. 58; also, see Elizabeth L. Eisenstein, *The Printing Press as an Agent of
Change* (Cambridge: Cambridge University Press, 1976), pp. 533–541.

[8] Carlo M. Cipolla, *Public Health and the Medical Profession in the Renaissance* (Cambridge:
Cambridge University Press, 1976), pp. 1–66.

[9] See: E. M. Carus-Wilson, *Medieval Merchant Venturers* (London: Methuen, 1954), pp.
1–97; E. M. Carus-Wilson and Olive Coleman, *England's Export Trade, 1275–1547* (Ox-
ford: Oxford University Press, 1963); Rosamund J. Mitchell, *John Free: From Bristol to
Rome in the Fifteenth Century* (London: Longman, Green, 1955); Alwyn Ruddock, *Italian
Merchants and Shipping at Southampton, 1270–1600* (Southampton: Southampton Records
Society, 1951); Alice Beardwood, *Alien Merchants in England, 1300–77* (Cambridge, Mass:
Harvard University Press, 1931); Eileen Power and Michael M. Postan, eds., *Studies in
English Trade in the Fifteenth Century* (London: Routledge and Kegan, 1933).

[10] Rosamund J. Mitchell, "English Students at Padua," *Transactions of the Royal Historical
Society*, 4th series, 1936, pp. 101–117; Charles D. O'Malley, "The Lure of Padua," *MH*,
14, 1970, pp. 1–9.

[11] Mitchell, "English Students at Padua," pp. 101–117.

1447; John Oxney, August, 1469: John Clerk, January, 1477; and Thomas Linacre, August, 1496.[12] Hatclif has been discussed in Chapter Three.[13] A royal physician, he was accomplished enough to take his M.D. after one year.[14] He may have been one of the few physicians to have military experience. Edward IV took him to France with the 1475 expedition as one of his two chief doctors, and it has been claimed that he served during the first battles of the Wars of the Roses.[15] Hatclif was also an author, and some of his recipes for his royal patients survive.[16]

There is less information about John Oxney. He is not listed by Talbot and Hammond, and his matriculation and degree from Padua are all that is known of his life or career.[17] Oxney probably remained and practiced medicine in Italy. There is more on John Clerk.[18] He was born in Leicestershire around 1440, and admitted as king's scholar to Eton in 1454.[19] He followed this by entering King's College, Cambridge, in 1459, and was incepted in Arts and awarded a B.A. in May, 1464. In 1469 he was admitted in Cambridge as an M.B. candidate on payment of twenty pence.[20] But he must have been unhappy or disappointed with the program, or simply longed for greener pastures, for he went abroad soon thereafter. Like Oxney, Clerk left no evidence of a medical practice, or embarked on a different career, if in fact he returned to England.

Linacre was most important in introducing Italian medicine to England and in the foundation of the Royal College.[21] He first went to Italy in 1487, already a fellow of All Soul's, Oxford, on a diplomatic mission

---

[12] *Ibid.* Others may have taken M.B.s, or matriculated without graduating. Alternatively, their records may be lost.

[13] See above, pp. 118–119; *T&H*, pp. 398–399.

[14] *T&H*, pp. 398–399.

[15] R. Theodore Beck, *The Cutting Edge: An Early History of the Surgeons of London* (London: Lund Humphries, 1974), p. 14, argues that surgeons did serve regularly, and picked up medical experience during the Wars of the Roses. I think he overstates his case.

[16] B.M. Harl. Ms. 168, ff. 155–56. Ironically, the recipes are traditional in scope and content. If he compiled them after his stay at Padua, Hatclif was little influenced by the medicine he learned there.

[17] Mitchell, "English Students at Padua," pp. 101–117.

[18] *T&H*, pp. 133–134.

[19] *Ibid.*

[20] *Ibid.*

[21] Francis Maddison, Margaret Pelling, and Charles Webster, eds. *Linacre Studies: Essays on the Life and Work of Thomas Linacre, 1460–1524* (Oxford: Clarendon Press, 1977), is a good collection of studies about his career.

for Henry VII.[22] He met the Bolognese humanist Angelo Poliziano, and may have attended lectures on medicine.[23] It is not clear how long he remained in Italy or whether he returned at some point to England. But he was a student early in 1496 and, like Hatclif, relied on his earlier English training to take his degree in August of that year.[24] He returned to England in 1499, where, unlike the other Englishmen who had taken medical degrees at Padua, he embarked on a long and glorious medical career.

Englishmen studying other subjects in Italy may also have brought back Italian medical ideas. Mitchell has discovered records of sixteen such students studying at Padua during the second half of the fifteenth century.[25] In addition to the four in medicine, one was a doctor of philosophy, seven were doctors of canon law, four were doctors of civil law, one took a degree in both legal fields, and four were doctors of theology. The degrees in law are particularly interesting because of the "middle-class" affinity that was suggested in Chapter Seven between doctors and lawyers. Padua's reputation was in medicine, not law, and its legal curriculum was far less distinguished than that at Bologna.[26] Yet many more Englishmen took degrees there in law than in medicine, a reflection of law's popularity and practicality, its general favor among the bourgoisie, and of the general prestige of the university.

There is some information about Englishmen who matriculated and took just M.B.s, who claimed to have taken M.D.s but for whom university records do not exist, or who simply attended for a while and dropped. Most famous was John Free.[27] Free was born about 1430 in Bristol, and matriculated at Oxford, probably Balliol, around 1445.[28] He took a B.A. in 1449, incepted as an M.A. in 1454, and in 1456 went off to the university in Ferrara, probably to attend the lectures of the

---

[22] *T&H*, pp. 348–389; *DNB*, 11, pp. 1145–1150.

[23] *T&H*, p. 346, from a comment made by Leland, in his *Itinerary*.

[24] Rosamund J. Mitchell, "Thomas Linacre in Italy," *English Historical Review*, 50, 1935, pp. 696–698.

[25] Mitchell, "English Students at Padua," pp. 101–117.

[26] Nancy G. Siraisi, *Arts and Sciences at Padua: The Studium of Padua Before 1350* (Toronto: Pontifical Institute for Mediaeval Studies, 1973), pp. 96–117. For Bologna, see Vern L. Bullough, "Medieval Bologna and the Development of Medical Education," *BHM*, 32, 1958, pp. 201–215.

[27] Mitchell, *John Free*. Also, see *DNB*, 15, p. 1,124, where he is listed as Phreas.

[28] *Ibid.*, pp. 20–43.

humanist Guarino de Verona.[29] In 1458, Free went to Padua, where he studied medicine; there is no record of his taking a degree, though his biographer presents an array of circumstantial evidence to suggest that he did.[30] Free's impact on English medicine was limited. He was interested in Greek, Hebrew, and civil law, and eventually took a position as secretary to John Tiptoft, Earl of Worcester, who was returning to England from the Holy Land via Italy, and wanted to take with him new translations of books.[31] Free eventually went to Rome, took up another secretarial position, and in 1458 was invested as the bishop of Bath and Wells.[32] But he died in Italy before making his way back to England, and never had the opportunity to demonstrate the skills he picked up at Padua.

Other Englishmen who studied at Padua made more of a medical mark. John Argentine too was discussed in Chapter Three.[33] Perhaps Italian by birth, in 1462 he was studying at Padua, where in 1465 he took an M.D. Argentine was in England by the late 1460s, and embarked on successful ecclesiastical and medical careers. John Chamber was, after Thomas Linacre, the most important purveyor of the new medical ideas from Italy.[34] Born about 1470, he took a bachelor's degree at Merton College, around 1491, and a masters in arts about 1495.[35] He was in Padua in 1503, and received his M.D. by 1505, which suggests that he like Hatclif and Linacre may have begun studying medicine in England. Chamber then served at the royal courts of Henry VII and Henry VIII, and was a founding father of the Royal College of Physicians in 1518.[36] He took many honors and royal favors and, as a cleric, preferments, for his service; he had a long and productive career, outliving by a year Henry VIII. By the 1520s he was a senior spokesman for

[29] *Ibid.*, pp. 44–82.

[30] *Ibid.*, pp. 83–120.

[31] *Ibid.*, pp. 98–113.

[32] *Ibid.*, pp. 121–133.

[33] See above, pp. 127–128; *T&H*, pp. 112–115; *DNB*, 1, p. 552. Also, see: Talbot, *Medicine in Medieval England*, pp. 112–13; and D. E. Rhodes, "Provost Argentein of King's and His Books," *Transactions of the Cambridge Bibliographic Society*, ii, 1956, pp. 205–212.

[34] *T&H*, pp. 131–132; *DNB*, 4, pp. 30–31.

[35] *T&H*, pp. 131–132.

[36] *Ibid.* The charter itself has been edited and printed several times. See Rymer, *Foedera*, Hvi, p. 1, 159; and Sir George Clark, *A History of the Royal College of Physicians in London* (Oxford: Clarendon Press, 1964), i, pp. 54–67.

London's physicians, and as an advocate of the methods of the Paduans a powerful force in the dissemination of their ideas.

Padua's curriculum and influential graduates were the most powerful influence for the new medicine. But there were also men and ideas from two other Italian medical schools, Pavia and Bologna. I have no records of Englishmen who studied at Pavia and then returned to England, but there were several aliens who studied at Pavia and then pursued careers in England. One of them was the Jewish physician Elias Sabbato, mentioned in Chapters Two and Three in his capacity as physician to Henry IV.[37] Henry hired him for a year, whereupon Sabbato returned to Italy and became physician to the pope.[38] But he was followed by other Pavians, notably David de Nigarellis.[39] Among those associated with Bologna was Henry Bagot.[40] Born in 1455, Bagot was granted a Master of Arts degree from Cambridge in 1479, then practiced medicine, apparently without a medical degree, in Norwich.[41] He seems to have gone to Bologna in the 1480s, and stayed there through the 1490s; then he returned to England, where he practiced until his death in 1525.[42] Thomas Linacre, as noted, seems to have studied at Bologna. This was part of an old tradition. Late in the thirteenth century Master Hugh, an Englishman, appeared in the Bolognese records.[43] Talbot and Hammond distinguish this Master Hugh from Hugh of Evesham, also of the late thirteenth century and in time a cardinal.[44] He was a student at Bologna, and a papal physician.[45] And two other Englishmen, Nicholas of Farnham and Thomas of Hamsterley, were professors of medicine at Bologna.[46] Indeed, before the Black Death ideas from Bologna had more influence on English medicine than those from Padua.

Important too was the coming of Italians to England. This was part of

[37] See above, p. 94; Rymer, *Foedera*, Hiv, i, p. 184. Also, Talbot, *Medicine in Medieval England*, pp. 204–205; *T&H*, p. 43.

[38] *Ibid*. See too Cecil Roth, *History of the Jews in Italy* (Philadelphia: Jewish Historical Society, 1946), pp. 160, 213–214.

[39] See above, p. 112. Also, Talbot, *Medicine in Medieval England*, p. 205; *T&H*, pp. 33–34.

[40] *T&H*, p. 75.

[41] *Ibid*.

[42] *Ibid*. See too Bagot's will, PCC, i, Porch, f. 29.

[43] *T&H*, pp. 91, 94.

[44] *Ibid*., pp. 92–93.

[45] *Ibid*.

[46] *Ibid*., pp. 223–225, 347.

the larger dissemination of Renaissance culture to northern Europe, beginning in the middle of the fifteenth century.[47] Henry VIII was a major
factor, an important patron who preferred Italian doctors and, much
like Edward III, wanted as cosmopolitan a court as possible. Henry's
first queen, Catherine of Aragon, was responsible for another trend, the
arrival of Spanish and Portuguese physicians.[48] The Iberians were not
as sophisticated as the Italians. But many of them had studied in Italy,
and the physic they practiced incorporated more anatomy and surgery
than that of the Englishmen trained at Oxford and Cambridge. Among
the most influential of the foreigners, Italians and Iberians, were John
Baptist Boerio, Ferdinand de Victoria, and Antony Ciabo.[49] All have
been discussed to some extent in Chapter Three because of their service
as royal doctors; all were influential, both at the royal court and among
London physicians. The Genoese Boerio, for example, was a close
friend of Erasmus, and used his friendship to further his own position.[50]
In effect, the combination of new ideas, dynamic Englishmen like Linacre and Chambers, royal patronage, and the presence in increasing
numbers of the teachers and purveyors of these ideas transfused new life
into moribund English physic.

Concomitantly, the barbers of the London company and the surgeons
of the Fellowship found themselves in increasing difficulty. In 1503, the
masters of the company made a fateful decision. They opened membership and hence the freedom of the barbery to *anyone* who could pay the
entry fees.[51] This was an immediate triumph for the barber-surgeons,
from whom the masters were drawn. Their mystery remained exclusive. But by opening the ranks of the barber-tonsors the company would
be assured a large membership, that, it may be recalled, having been the
key to its rise throughout the fifteenth century. For the barber-tonsors,
it was disastrous; there already were too many doctors at the lower end
of the medical scale, and now there would be many more. By 1510 the

[47] Weiss, *Humanism in England*, deals with this throughout his book. Also, see Margaret
Aston, *The Fifteenth Century: The Prospects of Europe* (New York: Norton, 1968), pp. 175–
208.

[48] See the data in Table 7.4.

[49] *T&H*, pp. 47–48, 49; 117–119. Also, see Beck, *Cutting Edge*, pp. 156, 169.

[50] *T&H*, p. 118.

[51] Jessie Dobson and R. Milnes Walker, *Barbers and Barber-Surgeons of London* (London:
Blackwell, 1979), pp. ix, 19.

barbers were the largest company in London, and probably in England.[52]

Ultimately, open membership was disastrous for all barbers. The
barber-surgeons never gained recognition as first-rank medical practitioners from the physicians, surgeons, or general public. They were
popular with patients because they were cheap. More importantly, all
barber-tonsors, even the newest entrants, were allowed to practice medicine. Before 1503, as the examination of Robert Anson, discussed in
Chapter One, showed, this could be kept under control.[53] But after
1503, with many new and inexperienced barbers practicing, all pretense
of regulation was dropped; the new amateurs were too numerous to police. As a result, the number of malpractice cases began to rise.[54] And,
as happened a century earlier, king, Parliament, and municipal officials
grew concerned with the quality of medical care. In 1511, Parliament
acted, passing "An Act Concerning the Approbation of Physicians and
Surgeons."[55]

The 1511 act was a milestone in governmental legislation of medical
practitioners.[56] It argued:

> Forasmuch as the science and cunning of physic and surgery to perfect
> knowledge whereof, be requisite both great learning and ripe experience is
> daily within this realm exercised by a great multitude of ignorant persons,
> of whom the great part have no manner of insight in the same, nor in any
> kind of learning, some also cannot read letters on the book, so far forth than
> common artificers, as smiths, weavers and women, boldly and customably
> take upon them great cures of things of great difficulty; in which they
> partly use sorcery and witchcraft, partly apply such medicines unto the
> disease as to be very noxious, and . . . great infamy to the faculties, and the
> grievous hurt, damage and destruction of many of the king's liege people;
> most especially of them that cannot discern the uncunning from the cun-
> ning. Be it, therefore, to the surety and comfort of all manner of people, by
> authority of this present Parliament enacted, that no persons within the

[52] *Ibid.*, p. 19.

[53] Guildhall Ms. 5244; Beck, *Cutting Edge*, pp. 149–150; Young, *Annals of the Barber-Surgeons*, pp. 69–70.

[54] See, for example, CCR, 1501, p. 47; CCR, 1503, p. 98; CCR, 1504, p. 131; CCR, 1508, p.
345.

[55] R. R. James, "The Earliest List of Surgeons to be Licensed by the Bishop of London
Under the Act of 3 Henry VIII," *Janus*, 41, 1937, pp. 255–260; Young, *Annals of the Barber
Surgeons*, pp. 72–73.

[56] See F.N.L. Poynter, "The Influence of Government Practice," pp. 5–15.

city of London, nor within seven miles of the same, take upon him to exercise and occupy as a physician or surgeon, except that he first be examined by the bishop of London, the Dean of St. Paul's, for the time being,
calling to him four doctors of physic and for surgery, other expert persons
in the faculty, and for the first examination, such as they think convenient,
and afterward always four of them that have been so approved, upon pain
of forfeiture, for every month that they do occupy as physicians and surgeons, not admitted, nor examined after the tenor of this act. . . .[57]

The next section extended the same procedure to the other dioceses in
England, though it is vague as to how these provincial examination
boards were to be constituted. Many county towns did not have four
university trained physicians. There were other contradictions. The
third section of the act, by not confirming or denying or superseding it,
allowed the universities to continue in their ancient privilege of licensing
their graduates as physicians. This meant that physicians, most of
whom had at least matriculated, were exempted from jurisdiction, leaving the bishops to police surgeons and barbers. The contractions notwithstanding, the act was confirmed by the Crown and became law in
1512.

The act helped the physicians. They were confirmed in their domination of medicine, both by the appointments of the medical boards, in
which they held the central positions, and by the fact that Oxford and
Cambridge were confirmed in their privileges. It did not affect too ad-
versely the surgeons of the Fellowship and their compatriots throughout
the kingdom. They were still the most skilled surgical practitioners, and
there were not many of them; they seem to have had little trouble passing the examinations, and the surgical examiners on the boards were
drawn from their ranks. Moreover, the act favored those with "book
learning." Surgeons were literate; many were authors and a few were
university graduates. If the act were well enforced—and the admission
records of 1514 suggest that it was—it would have been the barber-surgeons and especially the barber-tonsors who were most affected.[58] They
had to prove their proficiency in public rather than before their peers, as
had been the custom. Further, they lost some of their autonomy to the
church, an institution they were in no position to challenge. The Act of

---

[57] Vicary, *Anatomie of the Bodie*, pp. 197–198; Young, *Annals of the Barber Surgeons*, pp.
72–73.

[58] Young, *Annals of the Barber Surgeons*, p. 73, always conscious of the gains of the barbers and deterministic in his approach, argues that the act was not well enforced.

1511, therefore, put an end to seventy-five years of corporate successes. Now the barbers' medical futures lay in the hands of the physicians.

A number of events after 1511 suggest this. In 1513 Parliament exempted the surgeons from certain civic obligations.[59] This exemption, first sought in 1510 and later confirmed in 1514 and 1517, stipulated that the fellows were to be exempted because of their small numbers, but would be reconsidered if membership rose above twelve.[60] In the past, the barber-surgeons, always trying to keep pace with the surgeons, sought similar exemptions as soon as possible. But in 1513 they did not; their numbers were far too large, and the control of the barber-surgeons was beginning to weaken. Indeed, later in the year, over the objections of virtually all the members of the London Company, uplanders and foreigners were admitted to London practice.[61] This was an unforeseen result of the 1503 decision to broaden company membership. And in 1517 women were authorized to practice, despite the proscriptions of 1511.[62] This was good for women, but bad for the barber-surgeon establishment. It meant still more practitioners, and an association that, in the eyes of the male physicians, who had always discriminated against women, would further diminish the medical status of barbers. This loss of prestige was apparent in 1516 when a ranking of the London Companies was drawn up. The barbers were twenty-eighth of forty-seven.[63] And they continued to lose ground, for in 1532 they had fallen to thirty-second.[64]

---

[59] Letter Book N, f. 44b. See too Young, *Annals of the Barber-Surgeons*, pp. 74–75; and Beck, *Cutting Edge*, pp. 128–129.

[60] Letter Book N, 44b. See too the City of London Journal, ii, ff. 295b–296b.

[61] *Ibid.*

[62] Letter Book L, pp. xxx–xxxii; Young, *Annals of the Barber-Surgeons*, p. 260; Dobson and Walker, *Barbers and Barber Surgeons*, p. 24. Women had, of course, practiced barbering before this date. In 1485 the London citizen and barber Alexander Sly required his apprentice to finish his apprenticeship with his wife. And four years later Thomas Parkin did the same. See London Com. Court Wills Litchfield, ff. 11–12v; and 139.

[63] L–B N, f. 6b; London Rep Book 3, 1514–18, Corporation of London Record Office, f. 66b. Young, *Annals of the Barber Surgeons*, pp. 239–242, makes much of their "historic" claim to be seventeenth.

[64] Young. *Annals of the Barber Surgeons*, p. 240. This is not to say that the barbers did not play an important role in the medical and corporate life of sixteenth-century London. In 1533 another ranking of companies placed them eighteenth, so sudden a rise in one year's time that it casts doubt on the efficacy of the ranking system. Further, the sheer size of the company made it hard to ignore. But it is worth reiterating that the barbers' inferiority to

The surgeons too had problems.[65] It will be recalled that the Licensing Act of 1511 passed by Parliament gave the power of sanctioning surgery to local bishops and, in London, the dean of St. Paul's.[66] Oxford and Cambridge graduates were exempted from the jurisdiction. Hence while none of the graduates were trained to practice surgery and few probably had the inclination, they could have done so had they wished. The act was passed because of the alleged malpractice of surgery by non-professionals—"smiths, weavers and women, who . . . use sorcery, etc."[67] The Oxbridge physicians could not have been much more effective than these malpractitioners. Yet they suffered no restrictions, while trained surgeons—and barber-surgeons—were forced to undergo a test and take medical advice from clergymen who in most cases had absolutely no medical experience.

The surgeons had other troubles. One was the omnipresent problem of numbers. Of the seventy-two practitioners who took the licensing exam in 1514, just four were members of the Fellowship.[68] Thus in 1513–1514, the Fellows were again exempted from the night watch: there were just too few of them, twelve, to serve effectively.[69] And while such service was generally considered unimportant and banal and their exemption something of a coup, the Fellows' small numbers also meant that they were restricted in other, more important and prestigious, civic activities, the kind that confirmed and established municipal power and prestige.[70]

To make matters worse, the ranks of the surgeons continued to diminish. By 1514 there were just eleven Fellows, one having died and not been replaced.[71] The eleven are listed in Table 8.1. One of the wardens,

the physicians was heavily underscored. The right to license was no longer an internal affair, as it had been for most of the post-plague period.

[65] See George Unwin, *The Gilds and Companies of London*, 4th ed. (London: Frank Cass, 1966), pp. 71–82, 127–175.

[66] R. R. James, "The Earliest List of Surgeons," pp. 255–261.

[67] It has been reprinted many times. See Young, *Annals of the Barber-Surgeons*, pp. 72–74. The quote is on p. 72.

[68] James, "Earliest List of Surgeons," pp. 255–261.

[69] Young, *Annals of the Barber-Surgeons*, pp. 74–75; Vicary, *Anatomie of the Bodie*, p. 212; The Corporation of London Record Office, L–B N, f. 44b.

[70] Note should be made of the cautions of Charles Phythian-Adams, *Desolation of a City: Coventry and the Urban Crisis of the Late Middle Ages* (Cambridge: Cambridge University Press, 1979), especially pp. 189–278. He explains how expensive, even ruinous, public service in Coventry could be.

[71] Corporation of London Record Office, L–B N, f. 44b; Vicary, *Anatomie of the Bodie*, p. 212.

Thomas Thornton, first took office in 1488.[72] Thornton was a warden as late as 1517, and perhaps up to his death in 1525. This was a long stretch, and if he had begun at about age thirty he would have been close to seventy by his death. And his advanced age and considerable wealth notwithstanding, there is no evidence of noteworthy medical skills that earlier fellowship luminaries had.[73] There is no record of military service, of medical writing or commentary, a call to royal service, or even general statements attesting to his skills. There was, in short, nothing to distinguish Thornton from any other surgical practitioner, be he surgeon, barber-surgeon, or even barber-tonsor.

Nor were the other Fellows distinguished. The second warden was Thomas Roos.[74] Roos was a crucial figure in the changing perceptions of the members of the Fellowship, but in a negative way. In 1519 he was involved in a lawsuit with an Italian surgeon, to be discussed shortly, which showed just how far surgery had fallen. Roos was no more noteworthy than Thornton. Other than service as warden in the 1510s and 1520s, and the exemption of 1513, the only glimpse of professional achievement was his possible role as the translator of an edition of Henri de Mondeville's *Chirurgie*, of which he was the owner.[75] Roos was a reactionary, resistant to change and new ideas, claiming they were "for-

TABLE 8.1: Members of the Fellowship of Surgeons, 1514

| Surgeon | Other evidence |
| --- | --- |
| Thomas Thornton, warden | [*T&H*] |
| Thomas Roos, warden | [*T&H*] |
| Robert Beverley | [*T&H*] |
| Christopher Turner | [*T&H*] |
| Robert Hotchkins | [*T&H*] |
| Robert Marshall | [*T&H*] |
| | surgeon 1514 *Mary James* |
| John Rutter | [*T&H*] |
| Garet Ferris | [*T&H*] |
| | surgeon 1514 *Trinity Sovereign* |
| Thomas Monford | [*T&H*] |
| Thomas Palley | [*T&H*] |
| Edward Holloway | [*T&H*] |

[72] *T&H*, pp. 357–358.
[73] *Hustings Wills*, ii, p. 637.
[74] *T&H*, pp. 354–355.
[75] The manuscript is C.U.L. Peterhouse Ms, 118.

saking the truth," and were "against the right"—comments made against medicine from Italy, though there is no evidence that he ever read, let alone understood, it.

The others too left few records of professional activities and had unspectacular careers. Notice of exemption from civic duty is the only surviving reference for Robert Beverley, Christopher Turner, Richard Hotchkins, John Rutter, Thomas Monford, Thomas Palley, and Edward Holloway.[76] Robert Marshall and Garet Ferris did serve as naval surgeons on Henry VIII's 1513–1514 campaign, Marshall on the "Mary James," and Ferris on the "Trinity Sovereign."[77] But the rest of the practitioners selected by Henry—barring the omnipresent possibility of lost records—were taken from the barber-surgeons' mystery of the London Barbers' Company.[78] This would have been unthinkable in the fifteenth century. Not of course that Marshal, Ferris, or any of the barber-surgeons came away with combat experience. The efforts of the surgeons of the Fellowship between 1493 and 1518, such as they were, were directed at acquiring administrative privilege rather than the skills of the craft.

The best demonstration of this comes from the aforementioned legal suit between Thomas Roos and the Italian surgeon Balthazar Guercio.[79] Guercio was in service to Catherine of Aragon, and enjoyed a substantial practice on the side.[80] He complained first to Catherine and then to Henry VIII that the surgeons of the Fellowship, particularly Roos, were harassing him. Roos was bound over in £100 "not to molest Balthazar . . . or pursue information late put into the King's Exchequer, till he proves surgery is a handicraft."[81] Guercio was an advocate of the new anatomy and physiology that he learned in Italy, and it was to this that Roos objected, apparently under the assumption that these techniques, which he did not know, were the domain of physicians and would compromise the positions of denizen surgeons. Roos argued that Guericio's techniques would spread across England. The surgeons of the Fellow-

---

[76] For the individuals, see *T&H*, pp. 292, 29, 279, 178, 350, 353, and 41. They were also exempted—eight of them—in 1525. See Vicary, *Anatomie of the Bodie*, pp. 212–213.

[77] *LPFD*, 1, #2757, pp. 1128–1129.

[78] See above, pp. 157–167, for a discussion and a full list of the surgeons.

[79] *LPFD*, iii, Appendix 5, p. 1562. Also, see Beck, *Cutting Edge*, pp. 170, 180.

[80] For Catherine's patronage of medicine, see McLain, *Humanism and the Rise of Science*, p. 44.

[81] *LPFD.*, iii, Appendix 5, p. 1562.

ship rested their superiority over the barbers on their more advanced, sophisticated, and effective skills. Should the barbers, already drawn even with the members of the Fellowship in non-medical things—or perhaps it would be more accurate to say the surgeons had slipped back—master the Italian techniques, they might, with their superior numbers and organization, supersede the surgeons entirely. Roos saw Guercio's practice as a fundamental challenge to his social and medical position.

Roos was reactionary, but he was neither stupid nor ill-educated. In his defense he showed smatterings of a classical education that might have distinguished a university-trained physician. He drew on the ideas of Hippocrates, Galen, Isidore of Seville, Avicenna, Theodore of Lucca, Gilbertus Anglicus, Guy de Chauliac, Almansar, and, above all, Lanfranc of Milan. Roos based the rise of the London Fellowship on these authorities, and drew on Lanfranc's famous justification of surgery as a Greek creation.[82] Surgeons, he claimed, were "well made, temperate, handsome, had good manners, steady hands, were learned and honest." They put a premium on being ingenious and clever, and were well versed in natural philosophy, grammar, logic, rhetoric, and especially anatomy—herein, that of Galen. These claims were not new. Similar ideas had been expressed by earlier surgeons, including John Arderne.[83] But Arderne was not a slave to Galenic anatomy and physiology; indeed, he could not have been and remained effective. Nor was any surgeon with much clinical experience. Yet clinical experience was something Roos lacked.

Following Lanfranc, Roos defined surgery, or *chirurgia*, as *mannu operatio*, coming from the Greek *chir*, for hand, and *gios*, which he translated as operate.[84] Surgery, he continued, lay principally in the manual application of medicines, as in:

> staunching of blood, searching wounds with irons and other instruments, in cutting of the skull in due proportion to the pellicles of the brain with instruments of iron, counching of cataracts, sewing up flesh, lancing of boils, cutting of apostemes, burning out of chancres and other like, settling in of joints and binding them together with ligatures, letting of blood,

[82] Lanfranc of Milan, *Science of Cirurgie*, ed. Robert von Fleishhacken (London: EETS, cii, 1894), p. 7. Also, see Vicary, *Anatomie of the Bodie*, i, pp. 12–17.

[83] John Arderne, *Treatise of Fistula in Ano*, ed. D'Arcy Power (London: EETS, 139, 1910), pp. 42–52, for example.

[84] *LPFD*, iii, Appendix 5, p. 1562.

drawing of teeth, with other such like, which rests only in manual operation, principally with the hands of the workmen.[85]

Building further on his analogy and continuing to draw on classical
sources, Roos compared surgery and physic with carpentry and geom-
etry.[86]

Roos argued that surgery was a handicraft and surgeons fancy craftsmen. After a century and a half of trying to claim parity and alliance
with the physicians, then, a warden of the London Fellowship was arguing precisely the opposite, that the two branches of medicine were indeed distinct. Roos claimed that the Italian surgeon Guercio was really
a physician, and should practice as such. Ironically, it was Guercio and
the Italians who were arguing for the things that Thomas Morstede and
the other fifteenth-century leaders of the Fellowship had fought so hard
to attain—a union between physic and surgery. Roos wanted none of
this. He was, consciously or not, lumping the surgeons with the barbers, who claimed for themselves the sorts of skills and operations that
Roos said the surgeons should practice.[87]

What differences were there among the practitioners? The physician,
Roos argued, was concerned with the theoretical, with the application
of humoral theory to various environmental constraints. This kind of
physic was complicated, and took years of study to master: ". . . and
where the naturals do leave or put out, forsake, or be hurt accidentally,
there begin the leechcraft of medicine."[88] Roos went further. He cited
Avicenna and Gilbertus Anglicus, neither of whom enthused about surgery:

> These authors be authorized by our Mother, Holy Church [an odd allusion
> to make concerning the Muslim Avicenna], in whom as yet I have more
> belief, for their truth and their long countenance, and in the old and an-
> cient probable customs aforesaid, than in any new authors, as aliens and
> strangers, denying the authors aforesaid, and forsaking the truth and the
> doctors of their own faculty, intending in this realm of England custom-
> arily to be continued and dwell without license, law or contradiction
> against right and the due order of justice.[89]

[85] *Ibid.*
[86] *Ibid.*
[87] *Ibid.*
[88] *Ibid.*
[89] *Ibid.*

Ultimately, Roos's arguments proved unconvincing. Guercio won the suit and Roos had to post security against harassing him. This remarkable case shows well the conservatism of surgeons in the sixteenth century. And it reflects one thing above others—the desire of the surgeons to maintain their lock on the upper reaches of surgery against the encroachments of the barber-surgeons. Henceforth, new ideas about surgery would not come from the London Fellowship—or the barber-surgeons of the mystery. Rather, they would spring from those physicians steeped in the Italian methods, who had studied anatomy and physiology and had urged at least some clinical experience for physicians, and suggested the incorporation of surgery into physic.

This was the situation at the foundation of the Royal College of Physicians in 1518.[90] Physicians had won the battle of medical practitioners, and would dominate the other practices for the next two hundred years. But how enlightened was the new physic? The question can best be answered by looking at the college's foundation and principal founder, Thomas Linacre.[91] Linacre's studies in Italy had made him of the same mind as Balthazar de Guercio. He was witness to the municipal health system and public doctors that most large and middling sized towns had.[92] He saw too their systems of sanitation and quarantine. He had read the latest editions of Hippocrates and Galen, and knew of the anatomy and physiology of the surgeons of Padua. Indeed, Linacre himself had published six translations of works by Galen.[93] When he returned to England, he gave lectures in London on a range of classical and medical subjects, and in 1509 became the personal physician to Henry VIII.[94] He may have been influential in the passage of the 1511 Licensing Act, and certainly urged the founding of the Royal College of Phy-

[90] The major work for the college's early years is Clark, *History of the Royal College*, i, pp. 1–79.

[91] Clark, Webster and others have studied both; I will summarize, and try to put them in the context, not as the beginning of what Clark sees as the steady development of English medicine, but as the conclusion of the medieval medical era. See too Charles Webster, "Thomas Linacre and the Foundation of the College of Physicians," in Maddison, Pelling and Webster, eds., *Linacre Studies*, pp. 198–222.

[92] Cipolla, *Public Health and the Medical Profession*, pp. 1–66. See too Susan M. Stuard, "A Communal Program of Medical Care: Medical Ragusa/Dubrovnik," *JHM*, 28, 1973, pp. 126–142.

[93] Richard Durling, "Linacre and Medical Humanism," in Maddison, *Linacre Studies*, pp. 76–106; Talbot, *Medicine in Medieval England*, pp. 210–211.

[94] *T&H*, pp. 348–350.

sicians. Other elements were important in the foundation. Cardinal Wolsey, always important, supported it.[95] A severe epidemic struck London in 1517, bringing cries for better medical care.[96] And there were continuing complaints of malpractice, especially against surgical practitioners.[97] But Linacre was probably the moving force.

It has been suggested that the Royal College should be seen less as a vanguard of modernism than as a continuation of medieval corporatism.[98] Physicians had no guild, and while the universities provided some corporate identity, the Royal College would be far more effective. It was situated in London, the center of English medical practice, and close to the royal court. As a strictly medical corporation it was better than the universities in helping attain and preserve wealth, privilege, and dignity. Some physicians also believed that the college would guarantee the standards of medical practice. Indeed, by fixing the status of physicians, the college may well have helped destroy that seed of innovation planted by the new medicine from Italy. The college, in essence, assured that there would be little change in the quality of physic, for it ensured that physicians would have no rivals as doctors, little inspiration, and no basis for making changes in their techniques, especially as the threat of plague began to diminish.[99] For all Linacre's greatness and importance to medicine, his signal achievement, the foundation of the college, was less an accomplishment than has sometimes been claimed.[100]

It is also possible to overstate the importance of Linacre's translations of Galen.[101] They were more accurate than earlier versions. But in themselves they were neither revolutionary nor innovative enough to stir up a fresh medical mix. Perhaps most important of all, the foundation did not affect the status of the medical curriculum at Oxford and Cambridge. The university medical faculties continued to train students

[95] Webster, "Thomas Linacre," pp. 206–207.

[96] *Ibid.*

[97] Slack, "Mortality Crises and Epidemic Disease," pp. 13–21.

[98] Webster, "Thomas Linacre," pp. 198–222.

[99] Robert S. Gottfried, "Population, Plague and the Sweating Sickness: Demographic Movements in Late Medieval England," *The Journal of British Studies*, Fall, 1977, pp. 12–37.

[100] Clark, *College of Physicians*, pp. 55–67.

[101] Durling, "Linacre and Medical Humanism," pp. 76–106. It is ironic that Talbot, *Medicine in Medieval England*, p. 210, having trumpeted physic throughout his text, would deride Linacre's translations as "encouraging the very stagnation he purposed to remove."

in the old theoretical fashion, teaching them to treat patients with the same reserve and distance that English physicians had always employed. Italian physic had little real effect, at least for the first thirty years of the college's existence. And physicians, now protected by the Royal College, various acts of Parliament that restricted other practitioners, and still possessed of the traditional privileges of university graduates, could resist or ignore the new concepts if they wished.

The charter of the Royal College was drawn up in Latin, and had several corollaries.[102] It began with Henry VIII's reasons for the foundation: to eliminate quacks, fools, and malpractitioners, and ensure the health and well-being of his subjects. The charter claimed that control of medical practice was tighter and hence more effective on the continent, and that this benefited patients and the common weal. Here surely was the hand of Linacre, with, ironically, the king of England imitating the bourgeoisie of Italy. And to add to the college's prestige six prominent doctors were cited as co-founders. They were John Chamber, Thomas Linacre, Ferdinand de Victoria, Nicholas Halswell, John Francis, and Robert Yaxley.[103]

Chamber, Linacre, and Victoria have been discussed; and something is known of the others. Nicholas Halswell was admitted as a fellow of All Soul's Oxford, in 1468.[104] He was an M.D. by the 1480s, and had a successful ecclesiastical as well as medical career. His will, proved in 1528 in the Prerogative Court of Canterbury, provides glimpses of his professional life.[105] He left two medical books, *Liber aggregationum* and Rhases's *Liber dictis Elhavi*, to All Soul's.[106] Little is known of John Francis before he appeared on the charter.[107] This gives credence to Talbot and Hammond's claim that he was Italian, and was educated in Italy.[108] Francis eventually became physician to Wolsey, and like Balthazar Guercio was a long-time correspondent with Erasmus.[109] Yaxley took an M.B. from Cambridge in 1487, and an M.D. in 1498.[110] He was a phy-

[102] *LPFD*, ii, #4450, p. 1367.

[103] A seventh signature was that of Cardinal Wolsey. Wolsey probably played as great a role in the foundation as Henry VIII, and perhaps even Linacre.

[104] *T&H*, p. 226.

[105] PCC, 36 Porch.

[106] All Soul's Oxford, S.R. 49, ff. 5–6.

[107] *T&H*, pp. 145–146.

[108] *Ibid.*, p. 145.

[109] *Ibid.*, p. 146.

[110] *Ibid.*, p. 306.

sician to the royal family, a resident of London, and a successful practitioner until his death in 1540.[111] Like Francis, his will was proved in
the archbishop of Canterbury's court, an indication of considerable
wealth.[112] The six were, in all, the ideal mix of Englishmen and aliens,
royal and private physicians, Londoners and university men. They
were among the most successful doctors of their day, and their support
was important in the initial stages of the foundation.

The charter claimed that the Royal College's goal was to create a perpetual college of learned men, with controls over medicine similar to
those granted to the bishops by the Parliamentary acts of 1511.[113] Ironically, the 1511 act was never rescinded, nor was the original control that
had been vested in the university medical faculties. No one, however,
seemed to regard this as contradictory, supporting further the idea that
the college was perceived as just another medical corporation, this one
designed to prop up the physicians. A president was appointed for a
term of one year, and empowered to supervise medical practice, first in
London and later throughout the entire kingdom.[114] The college was
provided with a small endowment yielding an income of £12 per year.
This lack of funding proved to be a serious limitation, and was rather
surprising, given the largesse of the young Henry VIII.[115] But it was expected that the endowment would be supplemented with dues from its
members. Further, the college could sue and be sued, characteristics of
sixteenth-century corporations, and had control over the practice of aliens, characteristics of late medieval corporations.

Clark argued that the college was more than an elaborate medieval
guild.[116] He wrote that it was linked to two other colleges, that of arms,
the College of Heralds, and that of law, the Association of Doctors and
Law Advocates, founded in 1511, and probably best known to and an
inspiration for Linacre.[117] He believed that the College of Physicians
was a professional organization, and herein I agree.[118] But to some degree Clark's argument is moot. The Royal College's format and purpose

[111] *Ibid.*
[112] PCC, F, 18 Alenger.
[113] *LPFD*, ii, #4450, p. 1367.
[114] *Ibid.*
[115] *Ibid.*
[116] Clark, *History of the Royal College*, i, pp. 54–87.
[117] *Ibid.*
[118] *Ibid.*

were not teaching and instruction. These were left to the universities, something Linacre clearly recognized. In 1521 he began talking of establishing lectureships in medicine at Oxford and Cambridge.[119] These were to be supplemental to lectures already given, that is, devoted to the medicine from Italy. In 1523 he was provided with royal license to endow three lectureships, two at Merton College, Oxford, and one at St. John's, Cambridge.[120] This was finally accomplished in October 1524, just before he died.

It is likely, too, that the college was provided with a paltry endowment so that physicians would continue to be self-supporting.[121] Here again Linacre seems to have distinguished between the corporation designed to protect physicians and the one designed to educate them. In his will he left the college his house on Knightrider Street as a meeting place, and some of his books to serve as the kernel of a library.[122] But he gave the bulk of his library to Merton College, suggesting again that the principal goal of the Royal College was not the introduction and sponsorship of the new medicine, or even the growth and development of traditional physic: it was the protection of physic and physicians. In essence, the Royal College represented the interests of university-trained physicians practicing in London.

Perhaps this explains why the Royal College of Physicians was not an immediate success. Between 1519 and 1522 just six new members were added to the original six.[123] Then it began to grow. Thirty-one more members were added from 1522 to 1553, and demand grew so great that membership was restricted to just three new members a year.[124] One reason for this rapid expansion was continuing royal support; another was the gradual acceptance that comes with being around for a while. A third was the revision of the original charter. In 1523 the rather lax rules of 1518 were tightened. Entry and membership fees were established, with each member paying quarterly dues of twenty pence.[125] This mod-

---

[119] John M. Fletcher, "Linacre's Lands and Lectureships," in Maddison, *Linacre Studies*, pp. 107–197. The will was proved in the PCC, Bodfelde, f. 36.

[120] Rymer, *Foedera*, Hvi,ii,12.

[121] R. G. Lewis, "The Linacre Lectureships Subsequent to Their Foundation," in Maddison, *Linacre Studies*, pp. 223–264.

[122] PCC, Bodfelde, f. 36.

[123] Clark, *History of the Royal College*, pp. 68–88.

[124] *Ibid.*

[125] *Ibid.*

est sum was not enough to discourage perspective members, but was sufficient to provide a working budget, albeit a small one. And the directors of the college made the wise choice of using their funds to prosecute practitioners who operated without the strictures of the corporation. This was precisely what the members wanted, and was an incentive for non-members to seek admission. By 1529 an entry fee of six shillings, eight pence, was instituted.[126] Attendance at college meetings was made mandatory, and other rules were added.[127]

Other developments made the college attractive. When the foundation was granted in 1518, Parliament was not in session, and certain rights could not be confirmed. But in 1523, the college wardens petitioned a sitting Parliament to redress this omission.[128] Parliament confirmed the 1518 charter and granted new privileges. The members' jurisdiction was extended from greater London throughout the realm.[129] The bishops' authority over surgical practitioners, vested from 1511, and the universities' rights to grant degrees remained intact. But no one was allowed to practice physic unless they had first been examined by the physicians of the college.[130] Whether college authorities could actually enforce their authority in the countryside was another question. Yet this power, combined with that of the Quack Act of 1542, the Reformation, which curtailed ecclesiastical authority over doctors, and the continuing lack of interest in physic in the universities, especially concerning practice, made the college the centerpiece of English medicine.[131] When in 1540 Parliament merged the surgeons and barbers into a single company, even the remote possibility of a rival group of practitioners was ended. Hence, the physicians gained their stranglehold over medical practice without making any substantial innovations or improvements.

As external events were delineating their futures, the surgeons' and barbers' organizations in London were concentrating on protecting their corporate privileges. The only record of the Fellowship from 1518 to 1540 was the 1524–1525 watch exemptions; by that time, their numbers had dwindled to eight.[132] Thornton, Hotchkins, Marshall, Beverley, and

---

[126] *Ibid.*

[127] *Ibid.*

[128] *Ibid.*

[129] *Ibid.*

[130] *Ibid.*

[131] *Ibid.*

[132] Vicary, *Anatomie of the Bodie*, i, pp. 212–213.

Turner were dead, and just two new surgeons, Edward Clache and Christopher Dixon, had been selected to replace them.[133] There is more evidence, however, from the Barbers' Company, and it shows the wardens' inability to protect its members from the physicians. In 1520, the barber-surgeons' mystery asked for an exemption from the watch; they were turned down.[134] Yet in 1525, the year in which members of the Royal College got authority to put unlicensed practitioners of physic in prison, the barbers were commanded to serve on commissions of inquest.[135] By contrast, when in 1538 the physicians were asked to serve on the London constabulary and watch, they bought exemptions.[136] Whether the physicians gained exemption because they were rich or because such onerous duties were despised or both is immaterial. They could do it, and the barbers could not. This is also evident from the ranking of the Barbers' Company among the other companies of the city. As noted, in 1525, 1533, and 1535, they stood at best in the middle, and more commonly toward the bottom of the lists.[137] Even the barbers' triumphs were modest. When in 1525 they finally won a partial exemption from the night watch, it was a watered-down version of that granted to the surgeons.[138]

The ranks of the barbers remained full. From 1522 to 1540, the number of freemen entering the "worshipful company of barber-surgeons" was extraordinarily high.[139] The data, presented in Table 8.2, show the ease in becoming a barber-surgeon—and one must remember that the barber-surgeons were the elite of the Barbers' Company.[140] The mean figure for admission was almost eleven a year—more than the entire membership of the Fellowship of Surgeons and in sharp contrast to the

[133] *Ibid.* Dixon could be a surgeon exempted in 1517. See *T&H*, p. 28.

[134] Vicary, *Anatomie of the Bodie*, p. 215.

[135] *Ibid.*, p. 214. Young, *Annals of the Barber-Surgeons*, p. 76, reprints most of this.

[136] Vicary, *Anatomie of the Bodie*, p. 215.

[137] Young, *Annals of the Barber-Surgeons*, pp. 239–241; Corporation of London Records Office, London Rep Book 3, 1514–1518, f. 66b.

[138] Vicary, *Anatomie of the Bodie*, pp. 213-14; Young, *Annals of the Barber-Surgeons*, pp. 76–77; Dobson and Walker, *Barbers and Barber Surgeons*, pp. 7–8.

[139] London Guildhall Ms. 5265, "Register of Admissions to the Freedom of the Worshipful Company of Barber-Surgeons of London, 1522–1664."

[140] But the distinction between the mystery of barber-surgeons and the company of barbers in sixteenth-century London (though not the distinction between the practitioners called barber-surgeons and those called barber-tonsors) is often difficult to discern. This is not the case in the fifteenth century, when the distinction between the mystery and the company was always clear.

TABLE 8.2: Admission to the Freedom of the Barber-Surgeons' Company

| Year | Number | Year | Number |
|------|--------|------|--------|
| 1522 | 4  | 1537 | 6  |
| 1523 | 17 | 1538 | 17 |
| 1524 | 20 | 1539 | 9  |
| 1525 | 9  | 1540 | 10 |
| 1526 | 8  | 1541 | 17 |
| 1527 | 6  | 1542 | 6  |
| 1528 | 14 | 1543 | 12 |
| 1529 | 8  | 1544 | 11 |
| 1530 | 11 | 1545 | 16 |
| 1531 | 2  | 1546 | 22 |
| 1532 | 2  | 1547 | 17 |
| 1533 | 5  | 1548 | 11 |
| 1534 | 10 | 1549 | 7  |
| 1535 | 11 | 1550 | 13 |
| 1536 | 16 |      |    |

restrictive policies of the Royal College, even after its membership began to expand in 1523. This was not necessarily bad. In the fourteenth and fifteenth centuries the barbers of London had built up their corporate power on the basis of numbers rather than skills. But in the sixteenth century membership seems to have become indiscriminate; the standards of professionalism, if they were ever applied, had been abandoned.

There is more evidence of the size of the Barbers' Company. Power has shown that in the middle of the sixteenth century the number of apprentices presented annually was a staggering 150![141] Some, perhaps most, never became medical practitioners. But if in the 1550s and 1560s apprenticeships ran for the traditional seven-year period, the admissions figure meant there were over a thousand barber apprentices in London at any time. As physicians became more elite, barbers, now the principal surgical practitioners, became more common. The range of medical care must have been broader than ever, though of questionable quality. And, indeed, this is borne out by a 1537 count of freemen in all the London companies.[142] There were 185 barber-surgeons—though the rec-

[141] Sir D'Arcy Power, "The Education of a Surgeon Under Thomas Vicary," in his *Selected Essays 1877–1930* (New York: Augustus Kelley, 1970), pp. 71–75.
[142] Vicary, *Anatomie of the Bodie*, i, pp. 243–246.

ords are vague as to whether these were actually barber-surgeons or all barbers—making them the most numerous among all the companies.[143] Yet as evidence of the difference between numbers and status, the barbers ranked twenty-second in prestige. The mercers company, with fifty-five members, was first, and the drapers, with seventy-seven, were second.[144]

In 1530, under the sponsorship of Sir Thomas More, Parliament passed an ordinance that further affected surgery.[145] It was a general act, aimed at all companies in London, claiming that they could not make any more by-laws, no matter how particular and specialized, without first getting the approval of the king's agents. This further divided the surgical practitioners from those in physic, since the physicians were unaffected. And it was directed to the masters and wardens of the mystery of the craft of barber-surgeons, presumably the whole company and not just the elite mystery.[146] All freemen were to take an oath of al-

[143] The next most numerous companies were the skinners with 151 members, and the haberdashers, with 120. See Vicary, *Anatomie of the Bodie*, i, pp. 244–245. It is worth noting that Talbot, *Medicine in Medieval England*, p. 124, and Stephan R. Ell, "Barbers, Barber-Surgeons," *Dictionary of the Middle Ages*, ii, ed. Joseph R. Strayer (New York: Charles Scribner's Son, 1983), pp. 97–101, regard membership in the guild as open to other craftsmen. There is no clear evidence that this was the case.

[144] Vicary, *Anatomie of the Bodie*, i, pp. 245–246. The goldsmiths, with fifty-two, were fifth, and the grocers, with fifty nine, were sixth. There were a few medical triumphs. In 1528, the barber-surgeons mystery agreed to: ". . . provide and ordain a place and house convenient for the relief and comfort of the sick and sore people that have great sicknesses and diseases, they the said master, warden and fellowship [sic] . . . their assistants shall freely at their own expense, cost and charge minister unto them all such salves and plasters and other things belonging to the science and craft of surgery."

Here was a mix of the best and the worst. The city of London would provide a house to serve as a clinic, while the barber-surgeons would provide, gratis, the doctors to staff it. On one hand, the barber-surgeons surrendered some authority to the municipal powers of London. But, on the other, they must have engendered a considerable amount of good will unto themselves. They were providing an important public service—one that came one hundred and fifty years after comparable municipal services in Italy, but one which was forthcoming nevertheless. And they managed to get a leg up on the surgeons of the Fellowship, who, in any case, were not numerous enough to provide the staff for what potentially was a very busy clinic indeed. This incident is transcribed and discussed in Thomas Forbes, "The Barber-Surgeons Help the Sick Poor," *JHM*, 31, 1976, pp. 461–462.

[145] The 1530 Act of Parliament, called "Sir Thomas More's Ordinances," has been reprinted in full in Young, *Annals of the Barber-Surgeons*, pp. 579–586; and excerpted in Beck, *Cutting Edge*, pp. 156–157; and Vicary, *Anatomie of the Bodie*, i, pp. 249–260.

[146] Young, *Annals of the Barber-Surgeons*, p. 579.

legiance and obedience to the king, the London government, and the guild masters; this no doubt was one reason the wardens of the company were so anxious to see it approved. For the masters, of course, had obligations, pledging themselves to look after their members, and accepting accountability for their actions. The act made them responsible for surgery and barbery—as distinct from general medical standards. They were given power to punish violators and regulate aliens, apprentices, journeymen, and uplanders. Entry fees and dues were set, and the structure of organization renewed.

None of these regulations were new; in most cases they simply reiterated the original charter of 1376.[147] Generally, they followed the regulations passed down by Parliament to all the other companies. But there are some particular points of interest. One is the length of discussion about entry fees.[148] Such fees were a standard and accepted part of municipal life. Yet the barbers seemed to think that they were a more important qualification for membership than any tests of medical or even tonsorial skills, which were quickly passed over. By the middle of the sixteenth century the company wardens were more interested in numbers than quality. No member could take a patient from another. This too was an old rule, and part and parcel of corporate, guild practice. But it had bad medical connotations. There was worse. The rules stated that no man: "being free of the said fellowship shall take any sick or hurt persons to his cure which is in peril of death or maim . . . unless he shows the patient to the master or governors of the mystery . . . for . . . the safeguard of the king's liege people."[149] Here was an indictment of the medical abilities of the barbers, and it might well have been a demand of the physicians. In any case, it could only benefit the physicians. And without a strong fellowship of surgeons, it meant that physicians had a monopoly on all serious medical practices.

Barbers had by no means given up on medical practice. Some of regulations actually improved, at least in theory, on the nature of medicine. For example: "Every man enfranchised in the said Fellowship occupying surgery shall come to their hall to the reading of the lecture concerning surgery every day of assembly thereof and every man after his course shall read the lecture himself. . . ."[150] Further, it stated that surgeons,

[147] L–B H, p. 28.

[148] Young, *Annals of the Barber-Surgeons*, pp. 581–583.

[149] *Ibid.*, p. 584.

[150] *Ibid.*

presumably the members of the Fellowship, should attend as well. Young believed this to be a major advance in the barbers' medical practice.[151] In fact, the lectures were offered just twice a year. There is no evidence as to how many barbers actually attended, and, given their large numbers, few could have participated directly.[152] Indeed there were so many barbers that most of them may never even have practiced surgery, but restricted their medical activity to the most mundane sorts of treatment with salves and balms. And even if surgery had become the barbers' domain, barbery more clearly than ever was a craft. All surgical practitioners, even members of the Fellowship, who were acknowledged to be of a higher order, were labelled as craftsmen.[153]

The surgeons of the Fellowship were able to maintain some advantage over the barber-surgeons. The 1530 regulations, while restricting them to craft status, did acknowledge their superiority.[154] This was apparent in 1539, when the city's companies were arrayed for a muster.[155] The Fellows were given a prominent role, while the barbers, "a poor company, could not or would not go to the cost of the gay white sarcenet costs which other citizen soldiers bought for this grand march. . . ."[156] But "followed all the surgeons of the city, without harness, in white coats [trimmed with] black velvet. . . ."[157] What the account fails to mention is that by 1539 "all the surgeons" counted just eight Fellows.

This was prelude to the disasters of 1540. First, Henry VIII confirmed that physicians could practice surgery.[158] He claimed this would be beneficial to the sick and provide, ultimately, more surgeons, though

[151] Ibid., pp. 77–78.

[152] Dobson and Walker, Barbers and Barber-Surgeons, pp. 36–47, concentrating on the period from 1550 onwards.

[153] Vicary, Anatomie of the Bodie, p. 255.

[154] Ibid., 249–261.

[155] Ibid., p. 215.

[156] Ibid., pp. 172–174.

[157] Ibid., p. 173.

[158] Ibid., p. 202. The justification was as follows: "And for as much as the science of physic does comprehend, include and contain, the knowledge of surgery as a special member and part of the same, therefore, be it enacted, that any of the said company or fellowship of Physicians, being able, chosen, and admitted by the said president and fellowship of the physicians, may from time to time, as well within the City of London as elsewhere within this realm, practice and exercise the said science of physic in all and every members and parts, and act, statute or provision, made to the contrary notwithstanding."

the number of surgical practitioners could never have been the real issue. More disastrous still was "The Act Concerning Barbers and Surgeons to Be of One Company."[159] The act began by citing its reasons for action: ". . . it is very expedient and needful to provide for men expert in the science of physic and surgery, for the health of men's body. . . ."[160] Despite this, the act claimed, there were men and women in London who were incompetent in surgery. Parliament was acting in behalf of the people of the realm. To this end, a clear distinction was made in the Barbers' Company between barber-surgeons and barber-tonsors. Only barber-surgeons could practice medicine; barber-tonsors were to perform no medical activities "except shaving."[161] The reason for this was that the cutting of hair was considered dangerous and unsanitary—hence the separation. And to further the cause of surgery and because the surgeons of the Fellowship were unincorporated, they were to be united with the barber-surgeons of the mystery. There was no opportunity for appeal. Barber-tonsors were barred from the medical ranks, probably a good thing. Surgeons and barber-surgeons were combined—potentially a good thing, but limited by the reality that their practice was controlled and restricted by physicians, who still knew little about surgery or clinical practice.

There were other positive aspects of the 1540 act.[162] Four masters were appointed, two from what was the Fellowship, and two from the mystery. Moreover, the new company was to be given the bodies of four executed criminals to dissect every year.[163] This was to further their knowledge of anatomy and, if Thomas Vicary's accounts of dissection are to be believed, it probably did.[164] But the powers of the surgical practitioners were limited, and they remained under the thumbs of the physicians. Further, physicians were given control over apothecaries, and the apothecaries were now allowed to perform minor surgery.[165] In effect, the most important rights of practice and the most complicated

[159] "An Act Concerning Barbers and Surgeons Be of One Company," *House of Lords, Journals*, i, pp. 148–152. It is reprinted in Young, *Annals of the Barber-Surgeons*, pp. 586–590; and Beck, *Cutting Edge*, pp. 187–189.

[160] "An Act Concerning Barbers and Surgeons," p. 148.

[161] Young, *Annals of the Barber-Surgeons*, p. 589.

[162] "An Act Concerning Barbers and Surgeons," p. 148.

[163] Vicary, *Anatomie of the Bodie*, i, p. 125.

[164] *Ibid.*

[165] Young, *Annals of the Barber-Surgeons*, pp. 586–590.

aspects of surgery, traditionally dominated by the members of the Fellowship, were given over to the physicians. Thomas Roos's worst fears had been realized.

There was a final blow. In 1542, motivated by "consequence of licensed surgeons' greed," Parliament passed what has come to be known as the Quack Act.[166] The act allowed unlicensed practitioners—"common folk"—to "cure common ailments and outward wounds by Herbs, Waters, etc."[167] This opened the door once and for all to medical practice for anyone so inclined, and marked more clearly than ever the separation between respectable medicine, that of the physicians, and popular medicine, that of the craftsmen like surgeons, barbers, and apothecaries, and anyone else who wished to wield a scalpel, apply a leech, dispense a pill, or mix a powder. Any advances in surgery would have to come from the physicians.

This brings up another issue. How good were the physicians of the Royal College, influenced and infused as they were with new ideas? By concept and by law, the results of the acts of 1530, 1540, and 1542, surgery was now fair game for physicians. If the quality of physic was raised and its practitioners subjected to vigorous testing and screening, then perhaps Clark was right in picking 1518 as the beginning of modern English medicine. But his position is hard to defend. The medicine practiced at the Royal College and taught by the dons of Oxford and Cambridge was fundamentally unchanged from the previous three hundred years. Doctors Caius and Boorde, for all that has been written of them, were hardly more effective or enlightened than Gilbert Kymer or John Somerset.[168] Indeed, in 1540, Boorde wrote: "It is vain curiosity when we pry into the secrets of God which belong not to us."[169] Sound sentiments on theology, perhaps, but Boorde was writing about medicine.

Some scholars point to English Paracelsians as a new and dynamic force.[170] In many ways they were. They had a method, and based their conclusions on the results of research. They looked at nature in a new

[166] Vicary, *Anatomie of the Bodie*, i, pp. 208–209.

[167] *Ibid.*, p. 209.

[168] For Boorde, see *DNB*, 2, pp. 833–835.

[169] Andrew Boorde, *The First Book of the Introduction of Knowledge*, ed. F. J. Furnivall (London: EETS, e.s., 10, 1870), p. 226.

[170] Allen G. Debus, *The English Paracelsians* (London: Oldbourne, 1965).

way.[171] Further, by stressing iatrochemistry they were filling the crucial need in medical research for physical science. The iatrochemistry of the Paracelsians was wrong more often than it was right, but, following the argument of the importance of physical science through to a later period, it has been argued that Robert Boyle was as much a key in the emergence of modern medicine as was William Harvey.[172] Generally, the role of chemistry in the Scientific Revolution of the seventeenth century suffers when compared with that ascribed to, say, mathematics; while this is justified in interpreting the larger revolution, it is not the case with medicine.

But, giving the Paracelsians their due, it is difficult to see what concrete advances came of their labors. Their iatrochemistry, though well meaning and prescient, was inaccurate. Alchemy may have been practiced in the laboratory, but when its results were false it had more in common with magic than science.[173] Existing medical theory was already riddled with errors and superstition; a new ignorance, albeit one based on a different, pseudo-scientific method, was not much of an improvement. In the final analysis it is not clear that the preparations of the alchemists were much better than those of the apothecaries. Generally, it is difficult to sustain the arguments that the events of the early sixteenth century represented a new beginning in the history of English medicine. Rather, by killing the Fellowship of Surgeons, first professionally and then institutionally—and it should be remembered that because of their lack of military experience the Fellows of 1518 were far less effective than those of 1418—the physicians who founded the Royal College cut off the most innovative, dynamic part of late medieval medicine.

Further evidence of this is a comparison of English and Italian medicine in the early sixteenth century. Allusions have already been made to the latter systems. In Italy, surgery was brought far more effectively in the corpus of traditional medicine.[174] In many towns in northern and central Italy the division between physicians and surgeons was blurred,

---

[171] *Ibid.*; and Debus, *Man and Nature in the Renaissance* (Cambridge: Cambridge University Press, 1978).

[172] See, for example, Alan G. R. Smith, *Science and Society in the Sixteenth and Seventeenth Centuries* (New York: Harcourt Brace Jovanovich, 1972), pp. 149–151.

[173] This was of course pointed out by Lynn Thorndike in his *A History of Magic and Experimental Science*, especially vols iii and iv (New York: Columbia University Press, 1934).

[174] Cipolla, *Public Health and the Medical Profession*, pp. 11–66.

if not eliminated.[175] There was a long tradition for this fortuitous combination. The idea of a municipal surgeon was an old one, dating back to the twelfth century, and drawing on the idea that the poor ought to be provided with proper medical care, if necessary through public expense.[176] The Black Death made this need even greater, and the high mortality that came of it resulted in the idea of powerful central Boards of Health. The boards served as medical watchdogs, warning of pending epidemics, supervising the towns' medical practitioners, and policing sanitary regulations. Board members, who usually were drawn from town elites, had powers to impose quarantines, always a controversial decision since it impeded the trade that was most towns' bloodlines. They had staffs, including messengers, carters of the dead, and police, who accompanied the doctors and enforced the bans. They kept records and drew up bills of mortality similar to those the Henry VIII would begin in 1531.[177] By the middle of the fifteenth century the boards extended their control to hospitals, hostels, burials, and the manufacture and sale of drugs.

It is easy to see why Thomas Linacre and the other Englishmen who studied medicine in Italy were so impressed. It is easy, too, to understand why they would want to try to establish such boards and a similar kind of medicine in England. But in purely medical terms the Royal College of Physicians was not similar. In theory it provided regulation; in practice it offered its members protection. And however much Linacre and a few others wanted to incorporate surgery and anatomy into their physic, most physicians still gave it only lip service. It would in fact be easier to draw analogies between the Italian system of municipal medicine and public health and the 1423 College of Medicine than it would the 1518 College of Physicians.

In the end, then, late medieval English medicine did not realize its promise. In 1450 things looked bright. From the tragedy of recurring war came the opportunity for medical practitioners to gain the experience, devise the methods, and undertake the dissections necessary to proper clinical training. On the battlefield they performed operations denied them in civilian practice. It was these opportunities that pre-

---

[175] *Ibid.* See too Carlo M. Cipolla, "A Plague Doctor," in Harry A. Miskimin, David Herlihy, and A. L. Udovitch, eds., *The Medieval City* (New Haven: Yale University Press, 1977), pp. 65–72.

[176] Cipolla, *Public Health and the Medical Profession*, pp. 11–66.

[177] Paul Slack, "Mortality Crisis and Epidemic Disease," pp. 41–42.

pared John Arderne and Thomas Morstede to write their surgeries, to cut out tumors, to sift through skull fragments, to develop tools to help set bones, and to put together broken bodies.

Yet the older corporate mentality was never swept away. Some physicians may have tried to restrict surgical advances because they were jealous or felt threatened, or because they themselves could not master or even understand them. But most resisted on other grounds. They remained convinced that their methods were best. They believed Galen to be the true authority. And why not? The methods physicians used had been tried over a thousand years. Furthermore, by 1500, new and more accurate translations of the classical texts were available; old shortcomings might be attributed, not to Galen and other Greek masters, but to flaws in poor editions. But the new medical ideas from Italy were slow in circulating through the universities. Most physicians were still trained without clinical practice, even in 1530. Plague, though it remained a threat, was less so than it had been for almost two centuries.[178] Physicians, buoyed by the Royal College, had little threatening them, and no reason to make changes in their practice.

More importantly, and taken from another angle, surgeons in the sixteenth century were no longer dynamic. Ultimately, their medical superiority in the late fourteenth and fifteenth centuries had not been born of superior theory or higher moral standards or even greater commitment to medicine. They were better because of their clinical practice. When the wars stopped, so did the best kind of clinical practice. Surgeons grew prosperous, and prosperity made them conservative. Had they taken to the new medicine, had they been able to partake more fully of anatomy and redefine their physiology and combine it with continuing clinical practice, things might have been different. But they did not. Thomas Roos, in his defense of the old system, was typical of the Fellows. Like physicians, surgeons had become resistant to change. But, unlike physicians, they did not have a powerful institution to back their special interests. Under attack on one side from the academic learning of the physicians and the status that accompanied it, and bludgeoned on the other by the numbers and collective wealth of the barbers, they were helpless. Parliament literally legislated them into oblivion.

By 1530 English medicine was sunk in inertia. It was controlled by

[178] *Ibid.* Also, see Gottfried, "Population, Plague and the Sweating Sickness," pp. 12–37.

the physicians of the Royal College. There was much talk but little prac-tice of new ideas, and the gains of the fourteenth and fifteenth centuries went for naught. It is not surprising, then, that when William Harvey began his medical revolution in the seventeenth century he would have to go to Italy for inspiration.

# BIBLIOGRAPHY

## *Primary Sources*

### I. Catalogues and Guides

William Henry Black, *A Catalogue of the Manuscripts . . . Ashmole . . .* (Oxford: Oxford University Press, 1845).

*Catalogue of the Manuscripts Preserved in the Library of the University of Cambridge* (Cambridge: Cambridge University Press, 1856).

H. O. Coxe, *Laudian Manuscripts* (Oxford: Bodleian Library, 1973).

Henry Hallett Dale, *A Calendar of Printed Books in the Wellcome Historical Medical Library*, i (London: Wellcome, 1962).

J.S.W. Gibson, *Wills and Where to Find Them* (Chichester, Sussex: Phillimore, 1974).

Thomas Duffus Hardy, *Syllabus of Rymer's Foedera*, 3 vols. (London: Longmans, 1869).

Neil Ker, *Medieval Libraries of Great Britain*, 2nd ed. (London: Royal Historical Society, 1964.

—— *Medieval Manuscripts in British Libraries*, 3 vols., (Oxford: Clarendon Press, 1969–1984).

—— "Oxford College Libraries before 1500, in Josif Ijsewijn and Jacques Pacquet, eds., *Universities in the Late Middle Ages* (Louvain: Louvain University Press, 1978), pp. 294–311.

Philip E. Jones and Raymond Smith, *Guide to the Records in the Corporation of the London Record Office and then Guildhall Library Muniment Room* (London: English Universities Press, 1951).

Falconer Madan and H.H.E. Craster, *A Summary Catalogue of Western Manuscripts at the Bodleian Library at Oxford*, 5 vols. (Oxford: Clarendon Press, 1905–1953).

Albinia de la Mare, *Catalogue of Manuscripts . . . Lyell* (Oxford: Clarendon Press, 1971).

William D. Macray, *Catalogue Codicum Manuscriptum . . . Digby* (Oxford Clarendon Press, 1883).

—— *Catalogi Codicum Manuscriptorum . . . Rawlinson . . . A–Dii*, 5 vols. (Oxford: Oxford University Press, 1872–1900).

S.A.J. Moorat, *Catalogue of Western Manuscripts on Medicine and Science in the Wellcome Historical Medical Library*, i (London: Wellcome Historical Medical Library, 1962).

R.A.B. Mynors, *Catalogue of the Manuscripts of Balliol College, Oxford* (Oxford: Clarendon Press, 1963).

Rossell Hope Robbins, "Medical Manuscripts in Middle English," *Speculum*, 45, 1970, pp. 393–415.

—— "A Note on the Singer Survey of Medical Manuscripts in the British Isles," *Chaucer Review*, 4, 1970, pp. 66–70.

D. W. Singer "Survey of Medical Manuscripts in the British Isles Dating Before the Sixteenth Century," *Proceedings of the Royal Society of Medicine*, 12, 1918–1919, pp. 96–107.

Lynn Thorndike and Pearl Kibre, *A Catalogue of Incipits of Medieval Scientific Writings in Latin* (Cambridge, Mass.: Medieval Academy of America, 1963).

## II. Manuscripts

Bristol, England
   Public Library Ms. 10, Guy de Chauliac, "Medical Miscellany."

Cambridge, England
   1. University Library
      Add. Ms. 3120, Constantinus Africanus, "Breviarius."
      Add. Ms. 4087, Richard Fournival, "Liber alchyme."
      Add. Ms. 4407, "Collectianea."
      Add. Ms. 6000, Henri de Mondeville, "Tractus."
      Add. Ms. 6860, "De Proprietate Umbilici."
      Dd 3 52, Guido de Cauliaco, "Antidotary."
      Dd 4 44, "Cure for Horses."
      Dd 5 53, John Arderne, "Practica."
      Dd 5 66, "Medical Recipes."
      Dd 5 76, "De diversis et medicinis."
      Dd 6 13, "Medical Receipts."
      Dd 6 29, "Medica."
      Dd 8 22, Petrarch, "De Podogia."
      Dd 10 44, "Collection of Medical Works."
      Dd 11 45, "Collection of Medical Treatises."
      Dd 12 51, "De herbis medicinalibus."
      Ee 1 13, "Medica et Alchemica."
      Ee 2 20, "Miscellany."
      Ee 6 41, J. Platearius, "Breviarum de simplici medicinae."
      Ff 1 33, Hippocrates, "De gouvernement de sante."
      Ff 2 6, Henry Daniel, "Book of Urines."
      Ff 2 37, Gilbert the Englishmen, "Compendium."
      Ff 4 12, Robert Greene, "Collections."

Ff 4 13, "De phlebotomia."

Gg 1 1, "De sanguinis minutione."

Gg 3 29, Henry Daniel, "Libri tres uricrisiarum."

Gg 3 32, Orosius "Practica."

Hh 1 7, Poggio, "In laudem medicinae."

Hh 6 13, "Medical Recipe for a sore leg."

Ii 1 13, Bernard Gordon, "De astronomica medicorum."

Ii 1 16, Ricardus Anglicus, "Practica."

Ii 1 31, "Dieta . . . Ric . . . contra pestilentem."

Ii 2 5, "Medical Miscellany."

Ii, 3 17, "Rosarium medicum."

Ii 5 11, Aldobrandino of Siena.

Ii 6 17, Bartholomeus Franciscanus, "De urinis."

Ii 6 18, "Tractus urinarum."

Ii 6 43, "Medical Recipes in English."

Kk 6 30, "Alchemical and Medical Tracts."

Kk 6 33, "Medical Receipts."

Ll 1 18, "Of the Pestilence."

Ll 4 12, Hippocrates.

Ll 4 14, "Treatise on Physionomy."

Mm 1 17, Oribasius, "Extracts."

Mm 4 41, "Pondera medicinalia."

2. Emmanuel College

Ms. 69, John Arderne.

3. Gonville and Caius College

Ms. 190, John Arderne, "Fistula."

Ms. 336, "Medical Miscellany."

Ms. 451A, "Medical Miscellany."

4. King's College

Ms. 16 1, "Medical Miscellany.

Ms. 21, "Medical Miscellany."

5. Magdelane College

Ms. Pepys 1916, "Medical Sketchbook."

6. St. John's College

Ms. 19 (A. 19), Jan Yperman, "Chirurgie."

7. Trinity College

Ms. 992 (R. 14.52), "Medical Miscellany."

Ms. 1037, "Medical Miscellany."

Ms. 1102, "Medica."

Ms. 1148, "Medica" (includes a Henri de Mondeville, "Chirurgie").

Ms. 1153, John Arderne, "Practica chirurgia."

Ms. 1422, "Medica."

LONDON

　1. British Library

　　B.M. Add. Ms. 8928, "Medical Miscellany."

　　B.M. Add. Ms. 10440, Lanfranc of Milan, "Anatomy and Surgery."

　　B.M. Add. Ms. 15236, "Medical Tracts."

　　B.M. Add. Ms. 15692, "Medical Miscellany."

　　B.M. Add. Ms. 15813, "Anatomy."

　　B.M. Add. Ms. 17810, William of Saliceto, "Chirurgia."

　　B.M. Add. Ms. 18851, "Anatomy."

　　B.M. Add. Ms. 24453, "Inventory of John Hexham, apothecary."

　　B.M. Add. Ms. 27582, Thomas Forestier, "Tractus contra pestilentiam."

　　B.M. Add. Ms. 28725, "Medical Calendar."

　　B.M. Add. Ms. 29301, John Arderne, "Practica Chirgia."

　　B.M. Add. Ms. 34111, "Medical Miscellany."

　　B.M. Add. Ms. 36617, "Medical Miscellany."

　　B.M. Egerton Ms. 1624, Henry Daniel, "Urines."

　　B.M. Egerton Ms. 2572, "York Barbers' Guild."

　　B.M. Egerton Ms. 2724, "Medical Miscellany."

　　B.M. Harl. Ms. 541, "5 Richard II list of London Company Halls."

　　B.M. Harl. Ms. 1454, "Apothecary's Account Book."

　　B.M. Harl. Ms. 1735, "English Medical Texts."

　　B.M. Harl. Ms. 1736, "Old English Medical Manuscripts" (thought to include Thomas Morstede, "Fair Book of Surgery").

　　B.M. Harl. Ms. 3719, Thomas Florentine, "Medical Miscellany."

　　B.M. Harl. Ms. 5294, "Herbal."

　　B.M. Harl. Ms. 5311, "Bloodletting."

　　B.M. Royal 17 D1, Henry Daniel, "Of the Domes of Urines."

　　B.M. Royal 18 A VI, "Medical Miscellany."

　　B.M. Sloane Ms. 1, Guy de Chauliac, "Surgery."

　　B.M. Sloane Ms. 4, "Medical Recipes."

　　B.M. Sloane Ms. 5, Richard Dod, "Medical Miscellany."

　　B.M. Sloane Ms. 6, John Arderne, "Fistula in Ano."

　　B.M. Sloane Ms. 7, "Medical Miscellany."

　　B.M. Sloane Ms. 56, John Arderne, "Liber Chirurgia."

　　B.M. Sloane Ms. 59, John Malverne, John Somerset, "Treatise."

　　B.M. Sloane Ms. 75, John Gaddesden, "Rosa Medicinae."

　　B.M. Sloane Ms. 76, John Arderne, "Surgery."

　　B.M. Sloane Ms. 134, "Medical Miscellany."

　　B.M. Sloane Ms. 142, Aristotle, "Libros de Physico."

　　B.M. Sloane Ms. 249, "Medical Miscellany."

　　B.M. Sloane Ms. 335, John Arderne, "Liber Medicinarium."

　　B.M. Sloane Ms. 341, John Arderne, "Surgery."

B.M. Sloane Ms. 347, John Arderne, "Surgery."
B.M. Sloane Ms. 405, "Medical Miscellany."
B.M. Sloane Ms. 418, Bernard Gordon, "Medical Miscellany."
B.M. Sloane Ms. 420, "Medical Miscellany."
B.M. Sloane Ms. 421a, "Diseases of Women."
B.M. Sloane Ms. 563, John Arderne, "Fistula in Ano."
B.M. Sloane Ms. 635, "Medical Miscellany."
B.M. Sloane Ms. 795, John Arderne, "Practica chirurgie."
B.M. Sloane Ms. 963, Macer Floribus, "Medical Miscellany."
B.M. Sloane Ms. 1047, John Chamber, "Medical Miscellany."
B.M. Sloane Ms. 1100, Henry Daniel, "Of the Domes of Urines."
B.M. Sloane Ms. 1313, "Medical Miscellany."
B.M. Sloane Ms. 1721, Henry Daniel, "Urines."
B.M. Sloane Ms. 1977, "Medical Miscellany."
B.M. Sloane Ms. 1991, "Medical Miscellany."
B.M. Sloane Ms. 2002, John Arderne, "Fistula in Ano."
B.M. Sloane Ms. 2156, "Medical Miscellany."
B.M. Sloane Ms. 2250, "Zodiac Man."
B.M. Sloane Ms. 2463, "Medical Miscellany."
B.M. Sloane Ms. 3498, "English Medical Texts."
B.M. Sloane Ms. 3844, John of Arderne, "Fistula."

2. Corporation of London Records Office
Letter Book M, 1497–1515.
Letter Book N, 1515–1526.
London Rep Book 3, 1514–1518.

3. London Guildhall Library
Guildhall Ms. 1108, "Barber Surgeons' Company," Names of the Masters and Wardens.
Guildhall Ms. 5242, "Barber Surgeons' Company, Charter of Incorporations," 1462 (now with the Company).
Guildhall Ms. 5243, "Barber Surgeons' Company, Charter of Henry VII."
Guildhall Ms. 5244, "Barber Surgeons Company, Charter of Henry VIII."
Guildhall Ms. 5248, "Barber Surgeons Company, Ancient Ordinances Book" (now with the Company).
Guildhall Ms. 5249, "Barber Surgeons Company," Ordinances of Henry VIII, with Thomas More."
Guildhall Ms. 5265, "Barber Surgeons Company, Register of Freemen."
Guildhall Ms. 5278, "Barber Surgeons' Company," Masters and Wardens."
Guildhall Ms. 5278A, "Barber Surgeons' Company, Masters and Wardens, with Notes of Sidney Young."
Guildhall Ms. 5280, "Barber Surgeons' Company, Charters, Ordinances."

Guildhall Ms. 5281, "Barber Surgeons' Company, Ordinances."

Guildhall Ms. 9826, "Barber Surgeons' Company, Charity of Robert Ferbras."

Guildhall Ms. 9834, "Barber Surgeons' Company," Papers of Sidney
Young."

4. Public Record Office.
Exchequer Accounts E 101/47/10.
Exchequer Accounts E/101/48/3.
Exchequer Accounts E/101/56/10.

5. Royal College of Physicians
Ms. 09.61 (227a), Henri di Mondeville, "Surgery."

6. Royal College of Surgeons.
Ms. 129a 1.5, "De passionibus mulierum."

7. Wellcome Historical Medical Library.
Wellcome Ms. 22, "Alchemy."
Wellcome Ms. 38, Philip Aleyne, "Notebook."
Wellcome Ms. 49, "Apocalypse: Anatomical and Medical Tracts."
Wellcome Ms. 290, "Pseudo-Galen on Anatomy and Surgery."
Wellcome Ms. 397, Lanfranc of Milan, "Chirurgia Parva."
Wellcome Mss. 404–411, "Leechbooks."
Wellcome Ms. 457, Macer Floribus, "De viribus herbarum."
Wellcome Ms. 537, "Medical Miscellany, Practica."
Wellcome Ms. 542, "Collected Leechbooks."
Wellcome Ms. 564, Henri de Mondeville, "Chirurgia."
Wellcome Ms. 673, "Regimen Sanitatis Salernitanum."
Wellcome Ms. 784, John of Burgundy, "Uroscopy."
Wellcome Ms. 974, Andrew Boorde, "Breviary for Health."

OXFORD
1. Bodleian Library
Add. Ms. A 106 (Bodley 29003), "Medical Recipes."
Add. Ms. B 60 (Bodley 29179) "Medical Recipes."
Ashmole Ms. 5, Nicholas of Lynn, "Kalendarii."
Ashmole Ms. 8, "Calendar."
Ashmole Ms. 59, "Materia medica."
Ashmole Ms. 210I, Ricardus Anglicus, "Calendar."
Ashmole Ms. 210II, Hippocrates, "Medical Astronomy."
Ashmole Ms. 343, "Materia Medica."
Ashmole Ms. 345, "Pathology."
Ashmole Ms. 346, "Medical Miscellany."
Ashmole Ms. 370, Nicholas of Lynn, "Calendar."
Ashmole Ms. 391V, "Astrological Medical."

Ashmole Ms. 393, "Ars medicinae."

Ashmole Ms. 398, "Surgery."

Ashmole Ms. 750, "Materia medica."

Ashmole Ms. 789viii, "Medical Miscellany."

Ashmole Ms. 1389, "Materia medica."

Ashmole Ms. 1391, "Ars medicinae."

Ashmole Ms. 1393, "Ars medicinae."

Ashmole Ms. 1396, Lanfranc, "Treatise of the Science of Cirurgie."

Ashmole Ms. 1397, "Ars medicinae."

Ashmole Ms. 1402, "Ars medicinae."

Ashmole Ms. 1413, "Ars medicinae."

Ashmole Ms. 1416, "Midwifery."

Ashmole Ms. 1427, Simon de Herbred, "Materia medica."

Ashmole Ms. 1432, "Materia medica."

Ashmole Ms. 1434i, John Arderne, "Practica."

Ashmole Ms. 1434ii, Gerald of Cremona, "The Manner of Medicine."

Ashmole Ms. 1435, "Ars medicinae."

Ashmole Ms. 1437, "Medical miscellany." (Includes tracts by John Arderne, Arnald of Villanova, and John Argentine).

Ashmole Ms. 1438i, "Medical Miscellany."

Ashmole Ms. 1438ii, "Ars medica."

Ashmole Ms. 1443, "Materia medica."

Ashmole Ms. 1444, "Ars medicinae."

Ashmole Ms. 1447, "Ars medicinae."

Ashmole Ms. 1448, John Mirplace, "Phlebotomy."

Ashmole Ms. 1468, "Pathology."

Ashmole Ms. 1470, "Ars medicinae."

Ashmole Ms. 1471, "Ars medicinae."

Ashmole Ms. 1475, "Ars medicinae."

Ashmole Ms. 1477iii, "Medical Miscellany."

Ashmole Ms. 1481, "Medical Miscellany."

Ashmole Ms. 1498, Gerald of Cremona, "The Manner of Medicine."

Ashmole Ms. 1517, Henry Daniel, "Urines."

Bodley Ms. 67 (2136), "Ars medicinae."

Bodley Ms. 178 (2073), "Materia medica."

Bodley Ms. 181 (2081), "Ars medicinae."

Bodley Ms. 211 (2927), Roger Bacon, "Uroscopy."

Bodley Ms. 264 (2464), "Medical Miscellany."

Bodley Ms. 360 (2461), "Chirurgia."

Bodley Ms. 361 (2462), "Ars medicinae."

Bodley Ms. 362 (2463), "Ars medicinae."

Bodley Ms. 465 (2459), "General Science."

Bodley Ms. 484 (2063), "Materia medica."

Bodley Ms. 591, (2363), "Medical Recipes."

Bodley Ms. 608 (2059), John Gaddesden, "Rosa medicinae."

Bodley Ms. 624 (2158), "Speculum Regis Ed. III."

Bodley Ms. 682 (2696), "Medical Treatises."

Bodley Ms. 762 (2535), "Ars medicinae."

Digby Ms. 29, "Ars medicinae."

Digby Ms. 44, "Quaestiones Aristotelicae novem."

Digby Ms. 57, "Fragmentum ex tract. de medicina astrologica."

Digby Ms. 75, "De medicinis."

Digby Ms. 79, "De morbis mulierum."

Digby Ms. 88, "Ars medicinae."

Digby Ms. 95, "Liber de conservanda sanitate."

Digby Ms. 160, "Tractus de medicinis simplicibus."

Digby Ms. 161, "De diebus criticis varia."

Digby Ms. 176, "Notuli de corruptione pestilenti."

Douce Ms. 2 (Bodley 21576), "Ars medicinae."

Douce Ms. 45 (Bodley 21619), "Astral Medicine."

Douce Ms. 54 (Bodley 21628), "Medical Recipes."

Douce Ms. 78 (Bodley 21652), "Old English Poems."

Douce Ms. 84 (Bodley 21658), "Medical Recipes."

Douce Ms. 87 (Bodley 21661), "Medical Recipes."

Douce Ms. 290 (Bodley 21864), "Herbal."

Douce Ms. 304 (Bodley (21878), "Diseases and Medical Recipes."

Hatton Ms. 29, "Ars medicinae."

Laud Ms. 553, "Herbarium."

Laud Ms. 558. "Ars medicinae."

Laud Ms. 598, "Pathology."

Laud Ms. 617, "Ars medicinae."

Laud Ms. 685, "Pathology."

Laud Ms. Misc. 724, "Surgery."

Lyell Ms. 35, "Commonplace Books."

Lyell Ms. 36, "Scientific Miscellany."

Museo Ms. e 19 (Bodley 3500), "Surgical Miscellany."

Museo Ms. e 52, (Bodley 3510), "Medical Pieces."

Museo Ms. e 122 (Bodley 3560), "Medico Salernitano."

Museo Ms. e 146, "Ars medicinae."

Rawlinson Ms. A 273, "Medicinae parvae."

Rawlinson Ms. A 429, "Medical Miscellany."

Rawlinson Ms. B 174, "List of Physicians and Their Writings, 1320–1365."

Rawlinson Ms. B 235, "Speculum medicinae."

Rawlinson Ms. B 815, "Materia medica."

Rawlinson Ms. c 81, "Ars medicinae."

Rawlinson Ms. c 211, "Table for Calculating Whether Sick Men will Live or Die."

Rawlinson Ms. c 299, "Ars medicinae."

Rawlinson Ms. c 328, "Ars medicinae."

Rawlinson Ms. c 499, "De cibis et medicinis simplicibus."

Rawlinson Ms. c 506, Thomas Herne, "Medical Collections."

Rawlinson Ms. c 543, "De regimine" (includes a version of Gilbertus Anglicus).

Rawlinson Ms. c 550, "Recepta varia medicinalia."

Rawlinson Ms. c 814, "Ars medicinae."

Rawlinson Ms. c 817, "Nomina et species morborum."

Rawlinson Ms. d 210, "Ars medicinae."

Rawlinson Ms. d 238, "Nota de iv temperamentis corporis."

Rawlinson Ms. d 247, "De coloribus urinium."

Rawlinson Ms. d 248, "Summula de urinis."

Rawlinson Ms. d 251, "Astrological Miscellancy."

Rawlinson Ms. d 595, "Transcript of a Venetian Medical Book."

Rawlinson Ms. d 678, "Midwifery."

Rawlinson Ms. d 1210, "Ars medicinae."

Rawlinson Ms. d 1221, "Judicium urinarum."

Seldon Ms. Arch b 35 (Bodley 3349), Roger Bacon, "Treatises."

Seldon Ms. Supra 73 (Bodley 3461), "Ars medicinae."

Wood Ms. empt. 18 (Bodley 8606), "Medical Recipes."

Wood Ms. empt. 25, "Herbal."

2. All Souls College

Ms. 79, Gilbertus Anglicus, "Compendium medicinae."

3. Pembroke College

Ms. 10, "Medical Miscellany."

4. St. Johns College

Ms. 86, John Arderne, "Liber medicinarum."

YORK

Cathedral Ms. XVI.E32.


III. PRINTED MANUSCRIPTS

Arnald of Villanova, *Opera Medica, II Omnia*, ed. Michael R. McVaugh (Chapel Hill, N.C.: University of North Carolina Press, 1975).

Albertus Magnus, *The Book of Secrets . . . of the Virtues of Herbs, Stones and Certain Beasts*, ed. Michael R. Best and Frank H. Brightman (Oxford: Clarendon Press, 1973).

Albucasis, *On Surgery and Instruments*, trans. M. S. Spink and G. L. Lewis (London: Wellcome Medical Library, 1975).

John Arderne, *De Arte Phisicale*, trans. D'Arcy Power (London: J. Bale and Co., 1922).

—— *Treatise of Fistula in Ano*, ed. D'Arcy Power (London: EETS, 139, 1910).

Avicenna, *The First Book of the Canon*, trans. Oscar C. Gruner (London: Luzac and Co., 1930).

—— *Poem on Medicine*, ed. Haven C. Krueger (Springfield, Ill.: Charles C. Thomas, 1963).

D. C. Bain, "A Note of an English Medical Receipt Book," *BHM*, 8, pp. 1246–1248.

Andrew Boorde, *The First Book of the Introduction of Knowledge*, ed. F. J. Furnivall (London: EETS, e.s., 10, 1870).

Celsus, *De Medicina*, 3 vols., trans. W. G. Spencer (London: 1935–1938).

Guy de Chauliac, *The Cyrurgie of Guy de Chauliac* (London: EETS, 265, 1971).

—— *Chirurgia Magna*, ed. Bjorn Wallner (Lund: Gleerup, 1970).

—— *On Wounds and Fractures*, trans. W. A. Brennean (Chicago: 1923).

—— *Treatise on Wounds*, ed. Bjorn Wallner, 2 vols. (Lund: Gleerup, 1976–1979).

O. Cockayne, ed., *Leechdoms, Wortcunning and Starcraft of Early England*, 3 vols. (London: Rolls Series, 1864).

W. R. Dawson, *A Leechbook or Collection of Medical Recipes of the Fifteenth Century* (London: Macmillan, 1934).

Dioscorides, *De materia medica*, trans. J. Goodyer (Oxford: Oxford University Press, 1934).

John Gaddesden, *Rosa Medicinae*, ed. H. P. Cholmeley in *John of Gaddesden and the Rosa Medicinae* (Oxford: Clarendon, 1912).

Galen, *Hygiene*, trans. R. M. Green (Springfield, Ill.: Charles C. Thomas, 1951).

—— *On the Affected Parts*, ed. Rudolph Siegel (Basel: S. Karger, 1976).

—— *On Anatomical Procedures*, trans. Charles Singer (London: Wellcome Historical Medical Library, 1956).

—— *On Medical Experience*, trans. R. Walzer (London: Oxford University Press, 1944).

—— *On Natural Facilities*, trans. Arthur J. Brock (Chicago: Great Books, 1952).

—— *On Respiration and the Arteries*, trans. David J. Furley and J. S. Wilkie (Princeton: Princeton University Press, 1983).

—— *On the Use of the Parts*, trans. M. T. May (Ithaca, N.Y.: Cornell University Press, 1968).

Gilbertus Anglicus, ed. Faye Marie Getz, "An Edition of the Middle English Gilbertus Anglicus Found in Wellcome Ms. 537" (Ph.D Dissertation, University of Toronto, 1981).

George Henslow, *Medical Works of the Fourteenth Century* (London: Chapman and Hall, 1889).

Hippocrates, *The Oath, The Canon, The Science of Medicine, Prognosis, Aphorisms, The Sacred Disease, Dreams, The Nature of Man, A Regimen for Health*, ed. W.H.S. Jones (London: Loeb Editions, 1923–1931), vols. 1, 2, and 4.

—— *Fractures*, ed. E. T. Withington (London: Loeb Editions, 1928).

—— *On Diet and Hygiene*, ed. John Precope (London: William Lea, n.d.).

—— *Hippocratic Writings*, ed G.E.R. Lloyd (London: Penguin Books, 1983).

Ibn Ridwan, *On the Prevention of Bodily Ills in Egypt*, trans. Michael W. Dols (Berkeley: University of California Press, 1984).

Isidore of Seville, *The Medical Writings*, trans. W. D. Sharpe (Philadelphia: Transactions of the American Philosophical Society, 1964).

Lanfranc of Milan, *Science of Cirurgie*, ed. Robert von Fleishhacken (London: EETS, cii, 1894).

*The Liber de Diversis Medicinis*, ed. Margaret Ogdan (London: EETS, 207, 1969).

Nicholas of Lynn, *Kalendarium*, ed. Sigmund Eisner (Athens, Ga.: University of Georgia Press, 1980).

John Mirfield, *Brevarium Bartholomi et Florarium Bratolomi*, trans., Percival Horton-Smith Hartley and H. R. Aldridge (Cambridge: Cambridge University Press, 1936).

—— *Surgery*, ed. James B. Coltan (New York: Hafner, 1969).

Mondino dei Liuzzi, *Anathomia*, trans. Ernest Wickersheimer (Paris: Documents scientifiques, 1926).

Moses Maimonides, *On the Causes of Symptoms*, ed. J. O. Leibowitz and S. Marcus (Berkeley, Cal.: University of California Press, 1974). Henri de Mondeville, *La Chirurgie*, 2 vols., ed. A. Bos (Paris: Librairie de Firmin Didot, 1896).

—— *Chirurgie*, 2 vols., ed. E. Nicaise (Paris: Felix Alcan, 1893).

Ambroise Pare, *The Apologie and Treatise*, ed. Geoffrey Keynes (London: Falcon Educating Books, 1951).

*Regimen Sanitatis Salernitanum*, trans. John Harrington (London: Oxford University Press, 1924).

Soranus, *Gynecology*, trans. Owsei Temkin (Baltimore: Johns Hopkins University Press, 1956).

*Tacuinum Sanitatis*, ed. Luisa C. Arano (New York: George Braziller, 1976).

Theodoric, *Surgery*, trans. E. Campbell and J. Colton, 2 vols. (New York: 1955–1960).

Trotula of Salerno, ed. Beryl Rowland, *Medieval Woman's Guide to Health: The First English Gynecological Handbook* (Kent, Ohio: Kent State University Press, 1981).

Thomas Vicary, *The Anatomie of the Bodie of Man*, ed. Frederick J. Furnivall and Percy Furnivall, (London: EETS, 53, 1888).

IV. Printed Sources

1. General

F. D. Blackley and G. Hermanson, eds., *The Household Book of Queen Isabella of England, 1311–12* (Edmonton: University of Alberta Press, 1971).

*Calendar of Various Chancery Rolls, 1277–1326* (London: HMSO, 1912).

*Calendar of Charter Rolls, 1341–1516* (London: HMSO, 1903–1927).

*Calendar of Close Rolls, 1339–1500* (London: HMSO, 1916–1927).

*Calendar of Entries in the Papal Registers, Letters, 1342–1484* (London: HMSO, 1897–1960).

*Calendar of Entries in the Papal Registers, Letters, 1484–1492* (Dublin: Stationery Office, 1978).

*Calendar of Entries in the Papal Registers, Petitions, 1342–1419* (London: HMSO, 1896).

*Calendar of Fine Rolls, 1337–1485* (London: HMSO, 1915–1961).

*Calendar of Libertate Rolls . . . Henry III* (London: HMSO, 1916–1937).

*Calendar of Patent Rolls, 1340–1485* (London: HMSO 1900–1916).

J. Payne Collier, *The Household Books of John Duke of Norfolk and Thomas Earl of Surrey, 1481–1490* (London: William Nicol, 1864).

William Dugdale, *Monasticon Anglicanum*, 6 vols., ed. J. Caley, H. Ellis, and B. Bandinel (London: Longmans, 1817–1830).

E. F. Jacob, *The Register of Henry Chichele*, 2 vols. (Oxford: Oxford University Press, 1937).

*Letters and Papers, Foreign and Domestic . . . of the Reign of Henry VIII*, 4 vols. (London: Longmans and HMSO, 1862–1920).

W. Munk, *The Rolls of the Royal College of Physicians*, 2nd ed., 3 vols. (London: By the College, 1878–1955).

A. R. Myers, *The Household Accounts of Edward IV* (Manchester: University of Manchester Press, 1959).

N. H. Nicholas, ed., *Privy Expenses of Elizabeth of York and Wardrobe Accounts of Edward IV* (London: William Pickering, 1830).

*Ordinances and Regulations for the Government of the Royal Household* (London: Society of Antiquaries, 1790).

*Rotuli Parliamentorum, ut et petitiones et placita in parliamento (1278–1503)*, 8 vols., ed. J. Strachey (London: 1767–1832).

Thomas Rymer, *Foedera*, 4 vols., ed A. Clarke, F. Holbrooke, and J. Caley (London: Record Commission, 1816–1869).

—— *Foedera*, 10 vols. (The Hague: John Neaulme, 1735–1745).

Sidney Young, *Annals of the Barber Surgeons of London* (London: Blades, East and Blades, 1890).

2. BRIDGWATER

*Bridgwater Borough Archives, 1377–99*, Somerset Record Society, 53, 1938.

3. BRISTOL

F. Bickley, ed., *The Little Red Book of Bristol*, 2 vols. (Bristol: W. Croftor Hemmons, 1900).

H. A. Cronne, ed., *Bristol Charters, 1378–1499*, Bristol Record Society, 11, 1946.

D. Hollis, ed., *Calendar of the Bristol Apprentice Books, 1532–1565*, Bristol Record Society, 14, 1948.

4. BUCKINGHAMSHIRE

A. C. Chibnall and A. Vere Woodman, eds., *Subsidy Roll for the County of Buckingham, 1524*, Buckingham Record Society, 18, 1944.

5. CAMBRIDGE

A. B. Emden, *A Biographical Register of the University of Cambridge to 1500* (Cambridge: Cambridge University Press, 1963).

J. and J. A. Venn, *Alumni Cantabrigienses: A Biographical List of All Known Students* (Cambridge: Cambridge University Press, 1920–1927).

6. CANTERBURY

J. M. Cowper, *Intrantes: A List of Persons Admitted to Live and Trade in Canterbury from 1392–1592* (Canterbury: Privately printed, 1904).

—— *Roll of Freemen of the City of Canterbury, 1392–1800* (Canterbury: Privately printed, 1903).

7. CHESTER

*Chester Freemen's Rolls*, i, 1392–1700, The Record Society . . . Relating to Lancashire and Cheshire, 51, 1906.

8. COVENTRY

Alice Beardwood, ed., *Statute of the Merchant Roll of Coventry, 1392–1416*, Dugdale Society, 17, 1939.

Mary D. Harris, ed., *Coventry Leet Book*, 2 vols. (London: EETS, 1907–1913).

—— ed., *Register of the Guild of the Holy Trinity, St. Mary, St. John Baptists and St. Katherine of Coventry*, 2 vols., Dugdale Society, 13, 1935.

9. DORCHESTER

Charles H., Mayo and Arthur W. Gould, eds., *The Municipal Records of the Borough of Dorchester, Dorset* (Exeter: William Pollard, 1908).

10. EXETER

Margery M. Rowe and Andrew M. Jackson, eds., *Exeter Freemen, 1266–1967*, Devon and Cornwall Record Society, e.s. i, 1973.

11. LEICESTER

Henry Hartopp, ed., *Freemen of Leicester, 1196–1770* (Leicester: Corporation of the City, 1927).

12. LINCOLNSHIRE

H. E. Salter, ed., *A Subsidy Collected in the Diocese of Lincoln in 1526* (Oxford: Blackwell, 1909).

13. LONDON

R. R. James, "Earliest List of Surgeons to be Licensed by the Bishop of London Under the Act of 3, Henry VIII, CII," *Janus*, 41, 1937, pp. 255–260.

Philip E. Jones, ed., *Calendar and Memoranda Rolls of the City of London at the Guildhall, 1437–1482*, 2 vols. (Cambridge: Cambridge University Press, 1954–1961).

H. T. Riley, ed., *Memorials of London and London Life* (London: Longmans, 1868).

—— ed., *Monumenta Gildhallae Londoniensis*, 3 vols. (London: Rolls Series, 1859–1862).

R. R. Sharpe, *Calendar of Coroners Rolls* (London: HMSO, 1913).

—— ed., *Calendar of Letter Books . . . of the City of London*, A–L (London: J. E. Francis, 1900–1912).

—— ed., *Calendar of Letters from the Mayor to the City of London, 1350–1370* (London: J. C. Francis, 1885).

A. H. Thomas, ed., *Calendar of Plea and Memoranda Rolls . . . of the City of London at the Guildhall, 1364–1482*, 5 vols. (Cambridge: Cambridge University Press, 1929–1943).

14. LYNN

*Calendar of the Freemen of Lynn, 1292–1836*, Norfolk and Norwich Record Archeological Society, 1913.

15. NEWCASTLE

*The Register of Freemen of Newcastle-upon-Tyne*, Newcastle-Upon-Tyne Record Series, iii, 1923.

16. NORTHAMPTON

Christopher A. Markham, ed., *The Records of the Borough of Northampton*, 2 vols., 1898.

## 17. Norwich

William Hudson and John Cottingham Tingay, eds., *Records of the City of Norwich*, 2 vols. (Norwich: Jarrold, 1910).

Walter Pye, ed., *Calendar of the Freemen of Norwich, 1317–1603* (London: Elliott Stock, 1880).

Winifred Rising and Percy Millican, eds., *An Index of Indentures of Norwich Apprentices*, Norfolk Record Society, 29, 1959.

H. W. Sanders, *An Introduction to the Obedientiary and Manor Rolls of Norwich Cathedral Priory* (Norwich: Jarrold, 1930).

## 18. Nottingham

*Records of the Borough of Nottingham, 1155–1547*, 3 vols. (London: Bernard Quaritch, 1882–1885).

## 19. Oxford

H. Anstey, *Munumenta academica Oxoniensis*, 2 vols. (London: Rolls Series, 1868).

A. B. Emden, *A Biographical Register of Oxford*, 2 vols. (Oxford: Oxford University Press, 1957–1959).

S. Gibson, *Statua Antiqua Universitatis Oxoniensis* (Oxford: Oxford University Press, 1931).

## 20. Preston

W. Alexander Abram, ed., *The Rolls of Burgesses at the Guild Merchant, Borough of Preston, 1397–1682*, Record Society of Lancashire and Chester, ix, 1884.

## 21. Reading

J. M. Guilding, ed., *Reading Records: Diary of the Corporation, 1431–1602*, i (London: James Parker, 1892).

## 22. Shrewsbury

C. H. Drinkwater, ed., *A Burgess Roll and a Guild Merchant Roll of 1372*, Transactions of the Shropshire Archeology and Natural History Association, 3rd series, iv, 1904.

—— *Shrewsbury Gild Merchant Rolls of the 14th–15th Centuries*, Transactions of the Shropshire Archeology and Natural History Society, 3rd series, v, 1905.

H. E. Forest, *Shrewsbury Burgess Rolls* (Shrewsbury: W. B. Walker, 1924).

*Calendar of the Muniments and Records of the Borough of Shrewsbury* (Shrewsbury: L. Wilding, 1896).

## 23. Stratford-upon-Avon

J. Harvey Bloom, ed., *The Gild Register, Stratford-upon-Avon, 1406–1535* (London: Phillimore, 1902).

J. Harvey Bloom, ed., *The Register of the Gild of the Holy Cross, the Blessed Mary and St. John Baptist of Stratford-upon-Avon* (London: Phillimore, 1907).

24. SURREY

J. F. Willard and H. C. Johnson, eds., *Surrey Taxations Returns . . . 1332 to 1623*, Surrey Record Society, xi, 1922–1923.
*County of Surrey: Inventory of the Borough Records*, Surrey Record Society, 3, 1929.

25. WELLS

Dorothy O. Shilton and Richard Holworthy, eds., *Wells City Charters*, Somerset Record Society, 46, 1932.

26. YARMOUTH

*A Calendar of the Freemen of Yarmouth, 1429–1800*, Norfolk and Norwich Record Society, 1910.

27. YORK

*The Register of the Freemen of York, 1272–1558*, Surtees Society, xcvi, 1897.
*The Register of the Guild of Christ Church, York*, Surtees Society, 57, 1872.


V. WILLS AND WILL INDICES

1. PREROGATIVE COURT OF CANTERBURY

Wills in the Public Record Office, London.
E. F. Jacob, *The Register of Henry Chichele*, ii (Oxford: Oxford University Press, 1937).
J. Challenor and C. Smith, eds., *Index of Wills Proved in the Prerogative Court of Canterbury, 1383–1558*, 2 vols., British Record Society, 1893–1895.

2. BERKSHIRE

W.P.W. Phillimore, ed., *Index to Wills Proved in the Court of the Archdeaconry of Berkshire*, Oxford Historical Society, 1893.

3. BURY ST. EDMUNDS

Peculiar Court wills in the West Suffolk Record Office, Bury St. Edmunds.
V. B. Redstone, *A Calendar of Pre-Reformation Wills . . . at Bury St. Edmunds* (Bury St. Edmunds: Privately printed, 1907).
Samuel Tymms, ed., *Wills and Inventories from the Registers of the Commissary of Bury St. Edmunds and the Archdeaconry of Sudbury* (London: Camden Society, 44, 1850).

## 4. Canterbury

H. R. Plomer, ed., *Calendar of Wills and Administrations Now Preserved at Canterbury, 1396–1558*, Kent Archeological Society, Kent Records, 6, 1916.

## 5. Ipswich

Archdeaconry Courts of Suffolk and Sudbury wills in the East Suffolk Record Office, Ipswich.

F. A. Crisp, *Calendar of Wills at Ipswich, 1444–1606* (London: Privately Printed, 1895).

## 6. Kent

Leland Lewis Duncan, ed., *Calendar of Wills Relating to the County of Kent* (Canterbury: Charles North, 1890).

*Index of Wills, Consistory Court of Rochester*, Kent Archeological Society, Rochester Branch, ix, 1924.

## 7. Lancashire

Henry Fishwich, ed., *A List of the Lancashire Wills Proved within the Archdeaconry of Richmond . . . 1457 to 1680*, Record Society of Lancashire and Cheshire, x, 1884.

## 8. Lincoln

C. W. Foster, ed., *Lincoln Wills, 1271–1526*, i, Lincoln Record Society, 5, 1914.

## 9. London

Consistory, Commissary and Archdeaconry Court wills in the Guildhall Library, London.

Ida Darlington, ed., *London Consistory Court Wills, 1492–1547* (London: London Record Society, 1967).

Marc Fitch, ed., *Index to the Testamentary Records in the Commissary Court of London, 1378–1570*, 2 vols. (London: HMSO, 1969–1974).

——, *Testamentary Records in the Archdeaconry of London, 1363–1649*, i (London: British Record Society, 1979).

Edward Alexander Fry, ed., *A Collection of Wills in the Great Orphan Books, 1379–1674* (London: British Record Society, 1897).

R. R. Sharpe, ed., *Calendar of Wills Proved and Enrolled in the Court of Hustings, London, 1258–1688*, 2 vols. (London: J. Francis, 1889–1890).

*Index to the Archdeaconry Court of London*, 3 vols., London Guildhall Library Ms. 9054.

10. NORWICH AND NORFOLK

Consistory, Archdeaconry of Norwich, Archdeaconry of Norfolk, City Court of Norwich wills in the Norwich and Norfolk Record Office, Norwich.

M. A. Farrow, *An Index of Wills Proved at Norwich, 1370–1500*, Norfolk Record Society, xvi, 1942–1945.

Patrick Palgrave-More, "Index of Wills Proved in the Norfolk Archdeaconry Court, 1453–1542," *Norfolk Genealogy*, 3, 1971

11. SOMERSET

F. W. Wilson, ed., *Somerset Medieval Wills, 1383–1530*, 2 vols., Somerset Record Society, 1901–1903.

12. SUFFOLK

T. W. Oswald-Hicks, *A Calendar of Wills . . . of Suffolk Proved in the Prerogative Court of Canterbury* (London: Privately Printed, 1913).

W. R. and R. K. Serjeant, eds., *Index of the Probate Records of the Archdeaconry Court . . . of Suffolk*, 2 vols. (London: British Record Society, 1979–1980).

13. SURREY

*Surrey Wills, Archdeaconry Court, 1484–89*, Surrey Record Society, v, 1921.

14. SUSSEX

R. Garraway Rice, ed. *Transcripts of Sussex Wills*, Sussex Record Society, 51–53, 64, 1935–1937, 1941.

15. WESTMINSTER

A. M. Burke, ed. *Indexes to the Ancient Testamentary Records of Westminster* (London: Eyre and Spottiswode, 1913).

16. YORK

J. W. Clay, *North Country Wills, being Abstracts of . . . York, Nottingham, Northumberland, Cumberland and Westmoreland, 1383–1558*, Surtees Society, i, 1908.

*Index of Wills in the York Registry, 1389–1514*, Yorkshire Archeological and Topographical Association Record Series, vi, 1888.

*Index of Wills and Administrations Entered in the Registers of the Archbishop of York Being Consistory Wills, 1316–1822*, 2 vols., Yorkshire Archeological Society Record Series, 93, 1936.

*Index of Wills in the York Registry, 1514 to 1553*, Yorkshire Archeological and Topographical Association Record Series, xi, 1891.

*Index of the Original Documents of the Consistory Court of York, 1427 to 1658*, Yorkshire Archeological Society, Record Series, 73, 1928.

## Secondary Sources

Edwin H. Ackerknecht, *A Short History of Medicine*, 2nd ed. (Baltimore: Johns Hopkins University Press, 1982).

Thomas Clifford Allbutt, *Greek Medicine in Rome* (New York: B. Blom, 1900).

—— *Historical Relations of Medicine and Surgery to the End of the Sixteenth Century* (London: Macmillan, 1905).

John Alford, "Medicine in the Middle Ages: The Theory of a Profession," *Centennial Review*, 23, 1979, pp. 377–396.

C. T. Allmand, "The Civil Lawyers," in Cecil Clough, ed., *Profession, Vocation and Culture in Late Medieval England: Essays Dedicated to the Memory of A. R. Myers* (Liverpool: Liverpool University Press, 1982), pp. 155–171.

Mary N. Alston, "The Attitude of the Church Towards Dissection Before 1500," *BHM*, 16, 1944–1945, pp. 221–238.

Darrel W. Amundsen, "Medieval Canon Law on Medicine and Surgical Practice by the Clergy," *BHM*, 52, 1978, pp. 22–44.

—— "Medical Deontology and Pestilential Disease in the Late Middle Ages," *JHM*, 23, 1977, pp. 403–421.

Hedley Atkins, *The Surgeon's Craft* (Manchester: Manchester University Press, 1965).

C. A. Auden, "The Gild of Barber-Surgeons of the City of York," *Proceedings of the Royal Society of Medicine*, 31, 1927, pp. 70–76.

D. C. Bain, "A Note on an English Manuscript Receipt Book," *BHM*, 8, 1940, pp. 1,246–1,248.

Francis Pierrepont Barnard, *Edward IV's French Expedition of 1475: The Leaders and Their Badges* (Dursley: Gloucester Reprints, 1975).

Margaret C. Barnet, "The Barber-Surgeons of York," *MH*, 12, 1968, pp. 19–30.

C.R.B. Barrett, *History of the Society of Apothecaries* (London: Elliot Stock, 1905).

Guy Beaujouan, Yvonne Poulle-Drieux and Jeanne-Marie Dureau-Lapeyssonnie, *Médecine humaine et vétérinaire à la fin du moyen âge* (Geneva: Droz, 1966).

R. Theodore Beck, *The Cutting Edge: Early History of the Surgeons of London* (London: Lund Humphries, 1974).

—— "The Halls of the Barbers, Barber-Surgeons and the Company of Surgeons," *Annals of the Royal College of Surgeons*, 49, 1970, pp. 14–29.

H. S. Bennett, *English Books and Readers, 1475–1555*, 2nd ed. (Cambridge: Cambridge University Press, 1970).

J-N. Biraben, *Les hommes et la peste*, 2 vols. (The Hague: Mouton, 1975).

William J. Bishop, *The Early History of Surgery* (London: Robert Hale, 1960).

J. H. Bloom and R. R. James, *Medical Practitioners in the Diocese of London, 1529–1725* (Cambridge: Cambridge University Press, 1935).

William Bonsor, *The Medical Background of Anglo-Saxon England* (London: Wellcome Historical Medical Library, 1963).

J. Bromley and H. Child, *The Armorial Bearing of the Guilds of London* (London: Frederick Warne, 1961).

Laurel Braswell, "Utilitarian and Scientific Prose," in A.S.G. Edwards, *Middle English Prose: A Critical Guide to Major Authors and Genres* (New Brunswick, N.J.: Rutgers University Press, 1984), pp. 337–387.

Vern L. Bullough, *The Development of Medicine as a Profession* (New York: Hafner, 1966).

—— "Achievement, Professionalization and the University," in Jozef Ijsewijn and Jacques Pacquet, eds., *Universities in the Late Middle Ages* (Louvain: Louvain University Press, 1978), pp. 213–227.

—— "The Development of the Medical School at the University of Montpellier to the End of the Fourteenth Century," *BHM*, 30, 1956, pp. 508–523.

—— "Duke Humphrey and His Medical Collections," *Renaissance News*, 14, 1961, pp. 87–91.

—— "A Fifteenth Century Prescription," *JHM*, 16, 1961, pp. 421–422.

—— "Medical Study at Mediaeval Oxford," *Speculum*, 36, 1961, pp. 600–612.

—— "Mediaeval Bologna and the Development of Medical Education," *BHM*, 32, 1958, pp. 201–215.

—— "The Mediaeval Medical School at Cambridge," *Mediaeval Studies*, 24, 1962, pp. 161–168.

—— "The Mediaeval Medical University at Paris," *BHM*, 31, 1957, pp. 197–211.

—— "A Note on Medical Care in Mediaeval English Hospitals," *BHM*, 35, 1961, pp. 74–77.

—— "Population and the Study and Practice of Mediaeval Medicine," *BHM*, 36, 1962, pp. 62–69.

—— "The Teaching of Surgery at the University of Montpellier in the Thirteenth Century," *JHM*, 15, 1960, pp. 202–204.

—— "The Term 'Doctor,' " *JHM*, 18, 1963, pp. 284–287.

—— "The Training of Nonuniversity Educated Medical Practitioners in the Late Middle Ages," *JHM*, 14, 1959, pp. 446–458.

MacFarlane Burnet and David O. White, *Natural History of Infectious Disease* (Cambridge: Cambridge University Press, 1972).

Sona Rosa Burstein, "The Care of the Aged in England from Medieval Times," *BHM*, 22, 1948, pp. 738–746.

Jerome J. Bylebyl, "The School of Padua: Humanistic Medicine in the Sixteenth Century," in Charles Webster, ed., *Health, Medicine and Mortality in the Sixteenth Century*, (Cambridge: Cambridge University Press, 1979), pp. 335–370.

Anna Montgomery Campbell, *The Black Death and Men of Learning* (New York: Columbia University Press, 1931).

A. M. Carr-Saunders and P. A. Wilson, *The Professions* (Oxford: Clarendon Press, 1933).

Sir John Charles, "Roger Bacon and the Errors of Physicians," *MH*, 4, 1960, pp. 269–282.

Carlo M. Cipolla, *Public Health and the Medical Profession in the Renaissance* (Cambridge: Cambridge University Press, 1976).

—— "The Professions," *Journal of European Economic History*, 2, 1972, pp. 37–52.

Sir George N. Clark, *A History of the Royal College of Physicians*, 3 vols. (Oxford: Oxford University Press, 1964–1966).

Edwin Clarke, *Modern Methods in the History of Medicine* (London: Athlone Press, 1971).

Rotha Mary Clay, *The Mediaeval Hospitals of England*, 2nd ed. (London: Frank Cass, 1965).

Cecil Clough, ed., *Profession, Vocation and Culture in Late Medieval England: Essays Dedicated to the Memory of A. R. Myers* (Liverpool: Liverpool University Press, 1982).

A. B. Cobban, *The Medieval Universities: Their Development and Organization* (London, 1975).

Sir Zachery Cope, "The Treatment of Wounds Through the Ages," *MH*, 2, 1958, pp. 163–170..

W.S.C. Copeman, *Doctors and Disease in Tudor Times* (London: Oldbourne, 1960).

George W. Corner, "Salernitan Surgery in the Twelfth Century," *British Journal of Surgery*, 25, 1937, pp. 84–99.

Madelaine Pelsner Cosman, "Medieval Malpractice: The Dicta and the Dockets," *Bulletin of the New York Academy of Medicine*, 2nd series, 49, 1973, pp. 22–47.

G. C. Cruickshank, *Army Royal: Henry VIII's Invasion of France, 1513* (Oxford: Oxford University Press, 1969).

John Cule, "The Court Mediciner and Medicine in the Laws of Wales," *JHM*, 21, 1966, pp. 213–236.

Walter Clyde Curry, "Chaucer's Doctor of Physick," in his *Chaucer and the Medieval Sciences*, 2nd ed. (New York: Barnes and Noble, 1960), pp. 3–36.

Allen G. Debus, *The English Paracelsians* (London: Oldbourne, 1965).

—— *Man and Nature in the Renaissance* (Cambridge: Cambridge University Press, 1978).

Luke F. Demaitre, *Doctor Bernard de Gordon: Professor and Practitioner* (Toronto: Pontifical Institute of Mediaeval Studies, 1980).

—— "Nature and the Art of Medicine in the Middle Ages," *Mediaevalia*, 2, 1976, pp. 23–47.

Luke F. Demaitre, "Scholasticism in Compendia Written by University Teachers," *Manuscripta*, 10, 1976, pp. 81–95.

—— "Theory and Practice in Medical Education at the University of Montpellier in the Thirteenth and Fourteenth Centuries," *JHM*, 30, 1975, pp. 103–123.

D. DeMoulin, "Cutting for the Stone in the Early Middle Ages," *BHM*, 45, 1971, pp. 383–386.

Stephan D'Irsay, "Teachers and Textbooks of Medicine in the Medieval University of Paris," *Annals of Medical History*, 8, 1926, pp. 220–230.

Jessie Dobson and R. Milnes Walker, *Barbers and Barber-Surgeons of London* (Oxford: Basil Blackwell, 1979).

Rene Dubos, *Man, Medicine and Environment* (New York: Praeger, 1969).

Louis Dulieu, *La chirurgie à Montpellier de ses origines au début du xixᵉ siècle* (Avignon: Les Presses Universelles, 1975).

D. M. Dunlap, "Arabic Medicine in England," *JHM*, 11, 1956, pp. 166–182.

Richard J. Durling, "Linacre and Medical Humanism," in Francis Maddison, Margaret Pelling, and Charles Webster, eds., *Linacre Studies: Essays on the Life and Works of Thomas Linacre, c. 1460–1524* (Oxford: Clarendon Press, 1977), pp. 76–106.

Elizabeth Eisenstein, *The Printing Press as an Agent of Change* (Cambridge: Cambridge University Press, 1979).

Stephen R. Ell, "Barbers, Barber-Surgeons," *Dictionary of the Middle Ages*, vol. ii, ed. Joseph R. Strayer (New York: Charles Scribner's Sons, 1983), pp. 97–101.

Philip Elliott, *The Sociology of the Professions* (London: Macmillan, 1972).

Charles Ermatinger, "Averroism in Early Fourteenth Century Bologna," *Mediaeval Studies*, 16, 1954, pp. 16–36.

William S. Fitzgerald, "Medical Men: Canonized Saints," *BHM*, 22, 1948, pp. 635–646.

Percy Flemming, "The Medical Aspects of the Medieval Monastery in England," *Proceedings of the Royal Society of Medicine*, 22, 1928–1929, pp. 771–782.

John M. Fletcher, "Linacre's Lands and Lectureships," in Maddison, *Linacre Studies*, pp. 107–197.

Thomas Forbes, "Barber-Surgeons Help the Sick Poor," *JHM*, 31, 1976.

—— "By What Disease or Casualty: The Changing Face of Death in London," *JHM*, 22, 1976.

Robert Forster and Orest Ranum, eds., *Biology of Man in History* (Baltimore: Johns Hopkins University Press, 1975).

George E. Gask, "Historical Sketch of the Methods of Treating Wounds of the Chest in War From AD 1300 to 1900," in *Essays in the History of Medicine* (London: Butterworth, 1950), pp. 145–156.

—— "The Medical Services of Henry the Fifth's Campaign of the Somme in 1415," in *Essays in the History of Medicine*, pp. 94–102.

—— "The Medical Staff of King Edward the Third," in *Essays in the History of Medicine*, pp. 77–93.

—— "Vicary's Predecessors," in *Essays in the History of Medicine*, pp. 56–76.

Benjamin Lee Gordon, *Medieval and Renaissance Medicine* (New York: Philosophical Library, 1959).

Robert S. Gottfried, *The Black Death* (New York: The Free Press, 1983).

—— *Epidemic Disease in Fifteenth Century England: The Medical Response and the Demographic Consequences* (New Brunswick, N.J.: Rutgers University Press, 1978).

—— "English Medical Practitioners, 1340–1530," *BHM*, 58, 1984, pp. 164–182.

—— "Plague, Population and the Sweating Sickness: Population Movements in Late Fifteenth Century England," *Journal of British Studies*, Fall, 1976, pp. 12–37.

H. L. Gray, "Incomes from Land in England," *English Historical Review*, 49, 1934, pp. 607–639.

Edward Lee Greene, *Landmarks of Botanical History* (Palo Alto, Calif.: Stanford University Press, 1983).

George Griffenhagen, "Tools of the Apothecary," *Journal of the American Pharmaceutical Association*, 17, 1956, pp. 810–813.

Robert T. Gunther, *Early Science at Oxford*, 14 vols. (Oxford: Clarendon Press, 1925–1945).

E. A. Hammond, "Incomes of Medieval English Doctors," *JHM*, 15, 1960, pp. 154–169.

—— "Physicians in Mediaeval English Religious Houses," *BHM*, 32, 958, pp. 105–120.

—— "The Westminster Abbey Infirmarers' Rolls as a Source of Medical History," *BHM*, 39, 1965, pp. 261–276.

Marta Powell Harley, "The Middle English Contents of a Fifteenth Century Physician's Handbook," *Mediaevalia*, forthcoming.

John H. Harvey, "Mediaeval Plantsmanship in England: The Culture of Rosemary," *Garden History*, 1, 1972, pp. 14–21.

Charles Haskins, *The Ancient Trade Guilds and Companies of Salisbury* (Salisbury: Barnet Brothers, 1912).

Jozef Ijsewijn and Jacques Pacquet, eds., *Universities in the Late Middle Ages* (Louvain: Louvain University Press, 1978).

Eric W. Ives, *The Common Lawyers of Pre-Reformation England: Thomas Kebell, A Case Study* (Cambridge: Cambridge University Press, 1983).

—— "The Common Lawyer," in Clough, ed., *Profession, Vocation and Culture*, pp. 181–208.

Danielle Jacquart, *Le milieu médical en France du xxii<sup>e</sup> au xv<sup>e</sup> siècle* (Geneva: Droz, 1981).

R. R. James, "The Earliest List of Surgeons to be Licensed," *Janus*, 40, 1937, pp. 255–260.

—— "Licenses to Practice Medicine and Surgery Issued by the Archbishops of Canterbury, 1580–1775," *Janus*, 41, 1937, pp. 97–106.

Ida B. Jones, "Popular Medical Knowledge in Fourteenth Century English Literature," *BHM*, 5, 1937, pp. 405–451.

W.H.S. Jones, *Philosophy and Medicine in Ancient Greece* (Baltimore: Johns Hopkins University Press, 1946).

Edward J. Kealey, *Medieval Medicus: A Social History of Anglo-Norman Medicine* (Baltimore: Johns Hopkins University Press, 1981).

J. J. Keevil, *Medicine and the Navy, 1200–1649*, vol. i (Edinburgh: E. S. Livingstone, 1957).

Neil R. Ker, "Oxford College Libraries before 1500," in Ijsewijn and Pacquet, eds., *Universities in the Late Middle Ages*, pp. 294–311.

Pearl Kibre, *Scholarly Privileges in the Middle Ages* (Cambridge, Mass.: Medieval Academy of America, 1962).

—— "Arts and Medicine in the Universities of the Later Middle Ages," in Ijsewijn and Pacquet, eds., *Universities in the Late Middle Ages*.

—— "The Faculty of Medicine at Paris, Charlatanism and Unlicensed Medical Practice in the Later Middle Ages," *BHM*, 27, 1953, pp. 1–20.

—— "Cristoforo Barzizza, Professor of Medicine at Padua," *BHM*, 2, 1942, pp. 387–398.

—— "Dominicus De Ragusa: Bolognese Doctor of Arts and Medicine," *BHM*, 45, 1971, pp. 383–386.

—— "Hippocratic Writings in the Middle Ages," *BHM*, 18, 1945, pp. 371–412.

—— "Lewis of Caerleon, Doctor of Medicine, Astronomer and Mathematician," *Isis*, 43, 1952, pp. 100–108.

—— and Nancy G. Siraisi, "The Institutional Setting," in Lindberg, *Science in the Middle Ages*, pp. 120–144.

Lester S. King, *Medical Thinking* (Princeton: Princeton University Press, 1982).

—— *The Road to Medical Enlightenment* (London: 1975).

—— "Plato's Concept of Medicine," *JHM*, 9, 954, pp. 38–48.

Paul Oskar Kristeller, "Philosophy and Medicine in Medieval and Renaissance Italy," in S. F. Spicker, ed., *Organism, Medicine and Metaphysics* (Boston: D. Reidel, 1978), pp. 29–40.

—— "The School at Salerno: Its Development and Its Contribution to the History of Learning," in his *Studies in Renaissance Thought and Letters* (Rome: Edizioni di storia e letteratura, 1969).

George Lambert, "Barber-Surgeons," *Transactions of the London and Middlesex Archeaological Society*, 6, 1890, pp. 123–189.

Brian Lawn, *The Salernitan Questions* (Oxford: Clarendon Press, 1963).

Gordon Leff, *Paris and Oxford Universities in the Thirteenth and Fourteenth Centuries* (New York: John Wiley, 1967).

Jacques LeGoff, "Licet and Illicet Trades in the Medieval West," in his *Time, Work and Culture in the Middle Ages*, trans. Arthur Goldhammer (Chicago: University of Chicago Press, 1980), pp. 58–70.

Reuben Levy, "Avicenna—His Life and Times," *MH*, 1, 1957, pp. 249–261.

R. G. Lewis, "The Linacre Lectureships Subsequent to their Foundation," in Maddison, *Linacre Studies*, pp. 223–264.

David Lindberg, ed., *Science in the Middle Ages* (Chicago: University of Chicago Press, 1978).

Cameron Louis, *The Commonplace Book of Robert Reyes of Acle: An Edition of Tanner Ms. 407* (New York: Garland Press, 1980).

Francis Maddison, Margaret Pelling, and Charles Webster, eds., *Linacre Studies: Essays on the Life and Work of Thomas Linacre* (Oxford: Clarendon Press, 1977).

Leslie G. Matthews, *History of Pharmacy in Britain* (Edinburgh: E.&S. Livingstone, 1962).

—— *The Royal Apothecaries* (London: Wellcome Historical Medical Library, 1967).

—— "King John of France and the English Spicers," *MH*, 5, 1961, pp. 65–76.

—— "Royal Apothecaries of the Tudor Period," *MH*, 8, 1964, pp. 170–180.

—— "Ss. Cosmas and Damian—Patron Saints of Medicine and Pharmacy: Their Cult in England," *MH*, 12, 1968, pp. 281–288.

—— "Spicers and Apothecaries in the City of Canterbury," *MH*, 9, 1965, pp. 289–291.

—— "The Spicer and Apothecaries of Norwich," *Pharmaceutical Journal*, 198, 1967, pp. 5–9.

Charles F. Mayer, "A Medical Leechbook and Its Fourteenth Century Poem on Bloodletting," *BHM*, 7, 1939, pp. 381–389.

Max Meyerhof, *Studies in Medieval Arabic Medicine; Theory and Practice*, ed. Penelope Johnstone (London: Variorum, 1983).

Rosamund J. Mitchell, *John Free: From Bristol to Rome in the Fifteenth Century* (London: Longmans, Green and Co., 1955).

—— "English Students at Padua, 1460–1475," *Transactions of the Royal Historical Society*, 4th series, 19, 1936, pp. 101–117.

—— "Thomas Linacre in Italy," *English Historical Review*, 50, 1935, pp. 696–698.

Charles F. Mullet, "John Lydgate: A Mirror of Medieval Medicine," *BHM*, 22, 1948, pp. 403–415.

—— "Public Baths and Health in England, Sixteenth to Eighteenth Centuries," *BHM*, Supplement 5, 1946.

James K. Mustain, "A Rural Medical Practitioner in Fifteenth Century England," *BHM*, 46, 1972, pp. 469–476.

Antonia McLean, *Humanism and the Rise of Science in Tudor England* (New York: Neale Watson, 1972).

R.M.S. McConaghey, "History of Rural Medical Practice," in F.N.L. Poynter, *The Evolution of Medical Practice in England* (London: Pitman Medical Publishing Co., 1961), pp. 117–143.

—— "Medical Practitioners of Dartmouth, 1425–1887," *MH*, 4, 1960, pp. 91–111.

Thomas McKeown, *The Role of Medicine* (Princeton: Princeton University Press, 1979).

—— "A Sociological Approach to the History of Medicine," *MH*, 14, 1970, pp. 342–351.

Loren Mackinney, *Early Medieval Medicine* (Baltimore: Johns Hopkins University Press, 1937).

—— *Medical Illustrations in Medieval Manuscripts* (London: Historical Medical Library, 1965).

—— "Medical Education in the Middle Ages," *Journal of World History*, 13, 1956, pp. 1–13.

—— "Medieval Surgery," *Journal of the International College of Surgeons*, 27, 1957, pp. 393–404.

William H. McNeill, *The Human Condition: An Ecological and Historical View* (Princeton: Princeton University Press, 1980).

Michael McVaugh, "An Early Discussion of Medical Degrees at Montpellier by Henry of Winchester," *BHM*, 49, 1975, pp. 57–71.

—— "Quantified Medical Theory and Practice at Fourteenth Century Montpellier," *BHM*, 43, 1969, pp. 397–413.

Max Neuberger, *History of Medicine*, trans. E. R. Playfair, 2 vols. (Oxford: Oxford University Press, 1925).

Robert E. Nichols, Jr., "Medical Lore from Sidrak and Bokkus: A Miscellany in Middle English Verse," *JHM*, 23, 1968, pp. 167–172.

Vivian Nutton, "Velia and the School of Salerno," *MH*, 15, 1971, pp. 1–11.

Margaret S. Ogdan, "Galenic Works Cited in Guy de Chauliac's *Chirurgia Magna*," *JHM*, 28, 1973, pp. 24–33.

—— "Guy de Chauliac's Theory of the Humors," *JHM*, 24, 1969, pp. 272–291.

Nicholas Orme, *English Schools in the Middle Ages* (London: Methuen, 1973).

—— "Schoolmasters," in Clough, ed., *Profession, Vocation and Culture*, pp. 218–241.

Charles D. O'Malley, *English Medical Humanists* (Lawrence, Kans.: University of Kansas Press, 1965).

—— *The History of Medical Education* (Berkeley, Calif.: University of California Press, 1970).

—— "The Lure of Padua," *MH*, 14, 1970, pp. 1–9.

Janis L. Pallister, "Fifteenth Century Surgery in France: Contributions to Language and Literature," *Fifteenth Century Studies*, 3, 1980, pp. 147–153.

Katherine Park, *Doctors and Medicine in Early Renaissance Florence* (Princeton: Princeton University Press, 1985).

George Parker, *The Early History of Surgery in Great Britain* (London: A. C. Black, 1920).

—— "Early Bristol Medical Institutions, The Medieval Hospitals and the Barber-Surgeons," *Transactions of the Bristol and Gloucestershire Archaeological Society*, 44, 1922, pp. 155–177.

J. F. Payne, *English Medicine in Anglo-Saxon Times* (Oxford: Clarendon Press, 1904).

—— "On an Unpublished Anatomical Treatise of the Fourteenth Century; and Its Relation to the Anatomy of Thomas Vicary," *British Medical Journal*, 25, 1896, pp. 200–203.

Margaret Pelling, "Occupational Diversity: Barbitonsors and the Trades of Norwich," *BHM*, 56, 1982, pp. 484–511.

—— "A Survey of East Anglian Medical Practitioners, 1500–1640," *Local Population Studies*, 25, 1980, pp. 54–65.

—— and Charles Webster, "Medical Practitioners," in Webster, ed., *Health, Medicine, Mortality*, pp. 165–235.

T. F. Pettigrew, "History of the Barber-Surgeons of London," *Journal of the British Archaeological Association*, 8, 1853, pp. 95–130.

E. D. Phillips, *Greek Medicine* (London: Thames and Hudson, 1973).

Lucille B. Pinto, "The Folk Practice of Gynaecology and Obstetrics in the Middle Ages," *BHM*, 48, 1973, pp. 513–523.

Sir D'Arcy Power, *Selected Writings, 1877–1930* (New York: Augustus M. Kelley, 1970).

—— "The Place of Tudor Surgeons in English Literature," *Proceedings of the Royal Society of Medicine*, 20, 1927–1930, pp. 51–60.

—— and John Flint South, *Memorials of the Craft of Surgery* (London: Cassells, 1886).

Eileen Power, "Some Women Practitioners of Medicine in the Middle Ages," *Proceedings of the Royal Society of Medicine*, 15, 1928, pp. 159–172.

F. M. Powicke, *The Medieval Books of Merton College* (Oxford: Clarendon Press, 1931).

F.N.L. Poynter, "The Influence of Government Legislation in Britain," in Poynter, *The Evolution of Medical Practice in London* (London: Pitman Medical Publishing Company, 1961).

—— ed., *The Evolution of Medical Education in Britain* (London: Pitman Medical Publishing Co., 1966).

Dorothy MacKay Quynn, "A Medical Picture of the Hotel-Dieu of Paris," *BHM*, 12, 1942, pp. 118–128.

Hastings Rashdall, *The Universities of Europe in the Middle Ages*, 3 vols., F. M. Powicke and A. V. Emden, eds. (Oxford: Oxford University Press, 1936).

Caroline Rawcliffe, "Medicine and Medical Practice in Later Medieval London," *Guildhall Studies in London History*, 5, 1981, pp. 13–25.

Dennis E. Rhodes, "The Princes in the Tower and Their Doctor," *English Historical Review*, 76, 1961, pp. 304–306.

—— "Provost Argentein of King's and His Books," *Transactions of the Cambridge Bibliographic Society*, 2, 1956, pp. 205–212.

Henry G. Richardson, "The Early History of the Commissions of the Sewer," *English Historical Review*, 34, 1919, pp. 385–393.

John M. Riddle, "Theory and Practice in Medieval Medicine," *Viator*, 5, 1974, pp. 157–184.

David Riesman, *The Story of Medicine in the Middle Ages* (New York: Hoeber, 1935).

A.H.T. Robb-Smith, "Medical Education at Oxford and Cambridge Prior to 1850," in Poynter, *Evolution of Medical Education*.

R. S. Roberts, "Personnel and the Practice of Medicine in Tudor and Stuart England," i, *MH*, 4, 1962, pp. 363–382.

—— "Personnel and the Practice of Medicine in Tudor and Stuart England," ii *MH*, 7, 1964, pp. 217–234.

Rossell Hope Robbins, "John Crophill's Ale-Pots," *Review of English Studies*, 20, 1969, pp. 182–189.

—— "Medical Manuscripts in Middle English," *Speculum*, 45, 1970, pp. 393–415.

—— "A Note on the Singer Survey of Medical Manuscripts in the British Isles," *Chaucer Review*, 4, 1970, pp. 66–70.

—— "The Physician's Authorities," in Mieczyslaw Brahmer. ed., *Studies in Language and Literature in Honour of Margaret Schlauch* (Warsaw: PWN, 1966), pp. 335–341.

Sir Humphrey D. Rolleston, *The Cambridge Medical School* (Cambridge: Cambridge University Press, 1932).

—— "History of Medicine in the City of London," *Annals of Medical History*, 3rd series, 3, 1941, pp. 1–17.

—— "Medical Aphorisms, Chiefly in English," *BHM*, 10, 1941, pp. 544–566.

Fred Rosner, "Maimonides the Physician: A Bibliography," *BHM*, 43, 1969, pp. 221–235.

Cecil Roth, "Jewish Physicians in Medieval England," *Medieval Leaves*, 5, 1943.

Stanley Rubin, *Medieval English Medicine* (New York: Barnes and Noble, 1974).

Guido Ruggiero, "Status of Physicians and Surgeons in Renaissance Venice," *JHM*, 36, 1981, pp. 168–184.

Josiah Cox Russell, "Medical Writers of Thirteenth Century England," *Annals of Medical History*, N.S., 7, 1935, pp. 327–340.

Eric Sanguine, "Private Libraries of Tudor Doctors," *JHM*, 23, 1978, pp. 167–184.

John Scarborough, *Roman Medicine* (London: Thames and Hudson, 1968).

William D. Sharpe, "Thomas Linacre, 1460–1524," *BHM*, 34, 1940, pp. 233–256.

C. J. Shoppee, *Description of Pictures and Other Objects in the Hall and Court Room of the Worshipful Company of Barbers . . . of . . . the City of London* (London: G. Barber, 1883).

R. E. Siegel, *Galen's System of Physiology and Medicine* (Basel: S. Karger, 1968).

Henry Sigerist, *On the History of Medicine* (New York: M.D. Publications, 1960).

—— "Bedside Manners in the Middle Ages: *De Cautelis Medicorum* attributed to Arnald of Villanova," *Quarterly Bulletin of the Northwestern University Medical School*, 20, 1946, pp. 136–143.

—— "A Doctor's Family in the Fifteenth Century," *BHM*, 3, 1935, pp. 159–162.

Charles Singer, *The Evolution of Anatomy* (London: Kegan Paul, 1925).

—— *A Short History of Anatomy and Physiology* (New York: Dover, 1957).

Dorothy W. Singer, "Survey of Medical Manuscripts in the British Isles Dating Before the Sixteenth Century," *Proceedings of the Royal Society of Medicine*, 12, 1918–1919, pp. 96–107.

Nancy G. Siraisi, *Arts and Sciences at Padua: The Studium of Padua Before 1350* (Toronto: Pontifical Institute of Mediaeval Studies, 1973).

—— *Taddeo Alderotti and His Pupils* (Princeton: Princeton University Press, 1981).

—— "The Medical Learning of Albertus Magnus," in James A. Weisheipl, *Albertus Magnus and the Sciences* (Toronto: Pontifical Institute for Mediaeval Studies, 1980), pp. 379–404.

—— "Some Recent Work on Western European Medical Learning, ca. 1200–ca. 1500," *History of Universities*, 2, 1982, pp. 225–238.

Paul Slack, "Mirrors of Health and the Treasures of Poor Men: The Uses of the Vernacular Medical Literature of Tudor England," in Webster, ed., *Health, Medicine and Mortality*, pp. 238–273.

Charles B. Schmitt, "Thomas Linacre in Italy," in Maddison, *Linacre Studies*, pp. 36–75.

Susan Mosher Stuard, "A Common Program of Medical Care: Medieval Ragusa/Dubrovnik," *JHM*, 28, 1973, pp. 126–142.

Ernest W. Talbert, "The Notebook of a Fifteenth Century Practicing Physician," *Texas Studies in English*, 21, 1942, pp. 5–30.

Charles H. Talbot, *Medicine in Medieval England* (London: Oldbourne, 1967).

—— "Medicine," in Lindberg, ed., *Science in the Middle Ages*, pp. 391–428.

Charles H. Talbot, "A Medieval Physician's *Vade Mecum*," *JHM*, 16, 1961, pp. 213–233.

—— "Simon Bredon (c.1300–1372), Physician, Mathematician and Astronomer," *British Journal for the History of Science*, 1, 1962–1963, pp. 19–30.

—— and E. A. Hammond, *Medical Practitioners in Medieval England* (London: Wellcome Historical Medical Library, 1965).

Ian Tattersall, "Dental Paleopathology of Medieval Britain," *JHM*, 23, 1968, pp. 380–385.

F. Taylor, "Medieval Scientific Instruments," *Discovery*, 1950.

Owsei Tempkin, *Galenism* (Ithaca, N.Y.: Cornell University Press, 1973).

A. Hamilton Thompson, *Newark Hospitals and Colleges* (Leicester: E. Backus, 1937).

C.J.S. Thompson, "The Apothecary in England from the Thirteenth to the Close of the Sixteenth Century," *Proceedings of the Royal Society of Medicine*, 8, 1915, pp. 36–44.

James Westfall Thompson, *The Literacy of the Laity in the Middle Ages* (Berkeley, Calif.: University of California Press, 1936).

Henry Reynold Thompson, "Serjeant Surgeons to Their Majesties," *Annals of the Royal College of Surgeons*, 26, 1960, pp. 1–23.

Lynn Thorndike, *A History of Magic and Experimental Science: The Fourteenth and Fifteenth Centuries*, vols. 3 and 4 (New York: Columbia University Press, 1934).

—— "Fifteenth Century Patients," *BHM*, 28, 1954, pp. 252–258.

—— "Notes on Medical Texts in Manuscripts at London and Oxford," *Janus*, 48, 1959, pp. 141–202.

—— "When Medicine Was in Flower," *BHM*, 33, 1959, pp. 110–115.

—— and Pearl Kibre, *A Catalogue of Incipits of Medieval Medical and Scientific Writings in Latin* (Cambridge: Harvard University Press, 1937).

Sylvia L. Thrupp, *The Merchant Class of Medieval London, 1300–1500* (Ann Arbor, Mich.: University of Michigan Press, 1962).

—— "The Grocers of London: A Study of the Distributive Trade," in Michael M. Postan and Eillen Power, eds., *Studies in English Trade in the Fifteenth Century* (London: Methuen, 1933), pp. 247–292.

Geoffrey E. Trease, *Pharmacy in History* (London: Bailliere, Tindall and Cox, 1964).

—— "The Spicers and Apothecaries of the Royal Household in the Reigns of Henry III, Edward I, and Edward II," *Nottingham Medieval Studies*, 3, 1959, pp. 19–52.

—— and J. H. Hudson, "The Inventory of John Hexham, A Fifteenth Century Apothecary," *MH*, 9, 1965, pp. 76–81.

Edward F. Tuttle, "The Trotula and Old Dame Trot: A Note on the Lady of Salerno," *BHM*, 50, 1976, pp. 61–72.

E. A. Underwood, ed., *A History of the Worshipful Society of Apothecaries of London* (London: Wellcome Historical Medical Library, 1963).

George Unwin, *The Gilds and Companies of London*, 4th ed. (London: Frank Cass, 1963).

Huling E. Ussery, *Chaucer's Physician: Medicine and Literature in Fourteenth Century England* (New Orleans: Tulane University Press, 1971).

Linda Ehrsam Voights, "Editing Middle English Medical Texts: Needs and Issues," in Levore, *Editing Texts*, pp. 39–68.

—— "Medical Prose," in Edwards, *Middle English Prose*, pp. 315–335.

R. Milnes Walker, "The Barber-Surgeons of Bristol," *Bristol Medico-Chirurgical Journal*, 90, 1975, pp. 51–53.

J. J. Walsh, *Medieval Medicine* (London: A. C. Black, 1920).

Scott Warthin, *The Physician of the Dance of Death* (New York: Arno Press, 1977).

William Wartman, *Medical Teaching in Western Civilization* (Chicago: Yearbook Medical Publishing Company, 1961).

Charles Webster, "Thomas Linacre and the Foundation of the College of Physicians," in Maddison, *Linacre Studies*, pp. 198–222.

—— ed., *Health, Medicine and Mortality in the Sixteenth Century* (Cambridge: Cambridge University Press, 1979).

James A. Weisheipl, "Curriculum of the Faculty of Arts at Oxford in the Early Fourteenth Century," *Mediaeval Studies*, 26, 1964, pp. 143–181.

T. D. Whittet, "The Apothecary in Provincial Gilds," *MH*, 8, 1964, pp. 245–273.

Charles Williams, *Masters, Wardens and Assistants of the Gild of the Barber-Surgeons of Norwich* (Norwich: Jarrold, 1900).

—— "The Ordinances of the Guild of Barber-Surgeons of Norwich," *The Antiquary*, 36, 1900, pp. 293–295.

C. E. Winslow and M. L. Duran-Reynolds, "Jacme d'Argremont and the First Plague Treatises," *BHM*, 22, 1948, pp. 474–765.

Charles T. Wood, "The Doctor's Dilemma: Sin, Salvation and the Menstrual Cycle in Medieval Thought," *Speculum*, 56, 1981, pp. 710–727.

LIBRARY OF CONGRESS CATALOGING-IN-PUBLICATION DATA

Gottfried, Robert Steven, 1949–
Doctors and medicine in medieval England, 1340–1530.

Bibliography: p.
Includes index.
1. Medicine, Medieval—England—History.
2. England—History.—Medieval period, 1066–1485. 3. England—
History—16th century. I. Title. [DNLM: 1. History of Medicine,
Medieval—England. 2. Military Medicine—history—
England. 3. Physicians—England. 4. Surgery—
history—England. WZ 70 FE5 G6d]
R141.G67  1986   610'.942   86–8135
ISBN 0–691–05481–9 (alk. paper)